ON PHILOSOPHY IN AMERICAN LAW

In recent years, there has been tremendous growth of interest in the connections between law and philosophy, but the diversity of approaches that claim to be working at the intersection of these disciplines might suggest that this area of inquiry is so fractured as to be incoherent. This volume gathers leading scholars to provide focused and straightforward articulations of the role that philosophy might play at this juncture of the history of American legal thought.

The volume marks the seventy-fifth anniversary of Karl Llewellyn's essay "On Philosophy in American Law" in which he rehearsed the broad development of American jurisprudence, diagnosed its contemporary failings, and then charted a productive path opened by the variegated scholarship that claimed to initiate a realistic approach to law and legal theory. The essays are written in the spirit of Llewellyn's article: they are succinct and direct arguments about the potential for bringing law and philosophy together.

Francis J. Mootz III is the author of *Rhetorical Knowledge in Legal Practice and Critical Legal Theory* (2006) and *Law, Rhetoric and Hermeneutics* (to be published in 2010). He is editor of *Gadamer and Law* (2007) and *Nietzsche and Law* (2008, with Peter Goodrich). He is also the author of a law casebook, *Commercial Transactions: Sales, Leases, and Computer Information* (2nd ed., 2008, with David Frisch and Peter Alces). He has published numerous articles in a variety of journals, including law reviews and peer-reviewed journals. Professor Mootz is a regular presenter at academic symposia focusing on issues of legal theory. He is a member of the editorial advisory board of the interdisciplinary journals *Law, Culture and the Humanities*, and *International Journal for the Semiotics of Law* and is a member of the Organizing Committee of the Association for the Study of Law, Culture and the Humanities. He is an active member of the Association of American Law Schools, the North American Society for Philosophical Hermeneutics, the Law and Society Association, the Society for Ricoeur Studies, and the Rhetoric Society of America.

He currently is the William S. Boyd Professor of Law at the University of Nevada, Las Vegas. Prior to accepting this appointment, he was the Samuel Weiss Distinguished Faculty Scholar and Professor of Law at the Dickinson School of Law of the Pennsylvania State University.

On Philosophy in American Law

Edited by

Francis J. Mootz III
William S. Boyd School of Law
University of Nevada, Las Vegas

CAMBRIDGE UNIVERSITY PRESS
Cambridge, New York, Melbourne, Madrid, Cape Town,
Singapore, São Paulo, Delhi, Tokyo, Mexico City

Cambridge University Press
32 Avenue of the Americas, New York, NY 10013-2473, USA

www.cambridge.org
Information on this title: www.cambridge.org/9781107661240

First published 2009
Reprinted 2009, 20010, 2011
First paperback edition 2011

A catalog record for this publication is available from the British Library.

Library of Congress Cataloging in Publication Data

On philosophy in American law / edited by Francis J. Mootz III.
p. cm.
Includes bibliographical references and index.
ISBN 978-0-521-88368-9 (hardback)
1. Law – Philosophy. 2. Law – United States. I. Mootz, Francis J. II. Title.
B105.L3O5 2009
340'.1 – dc22 2008041386

ISBN 978-0-521-88368-9 Hardback
ISBN 978-1-107-66124-0 Paperback

Contents

Introduction

FRANCIS J. MOOTZ III

> The purpose of a book is never entirely justified. In any event, no one is required to display his motives or to entangle himself in a confession. To attempt it would be self-delusion. Yet, more than anyone, the philosopher cannot refuse to give his reasons.
>
> (Ricoeur 1970: 3)

This project has a distinct provenance, and so it might be instructive for the reader to know this history before engaging with the lively and diverse essays in this volume. On the other hand, it is always the case that a project outstrips its humble beginnings and takes on a life of its own; this is particularly true when the project involves thirty-seven individuals. I recognize that my effort to tell the story of an undertaking such as this book is, in the end, fanciful. Nevertheless, I must give my reasons.

I have long admired Karl Llewellyn's irreverent and sweeping prose. Llewellyn cast aside received wisdom about the nature of law in favor of looking at what really goes on in the activities that constitute law. In many ways he was similar to Nietzsche in form and attitude: incisive in his analysis, unique (sometimes odd) in his delivery,[1] committed to clearheaded investigation but rejecting scientism, tortured in his personal life, and maddeningly frustrating both to those who would erect a logical system of thought around his legacy and to those who would deride his efforts as an intellectual blind alley.[2] Llewellyn was committed to

[1] One of Llewellyn's reviewers made this point in a pithy manner while still extolling the value of Llewellyn's work, commenting that there "are many Gothic structures worth half a trip around the world – and this book is one of them" (Levy 1961: 1051).

[2] William Twining describes Llewellyn in a manner that could easily be applied to Nietzsche. Llewellyn, Twining (1985: 113–14) explained,

> imprinted his personality on everything he did, and even if it were desirable, it would be virtually impossible to exclude the strong flavour of the Llewellynesque from any study of his work. Few people could be indifferent to Karl Llewellyn. He frequently stimulated admiration and enthusiasm, but there were also non-enthusiasts. There is some consistency in the respective reactions of those who were definitive Karlo-phobes or Karlo-philes. The former tended to consider him a vulgar exhibitionist, sometimes brash and insensitive, sometimes

Dennis Patterson offered very helpful comments on an incomplete draft of this Introduction.

reforming American commercial legal practice as a Nietzschean "great lawgiver" who disdained the effete practice of academic philosophy, but he was enmeshed in the most vital discussions of his day regarding the philosophical problems posed by law. Llewellyn helped to pioneer modern legal anthropology in his work with the Cheyenne, he wrote a book in German that adopted a comparative law focus, and he was a central figure in the creation and adoption by the states of the Uniform Commercial Code. Simply put, he was deeply engaged in the real world of law but also was always informed by a critical assessment of what paraded as knowledge in this real world. Musty academics hiding in their book-lined offices have no easy task if they wish to dismiss the larger-than-life Llewellyn and his legacy.

Llewellyn's essay, "On Philosophy in American Law," is particularly interesting because it uses his customary succinct and clipped prose to explore far-reaching themes. In a period of great jurisprudential ferment Llewellyn produced a suggestive and wide-ranging essay in an impossibly concise format. This short piece is worthy of emulation because Llewellyn captured the moment in jurisprudential thinking in an arresting manner and also outlined a path of productive development. The origin of the present book can be traced directly to my embarrassing epiphany while reviewing Llewellyn's essay to check a quotation for use as an epigraph for a forthcoming book. Simply put, as I finalized my own lengthy monograph I doubted that I could match Llewellyn's example of speaking about the jurisprudential moment so abruptly and provocatively. A simple idea followed quickly on the heels of my prepublication self-doubt: wouldn't it be fascinating to charge a diverse group of scholars to present their own summations of the current status of jurisprudential thinking in Llewellyn's manner?

I am gratified that so many talented individuals have taken this task to heart in response to my call and have contributed such excellent essays to this volume. In doing so, they have inspired me to try to meet the same challenge. It must be emphasized that the subject of this book is neither Llewellyn nor his essay. The book addresses the connections between philosophy and law at this point in American legal history; Llewellyn serves as inspiration in form only. The diversity of approaches that claim to be working at the intersection of philosophy and law

> perverse, lacking in self-discipline and too erratic to be taken seriously. His admirers tended to emphasize his combination of humanity and brilliance: warm-hearted, gay, tolerant, uninhibited and vital as a person, stimulating and inspiring as a teacher, perspicacious and wise as a thinker. Taken together such judgments suggest a volatile genius. There is truth in this image, but on its own it is too facile.
>
> There is a strange aura about Llewellyn's writings which is unique in juristic literature. It fascinates some readers, repels others and perplexes most. This strangeness is often attributed to his prose style, which at its best is picturesque and memorable, but is often mannered, irritating and obscure. His use of language is idiosyncratic but it is quite clear that by itself Llewellynese does not explain the Llewellynesque. It is beyond my competence to try to emulate the brave biographer who seeks to give a rounded account of the relationship between the personality and the ideas of his subject. The pitfalls are too many and this study is, in any event, not intended to be in any sense a 'complete' biography. However, there are two aspects of Llewellyn's private life which have a direct bearing on his work as a jurist: his supposed 'artistic' qualities and his personal credo.

Twining did not intrude on the truly private dimensions of Llewellyn's life, but there are reports of his troubled relationships, depression, and alcoholism that suggest that he lived a life not wholly unlike Nietzsche's (Connolly 1998).

might suggest that this area of inquiry is so fractured as to be incoherent, and so it seemed helpful to invite a broad range of scholars to provide focused and straightforward articulations of the role that philosophy might play in American legal thinking. Each contributor was limited strictly to no more than 4,500 words and footnotes were discouraged. As a result, the book brings together succinct articulations of diverse assessments of the intersection of law and philosophy in a manner that makes the whole greater than the sum of its impressive parts. By asking leading scholars to deliver concise accounts of the relationship of law and philosophy and to offer their suggestions for future productive work, the book should focus and stimulate ongoing work in the field. By offering a side-by-side comparison of different perspectives presented in crisp and direct terms, the book should also prove useful to a wide audience. There was a risk of cacophony or radical polarization, but in the end the book presents a range of views in the manner of a vigorous and nonlinear dialogue. Perhaps the most important contribution of this volume is what lies between the essays – the unstated connections, disputations, and elaborations – that must be supplied by the reader. This book opens a fruitful conversation; it does not pretend to provide the last word.

LLEWELLYN ON PHILOSOPHY IN AMERICAN LAW

The volume begins with Llewellyn's essay, published seventy-five years ago. Llewellyn (1934: 205) makes clear that he adopts a pragmatic and functionalist view of philosophy, arguing that theoretical efforts gain traction with "life-in-action" only when they meet social needs. He sets out to investigate how we grow "into ways of doing which comport with some one philosophy and not with another . . . a process dependent largely on the felt needs of the persons concerned" (206). Philosophy is part of our lived reality – often plural, messy, and inconsistent – rather than an intellectual exercise that can bring clarity to social practices and issue definitive guidance about how to reform those practices (206). Llewellyn suggested that philosophers might help to shape social reality, but only by tapping into a "felt need of which no one had been conscious before" either by inventing a new philosophy or adapting the philosophical underpinnings to a changing society (206).

Working from this conception of philosophy, Llewellyn brashly describes the tides of legal philosophy over the previous two hundred years in terms of the adjustment of philosophy to social need. From natural law to Holmes and Cardozo, legal philosophy has found its resonance by answering the challenges posed by contemporary society. Llewellyn's description of the past is a breezy romp of half-sentences and allusions, but he ends with the serious questions that undoubtedly motivated him to write the article: why is legal realism the correct philosophy for American society in the 1930s, and why hasn't society expressly recognized its "felt need" for this changed philosophical outlook (211)? During the previous four years Llewellyn had battled for the realist camp in the great intellectual debate of his day, but his functionalist view of philosophy required him to consider – even if somewhat elliptically in this short essay – why the realist cause had not quickly succeeded. By acknowledging that law's leaders remained beholden to the ideology of business rapacity that had dominated the end of the previous century,

Llewellyn faced the possibility that the legal realism propounded by the professors was simply irrelevant to the practice of law.

Llewellyn's response to this dilemma is not unlike Nietzsche's: messianic yet coldly analytical. Nietzsche knew he was condemned to be a posthumous philosopher; although he could see clearly that God had already died, that the moralism of his peers was utterly decadent, and that scholars were blind to the vitality of will to power that animated life, he knew that it would be years before his lessons could be understood by the philosophers of tomorrow. Similarly, Llewellyn suggested that the "spear-point" of legal realism had "advanced" in the work of Pound, Frankfurter, Brandeis, Dewey, and others, and had been accepted in "the actual behavior of the better bar" despite its "hopelessly unorthodox" character; nevertheless, he acknowledged that legal realism remained on the fringes of conscious legal life. Legal practice would have to grow into legal realism, because there was as yet no expressly felt sense of the need to do so.[3] Just as Holmes slowly developed a cynical realism that even more slowly won over the Supreme Court in public law, Llewellyn (1934: 210) predicted that there would be a "lag" between insight into a vaguely felt need in private law and the instantiation of a new philosophy.

Moreover, Llewellyn understood that philosophies do not appear and disappear in a flash. Instead, they tend to cumulate and provide a heterodox account even as one or more become ascendant at a particular time. He argued that while the "profession at large" is still influenced by natural law, and even more by the positivism of the robber-baron era, nevertheless it was then beginning to incorporate realism into its practices (Llewellyn 1934: 212). Legal realism is not the better philosophy because it can tell practitioners how to go about their business, Llewellyn emphasized, but because it provided the orientation for practitioners to address the rapidly changing needs of society. Legal realism is the philosophy that will answer future needs, rather than the philosophy that will create the future.

LLEWELLYN'S REALIST CRITIQUE OF LEGAL PHILOSOPHY

Llewellyn's essay is cast in the context of the debates of the 1930s, but he raises fundamental questions about the nature of philosophy and its relationship to social practices such as law. Llewellyn's attitude about potential connections between philosophy and law is explained in greater depth by his biographer, William Twining. Llewellyn plainly evidenced a "dislike of professional philosophy and philosophers" (Twining 1985: 93) and rejected "what might be termed the Royal Tennis Tradition in jurisprudence" (173). But Llewellyn was equally adamant that his jurisprudence course was the most important course offered in the law school, with many of his students subsequently agreeing with this assessment. Llewellyn was not playing

[3] "We are all legal realists now" is a well-worn phrase that suggests that Llewellyn's assessment was correct, and that to some extent he was fated to be a posthumous jurisprude. But as Joseph Singer (1988: 467, 504) – perhaps the first theorist to endorse the phrase – suggests, the statement is true only with qualification. Although legal realism, as channeled through such diverse forms of modern legal theory as law and economics and critical legal studies, certainly holds sway in the modern academy, it has not yet succeeded as a philosophy that can describe legal practice satisfactorily (Singer 1988: 467–8). Perhaps the theoretical "spear-point" has not been advanced much since Llewellyn's day, although our lived experience has clearly become more realistic.

semantic games. He believed that legal theory should be simplifying rather than esoteric or specialized, and he considered jurisprudence the bringing to bear of "general serviceable life-wisdom" to issues facing lawyers and judges (Twining 1985: 116).

> While it is not uncommon for theorists to seek a *rapprochement* between "theory" and "practice," Llewellyn's persistent urge to operate at the level of participant working theory is rare in jurisprudence, if not unique. Many of those who have revolted against the Royal Tennis Tradition have rejected all jurisprudence as being esoteric and useless; few, if any, have rivalled Llewellyn's consistency in seeking to provide for participants usable theory, drawing on the best modern thought available in a variety of disciplines, whilst maintaining a broad perspective and liberal values.... With some justification Llewellyn considered this line of thinking to be his most original contribution to jurisprudence (Twining 1985: 370).

Llewellyn avoided the problem of relating theory to practice by steadfastly refusing to sever them at the outset of his inquiry.

Llewellyn was a legal realist but he adamantly dismissed the idea of a finely tuned realist school of thought, eschewing the reductionist sociological and psychological approaches taken by some of his colleagues. He embraced the powerful potential for modern social science to clarify pressing issues in law, but he consistently rejected a scientistic ideology that would commit the same mistake as the stultifying ideologies of an earlier day. "In short, he favoured a commonsense strategy for research, based on a realistic appraisal of the obstacles in the way of quick advance, such as the cost, the lack of glamour in much of the work, and the shortage of personnel with appropriate training.... [His] was a pragmatic and sensible approach which could form the basis for a rounded strategy for developing the subject, giving due regard both to the importance of theory and to likely practical difficulties" (Twining 1985: 196). Of course, the social sciences have made tremendous strides in the intervening years, leading Twining to wonder whether Llewellyn's cautious approach had, by the end of his career, become "complacent and unambitious in relation to the possibilities and the needs" (196).

There is good reason not to cast Llewellyn as a precursor of wholly empirical approaches to law. Dennis Patterson (1990: 577–9) has argued persuasively that the substance of Llewellyn's philosophical views anticipated Wittgenstein's later work. Patterson contends that Llewellyn firmly believed that philosophy leaves legal practice as it is, but that nevertheless there is important work to be done within the practice. "Like Wittgenstein, Llewellyn believed that we can never escape the realm of linguistic understanding. What this means for the critique of law is that the ground of critique must be internal to legal practice itself. The impossibility of transcending the (linguistic) limits of the practice and reaching a point outside the practice from which to critique it leaves only those within the practice as sources – and evaluators – of criticism" (599–600). It is this orientation that led Llewellyn to reject the stereotypical realist view that law should be subsumed into the social science departments of research universities (Ansaldi 1992: 711; Llewellyn 1962: 375–94).

We can sharpen this account of Llewellyn's approach to philosophy and law by turning to his (still untranslated) 1931–2 lectures on law and sociology that he delivered in Germany. Llewellyn emphasized the integrity of legal practice and its connection to sociological jurisprudence in ways that illuminate the brief remarks that he would write in the following year in "On Philosophy in American Law." He argued that philosophies arise to render developed practices such as law into a "science," by which he meant a reflective practice that is both descriptively accurate and critical (Ansaldi 1992: 746–9). Reflections on practice, Llewellyn contended, "generally lead to attempts to draw together everything theretofore learned about a particular branch of knowledge, to a 'science' in the old-fashioned sense of the term, a somewhat organized collection and classification of prior knowledge, but one that jumbles knowledge with beliefs, with value judgments and prejudices, a 'quasi-science.' This philosophy coexists with, but does not supplant, the skills by which people earn their living" (Ansaldi 1992: 747). Llewellyn (1932: 38) wrote that "in this topsy-turvy world the central problem of all of law has to do with this still almost completely neglected descriptive science, with this 'legal sociology,' this natural science of living law," but Llewellyn would have no truck with crude efforts to subordinate legal practice to the social sciences narrowly construed (Ansaldi 1992: 748). He regarded legal practice as a normative enterprise that could not be explained solely by sociological laws, although sociological inquiry was a necessary first step toward sharpening the outmoded legal philosophies of his day. Thus, one of his important tasks was to describe how judges decided cases, and to link this practice to broader perspectives that offered critical insight into legal practice.

Critics who allege that Llewellyn was an ivory-tower relativist who believed in law's absolute indeterminacy badly misread his work. Llewellyn found ample stability within the practice of law while at the same time acknowledging room for critique and reform (Patterson 1990: 580–1, 598–9). Llewellyn (1989: 11–12) wrote that the totality of the practice of law was one of the most "conservative and inflexible" of social phenomena, and yet every case offered the opportunity for the judge and lawyers to shift the direction of thinking. Llewellyn anticipated the central tenet of contemporary legal hermeneutics, arguing that the meaning of a legal rule is known only in its use, which always constitutes a reformulation of the rule (either by expansion or contraction) even when the case feels like a simple matter of deductive reasoning.

> Thus, the task of the judge is to *re*formulate the rule so that from then on the rule *un*doubtedly includes the case or undoubtedly excludes it. "To apply the rule" is thus a misnomer; rather, one *expands* a rule or *contracts* it. One can only "apply" a rule *after* first freely choosing either to include the instant case within it or to exclude the case from it. . . .
>
> Matters are no different, only more sharply highlighted, when a new case is such that one first must mull over whether to include it within an existing category, or must choose which existing category to include it in. . . .
>
> For we all, lawyer not least, are mistaken about the nature of language. We regard language as if words were things with fixed content. Precisely because we apply to a new fact situation a well-known and familiar linguistic symbol, we lose the *feeling* of newness about the case; it seems long familiar to us. The word hides its changed meaning from the speaker (Llewellyn 1989: 74–5).

His message was philosophically radical, but he was no linguistic skeptic, cultural nihilist, or political revolutionary.

Llewellyn argued that the impasse between the philosophical interest in achieving justice in the individual case and the practical interest in achieving regularity resulted in a "leeway, a space admittedly bounded, within which a judge may act freely" (Ansaldi 1992: 755), but this realm of freedom was not beyond the scope of jurisprudential assessment. Llewellyn's realist inquiry did not shun normative questions precisely because the practice under consideration was normative, and one of the goals of legal sociology was to better understand what law ought to be. "Accurate scientific knowledge of what legal rules 'deliver' in real life is desirable not just because it satisfies a disinterested spirit of inquiry, but also because such knowledge is an indispensable element in devising effective answers to questions about what the law in the real world 'ought' to be" (749n162).

CONTEMPORARY PERSPECTIVES ON PHILOSOPHY IN AMERICAN LAW

> In philosophy, opposing points of view must be heard, whatever their nature or their source. This is a fundamental principle for all philosophers who do not believe that they can found their conceptions on necessity and self-evidence; for it is only by this principle that they can justify their claim to universality.
>
> ....
>
> As no criteria are absolute and self-evident, norms and values invoked in justification are never beyond criticism.... for philosophy there is no *res judicata.* (Perelman 1980: 71, 75)

Llewellyn's instrumental conception of philosophy and his prescient approach to language provide a rich starting point for thinking about the connections between philosophy and law today. The nature of philosophical inquiry, the nature of legal practice, and the general relationship between theory and practice are as contentious today as they were seventy-five years ago. This volume provides a comprehensive, concise, and diverse collection of essays by some of the leading contemporary theorists working at the intersection of law and philosophy. The result is not a carefully organized department store in which one can hurriedly find the precise object one seeks. Instead, it is much more like a bazaar or open market, in which it is best to wander, circle back, and change one's mind about what looks appealing and merits a second look. Because of space limitations, these essays all point outside their borders to the work already completed by the author and by work proposed for completion. This open market is not convened to make a quick sale, then, but to invite the reader to join the contributors in an ongoing and festive spirit of inquiry.

Karl Llewellyn and the Course of Philosophy in American Law

This book is not just about Llewellyn, but several contributions discuss Llewellyn's contribution to, and continuing effects on, American jurisprudence. Jan Broekman draws from competing accounts of Llewellyn's life to consider the connections between life and law, and he situates Llewellyn's interventions in a historical story that has yet to come to fruition. The realist tendency is to assume a pragmatic subject who regards the strings of case names as real objects of reference rather than as nonrepresentational signs, and Broekman urges realism to take the next step by embracing the semiotic life in law. David Caudill argues that Llewellyn suffers from the same natural law hangover that he diagnosed in American jurisprudence. Caudill extends Llewellyn's insights by bringing him into conversation with Herman Dooyeweerd, a Dutch legal philosopher writing within the natural law tradition but in a critical vein. Caudill draws the lesson that we cannot avoid our hangover of pretheoretical commitments, but we can argue about these assumptions productively.

Three contributions seek to continue Llewellyn's effort to chart the broad course of philosophy in American law. Brian Tamanaha describes the deleterious effect of Llewellyn's realism, arguing that the instrumental view of law as a tool of social policy has displaced the rule of law. Without guiding agreement about what "good" social policy entails, the law has become a battleground for interest groups promoting their parochial visions, and to the victor go the spoils of power. Consequently, Llewellyn's belief that realism would unshackle law from the ideology of the robber-barons has not been achieved. Steven Winter embraces realism and notes that it grew and prospered in a variety of forms through the 1980s, but he argues that during the past thirty years things have gone "terribly wrong" in jurisprudence. The post-Soviet era has witnessed the decisive triumph of rule of law formalism, capitalist private law, and liberal constitutionalism, but Winter contends that this development has set jurisprudence back a century. Finally, Larry Backer offers an alternative to Llewellyn's historical narrative, arguing that the quest for perfection is the unifying theme in American jurisprudence. Competing accounts of law have been competing accounts of how to achieve perfection in the American social experience; Backer contends that this unifying quest below the tides of jurisprudential change is religious in character rather than strictly philosophical.

Philosophical Perspectives on Law

Several essays argue that one or more broad philosophical themes are important at this stage of the relationship of philosophy and American law. Robin West contends that questions of normativity – what makes a law good or bad – have not been prominent in recent analytic or critical jurisprudence and that this omission is for the worse. Arguing that natural law thinking became too thin, legal positivism began attending only to law after insisting on its separation from morality, and critical theorists have focused on the relationship of law and power, West counsels a reinvigoration of normative jurisprudence in the vein of work by Martha Nussbaum. Jack Balkin argues for a renewal of critical legal theory to attend to law's ambivalent character: law renders power legitimate by containing it within the legal structure, but it also legitimates the exercise of power after the fact. A critical legal theory must attend to law's plasticity and ambivalence, and in turn must be self-critical of its tendency to regard law just as a mystifying legitimation of unauthorized power. Penelope Pether locates in the widespread practice of courts to decertify opinions for publication an emergent crude realism that equates law with judicial fiat, and thereby yokes the realist impulse to atavistic politics. In response, she charts a more sophisticated approach to law, social science, and the humanities that can make good on Llewellyn's view of the liberating effects of realism.

George Taylor calls for an inquiry into creativity that moves beyond the simple model of applying a constant legal principle to a new set of facts by analogy. Guided by the hermeneutical principle that meaning occurs in application, Taylor draws on Ricoeur's argument that application is metaphoric and imaginative. There can be no methodology for ensuring a productive imagination: imagination always threatens to undermine progressive goals even as it promises to advance them, but it is only by engaging in metaphoric imagination that we can claim to make these distinctions. Robert Hayman and Nancy Levit champion the "new legal realism" that eschews a crude empiricism and focuses on the narrative dimension of law. Extending the work of Llewellyn and other realists requires attention to the elements of narrative truth, and so they call on critical storytellers to attend to the truth as they seek to undermine the officially sanctioned stories appearing in judicial opinions.

Areas of Philosophy and Their Relationship to Law

Philosophy is neither a unidimensional nor a univocal discipline. A number of essays connect specific schools of philosophy or areas of philosophical inquiry to law. Brian Bix argues that American thinkers unfairly have marginalized the British tradition of analytical legal philosophy despite the growing number of American theorists doing sophisticated work within this tradition. American tendencies to demand pragmatic cash value leads to undervaluing careful philosophy, but Bix argues that the analytic clarification of legal concepts and the philosophical foundations of various substantive areas of law does provide some useful connection to legal practice, even if philosophical inquiry should not always be judged instrumentally. Austin Sarat and Connor Clarke contend that contemporary political philosophy sheds light on the particularly vexing problem of prosecutorial discretion. Agamben's work on the state of exception provides the lens for understanding prosecutorial discretion as a political question rather than a question of administrative bureaucracy.

Matthew Adler notes that legal theorists inexplicably have neglected contemporary moral philosophy in their work, and therefore have failed to incorporate the substantial developments in this area during the past twenty years. This inattention leads to skewed understandings, given that prior borrowing of lessons from moral philosophy might now be challenged within the field. Perhaps qualifying this indictment, Lawrence Solum heralds the development of virtue jurisprudence to overcome the antinomies of contemporary legal theory just as moral philosophy has looked to Aristotelian conceptions to overcome its roadblocks in recent decades. He discusses the judicial virtues, the virtue of justice, and the virtue of practical wisdom as a means of demonstrating how the aretaic turn can advance the philosophy of law.

Adam Thurschwell suggests that Llewellyn's essay follows the form of Continental philosophy in the post-Hegelian tradition, and that reading it in this manner restores its critical edge. Using the example of affirmative action, he reveals how we can reframe debates and locate the ethical impetus for change by attending to the lessons of contemporary Continental philosophy regarding finitude and historicity. Jeanne Schroeder and David Carlson argue that freedom is the core issue in legal theory, and that a psychoanalytic jurisprudence derived from Lacan illuminates the legal character of the subject and law's inability to quell subjective desire. It is precisely this insight that reveals an inescapable freedom to choose and act despite the inability of law or philosophy to direct action in a determinant manner.

Philosophical Examinations of Legal Issues

A number of essays provide intriguing philosophical analyses of legal questions. Frank Michelman addresses the perennial question of the relationship of law and morality in a unique manner, suggesting that in some instances law may be the premise for moral commitments. In particular, he suggests that socioeconomic rights may be grounded in the morality of law in the sense that these commitments depend on the premise of a certain legal order. In the next essay, David Fisher examines how justice never fully achieves its goal of rising above the deep-seated urge to seek revenge. Working from Ricoeur's later work on justice, law, and ethics, Fisher calls for a nonbinary thinking that understands how law can join the goal of living in mutual reciprocity with others with the need to build institutions that can foster the use of practical wisdom in resolving conflict. Eugene Garver asks why we privilege freedom of thought over freedom of action now that the religious justification that salvation depends on one's beliefs has receded. Drawing on the Platonic dialogues for guidance he contends that love can explain this puzzle, that tolerating another's thoughts can be part of friendship and not just indifference.

After acknowledging the difficulty of making predictions, especially in light of the chastened aspirations of contemporary philosophy, George Wright outlines a number of complex problems including free will and the implications of artificially enhanced personhood that might become the focus of future thinking. He cautions that a new philosophical humility might have an overriding effect on how these issues are addressed. Finally, Anita Allen provides an antidote to the prevailing ideologies – what Llewellyn terms the atmospherics of a guiding philosophy – of maternalism and paternalism that shape the legal treatment of abortion rights. Accepting the reality that the law might justifiably protect some women from self-harm and cruelty does not justify contemporary atmospherics.

Law, Rhetoric, and Practice Theory

Philosophy and law might find more common ground, several contributors argue, if we draw on the traditions of rhetoric and practice theory. Eileen Scallen challenges the traditional philosophical quest for foundational truths by acknowledging that plural ground truths are experienced in practice, drawing from the traditions of ancient rhetoric, legal realism, and pragmatism. Scallen insists that this is not a move to irrationalism or skepticism, but instead is an effort to develop a more complete account that might better serve the ends of justice. My essay contends that law and philosophy have developed into insular guilds that can come into vital contact again only by finding common ground in the ancient art of rhetoric. Using rhetorical knowledge as a guiding concept rather than rational or empirical knowledge, philosophers and lawyers can work together to elucidate the demands of justice. Peter Goodrich suggests that Llewellyn's article indirectly undercuts traditional philosophy in favor of a hermeneutical and rhetorical approach that attends to the affective dimensions of law. As with dicta, rhetoric operates in a realm of persuasion that does not claim compulsory power.

Dennis Patterson contends that conceptual analysis has run its course in legal philosophy and should be replaced by a practice theory of law. In an attempt to make good on Hart's goal of a descriptive sociology of law, Patterson offers a Wittgensteinian account of law as a shared normative practice of ongoing activity rather than a regime of rules and principles. Robert Burns similarly contends that a philosophy of law must adopt a radically empirical focus on the normative practices that constitute law, principally by focusing on rhetoric and practical reasoning. Legal practice can never be naturalized, Burns insists, but he argues that the interpretations and critique of legal practice can still converge on the truth of the human situation.

Questioning the Relationship between Philosophy and American Law

This book would be deficient if it did not place in question the hypothesis that law and philosophy can have a positive relationship. Larry Alexander and Emily Sherwin suggest that legal practitioners should ignore philosophy because they are engaged in a rule-governed activity that employs reasoning by analogy. This is problematic because it is philosophically suspect to follow a rule that one regards as wrong, and there is no persuasive philosophical defense of analogical reasoning as a rigorous practice. Steven Smith contends that theorizing about law is nearly moribund, with legal positivism devolving into irrelevance beyond a narrow group of academics at the same time that reviving the classical theistic account has become highly improbable. But legal practice, he argues, continues to proceed as if the classical account was acceptable, thereby placing law in a quandary from which Smith sees no obvious escape.

In a decidedly more critical vein, Pierre Schlag challenges the intellectual fascination with law's propositional character, accusing legal theorists of assuming the discourse of judges rather than of genuine critics. He identifies the fetishism of rankings and culture of garish self-promotion that infects contemporary academia as a synecdoche of rampant anti-intellectualism. In a coda, he makes a bold suggestion for what real thinking will require of law professors. Philippe Nonet castigates both academic philosophy and law, arguing that philosophy as metaphysics is complicit with law as technique. He regards philosophical questioning of essential, and therefore unanswerable, questions as highly unlikely in the present circumstances of the modern research university, but in any event this activity of thinking could occur only outside of law. This is the pessimistic implication of his title, which places question marks after both philosophy and law. There are unfortunate Heideggerian overtones to his claim that one may only philosophize in certain languages; I trust that this volume, including Nonet's essay, rebuts this aspect of his thesis.

CONCLUSION

It seems clear that the relationship between philosophy and law is at once more sophisticated, diverse, and contested than it was when Llewellyn wrote his essay seventy-five years ago. The essays in this volume provide intriguing points of entry to some of the debates and questions that define the current moment. From calls to augment the philosophical analysis of legal questions to skeptical rejoinders placing both philosophy and law in question, the book ranges widely and deeply. Carlos Ball, Marianne Constable, and Michael Sullivan – a law professor, a professor of rhetoric, and a philosophy professor – provide intriguing reflections that bring the essays into conversation with each other in a manner that stimulates future work.

Ball suggests that the contributions reveal an optimism about the potential to enrich law through philosophy, even if most contributors are not satisfied with the current state of affairs. There are dissenters, of course, with Philippe Nonet's essay serving as the most stark expression of pessimism. Ball begins with the divide that exists currently between the legal academy and the practice of law, and he concludes that legal theorists are perhaps most divorced from the real world of practice that Llewellyn so highly prized. Nevertheless, considering the quality and vibrancy of the diverse dialogue about the relationship between law and philosophy, Ball expresses his own optimism.

Constable takes a different tack. Working from my initial charge to capture the moment in legal philosophy, Constable suggests that the essays collectively uncover the impossibility of capturing the moment and the inevitability of our striving to do so. She then effectively regroups the contributions along several different axes, helping to uncover the moment revealed by these strivings. She gestures to the unfinished task of thinking, which is certainly a fitting read of this volume.

Sullivan concludes the volume by considering some of the contributions in greater detail, but in a manner that fits with the thematic approaches developed by Ball and Constable. Sullivan suggests that the volume exemplifies Llewellyn's thesis that we must take a fresh look at law in action, inasmuch as the competing and complementary essays jar the reader to consider matters anew. Sullivan emphasizes that the variety of approaches are a benefit rather than a scandal: the very understanding of law and philosophy are contested, not to mention the relation between these two practices. We can conclude, Sullivan argues, that law and philosophy have a vibrant and contested meeting point at this juncture in our intellectual history. What this dynamic interaction will yield remains an open question.

Several years ago I thought that this project might provide a basis for stimulating thinking about how to move forward from the jurisprudential moment of our times. The resulting volume is not a road map to be followed; in some respects, it is as if I asked directions of numerous people speaking different languages and using different scales of the topography ahead. Of course, this isn't a mark of failure: how could things be otherwise? All too often, self-assured philosophers and law professors assert their disciplinary authority and proclaim how these disciplines may properly intersect, all the while cautioning against the ebullience that might be unleashed if thinkers who have not been properly vetted – who do not subscribe to the dogma of the day – are permitted to speak. Such cloistered conversations among those largely in agreement provide a measure of reassurance and security, but they promote only scholastic scribblings. This volume was conceived as a way to bring the boisterous conversation of the agora into a focused moment, providing the reader with a means of reflecting on the current state of law and philosophy. Those who seek a definitive answer, or confirmation of an answer that they already hold secure, will be disappointed. However, I hope that the inquisitive, searching minds of those who will define the future will be inspired by this volume to continue the conversation it begins.

WORKS CITED

Ansaldi, Michael. "The German Llewellyn." *Brooklyn L. Rev.* 58.3 (1992): 705–77.

Connolly, James J., Peggy Pschirrer, and Robert Whitman. "Alcoholism and Angst in the Life and Work of Karl Llewellyn." *Ohio N.U. L. Rev.* 24.1 (1998): 43–124.

Levy, Beyrl Harold. "Book Review: The Common Law Tradition–Deciding Appeals," *U. Pa. L. Rev.* 109.7 (1961): 1045–51.

Llewellyn, Karl N. "On Philosophy in American Law." *U. Pa. L. Rev.* 82.3 (1934): 205–12.

———. *Recht, Rechtsleben und Gesellschaft [Law, the Life of Law, and Society]*. Ed. Manfred Rehbinder. Berlin: Duncker & Humblodt GmbH, 1977 (1932 lectures). (Quotations are from translations included in Ansaldi 1992.)

Patterson, Dennis. "Law's Practice." *Colum. L. Rev.* 90.2 (1990): 575–600.

Perelman, Chaim. "Justice and Reason." Trans. Susan Rubin. In *Justice, Law, and Argument: Essays on Moral and Legal Reasoning.* Dordrecht: D. Reidel, 1980, 66–75.

Ricoeur, Paul. *Freud and Philosophy: An Essay on Interpretation.* Trans. Denis Savage. New Haven, CT: Yale Univ. Press, 1970.

Singer, Joseph William. "Legal Realism Now." *Cal. L. Rev.* 76.2 (1986): 465–544.

Twining, William. *Karl Llewellyn and the Realist Movement.* 1973. Reprint, Norman: Univ. of Oklahoma Press, 1985.

PART ONE. KARL LLEWELLYN AND THE COURSE OF PHILOSOPHY IN AMERICAN LAW

January, 1934

University of Pennsylvania Law Review
And American Law Register

FOUNDED 1852

VOLUME 82 JANUARY, 1934 NO. 3

ON PHILOSOPHY IN AMERICAN LAW*

K. N. LLEWELLYN†

"The inquiry as to a theory" remarks Pareto, "runs in terms of what it did for the man who made it—and of what it did for the men who accepted it." There is rarely a lack of the theories in the world, or even in the air—or of philosophies. Nor, for that matter, when the philosophies die do the books die with them which contain them. But life-in-action a theory can gain only when it serves men's needs. Life-in-action; I am

* As Pound has pointed out, the natural law thinking in which Mansfield was at home, and which was choked out in England by Eldon's time at least, continued to flourish here. It was Morris Cohen, I think, who made me see its recrudescence in the constitutional law cases in and after the '90s. Pound gives good reason for the first phenomenon; but I have never felt satisfied with his mere listing and description of our apparently inconsistent jurisprudential trends in the latter 19th century. It is not enough to know what they were, and whence they came. We must see why men adopted them, and above all, *how* they all fitted into the single picture. Nor is this all. Philosophers' writings and law-men's doings meet rarely on the same level of discourse, and part of the game is to find where they do, where they do not, and—if you can—the *why* of either. Finally, wherever writings are contrasted with doings, there is the question of the relative rôle of the great man and his times.

I grow impatient for some one to work these matters out. It is due our students that cases with dates ranging from 1780 to 1930 should be given some chart of the sweep, on which they can be plotted. How else are the individual cases to be grasped? Indeed there are a number of finished jobs which a second year law student is entitled to have before him. Some one should make clear to him the difference in "feel" and tendency between, say the approach in most phases of property and a few phases of commercial law from that in the flexible body of commercial law at large, the difference between the latter and the mutually diverse flexibilities of Equity and of Torts; some one should set for him the "feel" of Procedure against that of Public Law. I still feel my wattles grow red as I recall the shock with which, as a dyed-in-the-wool commercial lawyer, I met property phases of mortgage law which left me gasping. "One system of precedent" we may have, but it works in forty different ways. Some day, some one will help the second year student orient himself. Nor does any one bother to present to him the difference between logic and persuasion, nor what a man facing old courts is to do with a new vocabulary; in a word, the game, in framing an argument, of diagnosing the peculiar presuppositions of the hearers. I think the second year student is entitled to feel himself aggrieved. Meanwhile, while we wait upon the treading of the Angel, there is rushing in that calls for doing. Here is a start.

† B. A., 1915, LL. B., 1918, J. D., 1920, Yale; Betts Professor of Jurisprudence, Columbia University School of Law; Commissioner of Uniform State Laws from New York; author of numerous legal treatises and articles.

less concerned here with currency-in-words. Men may scorn philosophies, as philosophers are fond of making clear, without escaping the necessity of living in terms of some one of them—or of some inconsistent hodge-podge of a dozen. Thus what is here before the telescope is the changing array not of verbalized philosophies, but of philosophies-in-action as the history of law in these United States has gone its way. What those philosophies were, what needs they served—and whose. I am not so much concerned, I repeat, with the philosophers themselves, with whom indeed my acquaintance is but scanty. I am concerned with philosophy-in-action, with implicit philosophy, with those premises, albeit inarticulate and in fact unthought, which yet make coherence out of a multiplicity of single ways of doing. Where explicit writers happen to be mentioned, it is as persons giving fortunate expression to the living currents of their time. With an exception. The two most recent lines of premise mentioned (the sociological and the realistic) are found rather in writings than in life. I view them as *products* of their time, as attempts to adjust action to felt needs, as were the others. I view them also as probable heralds of the future. But of the *ways of the law-guild at large,* as lived, they are as yet a most inadequate expression.

It will thus be clear that I am viewing not the invention, but the *choice* of a philosophy—or better, the growing into ways of doing which comport with some one philosophy and not with another. And it will be clear that I view such fitting into a philosophy as a process dependent largely on the felt needs of the persons concerned. And it need hardly be added that I view conscious choice of a philosophy as rare, and the mere growing into one as the order of the day. But I trust to make it persuasive as well that once a philosophy has been established in the habits and attitudes of any person, it has effects; *a fortiori,* if such establishment comes to prevail among a group; and again *a fortiori* as the group in question grows larger or more solid. Finally, I shall urge that the inventor of a new philosophy, or of a creative adaptation of some ancient one to current needs, may with luck affect or deflect the current of his times. There is a certain—or better, an uncertain—leeway within which the individual contributes to the shaping of society. And there is a speeding or slowing (or turning) of the march of events, according as the needed intellectual formulations are or are not invented (or rediscovered) or are well or badly, or late or early, achieved. A lone man, by his formulations, may indeed make felt a need of which no one had been conscious before.

The United States began as such with natural law the atmosphere about them. "We hold these truths to be self-evident," wrote Jefferson. And signers signed. The separation of powers, whether derived from Montesquieu or Reason, was surely written into the Document as an expression of the "essential" nature of government. The Bill of Rights, itself originally omitted because self-evident, incorporates in intent the "natural" heritage of the individual citizen.

How far this, as a philosophy, affected in that day our governmental law, is beyond my power to say. But as applied to *private law,* the rôle of the philosophy of natural law is clear. Precedents were few. Judges had neither training nor experience at their back. England was hated. Lawyers were only by accident accomplished, nor was their standing high. And yet, there were disputes. And courts. And lawyers. Meanwhile, with a rapidity no man (save one) had courage to prefigure, the country rushed westward and spawned progeny. A call for law, for changing law, for law fitted to conditions in good part theretofore unknown, was met by a lack of materials to answer the call. There was a single body of law available in English: the common law tradition. Yet that tradition (though pressed, increasingly as time went on, by advocates) was distrusted by the populace. Consider Tory-expulsion, the French Revolution, and the War of 1812. And partly the tradition was ill-adapted to our needs. If ever situation cried out for one particular philosophy, this did. Natural law! The law which urges Reason *as the law.* The judge, if his experience reaches, has but to think, to see, and to decree as seen. The English cases—merely, in tacit theory, as suggestions—proceed to suggest; and by suggesting, to relieve; and as reliefs, to become received. For one can always vary from them, when the case requires. Story and Kent, in search of variant suggestion, can range among the Continental writers. Until the growing reception of English practice as well (along with English precedents) threatens to wall in variant growth, instinct and theory of right reason continue to correct reception of the English law.

Thus up to the '50s. As the slavery controversy draws off attention, I lose the trail of growth in private law. Indeed, as I look back over my own fields of work, it is a little startling to see the incidence of the creative precedents which I happen to have met halt in the late '40s, disappear during the '50s, and set in again as the '70s approach. I speak of course from casual observation, not from careful inquiry. But, in conjunction with the towering of the slavery issue, the doubt impends whether private law, along with other lines of interest, may not have suffered stagnation as the powers of a nation were channeled toward one crucial conflict.

But whatever the doubt before the Civil War, there is none after. Grant, and the nadir of political corruption. In New York, Tweed. In the South, Reconstruction. Union Pacific Railway—why go on? The era of the business buccaneer. Natural resources. A continent to be exploited. Fortune ahead, fist in your neighbor's belly, foot in his face, immigrants, and consumers, and the earth—and law—to be exploited. In this period, as

I see it, the Business Man took hold of the ideology of America. While business began to center on industrialization, with corporate development in an ascending scale as the inevitable consequence. One thing must be remembered. "Hold of the ideology of *America,*" was what I said. "Captain of Industry", the slogan ran. *National* welfare was identified with *laissez-faire*—and with some reason. Not only were we growing, not only was—for most—the standard of living rising, but the business buccaneers (as contrasted, I suspect, with the political or the financial) were giving the country more than value received. The elder J. P. Morgan perhaps (and at times) excepted, Rockefellers, Harrimans and Hills, as doers, stood out in startling contrast to such stockjobbers as a Gould.

It is against this background that we approach the philosophy that underlay the private law between 1870 and, say, 1900. Little thereof was explicit. It was no day for too explicit philosophizing. Men's minds were on doing, which meant exploitation. Yet the trend is obvious. "Natural law" had built up, in the course of the decades, its precedents, and borrowing from England had acclimatized the precedent system in two or three of its multiform variants. And business captains needed a stable footing in the law. Stable: that means, on the one hand, reckonable. So, let us say, with reference to the law of long-term contracts or of property. Stable: that means, on the other hand, sufficiently straitjacketed in out-moded moulds not to catch up too fast with novel predatory practices. Footing to foot on, plus room to move in: these were the needs the dominant philosophy of life required. The dominant philosophy of law proceeded to supply the needs, by way of case law. By way of decisions of judges, based on decisions of the judges who had gone before them. Legislation? *Buy it off!* (Or, as with the Union Pacific, buy it on.) The nadir, I believe I mentioned, of political morality inside these boundaries.

And what philosophy may hope for acceptance and utilization, in such a situation? Positivism. Let us forget "right reason"; let us forget the bastard something known as morality; let us acknowledge merely the obvious fact, in law, that law *as is,* is law. Justice may be an ideal; in actuality it is an accident. A legal system exists to preserve the law as is, and any other thinking is a somewhat absurd idealistic tendency, divorced from facts of life.

It had happened meanwhile (thanks to the prior reception of English practice) that this philosophy (explicit or implicit) was applied to a body of *case law.* It had happened, further, that the body of American case law itself had already been developed, with a philosophical presupposition of natural law as nurse and guide. It had happened finally (as indeed was inevitable) that particular cases ran discordant ways. Whence arose, ineluctably, the problem of dealing with discordant precedents. For precedents are positive, each one of them.

The result was a confused but (to the dominant interested parties) wholly satisfactory "resolution" of incompatible decisions. To wit: decisions which we *like* are "sound", and therefore precedent. But decisions which we do *not* like are "unsound", and therefore to be disregarded. The following of *consistent* precedents is a positivistic choice. The choice among *inconsistent* precedents (say, "on principle") was, on the other hand, an echo of the already decadent philosophy of immutable "natural law". Only in later years has it tended to become mechanized in terms of "majority view", or that of *Corpus Juris;* or been frankly based on policy.

To repeat, the system was one of precedent. Into a system of precedent the urges from historical jurisprudence fit with no shock at all to the prevailing positivism. The study of history merely "reveals" the prevailing rule, or helps the natural law to make a choice among prevailing rules which happen to conflict. Indeed the going back helps positivism mightily to divorce law from the life around us.

The urge was thus for clarity and certainty, for a firm foundation. The urge was for a *solid* something on which to build, of course, with the aforesaid exception for extensions made necessary by business needs. These extensions were provided by the selected bar. Selected? Selected by fees. Throughout the period under consideration, the best brains of the bar were in the service of the business captains, as the results attest. There was no lack of growth of corporation law. The labor injunction was invented. There was, as events proceeded, the turning of the trust to the uses which have connected the word with oil and beef. The legal structure of high financeering found willing carpenters as well as able architects.

Meantime the revolt of labor breaks into the public eye in '73, in the '80s, and again and crucially in the Pullman strike of '93. The farmers, from the resumption of specie payments in 1879, suffer the pinch, and push for "easy money". The small business man in the late '80s, and loudly in the '90s, cries out against the Trusts. Popular movements capture legislatures. No longer can all legislation be bought off. In the skilled hands of corporation counsel, the front of battle shifts. A new utility is discovered for "due process", and "equal protection of the laws". For this there were no precedents. The prevailing positivism, explicit or implicit, gave no footing. Again the approach was along the lines of natural law. *Right reason* is the guide. The indefinite void marked by the phrasing of the two amendments was filled by the judges' notions of the way things should be—filled to the entire satisfaction of those persons whose ideology and action indicated the proper way to fill it. Observe the ways of *implicit* philosophy. Natural law in the constitutional field rides hand in hand with positivism on the private side. Who cares for inconsistency? Both serve the need—the need of those persons whose need, as things were organized, was *"the* need". Observe also how an appeal to natural law which in the first half-century was a vital source of creation could at the end become in very truth the judicial "enactment of Mr. Herbert Spencer's social statics".

At this point it is time to look into the philosophy of one individual whose phrasings have had power. As one follows the growth of Holmes' thinking from his early writings in the *American Law Review,* through *The Common Law,* into his speeches, and culminating with *The Path of the Law* in 1896, one finds increasing precision in the development of a cynical realism. It might be summed up as "Look and see precisely what is there; and reckon with that, and nothing else". Or, as my friend Patterson prefers to phrase it, the judge's attitude becomes: "You have not shown enough to make me move". Even the splendid clarity of the contracts opinions cannot hide the essential conservatism of the point of view—as applied to private underlying law. The misrepresentation cases show no desire to expand. The torts cases are choked by ancient history. Even the celebrated dissent in *Vegelahn v. Guntner*[1] rests on unwillingness to *create* a precedent, where the other judges were prepared to do so in the interest of a waning point of view. The very early essay on grain elevators is a notable exception. It is striking as one works through Holmes' writings before the appointment to the Supreme Court, to find an almost total absence of discussion on public law. I can recall only one passing reference in 1896.

Mark now how the philosophy thus developed, and without change in its form, takes on a total difference in effect as the man moves into another sphere of action. "Look and see precisely what is there"—and as applied to constitutional limitations on legislation (as distinguished from the piled up precedents of common law) the answer is only a non-existent brooding omnipresence in the skies. Or, from the other angle: "You have not shown enough to make me move"—this time, not in favor of the plaintiff, but to strike down a statute. And what had been in effect a philosophy of conservatism becomes, without internal change, the "open sesame" of liberal reform. Holmes does not take the initiative. The legislature will do that. Holmes strikes down the barriers others would *by new creation* set up before the legislature. Natural law cannot maintain its substance to a cynical eye.

We see thus exemplified the rôle of the single man in social change, and the rôle of a philosophy once accepted, in the work of the single man. As in all but exceptional instances, with a lag. It took twenty years to win the Supreme Court to Holmes' point of view, and when it had been done there came a setback. While his philosophy in private law has waited close to sixty years to find acceptance. The acclaim that greeted *The Common Law,* here and abroad, was not for the analytical insight we prize today, but for its history.

[1] 167 Mass. 92, 44 N. E. 1077 (1896).

With the turn of the century the emotional revolt of laborers, farmers, and small business men had worked its way up into the thinking of the intellectuals. How far this is a parallel phenomenon to Roosevelt's progressivism, how far it was kindled from the political sphere, I have no means of knowing. Certain it is that vital thinking of a peculiarly high order appears in the first decade of the century. Dewey, James, Bentley, Sumner, even Ross. And Veblen. And, on the legal side, Brandeis as early as the '90s, Wigmore, the path-breaking work of Pound, Hohfeld and Cook, and in 1910 and 1911 Bingham as the forerunner of realism.

On the private law side Pound's sociological jurisprudence represents in essence a revolt against case law positivism, a re-introduction of ethics into the law, and ethics with a vigorous social flavor. The critique of the law is to proceed not from inside but from outside. Once again with a hangover of natural law thinking. For to discover social values one turns to Reason in the armchair (and, with a hangover of positivism, to the cases in the books), and to such desultory experience as he may have had about the matter. Still, on the private law side, Pound, not Holmes, is the prophet of the new dispensation. On the public law side, much more Holmes than Pound.

But it will be observed that, as indicated at the outset, we have now shifted the arena of discussion. No longer are we dealing with the implicit philosophy of the law-men at large. We have begun to speak of individual writers whose work is far from mirroring the action of their legal contemporaries in the bulk. The lag in the case of Holmes has been mentioned. The lag in the case of Pound is hardly smaller. Not until Cardozo undertook the job of re-interpretation of the fundamental point of view (beginning in 1925) may one regard sociological jurisprudence as even beginning to win general acceptance among the body of the guild.

This calls for explanation. The needs of the times were there, and felt. Sociological jurisprudence ought, it would seem, to have found an early echo. I find a number of factors to which one might appeal, yet have no great confidence in any of them being operative. The "law" under discussion was the law of the schools, and the law of the schools had for some decades been divorced from life. That may have helped to pen the tempest within the legal teapot. More important is probably that impatience called for *legislative*—or administrative—change, and so focussed attention on the constitutional field. It will be found, *e.g.,* that widespread realism in public law antedates realism among private law scholars by a good two decades. But most important of all I suspect to be the fact that leaders in legal practice had fallen hopelessly behind the times. Dominated by bourgeois, business, buccaneer ideology, serving and knowing only, as specialized office counsel, the interests of the "Ins", they had no ears for words that betokened change in an existing order. One still meets gentlemen who still voice their profound conviction that such conservative men as Holmes, or Brandeis, or Pound, are "dangerous".

Meantime, the spear-point had advanced. In the immediate post-war years a goodly body of thinkers, stimulated especially by Dewey, Boas, Watson, and Veblen, had begun to apply Holmes' way of seeing not only to the law, but to sociological jurisprudence. To make the latter *real* required more than armchair estimates. Pound and Frankfurter had indeed begun the work in the Cleveland crime survey. A similar and more sustained approach was required no less in private law. To apply the criterion of judging law by its effects called for more exact knowledge both of what law was and of what its effects might be. Indeed it called for more accurate knowledge of the conditions of society. (Here it seems to me Brandeis was in public law the major pioneer—at least in forcing facts before the court.) Hence, "Realism". The mixture of philosophic tendencies involved in that way of work is interesting. From the positivists, the realists take the insistence on concrete data, though they largely increase the scope of data to be insisted on. From Holmes (and Watson) they take a cynicism of vision, an insistence on treating words as mere tools in attempting to deal with things more tangible. From sociological jurisprudence they accept the criterion of criticism by way of social needs. From Dewey and James they take an insistence on results as the single test of validity.

As yet their views are hopelessly unorthodox. The profession at large still shows, at times, the influence of the natural law of one hundred years ago. More vitally its work is affected by the positivism that was at home in 1880. Beginnings of the influence of sociological jurisprudence can be seen in law-men's actions. The realists find as yet little echo among judges. But what makes them seem a wedge that is opening up the future behavior of the guild is that their lines of thinking are so much closer than any others to the actual behavior of the better bar, and that their judgments of policy come backed by facts.

2 Law in Life, Life in Law: Llewellyn's Legal Realism Revisited

JAN M. BROEKMAN

When the philosophies die, the books do not die with them, he writes. He ardently desires to live a full life, which for him is a life of action that is not hampered by theories that do not serve anyone's needs. Consequently, his life is not focused on "verbalized philosophies" that can be found in law books or philosophy books but rather on "philosophies-in-action as the history of law in these United States has gone its way" (Llewellyn 1934: 206). What ideas are implied in Karl Llewellyn's approach, and do they remain relevant for us today?

TWO BIOGRAPHIES, AMONG OTHERS

Revitalizing a life as it is – a realm of immediate experiences – requires one to eschew ossified concepts, prescribed linguistic patterns, and institutionally safeguarded expressiveness. This guiding idea leads Llewellyn to use *law* and *philosophy* as catchwords rather than as precise descriptions of this important contrast. Indeed, the entire essay *On Philosophy in American Law* operates as a catchword. Perhaps the central catchword lurking in this essay is *life*, and to explore the complex dimensions of this catchword we can turn to two biographical notes on Llewellyn that point toward a very different development.

In his well-known book, Fikentscher (1975: 285) explains

> Llewellyn's oeuvre becomes more understandable if one looks at his way in life. Born 1893 in a German-English-Irish family of the Middle West, the parents had educational problems with the young man, so that he was handed over to a stern uncle in Eastern Prussia. Due to an administrative error in the beginning of the First World War, he had to perform active military service in the German army. He only came out of the army after an intervention of the American consul, and returned to the United States. Llewellyn learned the English language anew, as it were for the second time. That explains his incredible linguistic feeling and his ability to perceive issues without prejudice and to understand them anew. His essential contribution to Law stems from this "see-it-fresh" attitude.

This biography raises two questions among others: why is a fresh look at legal problems so exceptional, and does it require such a multicultural life experience?

Brian Leiter (2001: 8999) offers a different biographical story:

> Karl Nicholson Llewellyn was born in Seattle, Washington on May 22, 1893, though the family soon moved to Brooklyn, New York. At age 16, he went to Germany to study for 2 years, before entering Yale College in 1911. When World War I broke out, he was studying in Paris. Staunchly Germano-philic, he joined up with the 78th Prussian Infantry, was wounded later in 1914, and subsequently received the Iron Cross! Returning to Yale, he completed his undergraduate studies and enrolled in Yale Law School.... He joined the Yale Faculty in 1922, moving to Columbia Law School in 1925; Columbia was then fertile ground of the new 'Legal Realism,' a movement in which Llewellyn soon emerged as the major figure.... From the 1940s until his death, he made his seminal contributions to the Uniform Commercial Code.

From this biography we might conclude that the passions involved in the Germanophile attitude exemplify how life can take priority over disciplined reason, which would be independent of the factual question of whether his service was due to administrative error or a personal decision. Georg Liebmann (2006) suggested the same by vividly describing Llewellyn's "sympathy with the German cause," an attitude that is differently understood in the European countries than in the United States, just as the meaning of *philosophy* is differently understood.

Moving beyond the drama of Llewellyn's military service in the Prussian army, Llewellyn's biography suggests a much more important influence on his thinking by an ideology arising from the German politics and philosophy of the time. Llewellyn taught as a visiting law professor in Leipzig, Germany, during the 1928–9 term, and he was involved in the free law movement, the *Freirechtsbewegung*, which proclaimed that law is not a matter for legal scholars offering doctrinal discourses on social reality but is instead for the people. The movement was not a scientific and systemic philosophy but rather a loose association of thoughts and popular opinions.

Similarly, the German historical school, the *Historische Schule*, of that same period influenced legal realism in a U.S. philosophical manner and was the predecessor of sociological jurisprudence. The historical school wanted to restrict or even abolish legal doctrine and formal judicial decision making in jurisprudence in favor of the insight that all law is embedded in a national context, a *Volksgeist* ("the spirit of the people"), that provided a historical context that lawyers should use as a guide for their decision making. Because the written doctrinal law can never fully grasp the moral, historical, attitudinal, or philosophical reality of the people, the limits of law and jurisprudence become obvious: promulgation of legal rules must always be checked against the reality of the people's life. Continental historians underlined how this view of law and lawyers already included a return to natural law and ultimately favored Nazism by supporting a general conformism among lawyers in the Third Reich.

Only a few years after Llewellyn became acquainted with the historical school, the influential German jurist Karl Larenz proclaimed that the *Volk* ("community," "people," "ethnicity") is the goal and origin of law. Law originates in the Volk and must return to it, seeking to conform to the people's life according to images of a genuine justice, which is produced by the people, as the ultimate expression of their very nature (Larenz 1936: 26). Lawyers should, as a consequence, embrace inductive reasoning and a strongly emotional approach to law rather than formalist deductions, similar to one of the themes in Llewellyn's struggle against Langdellian orthodoxy in which Llewellyn argued for "sticking to the details of the case at hand." One must conclude that Llewellyn's legal realism was not just his adoption of a new intellectual perspective but rather a conviction that was deeply rooted in a widely acclaimed twentieth-century ideology that formed an important part of Llewellyn's life.

The relevance of this ideology resurfaced a half century later when the German Constitutional Court positioned German law against and above the European Union's Maastricht Treaty (1993) in the 1994 European Union case, *Brunner v. European Treaty*. The court determined that "each of the peoples of individual States is the starting point for a state power relating to that people" so that "if the Union carries out sovereign tasks and exercises sovereign powers, it is first and foremost the national peoples of the member-States who . . . have to provide the democratic legitimacy." The court thus referred to the philosophical climate of the historical school that Llewellyn encountered when he visited the country. The convictions that framed this case still reverberate in the political reality of the union, and they build on the views articulated by Llewellyn. It was shocking to observe their revival when several EU members during the June 2007 summit suggested reconsidering the directness of the direct-effect doctrine in the union. Their considerations mirror the problematic mixture of ethnic sentiments (Volksgeist) and economic (self) interest that defined the earlier period.

The German Constitutional Court decided that the union is not a *Volk*, that it is not a demos in its ethnic sense of the word (a sense belonging to Llewellyn's biographical experiences), and that the EU therefore can provide only a supplementary democratic regime (*Brunner* 1994: 57). This case and its many legal and philosophical consequences engendered a vast literature on the substance and form of law in the contemporary European context (Broekman 1999: 260–77). The contemporary reemergence of older doctrines suggests that we should reread Llewellyn and reconsider his motives by recognizing that his *life in law* shaped his doctrine of *law in life.*

A GRAND STYLE

Llewellyn has often been praised for his prose style. That style may have been rooted in his multicultural education, which forced him to learn his mother tongue twice, but there are other motives at work that have legal-theoretical relevance. Liebmann (2006: 149) characterizes Llewellyn and his texts as "a rare example of a law teacher-poet; the chief architect of the most ambitious common-law code of recent times; the possessor of one of the most exotic prose styles in all legal literature." However, as the architect of a code and designer of legal realism, Llewellyn uses his prose not to philosophize but rather to promote a legal technology: "Realism is not a philosophy, but a technology. That is why it is eternal" (Llewellyn 1960b: 510; Twining 1986: 175–84). This statement raises an eternal question that is not limited to the case of

Llewellyn: is it possible for a legal technology, untied from philosophical grounds, to exist at all? In other words: can a legal discourse function while separated from its philosophical or ideological foundation? Do Llewellyn's writings seek a legal order purer than Hans Kelsen's positivism, and is his peculiar style of writing inspired by a possible identity of legal facts and social facts?

Llewellyn's desire for lawyers to see legal facts freshly, without philosophical and ideological connotations, was captured by his effort to define the Grand Style, which he opposes to the Formal Style. The Grand Style is founded on a possible identity of legal and social facts (social facts not engendered by a social theory, but facts of life), whereas the Formal Style resorts to formal language in order to manage the semantic differences between the two types of fact, a difference that remains contentious among legal scholars and judges. As a consequence, one must conclude that the Grand Style is not in the first place a matter of text but rather a matter of theory based on Llewellyn's interpretation of the very nature of facts that are before lawyers and judges. He insists that the "law-job" of mastering those facts should not focus on philosophies. Llewellyn's (1960b: 509–10) remark in *The Common Law Tradition*, "I am referring to a way of thought and work, not to a way of writing," leads to the basic issue of how to understand facts and how to investigate their nature – a problem that realists and idealists have debated for centuries.

The nature of legal facts, and the tension between law as formal and informal communication, has been a central topic in European legal theory during the past forty years. Viehweg's "Topical Jurisprudence," Teubner and Luhmann's autopoiesis, Perelman on argumentation and rhetoric, and Habermas on consensus and communicative dimensions of law – all have deepened and exploited the differences between the formal and informal character of law. They all focus, in Llewellyn's words, on "the way of on-going renovation of doctrine." The Grand Style as an encompassing legal theory underlines Holmes' (1991: 1) famous conclusion in *The Common Law*: "The life of the law has not been logic: it has been experience." And, one has to notice, experience strives for the informal, even in the case of law. But the puzzle remains: how is informality nested in the formal discourse of law?

The legal order of a society cannot be wholly depicted in texts. Although written documents fulfill a function in society, they cannot mirror all human relations in all of their aspects, and certainly not the full function of law in social life. A reliable representation of social life does not come from legal scholars and judges who focus on conflict situations and the need for authoritarian decision making in what Llewellyn (1941) termed "trouble cases." Through this lens we would obtain distorted images of law as a form of social action, distortions that are not easy to detect. The weakness of sociological jurisprudence is that sociological investigations can never provide a solid foundation for legal judgments. Llewellyn's investigations into the profile of the legal institution and the outlines of what he calls the "law-job" in *My Philosophy of Law* confirms this fact. He doesn't argue for realism as a theory of legal discourse that appropriately honors the informal, and so the Grand Style is certainly not a Grand Theory! Why not? The answer is that Llewellyn, especially in *The Common Law*, maintains an individualistic and person-directed analysis of law. Legal doctrine evolves "too close to the past," he suggests, "its mood is too craft-conscious, the need for the clean line is too great, for the renovation to smell of revolution or, indeed, of campaigning reform" (Llewellyn 1960b: 509). His analysis builds to an emphasis on the role of judges, who must balance commands of authority with the demands of justice, must care for the clarity of legal language, and must prudently ensure that the rules and their applications are well understood and received, "even by mediocre men." This is neither merely a style nor deserving of the term *theory*. Perhaps it is best characterized as an emotional appeal to compassion, to interpretative skill rather than strict formality, and to a broad teleological conception of a legal rule, all of which characterize contemporary judges in the United States. But the deep gap between a system dedicated to resolving conflicts and a system dedicated to building solidarity remains. Can Llewellyn's legal realism speak to the latter?

Llewellyn's Grand Style is based on his understanding of the nature of legal facts. This style is based on language and meaning – even if Llewellyn wants to exclude philosophical motives in order to obtain an undisturbed view of facts in law. We have to recur to dimensions of expressiveness other than the opinions of judges or rules of doctrine, because in these instances the formal character dominates. Such a linguistic reorientation is a shift from a philosophy of law toward a philosophy of language. Even if a legal discourse could exist without a philosophy of law (Llewellyn's doubtful premise), it certainly cannot exist without a philosophy of language! This is the challenge for Llewellyn's legal realism.

WHOSE REALISM, WHOSE LIFE?

Against the foregoing backdrop it is now possible to sketch Llewellyn's view on the position of philosophy in American law. I begin with three points of orientation.

First, Llewellyn obviously is not adhering to the typical German understanding and use of the concept of philosophy. There is no canon of texts that bothers him, no problem of interpreting actual insights in the light of Greek ancestors or of schools such as German idealism or even existentialism, and there is no typical philosophical technique of thought formation (working from a logic and metaphysics) in his legal scholarship. The philosophical heritage is very different indeed from legal reasoning by precedent cases, and by avoiding this philosophical heritage he hopes to open numerous possibilities to develop a *fresh look*.

Second, with his observation that "philosophers' writings and law-men's doings meet rarely," Llewellyn (1934: 205n*) aims at another type of philosophy. Does his understanding of philosophy represent American philosophy between the First and Second World Wars? If not expressing a German philosophy, one would expect that his work evidences an American approach. The answer is not so simple. To say, "I do not look to philosophy" implies a truly philosophical standpoint and recalls a philosophical approach to the subject adopted by the American statesmen Benjamin Franklin and Thomas Jefferson. Their philosophy outside the academy was more accepted in America than in Europe, with Ralph Waldo Emerson and Charles Sanders Pierce as leading examples.

The defining American philosophy of the twentieth century is pragmatism – as is globally recognized. Alexis de Tocqueville once wrote how American philosophy seeks to "échapper à l'esprit de système," (escape the spirit of system) an attitude that emphasizes legal, social, and life practices because only what works out in practice is valid. This attitudes suffuses Llewellyn's (1941: x) description in *My Philosophy of Law*: "the viewing of law as a going institution provides two vitally serviceable points of orientation which freshen eyes . . . a going institution has jobs to do, and its function is to get them done effectively and well. . . . And a going institution has results in life." It is simplistic as well as challenging to say that American philosophy would, for Llewellyn, be characterized by means of three expressions: (1) freshened eyes, (2) jobs done effectively and well, and (3) results in life!

Third, the consequence of the foregoing is that there is an emphasis on judges; their profession is to fulfill the role of the subject of the legal texts they create. The "Grand Style" is a theory of law only to the extent that its style is the manner of constructing utterances via the dominance of the first-person singular. In this context, Llewellyn's essay provides a bird's-eye view of the activities of judges, and that eye is often a very cynical one. His eccentric style of writing treats social facts as if they were all alike: names, social issues, historic developments, political stances, companies, geographies. And he represents everything in the first-person mood: slavery as well as private law, the powers of a nation and a historic conflict, a railway, a reconstruction ideal, natural resources, and signers and consumers. Law's style for him is the common law articulated by the judge, and its history is the history of American society. No vague philosophical considerations should form clouds that obscure the fact that realism is what law and its order need.

But what is the realism he proposes? *The realism of the subject.* And a major subject – in fact the only one in legal discourse – is the common law judge! Llewellyn's style excels in not naming that name, in hiding the subject's identity, in telling the reader: "you know to whom I refer," "you know what I mean," "you know . . . the Truth, the Document, the Signer, the conflict." The bird's-eye is his eye; history unfolds through that eye, when the subject perceives the subject as "other"! This perception mechanism becomes especially clear when judges are involved in name giving: cases and names form one and the same identity before Llewellyn's legally skilled eye. Legal realism is based on this semantic process, which creates identity through the jurisprudential *conditio sine qua non* of cases. Cases are given names and they become signs through those given names. Once they are named signs in the great common law, they sustain the life of law and citizens under the rule of (the common) law.

The sequence of cases, names, and signs forms a major backbone of legal thought formation for Llewellyn and continues to define contemporary thought in the United States. Its existence and foundational position has far-reaching consequences. Llewellyn attempts to understand these legal signs in a fresh light, but the fresh light is dispersed only locally and there is limited motivation to spread the light, as revealed by the title of his essay, which refers not only to American law but also to American philosophy. As emphasized earlier, the latter is not a philosophy in books and libraries, scholarly debates, and sophisticated essays; it is found in practices on the basis of "accurate knowledge of the conditions of society" (Llewellyn 1934: 212). His legal realism is a *jurisprudence in action*, which is to say a *law in action*, expressing the *philosophy in action* of American pragmatism.

But these patterns of action are conceivable only on the basis of a philosophical assumption that is concealed in Llewellyn's text: the assumption that language is a matter of one-to-one semantic relationships. A word must maintain a correspondence to a reality beyond language so that our words will mirror reality, the action of life. Law's speech, the word of judges in the first place, only makes sense if reality is empirically present and not the sole result of human expressivity and articulation. Speaking of law as a fictitious discourse or of legal fictions in jurisprudence is just a bad joke. Legal realism depends on judges who never speak out of touch with reality.

Contrast this assumption with raising the question of what happens when "judging cases under the best knowledge of all circumstances" occurs through nontrustworthy references, words, or meanings? Friedrich Nietzsche stated that all our references are based on a fiction, a fallacy. Our erroneous belief is that reality is always just there, and it is there in order to be articulated through our language. Western Continental philosophy characterized this fallacy as the metaphysics of presence, which forms the basis for a large majority of methods of legal analysis, explanation, reading, and interpretation. Jacques Derrida suggested how even the concept of a sign, or of a name or a representation, are all rooted in such a fallacy! That insight inspired his deconstructive efforts, which eventually causes fissure in the foundations of American pragmatism. This explains the vivid interest in Derrida's approach in the United States, particularly outside the philosophy departments. His ideas received more attention in the pragmatic climate of the United States than in Europe, where scholars already were comfortable reading Nietzsche. The insight of deconstruction provokes a breach in law's attempt to represent nonlinguistic reality through its proper discourse, but this is precisely the fallacy embraced by Llewellyn's Grand Style. The catchphrase "no philosophy" might be recast as an anticipatory defense against a deconstructive critique.

Llewellyn's essay demonstrates how important the relations between law and philosophy are, even if he ostensibly attempts to withdraw legal issues from philosophical consideration. It is significant that one of his most popular books, *The Bramble Bush*, refers to a period of judicial decisions (the "conditioning machinery") that was grounded in the belief in a complete and comprehensive legal system, with new forms of law strictly referring to existing law, and with rules of law in the books that dominate theory and practice through conceptualism and predictability. Llewellyn (1960a: 158) speaks about that period as the least happy days of our legal system. Recognize that this is not because of the fictitious character of legal reference but because of the beliefs that found the legal system! It is no surprise, then, that Llewellyn confirmed how Roscoe Pound's instrumentalism was perhaps even more influential than his own realism. By 1908, Pound had already coined the term that judges are in essence social engineers who need to make their engineering theories explicit, and he later elaborated this thesis in his 1913 essay *The Philosophy of Law in America*, which later provided the title of Llewellyn's article.

Legal scholars must understand that Llewellyn's legal realism has yet to come to terms with the fallacy that institutes the sequence of cases, names, and signs as the reality of the legal order; in other words, it has failed to come to grips with the metaphysics of representation. *Law in life* must treat cases as traces in a legal system that emerges – like life itself, Gilles Deleuze teaches. Llewellyn's Grand Style rests on a grand fallacy in order to unfold *law in life*, but no legal realist has been realistic enough to grasp how it desires to unfold beyond that concealed fallacy. Llewellyn's appeal to a sociological jurisprudence can at most be read as a sign or a trace of such a desire to awaken *life in law*!

WORKS CITED

Broekman, Jan M. *A Philosophy of European Union Law.* Leuven, Belgium: Peters, 1999.

Brunner v. European Union Treaty, 1 Common Mkt. L. Rev. 57 (1994).

Fikentscher, Wolfgang. *Methoden de Rechts. Band II: Anglo-Amerikanischer Rechtskreis.* Tübingen, Germany: Mohr Sieback, 1975.

Holmes, Jr., Oliver Wendell. *The Common Law.* New York: Dover Publications, Inc., 1991 (1881).

Larenz, Karl. "Vom Wesen der Strafe." *Zeitschrift für Deutsche Kulturphilosophie.* Vol. 2 (1936).

Leiter, Brian. "Llewellyn, Karl Nickerson (1893–1962)." In *International Encyclopedia of the Social and Behavioral Sciences.* Eds. Neil J. Smelser and Paul B. Baltes. Oxford: Pergamon-Elsevier Science, 2001, 8999–9001.

Liebmann, George W. *The Common Law Tradition: A Collective Portrait of Five Legal Scholars.* New York: Transaction Publishers, 2006.

Llewellyn, Karl N. *The Bramble Bush: On Our Law and Its Study.* New York: Oceana, 1960a.

———. *The Common Law Tradition: Deciding Appeals.* Boston: Little, Brown, and Co., 1960b.

———. *My Philosophy of Law.* Boston: Boston Law Co., 1941.

———. "On Philosophy in American Law." *U. Pa. L. Rev.* 82.3 (1934): 205–12.

Twining, William L. *Karl Llewellyn and the Realist Movement.* London: Weidenfeld and Nicolson, 1986.

3 On Realism's Own "Hangover" of Natural Law Philosophy: Llewellyn *Avec* Dooyeweerd

DAVID S. CAUDILL

"Ever since the era of the Legal Realists (such as . . . Karl Llewellyn)," remarks Litowitz (1997: 164), "lawyers have been aware that legal outcomes are somewhat indeterminate and unpredictable." Hence the saying, "We're all realists now." Then there was the joke among some law professors at the annual meeting of the American Association of Law Schools following the U.S. Supreme Court's handling of *Bush v. Gore* – which seemingly confirmed that law is politics (the slogan of critical legal studies) – that "we're all crits now." But Karl Llewellyn, describing in 1934 the state of philosophy in American law, identified a sense in which we were, and I believe still are, all natural lawyers. (It is only a sense, because we are obviously not all formal adherents of the natural law tradition, any more than we are all realists or "crits." But natural law, in a sense, is the fallback position for all of us.) And that sense on Llewellyn's part provides an unlikely link to a contemporary of Llewellyn (1893–1962), the Dutch legal theorist Herman Dooyeweerd (1894–1977) – unlikely, because Dooyeweerd was no realist, but rather a neo-Calvinist natural lawyer.

Dooyeweerd, like Llewellyn, was trained in law, not philosophy, but he became a leading philosopher in the Netherlands. As Llewellyn (1934) was writing "On Philosophy in American Law," Dooyeweerd was completing *De wijsbegeerte der wetsidee* (The Philosophy of the Law-Idea) (Dooyeweerd 1935–6), which was translated into English as *A New Critique of Theoretical Thought* (Dooyeweerd 1953–8). Dooyeweerd's four-volume work has a lot in common with, and offers exhaustive support for, some of the philosophical concerns in Llewellyn's eight-page essay.

Despite its brevity, Llewellyn's essay is overflowing with concerns about philosophy. But because of its brevity, the essay does not clearly define the term *philosophy*. Llewellyn (1934: 205) begins with the term *theory*, quoting Pareto, as something that a "man" makes and that "men" accept; later in the essay Llewellyn will say philosophies are also "invented" and sometimes adopted in society. Then Llewellyn says there is no shortage of theories or "of philosophies," but later on he conflates the philosophy of natural law, natural law thinking or approaches, and the theory of right reason. Ambiguities aside, Llewellyn discusses philosophy in one of its traditional senses as a centralized and foundational discipline, preceding more specific theories and functioning as an organizing theory of theory itself. Even as Llewellyn focuses on legal philosophy, he explores its influence as a generalized source of fundamental values and ideals, like justice and morality – it supplies needs, and it tells us what is right or sound or desirable when difficult choices are made. And a legal philosophy has legs – it provides an atmosphere and has influence without regard to whether its adherents recognize or can give an account of it. This seems to add another level or aspect to the realist claim that legal decisions often involve extralegal factors, in addition to doctrine or precedent, such as a judge's personal bias, economic interests, strategically employed language, social class, or political views. Each of these factors, Llewellyn suggests, can probably be traced to an explicit or implicit philosophical orientation that merits our attention. This is not to say that the forces identified by social scientists, psychologists, or language theorists are not significant but rather that philosophy is also an important enterprise.

The only footnote, the asterisk on Llewellyn's title, offers a context for his essay. We urgently need to return to philosophy for the sake of our "aggrieved" law students. In their disorientation, while learning a system of precedent that "works in forty different ways," they need more than a mere list of jurisprudential trends; they "must see why men adopted them, and above all, *how* they all fitted into the single picture." They need to be "given some chart of the sweep," to see the difference in "feel" and tendency in our various approaches to law (Llewellyn 1934: 205). Llewellyn's essay is intended to be a start for that project.

The obstacles, however, are numerous. Philosophers' "writings and law-men's doings meet rarely on the same level of discourse," though "part of the game is to find where they do" and do not, and why (Llewellyn 1934: 205). Philosophers are scorned, as if they are dispensable, and those in the field of philosophy perennially wince at such dismissal. Such scorn is, nevertheless, quite beside the point for Llewellyn, who was "not so much concerned . . . with the philosophers themselves, with whom indeed [his] acquaintance is but scanty." Rather, Llewellyn highlights "philosophy-in-action" or "implicit philosophy," the necessity of which cannot be escaped. Each of us will live and make things coherent "in terms of some one of them – or of some inconsistent hodge-podge of a dozen" – even if the premises are "inarticulate and in fact unthought." Some (rarely) will choose a philosophy, but everyone will grow "into ways of doing which comport with one philosophy and not with another" (206).

Llewellyn then turns to his brief history of jurisprudence as it has been lived in the United States. We began in a natural law atmosphere, with self-evident truths, the essential nature of government ("whether derived from Montesquieu or Reason"), and the natural "heritage of the individual citizen" (Llewellyn 1934: 206–7). Irrespective of its effect on government, the philosophy of natural law provided the foundation for private law, rendering English cases as merely suggestive for the "law which urges Reason *as the law*. The judge, if his experience reaches, has but to think, to see, and to decree as seen. . . . [I]nstinct and theory of right reason continue to correct reception of the English law" (207). After the Civil War, "the Business Man took hold of the ideology of America" and positivism became the dominant philosophy of law. Forgetting "right reason," "morality," and the accident of justice, a "legal system exists to preserve the law as is." But when positivism was applied to case law (nursed and guided by "a philosophical presupposition of natural law"), our discordant precedents were all positive (Llewellyn 1934: 208). "The choice among *inconsistent* precedents (say, 'on principle') was... an echo of the already decadent philosophy of immutable 'natural law.'" And when the "front of battle shift[ed]," and there was no precedent for "due process" and "equal protection," the "prevailing positivism, explicit or implicit, gave no footing. Again the approach was along the lines of natural law. *Right reason* is the guide.... Observe the ways of *implicit* philosophy. Natural law in the constitutional field rides hand in hand with positivism on the private side" (4: 209). So ends the nineteenth century.

Llewellyn then shifts his attention to new legal philosophies, realism, and sociological jurisprudence, promulgated by "writers whose work is far from mirroring the action of their legal contemporaries in the bulk." In Pound's sociological jurisprudence, which reintroduces ethics "with a vigorous social flavor" into the law, the "critique of the law is to proceed not from the inside but from the outside. Once again with a hangover of natural law thinking. For to discover social values one turns to Reason in the armchair" (Llewellyn 1934: 211). But to make sociological jurisprudence "*real* required more than armchair estimates," and to judge law "by its effects called for more exact knowledge both of what law was and of what its effects must be" as well as "more accurate knowledge of the conditions of society." Hence, "Realism.... From the positivists, the realists take [but increase the scope of] the insistence on concrete data.... From Holmes... they take a cynicism of vision, an insistence on treating words as mere tools.... From sociological jurisprudence they accept the criterion of criticism by way of social needs. From Dewey and James they take an insistence on results as the single test of validity." Llewellyn calls this perspective, his own, hopelessly unorthodox, and remarks that the "profession at large still shows, at times, the influence of the natural law of one hundred years ago" (though more vitally, the positivism of 1880, and some influence by sociological jurisprudence). Realists, finding "as yet little echo among judges," nevertheless are in "their lines of thinking... so much closer than any others to the actual behavior of the better bar," and "their judgments of policy come backed by facts" (212).

Then Llewellyn stops, without saying that a confessing realist judge's philosophy-in-action or implicit jurisprudence will be, like all other judges he discusses, natural law. Indeed, natural law "cannot maintain its substance to a cynical eye" (Llewellyn 1934: 210). Llewellyn here uses the term *natural law* quite informally to refer variously to belief in self-evident truths, to "[r]eason *as the law*" that allows judges "to think, to see, and to decree as seen," to the choice "on principle" among inconsistent precedents (decisions that we like are "sound"), and to "judge's notions of the way things should be" in the absence of precedents. Pound's sociological jurisprudence suffered a natural law hangover because he found social values in armchair reason and in his own "desultory experience as he may have had about the matter" (211). Realism avoids such estimates through concrete data (e.g., the Cleveland crime survey), exact knowledge of law and its effects, accurate knowledge of social conditions, and a focus on results. Realists, it seems, do not believe in determinative reason, self-evident truths, or immutable moral principles. And yet a realist judge who was a proto-Posnerian, in Leiter's

(2005: 58–9) terminology, "would tackle directly exactly the kinds of political and economic considerations a legislature would weigh," and "Llewellyn thought it was *good* that judges were inclined in commercial disputes to try to enforce the norms of commercial culture." Why are such policy decisions not "an echo of natural law?"

The answer is in Realism's "*temporary* divorce of Is and Ought for purposes of study.... [D]uring the inquiry itself into what Is, the observation, the description, and the establishment of relations between the things described are to remain *as largely as possible* uncontaminated by the desires of the observer or by what he wishes might be or thinks ought (ethically) to be" (Llewellyn 1931: 1236).

Even though "value judgments must always be appealed to in order to get objectives for inquiry," and even though "a permanent divorce would be impossible" when change is perceived as necessary, Llewellyn insists that Realism has no normative aspect (Llewellyn 1931: 1254). Realists, Llewellyn "hazards," generally agree on some things – the importance of court organization and the need to "face squarely" policy questions, to know the effects of rules, and to allocate risk – but not on what changes in law should be made (Llewellyn 1931: 1254–5). Leiter (2005: 58–9) therefore identifies in Llewellyn a certain "normative quietism;" Llewellyn of course had normative preferences, but he did not view realism as a normative guide for judges. Eventually, however, after the temporary divorce, after the acknowledgment of ethical pluralism, after detailed knowledge of legal concepts and socioeconomic contexts, and after examining social reality for its "customary practices and beliefs" or "immanent law" (Fischer, Horwitz, and Reed 1993: 170), decisions will need be made as to what is a "good" effect, a "sound" outcome, or a "right reason." According to Llewellyn's own historiography, these would seem to represent hangovers of natural law thinking.

I am not criticizing realism – I agree that law and legal doctrine are indeterminate, and that other factors are in play. And I agree that a deeper understanding of how law actually works and more knowledge of social conditions – facts – are always helpful. I even agree with Llewellyn that realism is closer than any other jurisprudence to the actual behavior of the best lawyers, who know that precedents are incomplete and flexible, and that judicial personalities as well as judges' political, economic, and moral prejudices are influential in the decision-making process, even when veiled by doctrinal rhetoric. Critical legal studies (CLS), which updated realism in terms of neo-Marxism and French critical theory, likewise highlighted those aspects of law. And even as CLS splintered into some versions of feminist legal theory, critical race theory, and postmodern approaches, its enduring legacy was the disclosure of ideology, belief structures, and presuppositions that functioned as faithlike commitments in all legal-theoretical thought. In Llewellynian terms, all jurisprudence has a natural law hangover in the sense that it cannot avoid recourse to norms, values, or principles grounded in something that looks like a religious commitment, even when God is replaced by reason, common sense, self-evident truths, or any understanding of the way things are and should be.

That was the view of Herman Dooyeweerd, a professor of law at the Vrije Universiteit Amsterdam from 1926 to 1965. In more than two hundred books and articles, he developed a complex philosophical system based on Abraham

Kuyper's neo-Calvinism, but he was influenced along the way by neo-Kantianism and phenomenology. One aspect of Dooyeweerd's thought is particularly relevant to Llewellyn's essay, namely, Dooyeweerd's view that human beings are necessarily "religious," even those who do not belong to a traditional religious faith or community. Dooyeweerd used the term *ground-motives* (*grondmotieven*) to describe the various philosophical orientations that provide ideals and motivation in culture generally. As to theoretical thought, there will always be pretheoretical commitments that function like religious beliefs, that ground theory. According to H. J. van Eikema Hommes, the successor of Dooyeweerd's chair in jurisprudence and his close disciple, Dooyeweerd's transcendental critique confirmed that theoretical thought is always "subject to fundamental, centrally religious motives which dominate a thinker at heart" (Hommes 1979: 1). In his popularized formulation of that view, Nicholas Wolterstorff, a philosopher influenced by Dooyeweerd, calls these fundamental motives "control beliefs," which function alongside data and "data-background beliefs" in theoretical thought:

> [O]ne remains cloaked in belief – aware of some strands, unaware of most. . . .
>
> For one thing, there will always be a large set of [data-background] beliefs such that one's holding them is a condition of one's accepting as data that which one does. . . .
>
> [I]t is even more important to bring to attention a second component in the cloak of beliefs . . . while weighing a theory. Everyone . . . has certain [control] beliefs as to what constitutes an acceptable *sort* of theory on the matter under consideration. . . . Because we hold them we are led to *reject* certain sorts of theories . . . control beliefs also lead us to devise theories. . . . We want theories . . . that comport as well as possible with those beliefs. (Wolterstorff 1976: 62–4)

In a more sophisticated formulation, Hendrik Hart, a philosophical heir and friendly critic of Dooyeweerd, highlights the challenge "to look for the extratheoretical factors needed to complete theory. Over twenty years before. . . . Polanyi's *Personal Knowledge* [1958] . . . , Dooyeweerd forcefully advanced the conviction that knowledge . . . is personal . . . , [which] reinforces the concept of the relativity of the rational aspect of human experience. Dooyeweerd never subscribed to the view which treats our conceptional faculties as autonomous, isolated and substantivized." Hence Dooyeweerd's exhaustive critique of "the pretended autonomy of reason"; because of the relativity of rational knowing, reason is not the "measure of the truth about . . . the world" (Hart 1985: 151).

Having acknowledged his own religious starting point, Dooyeweerd went on to construct a normative theory of law that is both part of the natural law tradition and highly critical of many natural law conceptions. For purposes of comparison to Llewellyn, however, Dooyeweerd's critical method parallels the realist effort to reveal the "heavily operative" factors (Llewellyn 1931: 1237) – apart from legal doctrine, itself indeterminate – that produce court decisions. Like Llewellyn, Dooyeweerd felt that philosophy mattered, and that a philosophical orientation is inevitable. As a practice, Dooyeweerd (1953–8: 4) defined philosophy as theoretical reflection directed toward "cosmic" coherence, but Dooyeweerd also acknowledged the cultural power of philosophical orientations even when they are unconscious and unacknowledged. His theory of Western ground-motives is a theory of implicit philosophy or philosophy-in-action, which Llewellyn (1934: 206) defined as the "premises, albeit inarticulate and in fact unthought, which made coherence out of a multiplicity of single ways of doing." Philosophies, for Llewellyn, become "established in the habits and attitudes" of social groups. Such analyses have numerous parallels in contemporary theory, from the ideology critique of neo-Marxian social theory and the postmodern critique of Enlightenment foundationalism (both of which inspired many critical legal scholars), to poststructuralist literary theory's sense of language as a social force, and to the history, philosophy, and sociology of science: "Michael Polanyi's theory of the scientist's indwelling in his framework of commitment, Jürgen Habermas's theory of the role of the human interest in science, Gerard Radnitzsky's theory of steering fields internal to science, and Thomas Kuhn's theory of the role of paradigms are all prefigured in the way Dooyeweerd worked out his theory" (Hart 1985: 145). Interest in the "role of extraconceptual factors in theoretical inquiry" and the "connections between theory and the ultimate commitments of those who theorize" is as evident today as it was in the work of Llewellyn and Dooyeweerd (Hart 1985: 150).

Just as Llewellyn identified the natural law hangover in Pound's recourse to social values, van Eikema Hommes (1979: 292) saw in the sociological approach to law a "*social-normative prognosis* [that presupposes the norms of social life] *and is meaningless without them.* In other words a prognosis of probable legal conduct, as well as the true expectations of the legal subjects presuppose legal norms and their real normative validity. If these norms were lacking the expectations would be baseless and the prognosis unfounded." And even as some realists tried to "eliminate the normative character of law and [attempt] to reduce law to the actual conduct . . . of judges," Hommes argues (1979: 312), legal norms "happen to occupy and essential and undeniable position in legal life" – they cannot be reduced to facts. Recourse to social well-being, the ideal of justice, human needs, or normative generalizations – each of them a highly contested conception – only serves to revive the natural law impulse identified by Llewellyn in the history of American legal philosophy.

And yet Llewellyn wants to avoid, in his realist methodology, the contamination of value judgments, and the term *natural law* obviously has a pejorative connotation throughout his brief essay on legal philosophy. Llewellyn admires Justice Holmes (1964: 82), who said that "jurists who believe in natural law seem to me to be in that naïve state of mind that accepts what has been familiar and accepted by them and their neighbors as something that must be accepted by all men everywhere." I understand that natural law adherents might claim a universal validity for their deep-seated preferences, while realists concede the social and historical relativity of their deep-seated preferences, but both sets of preferences function in the same manner. I even understand that a realist might be more self-critical than a naive natural lawyer and therefore call upon social science, concrete data, and empirical studies to back up policy decisions while remaining alert to rhetorical strategies in legal discourse. But in Dooyeweerdian terms, self-critical reflection will reveal that our knowledge "is not simply a direct and neutral given of observation, but . . . is in part a subjective cultural *product* of our subjective selves with all our underlying philosophical assumptions" (Hart 1985: 147). Llewellyn's warning, to those who scorn philosophy, that they cannot escape the necessity of living "in terms of some of them," applies to Llewellyn and the realists, and to all of us.

The sense in which Dooyeweerd is a realist is that self-evident truths, reason, the essential nature of government, the ideal of justice, social values, principles of soundness, and so forth, are belief structures – to view them as foundational is an uncritical prejudice. Dooyeweerd, and implicitly Llewellyn, level the playing field by suggesting that every theorist should reflect upon and become aware of his or her assumptions. Unlike Holmes (1964: 81), who said that "deep-seated preferences can not be argued about," Dooyeweerd thought that his transcendental critique could "pave the way for a real contact of thought among the various philosophical trends." He recommended a "merciless war against the masking of supra-theoretical prejudices as theoretical axioms" (Dooyeweerd 1953–8: 70), and he claimed no monopoly on truth for his own inquiry: "As a *philosophy* it does not in any way demand a privileged position for itself; on the contrary, it seeks to create a real basis for philosophical dialogue among the different movements . . . in terms of their own respective deepest spiritual backgrounds" (Dooyeweerd 1996: 4). Dooyeweerd therefore saw a lot of room for dialogue and argument about deep-seated preferences – identifying assumptions, challenging their status, inquiring about their sources, and defending their results as good for everyone.

To the likely distress of actual natural law philosophers, Llewellyn's (and my own) use of the term *natural law* to refer to any determinable value judgment or preference, including reason in the armchair, is probably unfortunate. In Llewellyn's defense, he does describe these phenomena as "echoes" of, as approaches "along the line of," and as "hangovers" of the philosophy of natural law (Llewellyn 1934: 209, 211). *Natural law* is just a catchphrase for a decadent tendency to pretend that personal preferences are somehow in accord with higher reason or immutable principles. Dooyeweerd would have referred to the uncritical dogma of the autonomy of reason, reserving the term *natural law* for his own style of jurisprudence (Dooyeweerd 1996: 19–25). But Dooyeweerd would also have referred to all jurisprudential movements as "religious," in the sense of their inevitable faith in pretheoretical assumptions, and he was of course not being pejorative.

The targets of Llewellyn's critical essay, and Dooyeweerd's critique of theoretical thought, are sometimes the same. Both emphasize concrete data, and Dooyeweerd argued that all disciplines must prove their worth in their fact-filled fields (Hommes even wanted to call Dooyeweerd's approach "transcendental-empirical"). Both are suspicious of reason as an allegedly universal source of guidance, because both see its relativistic foundation in a philosophical orientation. Llewellyn thought that such an orientation should be replaced by another orientation – one that would insist on concrete data, that would see words as mere tools, that would be grounded in social needs and validated by results. That new orientation, Dooyeweerd would point out, cannot avoid pretheoretical commitments. Every philosophical orientation involves claims that it is natural, that it describes the way things are and should be. In that sense, every philosophical orientation is religious, based on faith, such that a natural law hangover is inevitable.

WORKS CITED

Dooyeweerd, Herman. "Calvinism and Natural Law." Trans. A. Wolters. In *Essays in Legal, Social and Political Philosophy.* Eds. John Witte Jr. and Alan Cameron. Lewiston, NY: Edwin Mellen Press, 1996.

______. *Christian Philosophy and the Meaning of History.* Trans. J. Vriend. Lewiston, NY: Edwin Mellen Press, 1996.

______. *De wijsbegeerte der wetsidee.* 3 vols. Amsterdam: H. J. Paris, 1935–6.

______. *A New Critique of Theoretical Thought.* 4 vols. Philadelphia: Presbyterian and Reformed Publishing, 1953–8.

Fischer, William W., III, Martin J. Horwitz, and Thomas A. Reed, eds. *American Legal Realism.* Oxford: Oxford Univ. Press, 1993.

Hart, Hendrik. "Dooyeweerd's Gegenstand Theory of Theory." *In The Legacy of Herman Dooyeweerd: Reflection on Critical Philosophy in the Christian Tradition.* Ed. C. T. McIntire. Lanham, MD: Univ. Press of America, 1985, 143–66.

Holmes, O. "Natural Law." In *The Holmes Reader.* Dobbs Ferry, NY: Oceana Publications, 1964, 81–4.

Hommes, H. J. van Eikema. *Major Trends in the History of Legal Philosophy.* Amsterdam: North-Holland Publishing, 1979.

Leiter, Brian. "American Legal Realism." In *The Blackwell Guide to the Philosophy of Law and Legal Theory.* Eds. Martin P. Golding and William A. Edmundson. Oxford: Blackwell Publishing, 2005, 50–66.

Litowitz, Douglas E. *Postmodern Philosophy and Law.* Lawrence, KS: Univ. Press of Kansas, 1997.

Llewellyn, K. N. "On Philosophy in American Law." *U. Pa. L. Rev.* 82.3 (1934): 205–12.

______. "Some Realism about Realism – Responding to Dean Pound." *Harv. L. Rev.* 44.8 (1931): 1222–56.

Wolterstorff, Nicholas. *Reason within the Bounds of Religion.* Grand Rapids, MI: William B. Eerdman's Publishing, 1976.

4 On the Instrumental View of Law in American Legal Culture

BRIAN Z. TAMANAHA

Karl Llewellyn's "On Philosophy in American Law" was not a philosophical essay but rather a chronological survey of the impact of philosophical ideas about law in American legal culture since the founding. Llewellyn (1934: 206) made this clear at the outset of his essay: "Thus what is here before the telescope is the changing array not of verbalized philosophies, but of philosophies-in-action as the history of law in these United States has gone its way. What those philosophies were, what needs they served – and whose. I am not so much concerned with the philosophers themselves, with whom indeed my acquaintance is but scanty. I am concerned with philosophy-in-action, with implicit philosophy, with those premises, albeit inarticulate and in fact unthought, which yet make coherence out of a multiplicity of single ways of doing." It is important to consider the impact of philosophical ideas in this sense, Llewellyn wrote, because "once a philosophy has been established in the habits and attitudes of any person, it has effects" (Llewellyn 1934: 206).

An underlying theme of Llewellyn's survey is that philosophical ideas have time and again been enlisted in law to serve the powers that be. His sketch can be conveyed in a few strokes. Matters started off well enough at the founding and for several subsequent generations, Llewellyn suggests, during which judging was infused with ideas about natural law and right reason. This was a period of dynamic change in the country and economy, and judges (in a "Grand Style") used these ideas to adapt the inherited English common law to rapidly changing needs and circumstances, or invoked them to discard what could not be adapted successfully. The situation changed in the second half of the nineteenth century. What business captains required most from law were certainty, the protection of property, and the enforcement of contracts; questions about morality were relegated to secondary importance. Positivism, the idea that law *is* law, served this stage well. "Thus urge was for a *solid* something on which to build, of course, with the aforesaid exception for extensions made necessary by business needs" (Llewellyn 1934: 209) Historical jurisprudence and natural law ideas were enlisted along with positivism to sanctify whatever legal doctrine was revealed to be the right one (i.e., favorable to business). But a new threat emerged for business interests at the close of the nineteenth century, when popular movements, including labor, controlled legislatures and began using the legislative power to enact laws in their interests. Positivism (law *is* law) was no longer useful to the moneyed class under these circumstances, and it gave way to a new stage of interpretations by courts of the due process and equal protection clauses in natural law–type laissez-faire terms to strike legislation that was antithetical to business.

There matters stood, until Oliver Wendell Holmes Jr. entered the scene with his "cynical realism." Llewellyn characterized Holmes's approach as a sort of unphilosophical philosophy that can "be summed up as 'Look and see precisely what is there; and reckon with that and nothing else.'" Holmes's main approach was to strike "down the barriers others would by new creation set up before the legislature. Natural law cannot maintain its substance to a cynical eye" (Llewellyn 1934: 210). The turn of the century witnessed the revolt of labor and farmers and small businesses, the rise of progressivism, and the emergence of philosophical pragmatism (James and Dewey), and of new approaches in sociology (Ross) and economics (Veblen) that rejected laissez-faire thought. In law, Llewellyn observed, this new age was represented by Brandeis, Pound, Hohfeld, and Bingham. Pound's sociological jurisprudence was critical of the prevailing exclusive focus on law and insisted that law should be evaluated with respect to whether it serves social needs.

Not until the mid-1920s, however, did this way of thinking about law begin to gain acceptance (reflected in Cardozo's views), albeit recalcitrantly. Public and private law, which had lagged in their development under the influence of formalism, were failing to meet the needs of society. Progress in the new effort to measure law by its effects was hampered by scant "knowledge both of what law was and of what its effects might be" (Llewellyn 1934: 121).

Llewellyn thus arrived in his survey at the present, circa 1934: "Hence, 'Realism.' The mixture of philosophic tendencies involved in that way of work is interesting. From the positivists, the realists take the insistence on concrete data, though they largely increase the scope of data to be insisted on. From Holmes (and Watson) they take a cynicism of vision, and insistence on treating words as mere tools in attempting to deal with things more tangible. From sociological jurisprudence they accept the criterion of criticism by way of social needs. From Dewey and James they take an insistence on results as the single test of validity." This realistic view "as yet found little echo among judges." Natural law and legal positivism were still influential. Nonetheless, Llewellyn was optimistic about the future prospects for realism because he felt this approach more closely matched the actions and views of "the better bar" (Llewellyn 1934: 212).

That is where Llewellyn's essay on the role of philosophical ideas in American law left off. He believed that he stood at the cusp of a transitional moment, and he projected that the new realist ways of thinking about law, still in gestation, would ultimately win out. This was anything but certain at the time he made this prediction. Within five years of the publication of the article, the realist movement was in full retreat, a victim of the throes of World War II (Purcell 1973). But time has vindicated Llewellyn's prediction. Today, it is often said, "We are all realists now." Law is seen a means to an end, and the primary focus of legal analysis is on whether law is effective in achieving ends.

Yet this transformation has not brought the benefits that Llewellyn thought would accrue from an instrumental view of law. Along with the benefits of the instrumental approach came damaging consequences that he and other promoters failed to anticipate – consequences that we struggle with today.

The remainder of this essay will pick up where Llewellyn's essay left off, quickly elucidating the spread of an instrumental view of law within American legal culture. There are doubts about whether the instrumental view of law that Holmes, Pound, and the realists promoted qualifies as full-blown legal philosophy in a sense that rivals natural law and legal positivism (Moore 1984), although some theorists have made this claim (Summers 1982). There is no doubt, however, that this instrumental understanding permeates law and is "established in the habits and attitudes" of legal actors and nonlegal actors, with real consequences for law and society.

The core dynamic underlying the situation will be stated at the outset. The notion that law is an instrument was urged by its proponents in an integrated two-part proposition: Law is an instrument *to serve the social good.* The crucial twist is that, in the course of the twentieth century, the first half of this proposition swept the legal culture, while the second half became increasingly untenable (Tamanaha 2006). People came to believe that the notion of the common good is a fiction; or that there are different and irreconcilable goods attached to different groups in society; or that even if there is a common good, we have no way to discover or agree upon what it is. Under these circumstances, individuals and groups within society endeavor to seize or co-opt the law in every way possible; to fill in, interpret, manipulate, and utilize the law to serve their own ends; and to utilize the law as a weapon against others in social, political, religious, and economic disputes. Law is a means pure and simple, with the ends up for grabs.

Needless to say, this scenario is not what the promoters of the instrumental view of law had in mind (although Holmes occasionally described law in such terms).

THE PROBLEM OF ENDS

What Holmes, Pound, and the realists objected to, as Llewellyn indicated, was the prevailing mode of thought at the turn of the century that legal concepts and principles consisted of logically prescribed, autonomous, largely predetermined content, comprising an internally consistent, comprehensive body of law. Conceptual formalism kept the law in a frozen state that paid little heed to changes in society and to the needs of society. Against this view, Holmes (1897: 469) argued that "a body of law is more rational and more civilized when every rule it contains is referred articulately and definitely to an end which it subserves." Similarly, Pound (1908: 605) declared that "as a means to an end, [law] must be judged by the results it achieves, not by the niceties of its internal structure." Llewellyn (1931: 1236) identified this major precept of the realist movement: "The conception of law as a means to social ends and not as an end in itself; so that any part needs constantly to be examined for its purposes, and for its effect, and to be judged in the light of both and of their relation to one another."

To say that law is an instrument to serve ends does not, in itself, indicate how the appropriate social ends are to be specified. This is where social science came into play in their thinking. Holmes (1899: 462) espoused a utilitarian approach facilitated by science: "I have had in mind an ultimate dependence upon science because it is finally for science to determine, so far as it can, the relative worth of our different social ends." Pound held that competing social interests must be aligned in a balance that maximizes the totality, although he never identified how this was to be done. Llewellyn suggested that the question of "ought" should be set aside temporarily until we understand how law actually works. Most realists were silent on the question of ends.

Early critics of the instrumental view of law recognized the evident problems with determining appropriate ends. There are many ends in society, many of which are not good, and many of which cannot be mutually reconciled. One critic wrote, "Pragmatism has been frequently criticized because it is in a sense anarchistic and devoid of standards or principles. . . . It does not suffice to shuffle the mass of wants and claims of the litigants into a confused pile and then give effect to as many of them as we can in so far as harmony will permit" (Kennedy 1925: 69) In the minds of many, furthermore, the suggestion that law is an instrument of coercive state power with no built-in integrity brought U.S. law uncomfortably close to echoes of Nazi law. The realists retreated in the face of this attack (Purcell 1973).

Well before the emergence of the realists, doubts about moral principles had begun their inexorable march. The ultimate roots of these doubts trace back to the sixteenth-century Reformation and the eighteenth-century Enlightenment, which challenged the centuries-long dominance of Roman Catholicism and of tradition. By the late nineteenth century, faith in objectivity, universal values, and absolute truths was under siege. Philosophical pragmatism – which Holmes imbibed as a member of the Cambridge Metaphysical Club, and that Pound identified as an inspiration for his instrumental view of law – reflected this shift in thought. Non-Euclidean geometry, Einstein's theory of relativity, and Heisenberg's uncertainty principle raised serious questions about the purportedly objective truths produced in natural science. The realist Walter Wheeler Cook (1927: 306) surveyed these developments in ideas to remark presciently, in 1927, "The reign of relativity thus inaugurated by the basic sciences, is destined to work a corresponding revolution, deep, noiseless it may be, but inevitable, in all the views and institutions of man."

Although the realists were largely silenced by the end of the 1930s, their incisive critiques of former understandings of the law continued to influence legal thought. The legal process school that emerged in the 1950s accepted and built upon the notion that law is a means to an end. Legal process thinkers characterized courts, legislatures, and administrative agencies as coordinate legal institutions, each with its own unique strengths and limitations, and each engaged in a collaborative effort to shape the law to serve common social purposes. Their manifest confidence that common purposes could be worked out in law was a reflection of the consensus view that saturated American intellectual thought and popular culture in the golden 1950s. This consensus, however, was utterly shattered in the civil rights and antiwar protests that rocked American society in the 1960s and 1970s. It was an unprecedented period of turmoil: the assassinations of President John F. Kennedy and his heir apparent, Robert Kennedy; the murders of Martin Luther King Jr. and Malcolm X; political terrorism and bombings and bank heists; students killed at Kent State and Jackson State universities; sexual revolution and drugs;

corruption of Watergate; and oil shortages and high inflation combined with high unemployment and economic stagnation.

Law was caught up in the middle of this social schism, castigated from all sides. People on the Left saw law too often line up on the side of power and privilege, answering peaceful marches and sit-ins with police brandishing nightsticks and snapping dogs. People on the Right thought that defiant public displays of civil disobedience, encouraged by the meek response of law enforcement, undermined social order. Progressives cheered the Warren Court as the one legal institution doing the right thing, while conservatives despised the Court as activist usurpers who were writing their own personal liberal views into the Constitution. Observers thought it evident that a crisis of legal liberalism was at hand.

By the beginning of the 1970s, the two aspects of the core dynamic identified earlier – an instrumental view of law coexisting with a loss of faith in the common good (or in our ability to agree upon it) – were set in place. Both were noted in the legal literature at the time. The dean of Cornell Law School, Roger Cramton, wrote that legal instrumentalism had become "the ordinary religion of the law school classroom. Law today tends to be viewed in solely instrumental terms and as lacking values of its own." Law professors convey to students "an instrumental approach to law and lawyering," along with "a skeptical attitude toward generalizations, principles, and received wisdom" (Cramton 1978: 248). The legal historian G. Edward White, in 1973, remarked upon the evident widespread skepticism. Critics of government were "linked in their perception that terms such as 'public interest' and 'social welfare' have lost their meaning: the terms are capable of such wide, divergent, and contradictory interpretations that they are useless as standards of performance" (White 1973: 295). In the 1979 *Duke Law Journal*, the legal theorist Arthur Leff (1979: 1240) lamented the apparently insurmountable problems in law generated by the realization that "*[t]here is no such thing as an unchallengeable evaluative system*" (emphasis in original).

No one would think to utter these observations today, because we take for granted the instrumental view of law and skepticism about the public good and moral values. At the time, however, they were the subject of commentary because they were recognized as novel – although they had been gestating for generations – and worrisome. The legal historian Calvin Woodward, in 1968 (735), contrasted the spreading instrumental view of law with previous noninstrumental views, concluding his essay by asking: "does the [Realist] approach not teach all manner of men to look to law as an instrument for their private or personal disposal?"

THE PERVASIVENESS OF INSTRUMENTAL VIEWS OF LAW TODAY

We are so thoroughly influenced by this understanding that is unnecessary to detail the pervasiveness of the instrumental view today. I will merely list various ways in which instrumentalism courses through American legal culture. As already indicated, law professors teach law students to understand and treat legal rules and processes in instrumental terms. As Llewellyn put it (1960: 84), law students are taught to "analyze coldly, to see, and to see only, and manipulate the machinery of law." This instrumental approach to law also pervades the practice of law. Lawyers routinely treat the law instrumentally to serve the interests of their clients, to serve their own economic interests, or to serve the causes they attempt to advance. Robert Gordon (1988: 20) describes this instrumental mind-set toward lawyering: Lawyers "may, and if it will serve their clients' interests must, exploit any gap, ambiguity, technicality, or loophole, any non-obviously-and-totally-implausible interpretation of the law or facts." It is not the case (nor did Gordon contend) that all lawyers take this attitude all the time, but many do much of the time.

An instrumental understanding of law also pervades contemporary legal theory, occupying a central place in law and economics, in critical theory, in law and society studies, in legal pragmatism, and in the notion of the rule of law. "Part of the power of economic analysis is that it presents a largely instrumental approach to law . . . ; it forces the question, do these legal rules achieve the objectives at which they aim, and would alternative do any better" (Bix 2004: 190). The invitation to the inaugural critical legal studies conference (in 1977) declared that "law is an instrument of social, economic, and political domination." Critical feminism views law as an instrument of male domination; critical race theory views it as an instrument of racial domination. Law-and-society studies characterize law as instrumental in a multitude of different respects. Legal pragmatism promotes an avowedly instrumental approach to judicial decision making. The most influential theoretical account of the rule of law, articulated by Joseph Raz (1979: 226), construes law in purely instrumental terms: "Like other instruments, the law has a specific virtue which is morally neutral in being neutral as to the end to which the instrument is put."

Modern cause litigation – which took off in the 1960s and 1970s – perceives and utilizes law in entirely instrumental terms. As one cause lawyer put it, "The law has always been an instrument of change, of course, but in recent years it has become, through the deliberate, indeed passionate, efforts of a new breed of lawyer-activists, a favored engine of change" (Stoddard 1997: 263).

Judges and judging are also seen in increasingly instrumental terms – in two different senses. A great deal of judging, common law and statutory, explicitly considers social consequences and aims to achieve social policies. Constitutional decision making regularly engages in balancing competing interests to achieve an optimal end. But these modes of judging take place amid widespread suspicions that judges' determinations about proper social policy and optimal balancing are inevitably colored by their personal values. Consequently, at both the state and federal levels, competing groups and interests engage in often vicious campaigns to seat judges who share their ideological views, in the hope that the judges will instrumentally interpret the law to advance the goals they desire.

Legislation and administrative regulation have long been viewed instrumentally, so in this respect no real change has taken place. Critics have for at least two centuries charged that legislation is subject to capture and instrumental utilization by special interests – a commonplace complaint today (fueled by reports of the corruption of congresspeople, members of their staff, and administrative officials who exchange official legal actions for money and favors). What has changed that is that previously noninstrumental views of law still substantially held sway, at least among the legal elite (judges, scholars, and leaders of the bar), whereas presently the entire legal culture has come over to a consummately instrumental view. Now instrumentalism permeates every aspect of law. Remaining noninstrumental understandings of and approaches to law continue to circulate, but they have been shunted to the margins as the instrumental view sweeps through the legal culture.

WHERE WE ARE NOW

If law is nothing but an instrument of coercive state power, and if we cannot agree about the common good, then it makes sense that competing groups and individuals would strive to seize the law and use it to further their own interests or wield it as a weapon against others. Even those who would prefer to abstain from this contest over and through law might be forced to engage, if only defensively, to keep the power of the law out of the hands of less restrained opponents. The contemporary situation is marked by systematic efforts to control and wield the law: through careful ideological screening of prospective judges; by funneling huge sums to pliable legislators who will enact desired legislation; by securing the appointment of lobbyists to administrative positions who will then implement favorable regulatory regimes and actions; by staffing law enforcement agencies like the Justice Department with ideologically motivated individuals; and by aggressively bringing provocative lawsuits before judges perceived as friendly to the same ends.

There have always been battles over and through law, to be sure, and law has always been utilized instrumentally, notwithstanding the previously prevailing noninstrumental characterizations of law. One might argue, therefore, that adoption of an explicitly instrumental view of law has the salutary effect of bringing this reality out in the open for everyone to see. Perhaps, but one must also consider what has been lost. Former noninstrumental views insisted that law has a built-in core of integrity. This belief about law exercised a constraining effect, at least to some degree, in that legal actions had to be plausibly justified in terms consistent with this belief. Now law is seen as an empty vessel that can be utilized instrumentally to serve whatever ends prevail in various contests – litigation, elections, legislative or administrative proceedings – after which winners get the legal spoils. In this manner, the purely instrumental view may have rendered law even more subservient to powerful interests, which are better armed to engage in these contests.

Unlike Llewellyn, I will not close with a prediction about the future. Too much is uncertain to know what the next stage will bring, although my sense is that we are likely to remain mired where we are for some time. What I can assert with confidence is that, for the reasons articulated in this essay, American legal culture is in a hazardous state with no evident way out.

WORKS CITED

Bix, Brian. *Jurisprudence: Theory and Context.* Durham, NC: Carolina Academic Press, 2004.
Cook, Walter Wheeler. "Scientific Method and the Law," *A.B.A. J.* 13.6 (1927): 303–9.

Cramton, Roger C. "The Ordinary Religion of the Law School Classroom," *J. Legal Educ.* 29.3 (1978): 247–63.

Gordon, Robert W. "The Independence of Lawyers," *B.U. L. Rev.* 68.1 (1988): 1–83.

Holmes, Oliver Wendell. "Law in Science and Science in Law," *Harv. L. Rev.* 12.7 (1899): 443–63.

______. "The Path of the Law," *Harv. L. Rev.* 10.8 (1897): 457–78.

Kennedy, Walter B. "Pragmatism as a Philosophy of Law," *Marq. L. Rev.* 9.2 (1925): 63–77.

Leff, Arthur Allen. "Unspeakable Ethics, Unnatural Law," *Duke L.J.* 1979.6 (1979): 1229–49.

Llewellyn, Karl N. *The Bramble Bush: On Our Law and Its Study.* Dobbs Ferry, NY: Oceana Press, 1960.

______. "On Philosophy in American Law," *U. Pa. L. Rev.* 82.3 (1934): 205–12.

______. "Some Realism about Realism – Responding to Dean Pound." *Harv. L. Rev.* 44.8 (1931): 1222–64.

Moore, Michael S. "The Need for a Theory of Legal Theories: Assessing Pragmatic Instrumentalism." *Cornell L. Rev.* 69.5 (1984): 988–1013.

Pound, Roscoe. "Mechanical Jurisprudence." *Colum. L. Rev.* 8.8 (1908): 605–23.

Purcell, Edmund. *The Crisis of Democratic Theory: Scientific Natural and the Problem of Value.* Lexington: Univ. of Kentucky Press, 1973.

Raz, Joseph. *The Authority of Law.* Oxford, UK: Clarendon Press, 1979.

Stoddard, Thomas R. "Bleeding Heart: Reflections on Using the Law to Make Social Change." *N.Y.U. L. Rev.* 72.5 (1997): 967–91.

Summers, Robert. *Instrumentalism and American Legal Theory.* Ithaca, NY: Cornell Univ. Press, 1982.

Tamanaha, Brian Z. *Law as a Means to an End: Threat to the Rule of Law.* New York: Cambridge Univ. Press, 2006.

White, G. Edward. "The Evolution of Reasoned Elaboration: Jurisprudential Criticism and Social Change." *Va. L. Rev.* 59.2 (1973): 279–302.

Woodward, Calvin. "The Limits of Legal Realism: An Historical Perspective." *Va. L. Rev.* 54.4 (1968): 689–739.

5 When Things Went Terribly, Terribly Wrong

STEVEN L. WINTER

It is the kind of thing that, like aging, catches you unawares even as it happens in plain sight. You look up and the landscape of your face, your town, your profession has changed. One minute everyone is talking about paradigm shifts and the next thing you know they're back practicing phrenology (Schlag 1997). I remember the moment when the realization struck. It was the mid-1990s. A colleague on appointments asked me to read a manuscript forthcoming in one of the top journals. The committee was interested in the author as a potential lateral and wanted to move before the market got hot. The piece, something on criminal procedure written from a liberal perspective, was one I would naturally be sympathetic to. Halfway through I stopped in disbelief. It wasn't that the argument was wrong so much as that there was none: The piece exemplified Llewellyn's admonition: "Doctrine brittle and neat is the tool of tender minds in pursuit of policy that can be embraced without using one's intellect" (Twining 1973:116). Who, I wondered as I checked the proud citation on the first page, is publishing this? "Oh, right, Harvard." I later recounted the incident over lunch with a friend known for his efforts to reshape the academy in more intellectual directions. "When I entered the academy ten years ago, you could pick up any of the top law reviews and always find some really interesting piece on Hegel, deconstruction, or literary theory. Now, it's all law and economics or boring doctrinalism." He looked down at his plate sadly, not uttering a word.

I was raised on the grand narrative in which legal realism defeated Langdellian formalism, replacing empty doctrinalism with a careful legal craft founded on functionalist interpretation and robust policy argument. By the time I entered the academy in the mid-1980s, critical legal studies had called into question this postrealist complacency. Its law-is-politics and indeterminacy critiques challenged as yet more mystifications the purposive reasoning and balancing of competing interests characteristic of mainstream judicial decision making. Excesses aside (Winter 2001b; 1990), critical legal studies produced several sophisticated critiques of law's pretension to neutrality and objectivity, not least of which was a devastating reinvigoration of the legal realist critique of legal rules as insufficient to determine outcomes. By decade's end, even Judge Posner (1990: 48) seemed to embrace a Llewellynesque understanding of effective legal rules as those driven by "lay intuitions about right behavior."

And then things went terribly, terribly wrong. It would, no doubt, be an oversimplification to say that the collapse of the Soviet Union set jurisprudence back a century. Still, it would not be entirely wrong. The 1990s witnessed a thriving cottage industry in which American legal academics traveled to the former communist countries of Central and Eastern Europe (as well as South Africa) to advise them on their transition to democracy and market economies. These experts tended to stress American-style constitutional government complete with judicial review. By and large, they also championed clear, enforceable rules of property and contract as necessary preconditions of free markets and as essential elements of democracy and the rule of law. In both instances, their advice presupposed a rule formalism of precisely the sort called into question by twentieth-century jurisprudence. In both instances, the advice was also at odds with some of the most profound lessons of their respective disciplines.

Consider, first, the dogma about clear rules of property and contract. It rests on the premise that predictability is important to economic actors and, therefore, conducive to stable and efficient markets. But the dogma about clear rules of property and contract cannot be derived from this premise, however unassailable, for at least two reasons.

First, it cannot be that predictability per se is a necessary precondition of markets: after all, nothing is more notoriously unpredictable than a market, yet nobody thinks the existence of markets inimical to the formation of market economies. Markets, in fact, are extremely dynamic mechanisms for managing unpredictability (which is exactly what makes them superior to command-and-control forms of economic organization). The predictability thought necessary for markets must, therefore, refer to the reliability of one's expectations that other market actors will follow through on their bargains. The claim about the necessity of clear, enforceable rules of property and contract is really a claim that only a rule-governed regime can provide the reliability of performance necessary for markets to function. It is, in other words, a claim not about markets but about human behavior. As such, it is demonstrably false.

The reliability necessary for markets may be provided by the cultural factors reflected in the rule-of-law ideal, but as a historical and sociological matter many other cultural factors can also provide it. Ellickson (1986) documented how parties in a small cattle-ranching community effectively regulate their economic relations through informal norms. Various scholars (Bernstein 1992; Landa 1994; Richman 2006) have studied how the extralegal communal norms of ethnic or religious groups provide a comparative advantage that enables them to conduct commerce more efficiently because of lower transaction costs. The best known of these studies concern Orthodox Jews in the diamond trade. But, for those familiar with Jewish history, this is but a footnote to an old story. For four or five centuries before the Crusades, Jewish merchants held a virtual monopoly on trade among Christian Europe, the Muslim Middle East, and Asia. Two cultural factors enabled this monopoly: (1) a network of Jewish communities stretching from Spain to China, which provided the support and succor that made otherwise-hazardous travel possible, and (2) a system of financial instruments analogous to the modern letter of credit that made it possible to travel and conduct commerce without carrying hard currency. The use of these financial instruments dated from at least Roman times and was later codified in the Talmudic law of promissory notes. The system was enforced entirely by implicit community sanction and made international trade possible on an unprecedented scale (Agus 1965; Gil 1976; Rabinowitz 1948).

One might argue that clear rules of property and contract are necessary to ensure performance in a heterogeneous liberal society. If true, it would be strange, self-obsessed advice to press on other societies with very different demographics, cultures, and institutions. But the argument faces a more profound problem. The conventional notion of rules as clear and predictable rests on an unexamined circularity. Because most human categorization is not categorical, rules per se are unavoidably indefinite. The observed predictability of a rule is, as suggested earlier, a function of the degree to which it reflects the categories, concepts, and social practices that define the social expectations of those whose behavior it purports to govern. Clear rules of property and contract can provide predictability only within the kind of stable cultural context that renders them largely superfluous (Winter 2001a: 186–222).

Second, there is an odd disconnect between the dogma of clear rules and the implications of the Coase Theorem. Coase's (1960) basic point is that, in the absence of transaction costs, parties will bargain among themselves to achieve the optimal set of distributions. This means the following: (1) that the initial assignment of a property right in a resource will not determine its ultimate use, and (2) that markets are better mechanisms for regulating and adjusting behavior than are legal liability rules. It is hard to get from that insight to the claim that rules of property and contract are necessary for the existence of markets. Quite the contrary. Coase's whole point is that markets are more efficient than the existing legal rules.

It will be recalled that Coase's principal examples of inefficient – and conceptually indefensible – liability rules came from the law of nuisance: arguing that the railroad's laying track near the farmer's wheat field was no more the cause of the fire (subsequently ignited by a spark from a passing engine) than was the farmer's having planted the wheat near the train tracks, he pointed out that whoever was engaged in the economically more productive use would bargain with the other to refrain from the competing use. But the same will be true across the entire spectrum of basic rules of property and contract. Kennedy and Michelman (1980) have argued that, in the absence of transaction costs, there is no reason in economic theory to prefer a private property regime to a state of nature. Even laws against theft would be unnecessary; as long as the possessor values the property more than the thief, the two can always strike a bargain in which the possessor pays the would-be thief to desist. Consider their example of two people stranded on a desert island. The industrious castaway cultivates a small coconut plantation by day while the indolent one steals coconuts by night. The farmer responds by building fences and snare pits to deter the thief. But these time-consuming efforts eventually mean that his coconut crop drops 10 percent as a result of neglect. So the farmer offers the thief 5 percent of the yield if only he stops stealing. Both parties will be better off. One might think that, without background norms of possession and performance, the thief can always agree, receive his free coconuts, and then return to stealing an additional 5 percent. But if he does, the farmer will return to making snare pits. Both have adequate incentive to honor their bargain without the external constraint of abstract rules of property and contract.

Taking Coase to the limit of his logic, the background norms of possession and performance *should* be bargained away in a near-perfect market. Suppose the railroad mentioned previously has been paying the farmer not to plant wheat. A parasite emerges that wipes out much of the world's wheat supply. Because wheat is now more valuable than train travel, the farmer should renegotiate with the railroad to pay it to refrain from using its tracks. To insist on the prior bargain in this context would be to entrench the economically inefficient use. Moreover, the very existence of an enforceable contract right would give the railroad a strategic edge that would lead to rent-seeking behavior reflected in a higher, inefficient price.

There are, of course, always transaction costs. It might be argued that clear rules of property and contract are necessary to approximate what a frictionless market would produce. But it is difficult to see exactly how. The ability of legal rules to mirror market outcomes is one of the issues that Coase's critique calls into question. The conceptual element of the critique is the same as the earlier legal realist conclusion that the legal concept of causation is analytically empty: everything – the spark, the wheat, the wind – is a cause of the fire. A rule will, necessarily, employ some categorical element that stands at some remove from the considerations that market actors would evaluate in making their bargain. It will, therefore, systematically misallocate resources to the extent that the rule category diverges from the factors that a theoretical frictionless market would consider. All we can do to mimic the conditions of a perfect Coasean market is to assign initial entitlements in a way that minimizes transaction costs. The conventional wisdom is that clear rules of property facilitate Coasean bargaining by lowering information costs. But this seems true because we have focused on one factor in isolation. In the real world, the efficiency of the allocation depends not just (or even primarily) on the clarity of the entitlement but also (and perhaps more importantly) on the valence of informational (and other) asymmetries. Suppose we were to allocate the entitlement to the railroad (in this case, via a clear nonliability rule) because it is the party engaged in the economically more productive use. The result would deviate from Pareto optimality: as long as train travel remains more valuable, no Coasean adjustment will occur and the farmer will suffer the entire cost of the fire loss. If wheat becomes more valuable, existing railroads will be able to leverage their entitlement to exact a higher, inefficient price for desisting; where railroads have not yet arrived, the farmers will incur very high information costs identifying both which company is planning to lay track and where. Rules are linear and static, while the real world of economic activity is complex and dynamic.

If the law and economics preference for rules thus seems odd, the boosterism of the liberal constitutionalists is no less curious. By definition, judicial review removes issues from the realm of democratic politics and submits them for determination by courts pursuant to judge-made principles or rules. Democracy and judicial review, in other words, inherently conflict. For more than a century, the central debate in constitutional law has been about the proper role of judicial review in a system of democratic self-governance. To urge American-style constitutionalism on emerging democracies presupposes both that this conflict has in some sense been resolved satisfactorily and that principled or rule-governed judicial review is meaningfully possible. But, if twentieth-century constitutional law teaches anything, it is that neither of these propositions is true. To see why, consider three points.

First, mainstream constitutional discourse is characterized by the conflation of the first and second propositions (i.e., concern over the questionable democratic legitimacy of judicial review is expressed almost entirely, with one exception discussed subsequently) as a debate about proper interpretive method: should the Court be textualist, originalist, historicist, or organicist? This phenomenon is particularly acute among judges, who are understandably focused on the practical interpretive task at hand. But it is no less true of constitutional law scholarship (Winter 1991: 1919–23). While it makes sense to be concerned about appropriate constraints on judicial decision making in a democracy, it remains true that no set of interpretive constraints, however rigorous, can resolve the inherent conflict between democracy and judicial review. To act as if it were otherwise suggests a psychological defense akin to reaction formation – much like the person who manifests the darkest sexual impulses via overly fastidious public protestations.

Second, it is nearly a half century since Wechsler's (1959) notorious plea for neutral principles in constitutional decision making. There has been much debate over appropriate methodology since but very little consensus. The interminability of this methodological debate is itself instructive. More instructive still is what happens when one takes up Wechsler's call, as did the plurality in *Planned Parenthood v. Casey* (1992). Averring that "our contemporary understanding is such that a decision without principled justification would be no judicial act at all," the plurality nevertheless conceded the impossibility of the task: "Because not every conscientious claim of principled justification will be accepted as such, the . . . Court must take care to speak and act in ways that allow people to accept its decisions on the terms the Court claims for them, as grounded truly in principle. . . . Thus, the Court's legitimacy depends on making legally principled decisions under circumstances in which their principled character is sufficiently *plausible* to be accepted by the Nation" (62–63, emphasis added). As Wechsler's most insightful critic long ago demonstrated, consistency, generality, and principle in judicial decision making is objectively impossible because what counts as "neutrality" and as "principled" is, necessarily, historically and culturally contingent (Deutsch 1968).

Third, the one strand of constitutional thought that does engage the problem of legitimacy does so, ultimately, only by sacrificing any claim to being rule governed or lawlike. In the aftermath of the battle over the constitutionality of the New Deal, Chief Justice Stone proposed an overarching schema in which all legislation would be treated as presumptively constitutional unless it represented an interference with or breakdown of the democratic process (*Carolene Products*: 152, 152n4). While a full Court has never explicitly endorsed the second half of Stone's formulation, it does fairly characterize much of the Court's work over the following three decades and, in particular, the work of the Warren Court (Ely 1980). It is reflected most clearly in the two-tiered approach to equal protection that prevailed until the emergence of intermediate scrutiny in the gender cases of the mid-1970s.

The striking thing about the constitutional methodology that dominated this period (and still serves as the point of departure today) is the degree to which it dispenses with any pretension to a lawlike methodology. This is immediately clear in cases of social and economic legislation where the Court defers to legislative choice as long as there is any conceivable rational basis for the statute. But it is no less true of the obverse strict scrutiny test applied in cases of racial discrimination, freedom of speech and religion, and other fundamental rights. Just as the rational basis test has been castigated as an abdication of judicial review, the strict scrutiny test has been criticized as "strict in theory, but fatal in fact" (Gunther 1972: 8).[1] And so it is because it, too, lacks analytic content. Once strict scrutiny is invoked – requiring that the law be narrowly tailored to achieve a compelling state interest – the statute is bound to fail because every legislative classification, however expertly drawn, will always be under- and overinclusive relative to its underlying purpose. The two-tiered approach is not so much a doctrinal test as a simple on-off switch.

To see why, it is necessary only to trace the reason for its emergence. Among the traditional objections to *Lochner* (1905) was the criticism that it was too stringent in its means-end analysis. The majority had invalidated maximum-hours legislation because it did not bear a direct, real, and substantial relation (*Lochner*: 64) to what it deemed a bona fide health, safety, or welfare purpose. While Holmes rejected any limitations on the subject matter of democratic legislation (*Lochner*: 74), Harlan and the other dissenters accepted the majority's doctrinal premises. But they maintained that the statute should be upheld because, given the state of the then-extant expert knowledge, the reasonableness of the statute was something "about which there is room for debate" (*Lochner*: 72) and, therefore, properly left for legislative determination.

The rejection of *Lochner*, in other words, also entailed a skepticism about judicial capacity to engage in meaningful means-ends analysis. Just as the lesson of the fight over the commerce power was that there is no way to draw a rationally defensible line between interstate and merely intrastate commerce, the lesson of the battle over substantive due process was that there is no rationally defensible way to measure the adequacy of legislative means. Every legislative classification will bear a second-order relationship to the statute's motivating purpose and, therefore, will manifest a less-than-perfect fit (Tussman and tenBroek 1949). How much disparity is permissible? How much is too much? It is not that courts lack a superior methodology for making this determination so much as that they lack any methodology at all. (This is apparent from the gender cases in which the intermediate scrutiny standard – requiring that the law be substantially related to an important state interest – has yielded wildly uneven results.) Given the unavailability of any such method, the only sensible response is to leave the question to the democratic process. For the run-of-the-mill case of socioeconomic regulation, that is exactly what the rational basis test does. For issues that cannot be entrusted to the political process, the only available alternative is an unrealistically

[1] The contemporary Court has frequently denied this charge. But the fact of the matter is that, in the rare case that has survived strict scrutiny review, the Court has invariably applied a more deferential standard of review at at least one point in the analysis (see *Grutter* and *Korematsu*).

exacting judicial scrutiny that nevertheless leaves open the possibility that a more narrowly crafted statute might pass muster.

With respect to clear standards of judicial review, just as with clear rules of property and contract, the upshot of twentieth-century jurisprudence is this: we don't have them and, in any event, we are probably better off without them. So why the contemporary resurgence of rule-oriented approaches to law?

As Charles Taylor (1989: 307–8) and Martha Nussbaum (1990: 224) observe, philosophies emerge because they capture, thematize, rationalize, and justify our unreflecting social practices. This was Llewellyn's (1934: 206) point in the essay this volume celebrates: philosophy-in-action, as he dubbed it, concerns "those premises, albeit inarticulate and in fact unthought, which yet make coherence out of a multiplicity of single ways of doing." In the wave of triumphalism that followed the fall of communism in 1989 (see Fukuyama 1992), a certain amount of self-congratulatory exuberance was perfectly natural.[2] Suddenly, it seemed to many that history had vindicated all the things we in the West had been doing – democracy, free markets, judicial review, the rule of law. It was only good sense to urge them on others, freedom's new initiates. "But," as Llewellyn (1934: 205) warned, "life-in-action a theory can gain only when it serves men's needs." Not only did this surprising turn of events vindicate our society; it also valorized those in the academy as experts. Cognitive dissonance (Festinger 1957) necessitated that whatever dark doubts we harbored about the efficacy of law and legal rules had to be vanquished. Never mind bothering to dispute the various critiques of legal formalism or judicial review. Never mind that our free-market and rule-of-law proselytizing has yielded decidedly mixed results. Disputation and proof just were not relevant.

This was not the sole reason for the shift in jurisprudential understandings that characterized the past decade. By the fall of the Soviet Union, there were several developments already in train with respect to the networks by which social capital is distributed. In 1969, the John M. Olin Foundation began an active campaign to influence the American legal academy in a more conservative direction. It provided early support to the law and economics movement. In general, and not coincidentally, the foundation sought to fortify the role of traditional cultural institutions such as the university in maintaining the systems of constitutional government and private enterprise. In 1982, the Federalist Society was founded, funded in part by grants from the Olin Foundation. It has served as a quite successful networking and training ground for conservative judges, officials, and law professors. The remaking of the federal judiciary in the Reagan and first Bush administrations has substantially reworked the legal landscape. The appointment of Justice Scalia has proved particularly influential both because of his charismatic role and because of the network of smart, articulate, highly motivated former clerks who have become legal academics.

[2] So much so that some now claim that the process is natural: specifically, that the emergence of the Industrial Revolution in England was a product of fortuitous biological adaptations in that population during the Middle Ages that rewarded with reproductive success those with the repertoire of skills and dispositions that would give rise to modern economies (Clark 2007: 186–8).

The success of these social networks is, necessarily, a function of the larger cultural context in which they unfolded – including both the greater political conservatism of late-twentieth-century America and the triumphal effects of the end of the cold war. After all, appeals for a conservative reconstruction of our legal institutions could hardly have succeeded if they had not found receptive ground (see Winter 2001a: 320). But the striking reemergence of these atavistic understandings of law is also a function of a deeper contextual factor. As Unger (1983: 1–14) has observed, American legal thought has struggled for more than a century to escape the tenacious grasp of legal formalism and legal positivism. It is not just that much of the first-year curriculum continues to take as its point of departure formalist and positivist understandings of law (cf. Mertz 2007) nor, even, that those who fail to learn the lessons of the past are doomed to repeat it. Rather, the persistence of these atavistic understandings of law is, in part, a function of our core conception of law: we understand (or *mis*understand) law as an autonomous force that lays down the rules we are to follow and ensures compliance with law's constraints by threat of sanction (Winter 2001a: 332–40). In doing so, we unconsciously reify and substantially misrepresent a fluid social process as a static set of rules. The strange recrudescence of formalist understandings of law, notwithstanding the trenchant critiques to which they have been subject, is, in technical terms, a prototype effect arising from our deeply held cognitive model of law. And it has many unhappy consequences: not only do we give others questionable advice, but we also obscure from our own selves the value of a more profound and productive understanding of law (Winter 2001a: 332–40).

Which, notwithstanding Llewellyn's confidence in the "better bar" and the efficacy of reason "backed by facts" (Llewellyn 1934: 212), leaves us with quite a lot of work to do.

WORKS CITED

Agus, Irving A. *Urban Civilization in Pre-Crusade Europe: A Study of Organized Town-Life in Northwestern Europe During the Tenth and Eleventh Centuries Based on the Responsa Literature*, vols. 1–2. New York: Yeshiva Univ. Press, 1965.

Bernstein, Lisa. "Opting Out of the Legal System: Extralegal Contractual Relations in the Diamond Industry." *J. Legal Stud.* 21.1 (1992): 115–57.

Clark, Gregory. *A Farewell to Alms: A Brief Economic History of the World.* Princeton, NJ: Princeton Univ. Press, 2007.

Coase, Ronald H. "The Problem of Social Cost." *J. Law & Econ.* 3.1 (1960): 1–44.

Deutsch, Jan. "Neutrality, Legitimacy, and the Supreme Court: Some Intersections between Law and Political Science." *Stan. L. Rev.* 20.2 (1968): 169–261.

Ellickson, Robert C. "Of Coase and Cattle: Dispute Resolution among Neighbors in Shasta County." *Stan. L. Rev.* 38.3 (1986): 623–87.

Ely, John Hart. *Democracy and Distrust: A Theory of Judicial Review.* Cambridge, MA: Harvard Univ. Press, 1980.

Festinger, Leon. *A Theory of Cognitive Dissonance.* Evanston, IL: Row, Peterson, 1957.

Fukuyama, Francis. *The End of History and the Last Man.* New York: Free Press, 1992.

Gil, Moshe. "The Radhanite Merchants and the Land of Radhan." *J. Econ. & Soc. Hist. Orient* 17.3 (1976): 299–328.

Grutter v. Bollinger, 539 U.S. 306 (2003).

Gunther, Gerald. "The Supreme Court, 1971 Term – Foreword: In Search of Evolving Doctrine on a Changing Court: A Model for a Newer Equal Protection." *Harv. L. Rev.* 86.1 (1972): 1–48.

Kennedy, Duncan, and Frank Michelman. "Are Property and Contract Efficient?" *Hofstra L. Rev.* 8.3 (1980): 711–70.

Korematsu v. United States, 323 U.S. 214 (1944).

Landa, Janet T. *Trust, Ethnicity, and Identity: Beyond the New Institutional Economics of Ethnic Trading Networks, Contract Law, and Gift-Exchange.* Ann Arbor: Univ. of Michigan Press, 1994.

Llewellyn, Karl. "On Philosophy in American Law." *U. Pa. L. Rev.* 82.3 (1934): 205–15.

Lochner v. New York, 198 U.S. 45 (1905).

Mertz, Elizabeth. *The Language of Law School: Learning to Think Like a Lawyer.* Oxford: Oxford Univ. Press, 2007.

Nussbaum, Martha C. *Love's Knowledge: Essays on Philosophy and Literature.* Oxford: Oxford Univ. Press, 1990.

Planned Parenthood of Southeastern Pennsylvania v. Casey, 505 U.S. 833 (1992).

Posner, Richard A. *The Problems of Jurisprudence.* Cambridge, MA: Harvard Univ. Press, 1990.

Rabinowitz, Louis. *Jewish Merchant Adventurers: A Study of the Radanites.* London: Edward Goldston, 1948.

Richman, Barak D. "How Community Institutions Create Economic Advantage: Jewish Diamond Merchants in New York." *Law & Soc. Inquiry.* 31.2 (2006): 383–416.

Schlag, Pierre. "Law and Phrenology." *Harv. L. Rev.* 110.4 (1997): 877–921.

Taylor, Charles. *Sources of the Self: The Making of the Modern Identity.* Cambridge, MA: Harvard Univ. Press, 1989.

Tussman, Joseph, and Jacobus tenBroek. "The Equal Protection of the Laws." *Cal. L. Rev.* 37.3 (1949): 341–81.

Twining, William. *Karl Llewellyn and the Realist Movement.* London: Widenfield and Nicolson, 1973.

Unger, Roberto Mangabeira. *The Critical Legal Studies Movement.* Cambridge, MA: Harvard Univ. Press, 1986.

United States v. Carolene Products Co., 304 U.S. 144 (1938).

Wechsler, Herbert. "Toward Neutral Principles of Constitutional Law." *Harv. L. Rev.* 73.1 (1959): 1–35.

Winter, Steven L. *A Clearing in the Forest: Law, Life, and Mind.* Chicago: Univ. of Chicago Press, 2001a.

______. "Indeterminacy and Incommensurability in Constitutional Law." *Cal. L. Rev.* 78.6 (1990): 1441–541.

______. "The Next Century of Legal Thought?" *Cardozo L. Rev.* 22.3 (2001b): 747–72.

______. "An Upside/Down View of the Countermajoritarian Difficulty." *Tex. L. Rev.* 69.7 (1991): 1881–927.

6 The Mechanics of Perfection: Philosophy, Theology, and the Foundations of American Law

LARRY CATÁ BACKER

American philosophy of law is better understood as theology than as that traditional American academic or pragmatic discourse that styles itself *philosophy.* The mechanics of an American philosophy of law provides a basis in reason for an American theology of faith in the perfectibility of law. The relationship among reason, faith, and truth (perfection) better defines an American philosophy of law than do traditional, merely rational, conceptions. This essay first examines the archetypal framework within which Americans work through their theology and construct their rational analytic frameworks for that purpose through the prism of two foundational cases, *Swift v. Tyson* (1842) and *Erie Railroad Co. v. Tompkins* (1938), and its transposition to American legal positivism. It then suggests that Benedict XVI's 2006 articulation of the foundational relationship between faith (theology) and reason (philosophy) is a better basis for understanding the American theology of law, the function of philosophy within that theology, and the role of the magisterium of judges in its elaboration.

Since the settlement of Plymouth Bay and the Virginia colonies, Americans have been obsessed with the mechanics of perfectibility. Perfectibility is built into the constitutive documents of the American republic. The preamble to the American Constitution declares the establishment of the American union: "in Order to form a more perfect Union, establish Justice, insure domestic Tranquility, provide for the common defence, promote the general Welfare, and secure the Blessings of Liberty to ourselves and our Posterity." The objective is at once transcendental (reflecting universal eternal values) and immanent (immersed in a historical project to that end).

The philosophy of perfection, thus, can be subsumed under a greater objective – the search for perfect order. The amalgamation of *rechtsstaat* with the substantive basis of a *Sozialstaat,* the perfect order merges expression (law), means (government), and mechanics (philosophy) into a dynamic whole that ultimately achieves rest (the end of striving) and, thus, peace. American jurisprudence embraces, perhaps in an ironic way, the Augustinian insight about the messianic character of peace: "Peace between man and God is the well-ordered obedience of faith to eternal law. Peace between man and man is well-ordered concord. Domestic peace is the well-ordered concord between those of the family who rule and those who obey. Civil peace is a similar concord among the citizens. The peace of the celestial city is the perfectly ordered and harmonious enjoyment of God, and of one another in God. The peace of all things is the tranquility of order. Order is the distribution which allots things equal and unequal, each to its own place" (Augustine 1950: bk. 19, sec. 13, p. 690).

Perfection is an ideal state that is to be served through a philosophy or, better put, the rational pragmatics of law. This ideal state can be realized by embracing truth as it exists outside of an individual – either in divine command (or grace or law) or in the inspired will of the community at its most potent. It is (or apes) messianism, with or without religion, "What I call messianicity without messianism is a call, a promise of an independent future for what is to come, and which comes like every messiah in the shape of peace and justice, a promise independent of religion, that is to say universal" (Derrida and De Cauter 2006: 268–9). That is, perfection arrives from the top (the divine or the apparatus of government) down (the people and their customs), or from the bottom up; that is, it is organically constructed as an articulation of the community's aggregate beliefs and behaviors. How that occurs, through judge or legislature, is the substance of the philosophy of law.

The expression of that perfection is law, and government provides the means. The mechanics of perfectibility lies in a philosophy the elaboration of which has been marked by great and hotly contested battles. The theology of perfection is grounded in a faith that the attainment of perfection can be expressed by means of governmental action through a rational mechanics. Through these mechanics Americans can discern the spirit of perfection – as God or as the genius of the American community made manifest – to be embraced as the American nation relentlessly builds that *civitas dei americorum.* Logos – understood in its modern sense as the union of faith and reason, as the inherent rationality of the divine in a historically immanent form – serves as well as the ancient philosophy of American law. Law is the expression of the present state of the American search for perfection. The quest for perfection is accomplished through government and proceeds on the basis of the simultaneous application of philosophies or theologies of perfectibility embraced by the great stakeholders in the American system – lawyers, politicians, industrialists, religious leaders, and the media – on which "the people" depend.

Perfectibility in the American context is a messy business – it is the product of uncontrolled and uncoordinated efforts undertaken independently and in communion with like-minded allies and institutions by every stakeholder in American civic life. Disaggregated – into court cases, statutes, the efforts of particular courts and legislatures – the sense is of something chaotic and directionless. But appearances veil a different picture, one better appreciated in the aggregate and over the long term. From a distance, the pattern becomes clearer; and the pattern suggests a lurching toward perfection. American law at any moment is a snapshot of that aggregate lurching toward perfection that is always a case and a statute away. The expression, means, and mechanics of perfectibility – these form the essence of a philosophy of American law in the service of a paramount faith in that perfection.

THE EXPRESSION (AND MEANING) OF PERFECTION THROUGH LAW

The decisions in *Swift* and *Erie* are twin poles of reason joined by a shared faith in a rational basis for legal perfectibility. "Swift and Erie address the question of the nature of law and of the common, or unwritten, law in particular" (Braithwaite 1992: 774). The cases offer substantially irreconcilable conceptions of the state, law, the role of legislatures and judges, and the relationship between the higher law of the federal Constitution as an ultimate positive constitutive act and the law of the nation. Yet there is commonality. Both are founded on the same fundamental understanding of purpose, of the function of law as an expression of perfectibility. The differences between them, differences that keep American jurisprudence lively, center on the specifics of the relationship of law, the state, and its government.

Swift assumes a common national judicial project to approach the perfection of the common law by repeated communal application by the community of judges. Matters of a general nature, affecting the peoples of the states of the union in equal measure, general questions of law, were organic and required a common effort from all judges – whether state or federal – to the same task, "that is, to ascertain upon general reasoning and legal analogies, what is the true exposition of the contract or instrument, or what is the just rule furnished by the principles of commercial law to govern the case" (*Swift* 1842: 18). In this context, positive law was a derogation from the common law, the organic and communal law of the people, expressed by them and through their courts, and to which they, like their government, were subject. That subjection was conditional, with respect to those local matters on which government might direct a different result, that is, "to rights and titles to things having a permanent locality, such as the rights and titles to real estate, and other matters immovable and intraterritorial in their nature and character" (*Swift* 1842: 18). And it was immutable with respect to the higher law represented by the common law. The judge served the law, and law was an articulation of the lived customs and principles of communal organization of the people who came together in a political union. The obligations of all judges were general and the same – to work together to attain the highest, best, and most just expression of the organic law of the people to apply in any dispute brought before them. Judges thus exist beyond the mechanics of the various governments, and their role is not limited by the political and territorial restraints put on the various elected and administrative officials constituted through the higher law of the federal and state constitutions. Their relationship to law, and to the people, is direct and extends, like the common law, to the borders of the union. To abrogate or limit this common law is to abrogate or limit the substantive portion of the higher law of the federal (and state) constitutions, which both preceded and served as a foundation for the constitution of government that those instruments represent.

Erie assumed the necessary subordination of the judiciary and the common law of the nation to that of subordinate political units, the content and power over which were to be distributed in accordance with whatever formula their legislatures may declare. Its foundation is the princely state, in which the popular will is reduced to the positive and instrumental expression of a popular construct – the apparatus of state. Law loses its organic character, and the judge his or her role as the vehicle through which the customary will is articulated and applied. *Erie* assumes a legislative supremacy to define the confines of law and its character. It rejects "the assumption that there is 'a transcendental body of law outside of any particular state but obligatory within it unless and until changed by statute,' that federal courts have the power to use their judgment as to what the rules of common law are; and that in the federal courts 'the parties are entitled to an independent judgment on matters of general law'" (*Erie Railroad* 1938, 79: [quoting in part Justice Holmes]). *Erie* rejects the possibility of the judge as an instrument of the search for the ultimate truth or justice as expressed in law. Quoting Justice Field, Justice Brandeis turns the conceptual framework of *Swift* on its head. What passes for a general law of the United States "is often little less than what the judge advancing the doctrine thinks at the time should be the general law on a particular subject" (*Baltimore* 1893: 401 [Field, J., dissenting]). The law of the judge is thus both personal and uncontrolled. The judge is transformed into the unelected legislator usurping legislative authority. It is to the apparatus of government, rather than to the whim of the judge, that the appropriate measure of law lies.

GOVERNMENT AS THE MEANS TO PERFECTIBILITY

Neither *Swift* nor *Erie* rejects the possibility of perfectibility in general and perfectibility through law in particular. This point, perhaps one of the most potent in the cases, serves as the substance of the jurisprudential adventures of American legal philosophy for legal realists, postmodern critiques, and conservatives, each seeking to reduce further the authority of the judge and mold the positive acts of the legislature to its own program of legislation. Perfectibility becomes a political rather than a judicial act. American customary law is submerged in theory.

Perfectibility and the judge. Law in *Swift* was an organic construct, presided over by judges, into which the legislature sometimes intruded. The aggregation of that construct, the work of all judges wrestling with the same question, produced perfection, sometimes even against the will of the legislature expressed as statute. This reflects old knowledge. In *Dr. Bonham's Case* (1610: 275), Coke reminded us that "when an Act of Parliament is against Common right and reason, or repugnant or impossible to be performed, the Common Law will controll it, and adjudge such Act to be void." The judge stands between perfection and the political community. American constitutionalism, like American religion, functions on the basis of sin, of error. The source of salvation from error, that is, from the sin of unlawfulness, is then focused on the judge, as guidance from sin is vested in the priest. "The priest rules through the invention of sin" (Nietzsche 1888: sec. 49, 631); the constitutional judge rules through the elaboration of doctrine. As Friedrich Nietzsche reminds us, "Disobedience of God, that is, of the priest, of 'the Law,' is now called 'sin' [and] the means for 'reconciliation with God' are, [of course, the] means that merely guarantee still more thorough submission to the priest: the priest alone 'redeems'" (Nietzsche 1888: Ch. 26, 598). The judge becomes voice to perfection and the instrument of his or her own privilege. This serves as the measure of perfection within the philosophical foundation of *Swift* – but also in *Erie*. While *Swift* would rely on the judges for the task of rationalizing perfection, *Erie* looked to the legislature and statute. In either case, faith in law and in government becomes basic to the rational exercises that serve as its philosophy. And in both cases it is the magisterium of judges that controls.

Perfectibility and the political branches. Still, *Erie* points to the role of the political branches between perfection and its expression in law. The intermediation is represented as a necessary consequence of the construction of a system of divided power in which the community is deemed to have divested itself of direct regulatory power (i.e., of its relationship to the construction of a customary law) in favor of a government constituted to exercise all political authority. As Justice Scalia (1995: 40) is now fond of noting: "Modern governments . . . are thought to derive their authority from the consent of the governed, and the laws they prescribe are enacted by the people's representatives. Such a system is quite incompatible with the making (or the "finding") of law by judges – and most especially by unelected judges." The apparatus of state thus serves as the means of a perfection, the measure of which is its constitution and the guardian of which remains the judge.

This sort of institutional intermediation is also tellingly confirmed by the substitution of the great law codes for what remains of the common law in the United States. It is evidenced by the rise of great private bodies of public personages charged with the consideration and development of a harmonized expression of the ideal in law. This objective is represented by the great projects of informal legal codification of the American Law Institute (ALI) and the Uniform Law Commission (ULC, formerly known as the National Conference of Commissioners on Uniform State Laws).

The ALI has sought uniformity in common law by systematizing decisions, by synthesizing and pointing to the "correct" result in a manner reminiscent of *Swift*. Building on the "Bractonian and Blackstonian treatises, declaring the common law on the empirical foundations of judicial decisions," fearing the "chaos in a legal world of [forty-eight] states" (ALI 2005: vii), but afraid to undertake legislative codification, the ALI invented the form of the Restatement. Restatements constituted a synthesis of sorts, "analytical, critical and constructive" (ALI 2005: 5), seeking to reduce to a single systematic form the underlying principles that gave a legal field coherence "and thus [to] restore the coherence of the common law as properly apprehended." They serve at once to synthesize and to innovate (ALI 2005: 5) Although they are not binding, ALI Restatements have proved authoritative in many American courts.

The ULC has worked since 1892 on the unification of law through statutory projects more in conformity with the jurisprudential focus of *Erie*. As a nongovernmental organization whose members, representing all of the states and other territorial units, are for the most part regulated by statute, ULC commissioners "promote the principle of uniformity by drafting and proposing specific statutes in areas of the law where uniformity between the states is desirable" (ULC). Their uniform laws have become a pillar of state legislation and have moved the project of legislative uniformity – of the search for a pan-American legal ideal – closer to realization. It, too, then, serves as a potent illustration of the application of this development of a means to apply the mechanics of perfectibility expressed as law within the American political community. The mechanics of perfection are strikingly similar to that of the judge. But here the legislator becomes voice to perfection and the instrument of his or her own privilege.

Whether by means of judge or legislative command, or through the efforts of quasi-legislative endeavors of political elites, then, the expression of perfection remains law, realized through institutional techniques whose value are determined by application of a mechanics of the knowledge of the attributes of perfection. And that mechanics of knowledge joins law to philosophy or theology. It is this last point that this essay now considers.

LOGOS AND LAW: THE MECHANICS OF PERFECTION

The philosophy of law centers on a rationality of perfection and a systems approach to jurisprudence. Its grounding is entwined with order, and order folds back into rationality – whether subjective or objective. Faith in perfection is rationally expressed through and as systems of the production of law grounded in the "right" set of parameters in law. Control of the choice of the form of perfection becomes the theology (the *for* of faith) and sets the parameters of the method (philosophy) of its attainment.

The institutional Catholic dialogue between faith and reason provides useful insights with which we can contextualize the philosophy of American law within its theological (or faith) foundations. Within that context, *faith* becomes the truth of perfectibility, and *reason* the substance of and mechanics for its attainment. As articulated in John Paul II's encyclical *Fides et Ratio* (1998), one starts with the knowledge of revealed truth (para. 7), a transcendental truth that is also immanent, that is, "immersed in time and history" (para. 11). Faith is a fidelity to this revealed truth as both transcendental (eternal and ultimate – perfect) and immanent (leading to perfection; para. 13). "Between these two poles, reason has its own specific field in which it can enquire and understand, restricted only by its finiteness before the infinite mystery of God" (para. 14). Thus the foundation of the unity of faith and reason: "In God there lies the origin of all things, in him is found the fullness of the mystery, and in this his glory consists; to men and women there falls the task of exploring truth with their reason, and in this their nobility consists" (para. 17). God – perfection, peace – is thus encapsulated in the notion of Logos: "Logos means both reason and word – a reason which is creative and capable of self-communication, precisely as reason. John thus spoke the final word on the biblical concept of God, and in this word all the often toilsome and tortuous threads of biblical faith find their culmination and synthesis" (Benedict XVI 2006).

Where the community of the faithful includes the world (the founding postulate of universalist religions and philosophies), the internal workings of faith on reason become the paramount relationship. The body of the Divine defines the extent of reality; it serves without limit. Reason without faith, then, becomes method without purpose and reduces its object to individual satisfaction. Within religion, "any attempt to maintain theology's claim to be 'scientific' would end up reducing Christianity to a mere fragment of its former self. But we must say more: if science as a whole is this and this alone, then it is man himself who ends up being reduced"

(Benedict XVI 2006). Reason in the absence of faith and the faith community is reduced to the subjective and the partial. "The subject then decides, on the basis of his experiences, what he considers tenable in matters of religion, and the subjective 'conscience' becomes the sole arbiter of what is ethical. In this way, though, ethics and religion lose their power to create a community and become a completely personal matter. This is a dangerous state of affairs for humanity" (Benedict XVI 2006).

But in a world in which multiple communities of the faithful exist, and in which the scope of faith communities is functionally differentiated (e.g., political, economic), then faith and reason acquire a different direction – communication, collaboration, and evangelization (*diálesis*) rather than Logos. This is a world with many bodies of the Divine, internally infinite, yet externally limited by the body of faith. In this world, and within that *diálesis*, an overcoming of parochial faith (one that is inwardly infinite and outwardly limited) might be possible, or power relationships might play out.

From this is the great organizing principle of American legal philosophy. Self-constituted communities are bounded by the truth of their constitution, a truth that necessarily embodies faith and reason in the sense that John Paul II describes in *Fides et Ratio*. Political communities, like religious and social communities, are bounded by the truth of their constitution – rationally bounded by rules and understandings within which the infinite is possible. Faith provides the ongoing principles of that community – its morals, ethics, and theology. Reason serves as the means for incorporation and application of those principles. Together they provide the framework within which the search for truth – as perfection – is undertaken by means of government and expressed, ultimately, in law.

TERMINUS

There is thus an active and a passive element to the relationship between American law and jurisprudence, its philosophy and theology. On one hand, jurisprudence explains a mechanics of law eschewing any suggestion that it may affect the product. On the other, jurisprudence styles itself the source of a mechanics of law construction – but not just an explanation or a mechanics. American juristic philosophy, like the cultural-political framework in which it operates, is both fractured and is itself seeking that singular perfection of expression that would bring it in line with the sole, exclusive, and ultimate reality.

American jurisprudence reduces itself to the conceptual battles that *Swift* and *Erie* represent. "The major issue, thus, is to find the ultimate criterion of law, whether in the heaven of juristic ideals or in the earth of social reality.... In other words, we are advancing, let us hope, in the direction of agreement that the objective of jurisprudence is the same as for all science – to develop the truth" (Yntema 1947: 1106). And this reduction overcomes itself as well: "justice exceeds the law (*le droit*) but also motivates its movement, the history and becoming of juridical rationality.... [N]o justice without appeal to judicial determinations and to the force of law, no becoming, no transformation, history or perfectibility of law without the appeal to a justice that will always exceed it" (Derrida 1993: 266, translated and quoted in De Cauter 2006).

The philosophy of American law is rational and pragmatic: it seeks to serve its faith. Faith is grounded in perfection through law among the community of the faithful, who together constitute the citizens of the American nation. Together this community lives its faith through a commitment to the attainment of the more perfect union on which the American self-creation is based. That more perfect union is expressed in law by means of the apparatus of state – through which the collective genius of the community of the faithful is assembled and through which faith can be authoritatively manifested.

Yet it is the mechanics of this perfection, rather than its content, that continues to dominate the more dynamic aspects of the philosophy of the American theology of law. For Americans, the basic question of philosophy is more often reduced to who, rather than to what, and to how rather than why. From common law theory to liberal positivism, legal realism, natural law, and critical theory, all seek to serve as the mechanics of a singular perfectibility. These diverse mechanics provide the structure and context through which the ascendancy of different visions of the apotheosis of reason in perfection can be achieved, an American religion without religion (Caputo 1997: 116). The contests over the control of its mechanics are what keep American jurisprudence lively, a playing out as the endless battles over form. Thus Justice Frankfurter could mock *Swift* even as he affirmed its object. "Law was conceived as a 'brooding omnipresence' of Reason, of which decisions were merely evidence and not themselves the controlling formulations. Accordingly, federal courts deemed themselves free to ascertain what Reason, and therefore Law, required, wholly independent of authoritatively declared State law" (*Guaranty Trust Co.* 1945: 116). But that Reason is bound up in the form of the constitutional order, which itself is an expression of the form of perfection – the body of the Divine. "The operation of a double system of conflicting laws in the same state is plainly hostile to the reign of law" (*Guaranty Trust Co.*: 125) Or as Benedict XVI might suggest, "Not to act 'with *logos*' is contrary to God's nature" (Benedict XVI 2006).

WORKS CITED

American Law Institute. *Capturing the Voice of the American Law Institute: A Handbook for ALI Reporters and Those Who Review Their Work.* Philadelphia: American Law Institute, 2005.

Augustine of Hippo. *The City of God.* Trans. Thomas Merton. New York: Modern Library, 1950.

Baltimore & Ohio Railroad Co. v. Baugh, 149 U.S. 368 (1893).

Benedict XVI. "Faith, Reason, and the University: Memories and Reflections," address delivered at the University of Regensburg, Germany, Sept. 12, 2006 (available at http://www.vatican.va/holy_father/benedict_xvi/speeches/2006/september/documents/hf_ben-xvi_spe_20060912_university-regensburg_en.html).

Braithwaite, William T. "The Common Law and the Judicial Power: An Introduction to *Swift-Erie* and the Problem of Transcendental Versus Positive Law." In *Law and Philosophy: The Practice of Theory Essays in Honor of George Anastaplo.* Eds. William T. Braithwaite, John A. Murley, and Robert L. Stone. Athens: Ohio Univ. Press, 1992, 774–818.

Caputo, John D. *The Prayers and Tears of Jacques Derrida: Religion without Religion.* Bloomington: Indiana Univ. Press, 1997.

De Cauter, Lieven. "The Tyrant as Messiah: Messianism and Antinomianism in the Neoconservative Ideology." *The Brussels Tribunal*, Sept. 3, 2006 (available at http://www.brusselstribunal.org/Messianism.htm#_ednref2).

Derrida, Jacques. *Spectre de Marx l'état de la dette, le travail du deuil et la nouvelle internationale.* Paris: Galilée, 1993.

Derrida, Jacques, and Lieven De Cauter. "For a Justice to Come: An Interview with Jacques Derrida." In *The Derrida-Habermas Reader.* Ed. Lasse Thomassen. Edinburgh, Scotland: Edinburgh Univ. Press, 2006, 259–69.

Dr. Bonham's Case (1610). Hilary Term, 7 Jac. 1. In the Court of Common Pleas. Eng. Rep., vol. 8, page 113b (8 c. 107a [1610]), reprinted in *The Selected Writings of Sir Edward Coke* (Steve Sheppard, ed., Indianapolis, IN: Liberty Fund, 2003), 1:264.

Erie Railroad Co. v. Tompkins, 304 U.S. 64 (1938).

Guaranty Trust Co. v. York, 326 U.S. 99 (1945).

John Paul II, *Fides et Ratio.* Vatican City: Vatican Publication, 1998.

Nietzsche, Friedrich. *The Antichrist. In The Portable Nietzsche.* Ed. and Trans. Walter Kaufmann. 1888. Reprint, New York: Penguin Books, 1968, 565–656.

Scalia, Antonin. "Book Review." *First Things* 157 (2005): 37–46 (reviewing Steven D. Smith, *Law's Quandary* [Cambridge, MA: Harvard Univ. Press, 2005]).

Swift v. Tyson, 41 U.S. (16 Peters) 1 (1842).

Uniform Law Commission, "Organization," (available at http://www.nccusl.org/Update/DesktopDefault.aspx?tabindex=0&tabid=11).

Yntema, Hessel E. "Book Review." *Yale L. J.* 56.6: 1101–6 (1947) (reviewing *Interpretations of Modern Legal Philosophies: Essays in Honor of Roscoe Pound.* Ed. Paul Sayre. [New York: Oxford Univ. Press, 1947]).

PART TWO. PHILOSOPHICAL PERSPECTIVES ON LAW

7 Toward Normative Jurisprudence

ROBIN WEST

Lawyers, judges, legal scholars, and law students – collectively, the legal profession – all, at various times, criticize, pan, praise, or laud laws. So, lawyers are inclined to say, in any number of formal and informal contexts, this law is a good law or a bad law, or this regulation is a godsend or a calamity; that piece of legislation is a breach of trust or an act of good faith; that legal regime, even, is a boom or a bust for mankind. How do we do that? What is it that lawyers know, if anything, about law, society, or political morality that informs their nonadversarial critical work? Somehow, the scholar, judge, American Law Institute committee member, legislator, or student reaches a judgment, decidedly moral, that a strict liability rule with respect to automobile accidents or defective products is *better* than a negligence regime, that the holder of a promissory note *should* take that note free of defenses on the basis of fraud in the underlying transaction, that a sexually harassed worker *should* have a cause of action under Title VII of the Civil Rights Act, and that the First Amendment *should* protect purveyors of hate speech no less than advocates of evolution or creation science against state censure. Knowledge of the law that exists, alone, cannot possibly generate the basis of our conclusions regarding the law that ought to be – although it is surely true, as countless scholars have pointed out now for the past one hundred years, that our judgments regarding the law that ought to be influence our understanding of the law that is.

So, what fills the gap from the legal is to the legal ought, for the legal critic? Do lawyers have a sense, in any way different from that of nonlawyers, of the good that law, or a law, does, can do, or fails to do? Do lawyers have a better moral sense than nonlawyers, perhaps, of the attractions of legal utopias and the dangers of legalist dystopias? If lawyers don't have some distinctive moral knowledge, then against what base are they judging it, when they praise, laud, pan, or denounce law? And if they do have some distinctive moral knowledge, then what is it? What is the human good, or goods, that lawyers, distinctively, take to be law's goal, or a law's goal, or the rule of law's goal?

These questions – the nature of the "good" that a good law exhibits and that a bad law lacks – have not been defining questions of either analytic or critical jurisprudence for some time now. With a few exceptions, of course, neither camp asks what makes a good law good or what makes a bad law bad, or what the good is that law can, or should, accomplish, against which we might judge particular laws or legal regimes. We don't ask how we know that a good law is good or a bad law bad, or what lawyers generally seem to assume to be the case about a good law or a bad law, or whether those assumptions are warranted or unwarranted. Even more clearly, we don't ask what it is about social life that seemingly requires address by or recompense from the law, or how a good law might respond to a social ill in a desirable fashion, or how a bad law, or no law, might do so poorly. We ask neither ethical questions about a legal regime's or a law's moral goodness nor metaethical questions about our own or our fellow lawyers' unexamined practices regarding the legal criticism in which we all nevertheless engage.

This is a significant omission. These ought to be jurisprudential questions, on par with questions regarding the meaning of law, or the status of the unjust law, or the relationship of law and positive morality. But they are not. Because they are not, an entire family of questions about the criteria that lawyers use or should use in determining or debating the goodness of laws have been slighted, over the past half century or so, in the very field of legal studies to which those questions should be central. Jurisprudes do not ask themselves or one another or the rest of us particularly probing questions about the nature of the "legal good" and its relation to law. In fact, we are in flight from these questions, and our jurisprudence as well as our critical practices are the worse for it.

It clearly was not always thus. Until about the mid-twentieth-century mark, both jurisprudes and legal philosophers routinely asked these questions. But in our own time, while our three major contemporary secular jurisprudential traditions – natural law, legal positivism, and modern critical legal theory – ask jurisprudential questions that are surely related to these, they have nevertheless omitted questions regarding the nature of the legal good. Although in different ways, this has left a gap in each of these traditions.

Let me start with natural law. In *Natural Law and Natural Rights*, John Finnis's great and greatly underappreciated 1980 jurisprudential work, Finnis developed what still stands as the most thorough twentieth-century natural law that aims (partly) to answer precisely this question. The just law, Finnis argued, is the law that (in part) promotes the common good, which is itself nothing but the basic goods of the individuals affected by the law. Those goods, in turn, include, in part, the value of play, of life itself, of friendship, of knowledge, of practical reason, and of autonomy. Both law itself, Finnis posited, and our basic legal institutions such as contract, property, and marriage are necessary conditions for the cooperation required among even benignly motivated citizens to secure these basic goods. Thus – the just law promotes these basic goods of individuals, or the common good, while the unjust law does not. The good law likewise, then, is the law that promotes these goods. Criticism of law should reveal the relationship, or lack of relationship, between positive law and the human goods it ought serve.

Finnis's decidedly substantive natural law theorizing, however, did not persuade late-twentieth-century American jurisprudes, including even those who famously embraced natural law, for several reasons, some internal to Finnis's work, some external. First, the method Finnis espoused was overly intuitionist – the basic goods were to be understood by people with experience, intelligence, and a capacity and taste for speculation – but against their grasp of the goodness of the basic goods, no arguments were germane. How do we know the content of the good, or the common good, that law ought promote? The basic goods, Finnis argued, are simply understood as such by such good and intelligent people – they are good in themselves and need no further justification. This is clearly unsatisfying, methodologically, for any who find Finnis's list incomplete or in some way wrongheaded. Second, by the 1970s, political liberalism itself, and eventually the constitutional jurisprudence built upon it, had come to assume as axiomatic a theoretical structure at midcentury that explicitly disavowed any reliance on any conception of the good life as the object of state action, politics, or certainly of law. Finnis's work, and his approach, appeared to be illiberal when posited against a liberalism that claimed agnosticism toward all richly developed conceptions of the good life, and hence the basic goods. Third, Finnis's later writing and advocacy against same-sex marriage seemingly validated the worry that his substantive natural law, targeted on a law that would advance a full conception of the good and the good life, would prove unduly conservative and moralistic. Finally, the secularized but loosely Thomistic approach he embraced in *Natural Law and Natural Rights* – the attempt to specify a universal account of human nature that would inform, although by no means define, the human good, and to place the value of law within that framework, came to embody, by century's end, an ambition that was unacceptable to a critical consciousness that worried not so much about parochialism and a good deal about imperialism: any theory based on an account of human nature, even loosely understood, appears suspect. Finnis's early writing continues to influence, and heavily, the development of a catholic natural law tradition that views itself as decidedly outside the mainstream of the secular legal academy. His writing on the moral duty to obey just law continues to attract attention from his positivist critics. But his developed substantive natural law jurisprudence failed to significantly change the direction of natural law theorizing within the liberal legal academy of the late twentieth century. By 1970, natural law, at least in the United States, had taken a dramatically different, far less substantive, and only purportedly more liberal turn.

By the 1960s Lon Fuller, our midcentury's foremost American secular natural lawyer, asked much the same question as that which engaged Finnis and his catholic natural law colleagues but answered it by developing, in essence, a nonsubstantive, procedural alternative to natural law theories to which Finnis contributed: the goodness of a morally good law, Fuller argued, is to be found not in any relationship it might have to any substantive conception of the human good, the basic goods, or the common good but rather in its regard for what we now call process, or procedural justice (Fuller, 1965). Although the legal process school of the 1960s embraced, partially, his response, Fuller's so-called procedural natural justice did not prove particularly regenerative within jurisprudence proper over the next half century. The procedural notice, generality, transparency, and related process goals that Fuller demanded of law for it to be good, seem, collectively, not quite good enough – plenty of very bad laws possess all of these process virtues and more so. On the other hand, the analytic and philosophical claim Fuller insisted on – that laws that fail to meet procedural criteria of goodness are not and ought not be regarded as law – seemed, to many, far too stringent: plenty of laws that lack the requisite goodness, defined by his criterion, seem to all the world except Fuller, perhaps, to be law nevertheless. Thus, Fuller asked the right question – what is the good that a good law possesses? – but his answer, procedural purity, notably failed to convince.

Thirty years later Ronald Dworkin offered a very different, albeit equally secular, natural law understanding of the legal good: perhaps the good law, or at least the good judicial decision, Dworkin (1985, 1986, 2005) argued, is one that logically and politically fits within a pattern of institutional arrangements established by a prior web of such decisions and is at the same time consistent with some defensible conception of political morality. A judicial declaration that meets this two-pronged test might be properly called both just and law, while one that fails either prong is neither. Although it has had a longer shelf life than Fuller's account, Dworkin's account of the goodness of a good law as well – that legal doctrine, articulated by judges, is both law and good when it is consistent with past legal practice and not dramatically at odds with a decent conception of political morality – also seems to be waning in influence. Dworkin's reliance on integrity with past legal practice as the test of both the legality and the moral goodness of judicially created law struck many as unduly Burkean or tradition bound at best, and pandering at worst – plenty of very bad laws will meet his test of goodness, if the historical web of traditional legal and political decisions have themselves been bad or unjust. And, as was true of Fuller's, the analytical jurisprudential claim at the heart of Dworkin's jurisprudence – that law consists only of those actual and potential and idealized pronouncements that meet these moral tests – like Fuller's, seemed both over- and underinclusive: it contains principles that do not strike anyone but Dworkin as the stuff of law, and it excludes ordinary legal pronouncements that may not meet the moral test but nevertheless seem to be law.

Both Fuller and Dworkin, for all their differences, put forward accounts of the legal good, but in both cases, the claims seem, and have seemed to their readers, too thin. Neither procedural purity nor institutional fit with the past are sufficient to ensure the goodness of law, and neither, perhaps, is even necessary. Perhaps more to the point, their moral claims about the content of the good that a good law possesses in both cases was overshadowed by their analytic claim: that a law that lacks goodness is therefore not law. The latter claim, which for different reasons also failed to convince their critics, captured the legal academy's attention more so than either theorist's account of the goodness that good law (or simply law) possesses. For whatever reason, however, with Finnis's substantive natural law contributions largely influential only within Thomistic traditions, Fuller's influence discernible only in occasional traces, and Dworkin's influence likewise on the wane, there is simply no secular natural law movement active in the legal academy that is putting forward a serious claim regarding the nature of the goodness that a good law exhibits – or an account of how we know it when we see it. For those of us who take quite seriously the importance of the moral question Finnis, Fuller, and Dworkin asked, and who have a high regard for those natural lawyers in our history who have tried to answer it, this is a profound lack indeed.

And what of legal positivism, once again the reigning philosophical and jurisprudential framework of the legal academy? Here, as well, we find little inquiry into the nature of the good law, at least since H. L. A. Hart's (1995) badly titled attempt to spell out the minimal natural law content of positive law. There's a profound historical irony here: nineteenth-century positivists, at least from Bentham forward, insisted on the separation of law and morality, in large part, to facilitate a clearer critical posture toward the law that is – only by separating the is and the ought, Bentham and his colleagues thought, could we see the injustice or possibly the evil of some of the law that is. Bentham's embrace of legal positivism, then (whatever might have been true for Austin), was clearly motivated by a desire to facilitate clearheaded moral criticism of law – that law is the command of the sovereign, and nothing more, permits the critic to put the rose-colored glasses aside and adjudge its utility, and hence its value, or its goodness – apart from its claim to legality. Only by first seeing law as it is can we hope to evaluate its goodness. Understand clearly the law that is, so that one can better adjudge its utility – and then criticize freely, and ultimately reform.

H. L. A. Hart continued this Benthamic understanding of the critical root of legal positivism, although without the utilitarian overlay: Hart, too, developed legal positivism as a jurisprudence that would complement and facilitate liberal, and critical, political engagement with extant law. Post-Hartian contemporary positivists, however, have not followed through on the invitation to use legal positivism so as to clarify the basis of (and need for) the moral criticism of law – and hence pave the way for legal reform. Rather, contemporary legal positivists who inquire into various definitional accounts of law, including the relationship of law and a community's positive law, or the relationship of law to true morality, do so, for the most part, to investigate the nature of the relationship of law to some moral standard, not to the content of the moral standard itself. The question for our contemporary legal positivist is how we determine whether some norm is a law, and whether in answering that question we must first say something about its moral value. The question is not, however, the content of the moral good – or even how we determine that moral value or lack of it. Contemporary legal positivists, not unlike contemporary secular Dworkinians or Fullerians, have focused overwhelmingly on the analytic part of positivism – the claim that the content of law must be determined by a nonmoral metric – and have neglected the moral motive for doing so: to better subject the law that is to the light of critical reason.

Finally, critical legal theorists, their self-appellation notwithstanding, have for the most part likewise not sought to elucidate the nature of the legal good. Rather, critical legal theorists for forty years now have asked probing questions about the relationship of law to power: Is law nothing but the product of power? If so, is that something to bemoan, celebrate, or simply acknowledge? What is the relation of law, some critical theorists ask, to patriarchal power, or, others ask, to the power of capital, or, still others, to white hegemony, or, recently, to heteronormativity? Does law legitimate these sources of cultural or social power; does law further the false and pernicious perception that these and other hierarchical arrangements are necessary? These are good questions all, but their answers do not imply anything one way or the other about the goodness or badness of the law so unmasked, revealed as contingent rather than necessary, or delegitimated. Rather, the focus of the contemporary critical theorist is relentlessly limited to the relationship of law to the power that perverts, produces, or constrains it, or alternatively to the social, cultural, or political power that is legitimated and mystified by the hegemony that is law's product. The nature of the legal good – what makes a good law good and what virtues a good law ought to have – is decidedly not the object of study, beyond showing the relationship of such a question itself to deployments of social or cultural or legal power.

Here, as well, this stands in contrast to the work of earlier generations of critical theorists who influenced the philosophical orientation of our critically minded peers and selves, notably the early-twentieth-century legal realists and American pragmatists who so influenced our understanding of law, for whom questions of the nature of the human good that might ideally be served by law, and against which existing law ought be criticized, were real and pressing (Cohen, 1993; Dewey, 1922, 1930). Likewise, the realists were not averse to explicitly moral critique of existing law and debate over the nature of the human good that good law ought to serve. Morris Cohen, John Dewey, and the architects of the New Deal had contestable but nevertheless articulable understandings of our nature and what law might do to contribute to human well-being. Contemporary critical theorists have in essence retained the realists' and the early critical theorists' insistence on power's pervasiveness, but they have dropped their constructive moral ambition: the ambition, that is, to specify a speculative account of human nature, from which one might imply an account of the good that law might do, and then criticize law accordingly. From our critical jurisprudential traditions, we get a powerful critique of law's sometimes-hidden political basis. We do not get the basis for a moral critique of power or of the law that is its product.

In the absence of a jurisprudence specifically focused on questions regarding the nature of the legal good, how, then, *do* lawyers criticize law? For the most part, lawyers and legal scholars moving from the legal is to the legal ought tend to use, and to assume, values drawn very loosely, and for the most part nonreflectively, from some version of these three traditions. Thus, for many traditional legal scholars and likely for most lawyers, the goodness and the justice of a legal decision is a matter of its fit with prior decisions, in a manner not dissimilar to what Dworkin described forty years ago for his idealized Judge Hercules. For these lawyers, that a judicial decision is in accordance with law – that it has integrity; that it fits with prior precedent; that it is, in short, legally just – is all that need be said on the question of its goodness: if the decision is just, meaning in accord with prior institutional arrangements, then it is good, and if it is unjust, meaning that it fails to fit, then it is bad. Whether or not a decision is just depends upon its fidelity to preexisting law. Ergo, legal doctrine itself, read in its best light and over an expansive period of time, exhausts the normative basis upon which at least legal decisions, if not new law in its entirety can be judged. The good decision is the just decision, and the just decision is the decision that accords in some deep and perhaps indiscernible way with past law. For other lawyers, the source of the value that accounts for the move from the legal is to the legal ought is roughly a tally of costs and benefits: that a law or regulation is efficient or inefficient, likely to create more wealth than costs, is all that one need know to ascertain the goodness of a law. Particularly for lawyers influenced by the normative wing of the law and economics movement, that a law or judicial decision promotes efficiency or increases wealth is sufficient to establish its goodness. The lawyer's expertise, if any, is simply to complement that of the legal economist, to add legal acumen to the economic calculation where need be. And to the rest of us, that either a law or legal decision – and it doesn't matter which – does or doesn't entrench established structures of power is basically all we seek or need to know. If a law can be shown to legitimate power, promote hegemonic values of various dominant political groups, mystify the nature of the contingent and socially constructed world we live in, or create an illusion of false necessity, it is therefore a bad law. If it delegitimates power, complicates the hegemonic power of dominant groups, demystifies what appears to be necessary as contingent, then it is good.

One can easily see the influence of natural law, positivism, and critical theory, respectively, in these common ways of evaluating law: the traditional doctrinalist echoes the Dworkinian natural lawyer's understanding that the good decision is the just decision that accords with the past; the legal economist echoes the classical legal positivist's insistence that welfare or utility, and not tradition or past decisions, ought to be the metric against which new law is judged, and the egalitarian echoes the critical legal scholar's focus on uncovering the politics behind law and mainstream criticism both. The legal community quite generally has embraced these three criteria – integrity, efficiency, and equality – for the moral evaluation of law and legalism. Jurisprudence proper, however, has eschewed the careful and dialogic consideration of precisely the questions that generated them.

Yet, these criteria – criteria pertaining to the institutional fit, efficiency, or politics of law – and the possible answers they suggest do not exhaust the criteria we do or should use in debating or pondering law's goodness. That a decision is just – perhaps because it fits well with prior rules or decisions raising comparable facts – neither implies nor disproves the goodness of the rule with which the decision comports. And, as truly countless scholars have pointed out, that a law is efficient, maximizes wealth, or leads to a net increase of benefits over costs does not make it, therefore, a good law. Many of us can imagine or point to many a law that is efficient, wealth maximizing, or conducive to more benefits than costs that we would nevertheless regard as a travesty, and those who cannot so readily imagine, nevertheless tend to concede the validity of the exercise. There is a gap between the goodness of a law and its efficiency, just as there is a gap between human welfare and wealth. Finally, that a law or decision or body of law, legitimates, mystifies, reifies, or reflects social power doesn't imply that it is therefore a bad law; its value depends entirely upon the value of the use to which that power is put. Likewise, a law that furthers hegemony or that legitimates the power of patriarchy or capital or the state or corporations, may or may not be bad – or good – by virtue of those facts.

There are reasons, internal to each strand of jurisprudence, for the diminishment in importance of the inquiry into the legal good. Both Dworkin and Fuller, our secular natural lawyers, invited an identification of constitutional and moral criteria of evaluation, thus conflating the legal is and the moral good, thereby conflating as well the determination of law with the determination of its merits.

This has the effect, desired by Dworkin and Fuller both, of morally enriching the legal craft, but it also had the effect of subjecting the law only to internal legal – albeit higher or constitutional – critique, but legal all the same, thus muting both the purely moral criticism of law, and jurisprudential inquiry into law's potential goodness. Within legal positivism, utilitarians, economists, and legal theorists have tended to uncritically embrace an identification of the good with the desired, and hence of human welfare with the product of choice and preference, thus conflating the moral inquiry into law's goodness with various empirical questions regarding the relation of legal constraints with market and democratic outcomes. Within critical theory, legal critical theorists tend to identify the project of critique with the project of unmasking power, and to equate goodness with egalitarian outcomes, thus neglecting the work of identifying and promoting the human good. All of these intramovement trends have occurred over the past half century or so, and all have left our jurisprudence remarkably hollow. The nature of the good, and hence the good law, has been equated within secular natural law with constitutional norms (both procedural and substantive); equated within positivism with desire, preference, and choice; and equated within our critical jurisprudential movements with the eradication of power. While other interdisciplinary movements – law and economics, law and humanities – have to some degree filled the gap, we have no sustained jurisprudential inquiry, within natural law, legal positivism, or critical jurisprudence, into the nature of the human good that law, a law, or the rule of law might do.

We need a rejuvenated normative jurisprudence that centralizes, rather than marginalizes, the concept of the human good, and the varying accounts of human nature that might inform such understandings. Why? First, we need to be able to ask what social or private or political injustices might prompt us to desire new law, where such law is absent, and when we should create law rather than simply how we should interpret the law we have. We need to be able to ask whether a law might improve a less regulated or unregulated social environment. We cannot do this with a jurisprudence that is court centered and focused on the virtue of maintaining continuity with the past rather than focused on legislative creativity and the virtue of meeting social need. Second, we need to be able to ask whether our most basic legal institutions are good or bad and why. We cannot do this with a normative jurisprudence that looks at most for integrity with past legal practice, tabulates cost and benefit that assumes current preferences as given, or asks too minimally whether a legal institution furthers or promotes social hierarchy. Third, we need to be able to ask whether the conceptions of human nature that current critical practices implicitly assume, or that implicitly inform our conception of the good and the good human life, are true or false, underinclusive of our human community, or denying of aspects of our nature – whether, for example, a myopic fixation on our autonomous individualism has blinded us to the universality and centrality of our dependencies on others, our vulnerability to calamity and disease, even our mortality. We cannot do that with a jurisprudence that resolutely denies the relevance or the appropriateness of inquiry into human nature and the human good, as does much of our critical jurisprudence. Briefly, we need to ask, as a matter of jurisprudence and political philosophy both, what good law can do and all the questions that basic inquiry implies: What does it mean for human beings to flourish, and how can law and legalism contribute? In what way does law or a particular law or a legal regime or a field of law increase our well-being? When and where is law needed? What makes a good law good, and what makes a law necessary, and what makes it inefficacious or worse? These questions have in the past been central to jurisprudence and to its philosophical forefathers, in the writings on human nature and well-being from Aristotle to Aquinas, and in the writings on human happiness and welfare from Jeremy Bentham to John Dewey. They lurk in the writings of some of our contemporary public philosophers, notably the neo-Aristotelian and neo-Marxist writings of Martha Nussbaum (2000) and the theorists of the capabilities approach to moral and political philosophy. But questions regarding the good, and hence the legal good, have been sadly absent in our contemporary jurisprudence, and we are all the worse for it.

WORKS CITED

Cohen, Morris. *Law and the Social Order.* New York: Harcourt, Brace, 1933.
Dewey, John. *Human Nature and Conduct.* New York: Henry Holt, 1922.
———. *Individualism Old and New.* Amherst, MA: Prometheus Books, 1930.
Dworkin, Ronald. *Law's Empire.* Cambridge, MA: Belknap Press, 1986.
———. *A Matter of Principle.* Cambridge, MA: Harvard Univ. Press, 1985.
———. *Taking Rights Seriously.* Cambridge, MA: Harvard Univ. Press, 2005.
Finnis, John. *Natural Law and Natural Rights.* New York: Oxford Univ. Press, 1980.
Fuller, Lon. *The Morality of Law.* New Haven, CT: Yale Univ. Press, 1965.
Hart, H. L. A. *The Concept of Law.* New York: Oxford Univ. Press, 1997.
Nussbaum, Martha. *Women and Human Development.* New York: Cambridge Univ. Press, 2000.

8 Critical Legal Theory Today

JACK M. BALKIN

Among the many topics in the philosophy of law one has always been central to me: the relationship between law and justice. Law does many things: it creates institutions, facilitates transactions, gives incentives for socially beneficial behavior, deters misconduct, manufactures social realities. But one thing law does especially is legitimate power, both just power and unjust power. Law's ability to legitimate is the source of the nested opposition between law and justice. Law is never perfectly just – indeed, it is often not very just at all. And yet it is an indispensable condition for justice.

Legitimate, like *sanction*, is a Janus word, one that refers simultaneously to a concept and its opposite. To legitimate means to bring power under the rule of law so that it is (sufficiently) just, impartial, or otherwise worthy of respect. But to legitimate also means to apologize for or mystify the exercise of power so that it seems to be just, impartial, and worthy of respect, whether or not that is so.

The dual nature of *legitimate* is the central concern of a critical theory of law. Critical theories ask how law legitimates power in both senses of the word: how it shapes, channels, and restrains power and how it mystifies, disguises, and apologizes for it. In addition, a critical theory of law asks how the very acts of making, interpreting, and applying law produce and proliferate ever-new forms of power, both just and unjust.

You might think that a critical theory would focus primarily on law's ideological effects. But there is more to it than that. First, a critical theory must be as concerned with how law might succeed in furthering justice as it is with how law disguises injustice. Second, older Marxist-inspired models of ideology as obfuscation or distortion hardly do justice (pardon the pun) to law's versatile powers of legitimation. Law does not merely mask or apologize for power; nor does it merely restrain it. Instead, law creates ever-new forms and methods for exercising power. Here Foucault's model of social relations is at least as important as Marx's. Law proliferates power by making itself true in the world. It generates new institutions, new conventions, and new social realities, and it generates new forms of professional knowledge about all of them. Law shapes the imagination of those who live under it around the categories and institutions that it produces. Law does not simply distort the world – or even merely represent it correctly; rather it makes a world, one in which and through which we live, act, imagine, desire, and believe.

A critical theory views law ambivalently as a method for legitimating (in both senses of that wondrous word) the exercise of power in society. The word *ambivalence* comes from Latin; it means having strength or effects on both sides. (And hence, this dual effect often produces mixed emotions.) We should distinguish an ambivalent conception of law from a pejorative conception. A pejorative conception views law fundamentally as an ideological practice for mystifying and legitimating injustice. By contrast, an ambivalent conception of law means that we see both the beneficial and harmful aspects of law – both law's ability to further its purported goal of a just social order and its ability to fall away from that goal and to mystify and apologize for that failure. Law may offer an unjust and unwieldy system for apprehending, incarcerating, and destroying human beings. It may also offer important elements of procedural fairness, equality, and human dignity. It does both of these things simultaneously, and it may be difficult to fully separate its harmful and beneficial aspects in practice. Justice and injustice, responsiveness to the world and mystification, are often inextricably bound together. In the pejorative conception, law is simply idolatry, a confused and contradictory mode of discourse, a technique of apology and disguise. In the ambivalent conception, law is both ideology and promise; it can be one resource among others in a project of political redemption.

Critical legal theorists of the 1970s and 1980s asked whether law was a kind of politics, and whether the discourse of rights was beneficial or harmful to justice and human flourishing. When people speak of the relationship between law and politics, they mean law's relationship to the many different forms of power – economic, social, cultural, political, military, and technological – that law might constrain, enable, or propagate. They also mean the ideals, ideologies, and arguments that people use to justify these forms of power. *Politics* refers to people's contrasting visions and to the values that they want to realize or recognize in public life. But it also refers to the power to realize or recognize those values and visions. So, when we consider the relationship between law and politics we are also interested in the question of law and power – how people justify and legitimate power, either directly or indirectly – through law. And we must also account for law's methods of proliferating its own power, whether they be through legal concepts, legal institutions, legal culture, legal education, legal officers, or the legal profession.

In any case, law is not simply politics; rather, it is a surprisingly plastic medium of discourse about power and for the exercise of power. Law mediates, colonizes, and transforms political and cultural struggle into legal doctrines and legal disputes. In doing these things, law constructs a new kind of power – the power of legal knowledge and institutions – that hopes to become indispensable to every other form of power. Law is implemented and spreads through institutions and practices that call on law or depend on law, and through a professional culture that treats law as of the highest importance, indeed, as central to civilization itself. Through legal arguments and legal institutions, political struggle and ideological disagreement become refracted and displaced, only to resurface in ever-new guises. Legal institutions and legal argument facilitate the exercise of power (and struggles over power) while tempering and redirecting them. Law simultaneously channels and facilitates, restrains and multiplies, the different forms of power in society – whether economic, social, cultural, political, military, or technological – while proliferating its own forms of power, its own professional culture, and its own authority. This complicated relationship between law and power is law's relative autonomy.

Three decades ago, critical legal scholars saw relatively little value in law's relative autonomy. They pointed out that if law were only relatively autonomous in this way, law would usually tend to reflect the most powerful interests in society at the expense of weaker interests. Worse yet, legal institutions and legal arguments would disguise this phenomenon, attempting to show that injustices committed in the name of law were required by legal reasoning, by legal impartiality, by procedural regularity, and by the values inherent in the rule of law. Law would contribute to and apologize not only for the dominant forms of power in society but also for many different forms of subordination and injustice.

The argument was twofold. First, legal rhetoric often mystifies and legitimates injustice perpetrated through law. Second, despite the surface appearance of reasoned elaboration, procedural regularity, and impartiality, legal reasoning is often indeterminate or underdeterminate. Substantial parts of the law or aspects of the law (like procedure and fact-finding) are sufficiently open textured in enough areas and on enough questions that clever lawyers and judges can often reshape its doctrines or its application with sufficient cognitive effort. By generating new ways of interpreting laws and precedents, by jousting over application and procedure, and by describing and redescribing the facts, the most powerful forces in society can often shape the practical force of law largely to their liking. They can do this both in terms of the substantive content of legal doctrines and in terms of how they would be applied to facts – as the law found and interpreted those facts. Even if doctrine is clear, application may be contested, even if application is straightforward, fact-finding can be controverted, even where the facts are clear, procedural hurdles can be erected. All other things being equal, the most powerful groups and individuals tend to enjoy greater success in shaping the content, force, and application of law because they often enjoy greater access to lawmakers, courts, and quality legal counsel, because they can devote more resources to legal representation and lobbying, or because they can afford to make systematic and strategic use of the legal system over extended periods of time.

Because lawyers' and judges' rhetorical efforts can take advantage of law's many opportunities for innovation and contestation, the practical effect of legal rules and their application tends toward the vector sum of the different modes of power in society. The most powerful forces generally make the greatest use of law; they will tilt the substantive content of law to their interests or, failing that, the way that the law is applied and enforced in practice. Conversely, the substantive content of law often proves least helpful to the least powerful groups and often will be applied and enforced in practice to their relative detriment. Oliver Wendell Holmes Jr., speaking of his career as lawyer and judge, once said that his epitaph should read, "Here lies a supple tool of power." Critical scholars might argue that Holmes's epitaph describes not only his career but also the entire legal system. Law – even a relatively autonomous law – is a supple tool of power.

Critical theory's concern with law's underdetermination and plasticity captures only half the story. Indeed, there is no necessary correlation between indeterminacy and illegitimacy. Law's plasticity and indeterminacy might help disguise and mystify injustices, but they might also promote adaptability and facilitate progress. A determinate law might avoid manipulation by powerful interests. But determinate legal norms – even when applied impartially – can be substantively unfair or tilted toward the interests of the powerful. Determinacy foments injustice as much as indeterminacy ever did if the rules are unjust rules, or if they tilt inequitably toward some groups over others.

Perhaps even more important, implicit in the idea of law's relative autonomy is a contrary point. Even if law is a supple tool of power, law also serves as a discourse of ideas and ideals that can limit, channel, and transform the interests of the powerful, sometimes in unexpected ways that the powerful cannot fully control. Law is a tool of power that can become important and even indispensable to power. People have to justify what they want to do through it. Perhaps the tools of law cannot fully dismantle the forces of injustice. But the proliferation of law and legal institutions also shapes and constrains how people can justify their actions and what they can do, both for good and for ill. In this way law and legal culture – as technologies and methods of justifying and shaping power – also become political resources for limiting and channeling what powerful people and institutions can do.

The relative autonomy of law from politics – rather than its complete autonomy – simultaneously poses a threat and a promise. The threat is that law will fail to do much more than ratify and legitimate the interests of the powerful; the promise is that it might hold off the worst excesses of power by giving people discursive and institutional tools to talk back to power; to restrain its selfishness and inhumanity; and to imagine finer, better visions of human association.

The threat and the promise of law are joined together inseparably. What gives law its power to legitimate is its ability to redescribe unjust and unfair events, social practices and institutions in terms of valued ideals of human association like consent, freedom, dignity, equality, and fairness. In the hands of lawyers and politicians, law can disguise, mystify, and legitimate great injustices using the very ideas and ideals we admire. But law can do this only because it appeals to these values and claims that it is trying to realize them through law. Recourse to law forces the powerful to talk in terms in which the powerless can also participate and can also make claims.

From this standpoint, law is not simply an efficient tool of power that powerful people and powerful groups can wield any way they like. They do not merely shape the world with it; rather, it shapes them and their world, because they have bought into law as a means of achieving and wielding power. Law shapes their beliefs and desires, their sense of the appropriate and the inappropriate, their conceptions of the possible and the impossible. Law generates its own institutions and its own demands; it creates its own culture; it is its own form of life; it struggles with other forms of knowledge and power for dominance. That struggle might lead to yet another form of professional power displacing older forms. But it might also offer a space for something far more beneficial and noble.

The critical approach to law – or at any rate, my version of it – has always been doubled, has always reflected the Janus word *legitimate*. On the one hand, powerful people have used law to subordinate others and to secure their own interests under the guise of promoting laudable goals like freedom, equality, liberty, consent, community, and human dignity. On the other hand, by choosing to speak in the language of law, powerful people and interests can sometimes be called to account because they try to legitimate what they are doing in those terms. The people they take advantage of can argue that this is a misuse of law, an illegitimate attempt at mystifying rhetoric. They can appeal to the values that law seeks to protect to promote better, more just, and more humane practices and forms of human association.

Important theoretical debates among critical scholars in the 1970s and 1980s revolved around which conception of law was the best one. Some critical scholars adopted a largely pejorative conception, focusing primarily on law's defects. They argued that the rule of law was enmeshed in irreconcilable contradictions; they denounced rights talk as sterile, useless, and counterproductive. Others, especially feminist and critical race theory scholars, pointed out that rights discourse and rule-of-law values were among the few resources that disempowered people had. Rule of law and rights talk were potentially emancipatory discourses. They held a limited but important potential for liberation and for contesting the arbitrary and unjust use of power.

These feminist and critical race theorists understood the deemphasized elements – the other side – of critical claims about the relative autonomy of law. They well recognized that rule-of-law values and rights discourse were hardly perfect – after all, they had been used repeatedly to justify slavery and the subordination of women – but that they had also allowed people to speak out against and to restrain the worst excesses of power. Even in a period of deep skepticism and disillusionment about what law could do, these critical scholars retained a sense of the political importance of rule-of-law values and rights discourse. That is not because they believed in a strict autonomy of law from politics, but because they understood the political values that legal culture and rights discourse might serve.

The best version of critical theory, I think, employs an ambivalent conception of law rather than a pejorative conception: it recognizes law's relative autonomy from other forms of power in social life, and it understands the dual or Janus-faced nature of that relative autonomy. It sees both law's limitations in the face of power and its possibilities as a means of channeling power and preventing its most serious injustices.

Moreover, I think that a critical approach must always be self-critical – it must recognize that how we make and apply legal theory arises out of the circumstances in which we recognize problems and articulate solutions. Theory may purport to be timeless, but what theory means in practice, how we should apply it, and which of its elements gain particular relevance will change with changing times. A critical theory of law must recognize how different aspects of law – and of a critical theory of law itself – become newly salient or refigured in different circumstances, and how the seemingly timeless verities of one historical period are conditioned by the assumptions and expectations of that time. Critical legal theory is no exception. If a critical theory of law looks different today than it appeared thirty years ago, that is because the world itself looks different.

The critical project in American law arose in a unique period in American legal history. During the 1960s American law had made enormous gains in promoting equality for the poor, for racial minorities, and for women, and had greatly expanded the scope of civil liberties. In a few short decades the country had become far freer and more equal, and law – and the discourse of rights – had seemed to play an important part in the transformation. When the Nixon administration tried to subvert American democracy in the early 1970s, the Constitution and the rule of law seemed to provide key elements in the resolution of the crisis. Both the Watergate scandal and the civil rights revolution seemed to demonstrate that law and rights discourse played an important role in promoting a just society. The law could not have succeeded without political mobilization and political will behind it. But law was a key institutional medium – and the language of rights a key discourse – through which progress was achieved.

But these gains – and the power of law to effect them – had stalled and slowed by the middle of the 1970s due to a series of reactions and countermobilizations from different segments of society. The result was continuing improvement in some areas, retrenchment in others, and stalemate in still others. There was no promise anytime soon of another round of truly transformative changes toward greater liberty and equality. Instead, progress was halting and inconsistent.

The critical movements in American law arose in this period, when the liberatory edge of law had been blunted and the tectonic plates of American politics had slowly shifted. From this perspective, key critical claims – that law reflected political struggles and political power, that rights discourse was manipulable and could easily be turned against progressive ends, and that legal argument often apologized for continuing injustices – made particular sense. As forces of reaction set in, the law once again appeared as a flexible tool of the powerful, and claims of law's impartiality as a powerful rhetoric of mystification.

Critical scholars rebuked their liberal colleagues in the academy as apologists for a status quo that, they believed, still had far to go. Frustrated with law's inability to do good and disgusted with complacent assertions of law's impartiality, they attacked the liberal defenders of the rights revolution and the rule of law as little better than their conservative adversaries. Whether or not this accusation was fair, it was surely deeply ironic. At this very moment in history the United States had already entered a period of political retrenchment in which liberals would lose most of their influence and authority over the development of American law, although at the time people had no idea how long the period of retrenchment would last and how deeply it would run. By directing their critical focus at the liberal legal academy, critical scholars ironically (and contrary to what their own theories would have advised) paid far less attention to the most powerful forces in American society, forces that would significantly change the direction of law in the next several decades.

By the turn of the twenty-first century, new conservative social movements dominated American politics. Their agenda was very different from that of the progressive forces of the 1960s – indeed, it was in some sense a reaction to it.

Today the critical project of debunking legal liberalism and rights discourse to clear space for greater justice seems beside the point. The problem today is not that liberal theories of law mask deep injustices, but that the rule of law itself has been cavalierly discarded in the quest for political power. The events of the early twenty-first century have made the other side of the ambivalent conception of law particularly salient.

As the new century began, the Supreme Court of the United States settled a disputed presidential election in *Bush v. Gore* by inventing a novel legal theory that did not even justify its remedy of stopping all recounts and that, the Court suggested, it would be unlikely to apply to any future decisions. The reasoning was so weak and ad hoc by professional standards of legal argument that it appeared that the majority simply wanted to end the contested election in favor of the Republican candidate, George W. Bush.

Once in office, the Bush administration's proclamation of a "war on terror" following the September 11, 2001 terrorist attacks made repeated assaults, some subtle and some not so subtle, on key rule-of-law values of transparency, accountability, and constraints on arbitrary power, particularly executive power. To give only a few examples: The administration rounded up thousands of Arab and Muslim immigrants shortly after the September 11 attacks and held them for months without charging them or disclosing their identities to the public. It held two American citizens in military prisons and claimed that they had no right to an attorney or to a judicial hearing to contest their designation as enemy combatants. Its secret "torture memos" justified torture and prisoner abuse by defining torture absurdly narrowly and by claiming presidential power to disregard statutes and treaties banning torture and cruel, inhuman, and degrading treatment. It maintained secret prisons overseas, where it tortured and abused detainees; it sent others off to be tortured by different governments, and it stashed still others at Guantánamo Bay, Cuba, to avoid the reach of American courts. It created military commissions to hold secret trials that permitted secret evidence the accused could not examine and secret witnesses whose identity the accused could not know. It began a series of secret and illegal domestic surveillance programs whose nature and scope it would not divulge, asserting that any attempt to litigate their validity would endanger national security and aid terrorists. And yet, as troubling as all these actions have been, the erosion of legal institutions may become far worse if Americans experience a second terrorist attack.

To be sure, one might insist that recent events have merely demonstrated conclusively that law was politics, that the rule of law was useless in combating injustice or constraining power, and that rights discourse was indeterminate and manipulable. *Bush v. Gore* did make legal arguments, even if they were transparently bad ones. Legal claims accompanied every incursion into American constitutionalism in the years following September 11, and well-trained lawyers have been only too happy to justify the Bush administration's every move – no matter how egregious – as fully consistent with the law. Indeed, government officials working in the vice president's office and in the Justice Department's Office of Legal Counsel developed novel legal theories claiming that when the president acted in his capacity as Commander-in-Chief, he could not constitutionally be bound by laws

Congress had passed, much less by international human rights treaties. According to these theories, none of the president's actions were outside the law; rather, the law effectively gave him the powers of a king or a dictator.

Moreover, in some cases the administration did not even need to manipulate the law. It repeatedly used the threat of terrorism – and accusations of being soft on terrorism – to goad Congress into passing new laws that created military commissions, authorized searches without judicial supervision, abolished habeas corpus for suspected aliens, and expanded the government's powers of electronic surveillance.

Yet even while professional discourses and institutions of law assisted these actions, they also provided methods for restraining the administration's worst excesses. Courts repeatedly rejected the president's most outrageous claims even if they upheld more modest powers. The professional discourse of law served as a partial check on executive aggrandizement. Perhaps equally important from the perspective of a critical theory, the political ideals of the rule of law – that legal institutions should restrain arbitrary power and impose norms of procedural fairness and impartiality – served as a powerful force both in American popular thought and in American legal culture. Whether or not any particular law or decision lived up to the ideals of the rule of law, both the American public and American lawyers and judges believed in those ideals. They fought back when they believed those values were threatened.

The ideals of human association embedded in the concept of the rule of law – like the ideals of liberty and equality – are well worth fighting for and realizing in our legal institutions, even (and especially) if we realize that all efforts to instantiate them in law are always subject to evasion, capture, and manipulation. In the world of the 1970s, critical theory noted how law failed when it was not supported by a robust politics; in doing so, it deemphasized and marginalized the positive elements of law and legal culture that were always implicit in an ambivalent conception. But in a world of executive arrogance, authoritarian posturing, and blatant disregard for rule-of-law values, those elements must necessarily come to the fore in any critical account. Critical scholars have prided themselves on their deconstructive acumen – their ability to elucidate the hidden and marginalized values and assumptions that bodies of legal doctrine deemphasized but on which they secretly depended. We should apply those same deconstructive techniques to critical legal theory itself.

The focus of a critical approach to law – and its ambivalent conception – will inevitably shift as we introduce it into new contexts of judgment. Deemphasized aspects will emerge. Sometimes a critical approach to law will focus on how rule of law norms, legal institutions, and legal culture serve important political values; but not because law is independent from politics or because law does not apologize for and legitimate injustices. Rather, legal culture and institutions are valuable to critical theories of law because they are a way of doing politics, in the sense of shaping, restraining, and challenging power.

In like fashion, a critical approach will not view the rule of law as simply a formal legal principle – for example, the requirement that like cases must be treated alike. Nor should one confuse it with a formalist hope that if we design legal doctrines carefully enough, they can conclusively determine all important and contested cases or prevent all injustices and abuses. Rather, the rule of law, like liberty or equality, is a political value. It is a value one struggles for and struggles with. It demands that legal institutions and professional culture should work to restrain the arbitrary and unjust exercise of power, and that we should build, preserve, and protect legal and social institutions to that end. Like most political principles, the principle of the rule of law does not determine the scope of its own extension; hence, it can be fought over and co-opted. But like other political principles – such as human dignity or equality – it is no less valuable to social life because it is underdetermined and co-optable.

History deconstructs; it shows how the conceptions of the past appear ever different in ever new contexts, how things we once thought naturally opposed are now joined together, and how things we thought were indelibly joined together now come apart. So it is with critical theories of law: in one era a critical approach lets us understand law's threat; in another, it reveals law's promise. The British historian E. P. Thompson famously argued that the rule of law was an unqualified human good. An unqualified good it will not be, at least to the ambivalent conception, for there always lurks the danger that law will become a form of idolatry and a technology of oppression. Yet there is no doubt that law and the rule of law are genuine human goods and indispensable elements in a humane civilization. It does not take a critical theory of law to recognize that fact. But without recognizing it, no theory of law can truly be critical.

9 Reviving the Subject of Law

PENELOPE PETHER

Legal realism seems to appear much in the recent (U.S.) news. The constitutional law scholar Carl Tobias (quoted in Doyle 2007) recently opined that the high level of 5–4 decisions by the Roberts Court signals that we – or at least they – are all (naive) realists now. Appropriating the realist thesis that judicial decisions are the product of judicial ideology, which in turn informed the critical legal studies perception that "law is politics," to characterize the emergent jurisprudence of the current iteration of the nation's Constitutional Court, he suggested that the following conclusion is unexceptionable: the Justices do not behave as if law exists; rather, they vote their guts or their prejudices, their political or ideological commitments.

If he is right, the nation's Constitutional Court of final jurisdiction presently manifests an attitude toward making law that has come to characterize the decision making of the federal courts in the half century from *Brown v. Board of Education* to the post–September 11 constitutional jurisprudence of emergency. Confronted in the early 1960s by burgeoning appeals from prisoners and civil rights plaintiffs, the U.S. Court of Appeals for the Fourth Circuit, based in Richmond, Virginia, the heart of "massive resistance" to desegregation, developed a response to appeals it considered peculiarly burdensome. I have called this practice, now institutionalized nationally in federal and state appellate courts and in federal trial courts, the institutionalized unpublication of judicial opinions.

Institutionalized unpublication enables judges or court staff to identify a small group of opinions as "published" and precedential, and the vast majority as "unpublished" and nonprecedential, and thus not required to be followed in factually analogous cases. This categorization is made in advance and by fiat, frequently in breach of courts' own guidelines as to what kinds of cases should fall into each category. Next, institutionalized unpublication diverts the processing of and thus usually the deciding of appeals from the outset to the nonprecedential track, where they are processed, in the absence of oral argument, by court staff. Third, on many courts, this delegated exercise of what, at the federal level, is Article III judicial power is performed without meaningful judicial oversight, and far too frequently without recourse to practices that would tend to provide safe results: for example, decision makers may not read either briefs or transcripts of evidence before passing judgment.

Unsurprisingly, there is substantial evidence that institutionalized unpublication produces inequality effects: powerful litigants manipulate it to stack the precedential deck in their favor; it confers predictive advantages on the information rich by making records of what the courts do differentially available to them; the comparatively powerless are much more likely to have their de jure appeals processed this way than are the comparatively powerful; and judges are on record both condemning the quality of staff work on their cases and claiming, against the weight of evidence, that they carefully decide these cases themselves.

Perhaps most troubling, there is evidence that when staff decide cases brought by the comparatively powerless, they characteristically find against them at rates much higher than even the conservative end of the bench, rates not justified by differential merit. That is, institutionalized unpublication is the product of a culture that adjudges normative – and thus normalizes – a profoundly hierarchical status quo with an ingrained tolerance of second class "justice" for the powerless, a profound lack of concern about the values expressed in the material practices of law work, and an evident comfort with legal decision making that does not reflect commitment to any recognizably legal method.

In "On Philosophy and American Law" Llewellyn focused some of his sweeping and yet cluttered survey of American law on precedent. Significantly for my purposes here, that survey was taken a year into the burgeoning "state of exception" that did away with a meaningful – that is, not merely positivistic or authoritarian – rule of law in Germany in the period from 1933 to 1945. To the extent that Llewellyn's account of precedent reaches a conclusion, it characterizes it as both positivist and available for unprincipled manipulation by those with economic and thus political power. Thus far, then, Llewellyn and I see the (judge-made) American law of our respective eras in similar ways.

There is a difference, however, in our conclusions about what might or ought to be done in response. For Llewellyn, legal realism provided a totalizing philosophy of law that could account for interpretive practices lacking coherent or conventionally principled grounds. Social science in the hands of those who have come to be euphemized as progressive skeptics provided a method of predicting and providing reasons for judgment superior to any distinctively legal method. As Tobias suggests of the Roberts Court, for Llewellyn there was no law there, and this troubled the philosopher as little as it apparently does the justices.

As Llewellyn signally fails to register, yet as is implicit in Tobias's account of the workings of the Roberts Court and my own account of the law-making practices that have come to characterize the nation's courts more generally, legal realism might be complicit with ends that do not advance the liberal or progressive "social needs" (Llewellyn 1934: 212) political agenda that the realists laid claim to. This should not surprise us: the sociologist of the professions Pierre Bourdieu has identified the juridical field as a site of permanent interpretive struggle for control of the meaning of law's texts.

On the other hand, the implications of Tobias's insight, contextualized, might provide at once a shock of recognition and an estrangement of the normal. In "American Constitutionalism as Civil Religion: Notes of an Atheist," Duncan Kennedy (1994–5) suggests that legal realism took root as powerfully and flourished as vigorously as it did in America because the high stakes created by both U.S. constitutionalist "civil religion" and the conservative Supreme Court doctrine on property rights of the late nineteenth century "created a vested interest for . . . progressives in demystifying legal reason." He concludes with an allusive and perceptive insight about legal realist thought's comparative lack of influence during the decade after Llewellyn's essay in Europe, from whence, sourcing itself in the German free law movement, it had been borrowed. "[F]ascism and Stalinism," he writes, made "the realist impulse look positively obscene in Europe" (Kennedy 1994–5: 921).

My reprise of Llewellyn's essay does not rest with diagnosis, and in its project of restoring the subject of American law to the "possibility of Justice," it departs not only from his conclusions but also from his method in three critical ways. First, it focuses on theory, specifically critical theory, rather than a totalizing philosophy of law, and it interests itself in what David Kairys called the politics of law rather than in law reduced to politics. Second, it is substantially more suspicious than Llewellyn about the uses of social science for law. Third, its candidates for interdisciplinary knowledge that might unsettle or supplement, rather than substitute for legal knowledge and thus enable a thick understanding – a philosophy, if you like – of what law is and how it does its work, lie largely in the humanities rather than in the social sciences, specifically in the disciplines of history and of literature and other linguistic humanities: rhetoric, cultural studies, critical linguistics, and so on. So much for the subject of law as discipline. Redressing the impoverishment of the philosophy of the nation's law depends not merely on reimagining the law as discipline, discourse, epistemology, and hermeneutics, however; it depends equally on enabling the formation of different kinds of legal subjects.

How would I reimagine Llewellyn's account of philosophy, and of philosophy's relationship with law, in this project of reviving the subject of law? First, privileging theory over philosophy draws on a scholarly tradition that does not seek to totalize, to give "a general account of interpreting that provides guidelines for guaranteeing correct interpretation" (Mailloux 2002: 40–1). Rather, it enables the familiar to be seen with estranged eyes, enabling "change in the currently prevailing discourse of authority and power" (Norris 1988: 41).

Next, I would make a move left unmade in Llewellyn's frozen jurisprudential moment and hold philosophers of law – which for my purposes means the members of the legal academy in their role as scholars and teachers of law – responsible for making law, just like judges, legislators, and regulators. On his account of public and private law making in the United States from the Declaration of Independence to the end of the first third of the twentieth century, Llewellyn suggests that the law is to be found not only – or perhaps not at all – in the texts of those whose positivistic charge it is to "lay down the law": judges, legislators, those authorized to issue regulations. Rather, it is to be found in the interpretive, predictive, analytical work that lawyers – or at least those to whom Llewellyn (1934: 212) referred when he invoked "the actual behavior of the better bar" – do.

This broader account of what law is understands law as always and only made in its varying forms of practice, including that which legal theorists, shadow practitioners of the work of highly skilled practicing lawyers, do. This is not, or ought not to be, all of the stuff of the law we make, however. Its reductiveness brings legal theorists close to eliding their responsibility for making law, confines them to documenting the work of others, reduces their law-making role to whatever little influence they can have on judges, and loses sight of their implication in the subject formation of lawyers. The law is also, then, and perhaps most importantly, what we teach.

Applied legal realism is also discernable in what the nation's news media signally and persistently failed to lose interest in as I wrote this essay: symptoms of the politicization, or more or less frank adoption of political results–oriented cronyism as personnel policy in action, in what it has become increasingly ironic to call the "Justice Department." The symptoms of this manifestation of the politicization in the making of U.S. public law in its material practice ranged from the simmering not-quite scandal of the firing of select U.S. Attorneys and their replacement with what appear to be paradigmatic executive loyalist hacks, with a view to selectively rig election law and thus national political power, to the egregious yet tragically predictable (to any modestly introspective U.S. legal educator with an eye for the structural and a grounding in critical sociology) Monica Goodling's apparent infractions of the Hatch Act in shaping career attorney hiring practice.

Goodling's approach to applied human resources theory was evidently informed by the way things were done at Regent University. This might be predicted from Pierre Bourdieu's account of the *habitus*, the embodied experience of the world that constitutes subjects and makes them constitute the world in its – and their – image in its turn. Another recent symptom of the politicization of U.S. public law evokes an analogous example of the contextually transposable reproduction of aspects of the *habitus*: the current administration's adoption of immigration court appointment practices that blend cronyism and a confidence in the appropriateness of a lack of expert qualification to do the job of passing judgment on the most vulnerable of the dominant culture's "others" as a criterion for appointment to this specialized adjudicatory office, yet another advance on the continuum of practices to systematically eradicate adjudicatory independence in immigration cases, carefully documented by Stephen Legomsky (2006).

The recent events I have chronicled thus far suggest the appropriation of (opportunistically naive) legal realist thought translated into action to reinforce the hegemonic status quo. What other insights into the current state of the relations between law and philosophy in the United States might be enabled by thinking them through critically, with estranged eyes? What impetus to transform those relationships might this impel?

First, the impoverishment of both the national practices of legal subject formation and its legal institutions, as of legal discourse and its theorizing, both likewise evident in the material practices of institutionalized unpublication, has left American law profoundly and critically adrift. Next, my project is to suggest a means to and the utility of using theory to recover the *subject of law*, by which I mean two things. The first involves accounting for law as a set of institutions, discourses, and practices distinct from politics, as from theory understood as doctrine or legal science on the one hand or law understood as (social) science manqué, on the other. The second suggests a way out of what my recent scholarly work has revealed: both a crisis of the national judicial ontology, evidenced by a massive, institutionalized, national failure in judicial ethics and judicial accountability, and the shoddy, intellectually etiolated, or disingenuous ragtag of business as usual that stands in for a conscious theory and practice of passing judgment and laying down the law in judgment's texts; and the systematic material institutional practices of production of impoverished and impoverishing legal subjects for which Monica Goodling – the U.S. legal academy's collective Frankenstein's monster – might serve as an exemplar.

The material results of the current administration's approach to appointing law makers are suggested by Ramji-Nogales, Schoenholtz, and Schrag's (2007) study of disparities in asylum adjudication at the immigration court level, a study that supplements my recent reinterpretation (Pether 2007) of David Law's (2005) study of Ninth Circuit appellate asylum jurisprudence: there is no better account of how law is made in this area than that provided by the politics of lawmakers. Ramji-Nogales and colleagues (2007: 1) conclude that

> in asylum cases, *which can spell the difference between life and death*, the outcome apparently depends in large measure on which government official decides the claim. In many cases, the most important moment in an asylum cases is the instant in which a clerk randomly assigns an application to a particular asylum officer or immigration judge. (Emphasis added.)

Law (2005: 861) concluded that a small number of Democratic appointees to the Ninth Circuit bench decided asylum cases "strategically"; that is, they "demonstrated a heightened tendency to vote in favor of the asylum seeker" in published, formally precedential, judicial decisions, for the purposes of "mak[ing] 'good law,' and to avoid making 'bad law' by casting 'good' (ideologically preferred) votes in published cases, while restricting 'bad' (ideologically disfavored) votes to unpublished [nonprecedential] cases."

Read against information revealing that while judges formally made these decisions, in practice court staff, particularly staff attorneys, made a sizable majority of unpublished asylum decisions, my own reinterpretation of Law's data shows that junior court staff, usually new law graduates, characteristically decide these cases against asylum seekers and for the government, at rates much more marked than those of Republican-appointed judges, which evidences a progovernment bias not accounted for by the merit of the cases involved. I conclude that these de facto Article III judicial officers have learned very well, from their law school teachers as from the judges whose work they do, the apparently compelling logic of hierarchy, as of an unreflective approach to the work of making the law; their work bears the imprint of an impoverished philosophy of law as indistinguishable from politics.

These two examples of social scientific work on asylum jurisprudence have much to teach about the uses of social science for postrealist legal theory. Legal realist thought had a paradoxical faith – given its debunking of Langdellian legal science – in sociology's ability to supply truth to, rather than merely knowledge about, law. To the extent that theory work, generally, and work in the humanities and human sciences understood as such rather than as pseudoscientific, is of use in reviving the subject of law, it might be deployed to generate a thick account of what law is and might be; of how its institutions, discourses, texts, and subjects are formed in culture and history, and of how legal subjects reproduce culture and make history in their turn.

The study by Ramji-Nogales and colleagues is useful in accounting for law precisely because it generates knowledge about legal subjects and their practices; other useful social scientific work might likewise give us information about legal institutions or discourses. The Law study manifests symptoms of the dangers that overreliance on legal realist social science poses when it seeks to theorize the "real" reasons for legal decisions in politics, both party line and professional, rather than interrogating its data for knowledge about legal subjects and the work that they do, knowledge capable of informing legal theory.

To the extent that interdisciplinary work in the human sciences might be employed in reviving the subject of law, it is most useful not as a substitute for legal knowledge that can unveil the "truth" that law's methods cannot; or yet in seeking substitutes in other social sciences for the contingency of legal knowledge; or in seeking to rehabilitate law from, or alternatively to substantiate, the claim that its real practitioners, the judges, are unprincipled because they practice politics rather than law. Rather, interdisciplinary (rather than alternative disciplinary) work in social science and law is most usefully deployed in illuminating our own institutions, discourses, and modes of subject formation, thereby generating ways of seeing what the law cannot see about itself or that which it occludes from vision. It does this to better understand the way that legal institutions, discourses, and subjects do their work; how they produce disciplinary truths; and how supplementary knowledge brought into intertextual relationships with law's texts and their modes of production, consumption, interpretation, and use in law work might unsettle business as usual.

Modes of interdisciplinary law and social science scholarship that are particularly apt to revive the subject of law include sociology of legal education or cultural psychology of the kind practiced by Guinier and colleagues (1997) or Susan Daicoff (1997), Pierre Bourdieu's theoretical sociology of the professions in general or the juridical field more specifically, and Elizabeth Mertz's linguistic anthropology. Mertz's study makes a powerful case why careful interdisciplinary recourse should be had to the linguistic humanities in the project of reviving the subject of law. She understands law as made in significant part in its discourses, language as much more thoroughly constitutive of what law is as well as what it ought to be than did Llewellyn, who saw it merely as a means to get at truth, which he called "the real" (1934: 212). A strong strategic argument for the utility of the linguistic humanities – including rhetoric, literary theory, critical linguistics, poetics, and cultural studies and semiotics, if we think of language broadly – in reviving the subject of law might be to suggest law's identity as a humanity, a discipline that produces knowledge about the institutions, discourses, subjects, practices, and texts of the law rather than truth, or totalizing systems of knowledge, which for Foucault were the selfsame thing.

If legal realist thought is identifiable by its commitment to "concrete data" and "facts" (Llewellyn 1934: 212) and its limited understanding of law's relation to language, the humanities' cultural texts provide supplementary narratives to those of the texts of judgment and other legal textual genres. They deny law's claims to completeness in accounting for society and enable insights into how the law legitimates particular ways of understanding and thus of ordering the world. The humanities disciplines of rhetoric and poetics have special claims to unsettle law's claims to totalizing knowledge, as Peter Goodrich has suggested: rhetoric because of its history as law's uncanny disciplinary double (2001); poetics because it tells tales out of school about what legal texts, method, epistemology, and hermeneutics seek to forget about themselves (1996).

Llewellyn (1934: 212) laid claim to the strength and promise of the realist school of legal theorists in part because their ways of thinking about the law were closer to the practices of "the better bar," genuinely sophisticated practicing lawyers, than to those of positivist legal philosophers or natural law theorists. Humanities scholars in the critical theoretical traditions share methods with those sophisticated lawyers: critical close reading of law's texts and of law's equivalent of interpretive literary biography applied in this discursive context in the service of prediction; and rhetorical expertise in deploying law's genres, discourses, figures, and tropes. Like scholars of literary theory in their work with that discipline's canonical texts, skilled practicing lawyers are also viscerally aware of law's instability, its contingency and indeterminacy, of what Peter Goodrich has identified as its rhetorical insistence that it is science, not a hybrid of literature and poetics. They are constitutionally skeptical of law's insistence that it does justice, never violence or, even less admissibly, systematic injustice. They recognize their own agency in the production of the one or the other.

Such lawyers understand, too, what adherents of critical historiography know about history: that the discipline makes stories out of the discipline of history's evidentiary material. Critical attentiveness to history can inoculate against complicity with what Judith Resnik (1999: 692) has called law's "*McCleskey* problem": legal culture's "self-regard and self-celebration," which make it "difficult to convince the unconvinced in law of a relationship between an individual instance and a larger social phenomenon, when both the individual instance and the larger phenomenon are claimed to betray liberal legal democracy's commitments to fairness and inclusion." It might counsel such legal professional practices as maintaining an abiding attentiveness to the nation's defining historical moments, involving as they do structural subordination on the basis of race, paradigm of otherness, and of exceptionalism.

Similarly, as the reference to *McCleskey v. Kemp* suggests, attentiveness to the lessons and methods of history might advocate acute awareness of the contexts in which legal issues arise. Just as it is in the litigation over the institutionalizing of the paradigmatic jurisdiction of exception, Guantánamo Bay, and in recent immigration and asylum jurisprudence (Morawetz 2006–7), the prerogative writ of habeas corpus was especially politically charged in the 1950s and 1960s. Like desegregation, this aspect of the Warren Court's criminal procedural revolution caused widespread anger among conservatives, especially in the South, including those who originated institutionalized unpublication, making the jurisprudence of hierarchy characteristic of Jim Crow revivify and spread silently to create a characteristic national jurisprudence of exception, which is today most starkly evident in asylum adjudication in the federal courts. If one product of the aftermath of the Holocaust, telos of the paradigmatic state of exception, is the origin of modern comparative constitutional law, then even U.S. constitutional law might be reminded that to the extent that it is constitutionalist, rather than merely constitutive, it cannot regard itself as a manifestation of American exceptionalism.

Comparative legal studies drive the subject qua discipline of law to engender knowledge of itself, legal subjects to a disciplined practice of self-searching. The most important lesson that a theorist of law seeking to engender a thick account of the subject of law, its institutions, and its discourses might take from both the governance of Germany as a state of exception in the years from 1933 to 1945, and the pall of obscenity it cast on realism, is that legal subjects enabled the locating of law beyond the purview of distinctively legal institutions, that is, the courts. Which is to say that the ontology of legal subjects, as much as if not more than a coherent and principled account of legal epistemology and hermeneutics, is, at present, the most critical project for those of us who profess the philosophy of American law.

WORKS CITED

Daicoff, Susan. "Lawyer, Know Thyself: A Review of Empirical Research on Attorney Attributes Bearing on Professionalism." *Am. U. L. Rev.* 46 (1997): 1337–1427.

Doyle, Michael. "Supreme Court Divided Over Hot Topics; Appeals Court Ruling Over Juror Rescinded." *The Belleville News-Democrat* June 5, 2007: A3.

Goodrich, Peter, "Law." In *Encyclopedia of Rhetoric.* Ed. Thomas O. Sloane. New York: Oxford University Press, 2001, 417–26.

———. *Law in the Courts of Love: Literature and Other Minor Jurisprudences.* London and New York: Routledge, 1996.

Guinier, Lani, Jane Balin, and Michelle Fine. *Becoming Gentlemen: Women, Law School and Institutional Change.* Boston: Beacon Press, 1997.

Kennedy, Duncan. "American Constitutionalism as Civil Religion: Notes of an Atheist." *Nova L. Rev.* 19.3 (1994–5): 909–21.

Law, David S. "Strategic Judicial Lawmaking: Ideology, Publication, and Asylum Law in the Ninth Circuit." *U. Cin. L. Rev.* 73.3 (2005): 817–66.

Legomsky, Stephen H. "Deportation and the War on Independence." *Cornell L. Rev.* 91.2 (2006): 369–408.

Llewellyn, Karl N. "On Philosophy in American Law." *U. Pa. L. Rev.* 82.3 (1934): 205–11.

Mailloux, Steven. "From Segregated Schools to Dimpled Chads: Rhetorical Hermeneutics and the Suasive Work of Theory." In *Rhetoric and Composition as Intellectual Work.* Ed. Gary A. Olson. Carbondale: Southern Illinois Univ. Press, 2002, 131–42.

Morawetz, Nancy. "Back to Back to the Future? Lessons Learned from Litigation over the 1996 Restrictions on Judicial Review." *N.Y.L. Sch. L. Rev.* 51.1 (2006–7): 114–31.

Norris, Christopher. "Law, Deconstruction, and the Resistance to Theory." *J.L.S.* 15.2 (1988): 166–87.

Pether, Penelope. "Sorcerers, Not Apprentices: How Judicial Clerks and Staff Attorneys Impoverish U.S. Law." *Ariz. St. L.J.* 39.1 (2007): 1–67.

Ramji-Nogales, Jaya, Andrew L. Schoenholtz, and Philip G. Schrag. "Refugee Roulette: Disparities in Asylum Adjudication." *Stan. L. Rev.* 60.2 (2007): 295–411.

Resnik, Judith. "Singular and Aggregate Voices: Audiences and Authority in Law and Literature and in Law and Feminism." In *Law and Literature: Current Legal Issues*, vol. 2. Eds. Andre Freeman and Andrew D. E. Lewis. Oxford: Oxford Univ. Press, 1999, 687–727.

10 Law and Creativity

GEORGE H. TAYLOR

In today's world we face the prospect of rapid change in many areas such as medicine, international trade, information technology, and the use of terror. *Innovation* is the buzzword in the business world. How able is the law to keep up with these changes?

We can contemplate several types of responses to this question. The first would argue that legal principles can extend to encompass new situations. The principles don't change, but their applications do. A second response would claim that the legal interpretation (whether common law, statutory, or constitutional) changes in a common law fashion: principles are modified, but slowly, incrementally, with a significant attention to the past and precedent. A third response would argue, as for example in a Posnerian pragmatism, for more robust attention to consequences rather than the past and would allow for greater deviation from existing law. A fourth and final response would focus on legal change occurring at the legislative or regulatory levels.

While I regard the first response as insufficient, my concern lies not with which of the latter three is a more accurate or appropriate assessment of the legal system. Instead, I want to probe how philosophy might assist reflection on the nature of legal change at whatever point and in whatever manner such change is deemed appropriate. How does philosophy help us understand how legal creativity occurs? My inquiry is basically descriptive, but there is an underlying normative element also to the extent that the inquiry opens a space alternative to rule formalism and the recourse only to the past, both of which can often be stultifying for both the law and the legal profession (Stefancic and Delgado 2005).

I rely principally on approaches in continental philosophy, particularly hermeneutics and the work of Paul Ricoeur on metaphor and imagination.[1] I also advert to recent work in cognitive theory that helps deepen the philosophical insights. While legal scholarship has debated the nature of legal creativity in the context of analogy, my claim is that the resources on which I draw allow a more precise, sophisticated, and illuminating rendering of this subject. I begin with

[1] A more expansive treatment would include as well important work in analytic philosophy (McGinn 2004; Rescher 2003; Warnock 1976).

exploration of the customary case of the extension of a legal principle to a new factual circumstance and then expand from that basis to larger arenas of legal creativity.

H. L. A. Hart (1958: 607–15) famously discusses a hypothetical legal rule that prohibits vehicles in a public park. A car is prototypically prohibited. It is not so clear, however, whether a bicycle is permitted entry. It might be possible to interpret the statute at a sufficiently high level of generality that the bike is definitely permitted – a vehicle is defined, for instance, as a motorized form of transportation – but that definition may seem imposed upon the term *vehicle* rather than its exposition. This act of definition does not avoid creative judgment because it is itself an operation of creativity. Suppose, in contrast, that a park announces that it is for pedestrians only, so no vehicles are permitted. Bicycles would seem not to be allowed there. Beyond the standard case (whose boundaries could themselves be revisited over time), a judgment is necessary about whether a new situation falls within or without the statute. The decision is not determined by the terms of the statute; legal creativity is required.

As another illustration of the potential role that legal creativity plays, consider whether states should grant the rights of marriage to gay and lesbian couples. Some Americans may accept that marriage should be available to any consenting adult couple, but for many others today the definition of marriage requires heterosexuality and, potentially, norms of procreation and fidelity that heterosexual marriage is assumed to imply and that same-sex marriage is assumed not to imply. The contest is over whether the meaning of marriage will – or should – change if same-sex marriage is granted. Against traditional norms that marriage is between a man and a woman, the question of same-sex marriage requires appraisal of the legal creativity that conjoins those two terms.

In the cases of both the bicycle in the park and same-sex marriage, the potential reinterpretation of meaning required at the moment of application is a basic theme of hermeneutics. The relationship between meaning and application is not one of subsumption; rather, application involves "co-determining, supplementing, and correcting [a] principle" (Gadamer 1992: 39). Meaning is not determined once and for all at the moment of origin but must be reassessed as the meaning is applied to new circumstances. Meaning can change as it is applied; the determination of meaning requires judgment.

Our understanding of the interrelation between meaning and application can be enriched, I would argue, by describing the interrelation as metaphoric. Paul Ricoeur (1977: 22) focuses on the "rifts" that metaphor creates in an existing order, the processes by which it "disturbs and displaces" order. The ground for metaphoric predication arises when customary meaning is challenged. Metaphor can cross the gap between terms – *same-sex* and *marriage* – that as presently understood (by many) offer a lack of literal fit. In metaphor, writes Ricoeur (1977: 196), "'the similar' is perceived despite difference." Metaphor is a creative act that can expand a category. In the interrelation of meaning and application, we may see resemblance where we had not before. The analytic point is appreciation of how legal creativity operates, not whether we necessarily agree with the particular creative judgment. While the metaphoric judgment that conjoins same-sex and marriage leads to a result that is more politically liberal, in other cases, as we shall see, the result will be conservative.

I extend analysis a step further by considering how the interrelation of meaning and application in legal judgment is not simply metaphoric but imaginative. The creation of metaphoric resemblance is an act of imagination. The relationship between meaning and application is not one of deduction of the particular from the general principle but rather of a transfer of meaning. Making the transfer requires imagination. "Imagination . . . is this ability to produce new kinds of assimilation and to produce them not above the differences, as in the concept, but in spite of and through the differences" (Ricoeur 1979: 146). The process of legal application is both metaphoric and imaginative: the imaginative interrelation of general and particular can create some new metaphoric resemblance across the initial divide. The process of application generalizes the imaginative productivity at work in creative legal judgment.

Ricoeur particularly wants to insist that the assimilation, the resemblance, produces something new. In his larger elaboration of a theory of imagination, Ricoeur differentiates between the West's preponderant attention to reproductive imagination, while he wants to promote productive imagination. Imagination is typically subsumed in Western philosophy under the study of what it is to have an image. A distinction is drawn between an original (reality) and a copy (the image or the imagination), and the copy is always less than the original. For Ricoeur, this model of original and copy exemplifies reproductive imagination. The image as copy is derivative of the original – from reality.

Productive imagination does something different. Ricoeur claims that we can conceive of a place that, unlike an image, is not duplicative of, not determined by, an original. Ricoeur offers as an example the social utopia. The utopia is a presently nonexistent reality that points to a new kind of reality. It expands our sense of reality and reality's possibilities. Ricoeur argues more generally that the "nowhere" not bound by an original can be found in fiction. "Because fictions don't reproduce a previous reality, they may produce a new reality. They are not bound by an original that precedes them" (Ricoeur 1975: 19.1).[2] Productive imagination introduces a fiction, an image without an original, something from nowhere. When Ricoeur locates the productive imagination in the nowhere that fiction provides, the paradox is that fiction can provide a new dimension of reality.[3] No longer is truth defined as adequation, a conformity between judgment and existing reality, because the potential disclosure of new reality has more to do with a concept of truth as manifestation (Ricoeur 1975: 19.12, 2.20).

In more recent work, Gilles Fauconnier and Mark Turner (2002) have further deepened our understanding of the operation of metaphor and imagination in their development of a theory that argues that human cognition often proceeds on the basis of "conceptual blending." In the type of "double-scope network" that they particularly emphasize, different organizing conceptual frames contribute to

[2] These unpublished lectures are cited from verbatim transcriptions by lecture number and then page number internal to the lecture.

[3] This connection of productive imagination with ontology differs, Ricoeur (1975: 19.13) notes, from Kant's employment of productive imagination.

a blend that is not a mere combination of the prior frames but one that generates its own emergent structure, a structure that is new, imaginative, and creative (Fauconnier and Turner 2002: 131). Fauconnier and Turner offer same-sex marriage as an example of this blending (134, 269–70).[4]

Significantly, for both hermeneutics and for Fauconnier and Turner, the changed meaning that arises at the moment of application or in the conceptual blend is not an extraordinary event but a quite ordinary human process. "Imagination is at work, sometimes invisibly, in even the most mundane construction of meaning, and its fundamental cognitive operations are the same across radically different phenomena, from the apparently most creative to the most commonplace. These operations are characteristic of the human species" (Fauconnier and Turner 2002: 89).

I would argue similarly that the law is replete with examples of conceptual blending and interrelations of meaning and application. These examples extend not only to more visible and dramatic instances such as deciding whether to extend the rights of marriage to same-sex couples, but also to more ordinary and routine elaborations such as determinations of what forms of locomotion are vehicles and so prohibited in the park. Unfortunately, the law too frequently hides these instances of imagination and creativity and often discourages the cultivation of imagination, which may leave the law trailing a distance behind unfolding events or external forms of organization.

If part of the message of metaphor, imagination, and conceptual blending is their ubiquity, a ubiquity that needs to be recognized in law, then law also needs to appreciate the larger possibilities presented by these terms. Law often focuses on day-to-day needs and neglects a larger vision or goal for itself. Imagination in particular, though, has the ability to redress that imbalance and attend law's prospective, aspirational role. As previously mentioned, in his work on social and cultural imagination, Ricoeur describes its productive power as utopian. The utopia exists nowhere and is a fiction, but it is a fiction that can change reality. A utopia can "shatter" or "break through the thickness of reality" and can "shape a new reality" (Ricoeur 1986: 309–10). The utopia's clash with reality may act as a metaphoric moment where new resemblance – a transformed reality – is pursued and created across the gap.

Yet in describing the roles that imagination, metaphor, and conceptual blending have – and should have – in law, we need to be careful not to exalt the value of these roles as ineluctably positive and beneficial. Legal liberals, for example, should not assume that the trajectory of imagination is necessarily progressive. While important liberal legal scholars have written on the potentially positive aspirational

[4] Fauconnier and Turner's work on conceptual blending is in part an outgrowth of prior work in cognitive theory by George Lakoff and Mark Johnson (1999). Both sets of authors emphasize the role played by metaphor in human cognition. Yet Fauconnier and Turner's emphasis on the double-scope network, in which both frames contribute to a new, emergent meaning, is distinctive. By contrast, Lakoff and Johnson (1999: 91) urge that conceptual metaphor "allows us to conceptualize one domain of experience in terms of another, *preserving* in the target domain the inferential structure of the source domain" (emphasis added). For Lakoff and Johnson the conceptual structure does not significantly change in the imaginative moment; for Fauconnier and Turner (and Ricoeur), it can.

role of imagination in law (Cover 1983: 4, 9; West 2003: 9), we are in a period that more prominently features a conservative legal and political imagination. This conservative imagination argues, on the one hand, in an aspirational fashion for consolidation of governmental power in the executive branch to address the rise of terror. On the other hand, it also argues for originalist interpretation of the Constitution to return to judgments of a perhaps mythical past. The latter might be called a conservative utopia (Mannheim 1936: 229–39). Both conservative perspectives invoke imagination.

So in a time when the liberal David Cole (2006) contends for a "return to established Fourth Amendment jurisprudence" to oppose conservatives endorsing legal creativity to allow for electronic surveillance by warrantless wiretapping, it is apparent that creativity and imagination in and of themselves align with no necessary legal valence. How then can legal imagination be policed? How do we determine whether its invocation is appropriate? One response might be to seek to curtail as much as possible the use of legal imagination, whether by emphasis on legal tradition or, say, judicial minimalism. These approaches, however, may neglect the pervasive role that imagination may play in law's ordinary transactions; they may adhere to a conservative form of imagination themselves and may not allow the law readily to evolve to meet new circumstances, though judgments of aptness here will often be disputed. Further, we have recently seen – particularly graphically in the political sphere – the costs of failures of imagination. Contrary to the assumptions of the Bush administration, the Iraqi people have not welcomed U.S. forces with open arms. Another example, *The 9/11 Commission Report* (2004a: 339), strikingly observes that of the kinds of governmental failures revealed in the attacks that day, a principal failure was one precisely in imagination.[5] We are poorer as a nation to the extent that we individually and collectively do not reach across the gap and attempt to imagine what it means to be of a different race or ethnicity or to dwell in a different land (Black 1986: 6–7). We must try to discover aspects of resemblance where we now only find difference.

Yet if imagination is not only pervasive but also, at least at points, normatively desirable, on what bases can we distinguish valuable from deleterious uses of imagination? First, we must appreciate that imagination is not unfettered. Current scholarship underscores that imagination does not arise from nowhere; we are far from the romantic view of imagination as simply free and spontaneous. Imagination is constrained conceptually by existing mental structures; novelty arises out of the clash and blend of these structures. The political and legal imagination is also constrained by the tradition or traditions out of which it arises. Imagination is innovative and adds to and changes prior tradition, but – for good and bad – its roots also lie in prior tradition as well.

Second, analytic distinctions may assist differentiation of positive and distortive uses of imagination. Ricoeur's discussion of utopia may again be fruitfully invoked. If the best function of utopia is its "exploration of the possible," its ability to manifest new realities and new truths, the pathology of utopia is its flight into

[5] The executive summary to the report goes even further and states: "The most important failure was one of imagination" (*9/11 Commission Report* 2004b: 9).

fancy, its escapism, its turn to the "completely unrealizable," its "magic of thought" (Ricoeur 1986: 310, 302, 296). As Ricoeur urges more generally, conceptual and social scientific thought can evaluate and test imaginative insights. Yet as he also recognizes, these tests – which are based on existing criteria – may be outrun by imagination, which introduces something new. In law we honor today many judicial dissents whose judgments were criticized and rejected at the time of their announcement. The use of imagination includes an ineliminable element of risk. The possibilities of imagination include loss and miscalculation but also benefit and significant gain.

Let me conclude this assessment of the potentially positive role imagination may play in law and the legal profession by a call for imagination's greater inculcation in legal education. As I have suggested, we need not disparage existing legal traditions or doctrines to acknowledge their current limits. In a world of rapid change on many fronts, the question is both whether present law satisfactorily keeps up and whether our students' legal training will allow them to keep up as well. Rhetoric that we want those entering the legal profession to be proactive rather than simply reactive, to be legal architects rather than simply legal mechanics, is not platitudinous. Business students focus on the need for innovation; medical students learn that much of what they are taught will need later to be revised on the basis of new scientific knowledge. Law students should not be taught only to look to the past or to the case on point. They need to learn how to exercise their muscles of imagination. Problem-based learning, simulations, and negotiations all offer not only more active student participation but also concrete and contextual forums in which students can begin to discover the need for and ability to undertake creative legal analysis.

WORKS CITED

Black, Charles L., Jr. *The Humane Imagination.* Woodbridge, CT: Ox Bow Press, 1986.

Cole, David. "How to Skip the Constitution." *N.Y. Rev. of Books.* Nov. 16, 2006 (available at http://www.nybooks.com/articles/19595).

Cover, Robert M. "The Supreme Court 1982 Term – Foreword: Nomos and Narrative." *Harv. L. Rev.* 97.1 (1983): 4–68.

Fauconnier, Gilles, and Mark Turner. *The Way We Think: Conceptual Blending and the Mind's Hidden Complexities.* New York: Basic Books, 2002.

Gadamer, Hans-Georg. *Truth and Method,* 2d rev. ed. Trans. Joel Weinsheimer and Donald G. Marshall. New York: Crossroad, 1992.

Hart, H. L. A. "Positivism and the Separation of Law and Morals." *Harv. L. Rev.* 71.4 (1958): 593–629.

Lakoff, George, and Mark Johnson. *Philosophy in the Flesh: The Embodied Mind and Its Challenge to Western Thought.* New York: Basic Books, 1999.

Mannheim, Karl. *Ideology and Utopia.* New York: Harcourt, Brace and World, 1936.

McGinn, Colin. *Mindsight: Image, Dream, Meaning.* Cambridge, MA: Harvard Univ. Press, 2004.

The 9/11 Commission Report: Final Report of the National Commission on Terrorist Attacks upon the United States, 2004a (available at http://www.9-11commission.gov).

The 9/11 Commission Report: Final Report of the National Commission on Terrorist Attacks upon the United States: Executive Summary, 2004b (available at http://www.9-11commission.gov).

Rescher, Nicholas. *Imagining Irreality: A Study of Unreal Possibilities.* Chicago: Open Court, 2003.

Ricoeur, Paul. *Lectures on Ideology and Utopia.* Ed. George H. Taylor. New York: Columbia Univ. Press, 1986.

______. *Lectures on Imagination.* 1975 (unpublished lectures delivered at the University of Chicago).

______. "The Metaphorical Process as Cognition, Imagination, and Feeling." In *On Metaphor.* Ed. Sheldon Sacks. Chicago: Univ. of Chicago Press, 1979, 141–57.

______. *The Rule of Metaphor: Multi-Disciplinary Studies of the Creation of Meaning in Language.* Trans. Robert Czerny. Toronto: Univ. of Toronto Press, 1977.

Stefancic, Jean, and Richard Delgado. *How Lawyers Lose Their Way: A Profession Fails Its Creative Minds.* Durham, NC: Duke Univ. Press, 2005.

Warnock, Mary. *Imagination.* Berkeley: Univ. of California Press, 1976.

West, Robin. *Re-Imagining Justice: Progressive Interpretations of Formal Equality, Rights, and the Rule of Law.* Burlington, VT: Ashgate, 2003.

11 The Stories of American Law

ROBERT L. HAYMAN JR. AND NANCY LEVIT

Caleb was finishing the first grade, and although it couldn't be said that he loved school, he certainly did love his teacher. Ms. Casey was her name, and she seemed to adore all the kids.

One of the kids in Caleb's class was named Gabrielle, and late in the school year, Caleb announced to his parents, "Ms. Casey likes Gabrielle the best." He said it matter-of-factly, without a hint of envy or disappointment, but still, it wasn't the kind of thing that his parents wanted to let stand.

"We are sure," they told him, "that Ms. Casey likes all the kids equally."

"Yeah, probably," he replied, "she likes all the kids equally." He took off his glasses, and rubbed his eyes. "And she likes Gabrielle the best."

They knew better than to argue the point. As parents, they had learned what lawyers too often forget: that some arguments are not worth having. Instead, they asked him: "What makes you think Ms. Casey likes Gabrielle the best?"

He pondered it. "Well, Ms. Casey put a sign on Gabrielle's desk."

"Well, what did the sign say?"

"I don't know, "he said, "I can't read. Don't you remember that?"

"Yes, we remember. Well, what do you think the sign said?"

"Hmm," he literally stroked his chin, assuming his most pensive pose. "Probably," he offered, "the sign said 'I like Gabrielle the best.'"

You most likely see where this is heading more clearly than Caleb's parents did at the time; there was no persuading Caleb that he was wrong. He saw in that sign – or claimed to see in that sign – what he believed to be the case, and unless his parents produced that sign to show him otherwise, he wasn't budging from his view. And frankly, even if they had that sign, we doubt that he'd trust their translation.

* * *

We felt bad when we first read that young Andy Meeks "suffered from attention deficit hyperactivity disorder and dyslexia," and that he couldn't go to the Seattle school that was arguably best for him. It was Chief Justice John Roberts who told us about Andy – he did it in his opinion for the Court in *Parents Involved*, the last desegregation case – and we're pretty sure that he wanted us to feel bad. We think, though, that he wanted us to feel bad – or maybe even angry – because Andy was being victimized because of his whiteness, which was preventing him from going to a school were there were already too many white kids.

But that's not why we felt bad. We felt bad – and yes, a little angry – to learn that another kid was being made to suffer from his perceived disabilities. We have seen too much of this sort of suffering. And we thought that it was wrong for the chief justice to exploit Andy this way, particularly seeing as how it was the Court's crabbed interpretations of the Individuals with Disabilities Education Act and section 504, and its regressive conceptions of disability and equality, that to a very significant degree likely caused Andy needlessly to suffer.

A lot of the suffering in the world is the result of the way that we have constructed disability. And a lot of the suffering in the world – and especially in the United States – is the result of the way that we have constructed race. In both cases, isolation causes a lot of the suffering, an isolation that follows from a construction of differences as something abnormal or subnormal.

We think that's what racial segregation was all about, and we think the boldness – and the beauty – of the opinion in *Brown v. Board of Education* rested principally in its willingness to confront this truth. Enforced segregation – even if it was enforced equally on everyone – was harmful. It was not harmful in some abstract, theoretical, first-principle-violating sort of way, but it was harmful in concrete, experiential, people-hurting kinds of ways. And the harms of segregation were inflicted – intentionally and obviously – on African Americans, whose perceived inferiority was both the *causa causans* of Jim Crow and its inevitable effect.

Racial segregation caused African Americans to suffer. Because it caused suffering, it was bad; because the suffering was visited unequally on African Americans, it was also unconstitutional.

That is the argument made over and over again in the *Brown* briefs, and in the oral arguments. It is the argument ultimately accepted by the *Brown* Court, which felt compelled to support its conclusion with a fairly cursory reference to the social science evidence, documenting the unequal harms of segregation. And the broader societal harms of segregation – elaborated on at considerable length in the amicus submissions from the United States – stem entirely from this injustice, from discrimination against minority groups, and from its consequent impacts on America's standing in the world.

Segregation was part of a racial caste system. That's why it was harmful. And that's why its defenders clung to it so desperately.

Hadn't it always been about caste? We thought that's what we had read in the record of the Reconstruction congresses. We thought that's what we had read in Justice Harlan's dissent in *Plessy* ("There is no caste here."). We thought that's what we had read in the *Brown* briefs, and in the histories of resistance to desegregation.

But that's not what we read in the opinion of the Court in *Parents Involved*; it says not one word about caste. It says not one word about the harms of racial segregation. The only harms it recognizes are the harms that inhere in the bare invocation of race. Race consciousness, it advises, is harmful, regardless of its motives, and the proof of that critical fact is to is to be found in, well, a few scattered opinions of fairly recent vintage, mostly concurrences and dissents, which do indeed say that, over and over again (the Court "apparently believing, with the Bellman, that what it says three times must be true"; Cohen 1935: 820).

Oh, and the *Brown* briefs. There's proof there, too, according to the *Parents Involved* Court – a sentence broadly condemning differential treatment based on race. And, the Court says, the oral arguments: Robert Carter, lawyer for the schoolchildren, had argued that no state could "use race as a factor" under the Fourteenth Amendment.

Judge Carter, now ninety, was not pleased by this appropriation of his words. "It's to stand that argument on its head," he responded, "to use race the way they use it now." But the fact of his displeasure, clearly, should not interfere with a good story.

Maybe Judge Carter is wrong. Maybe he really was arguing for color blindness, not against caste. And maybe Jack Greenberg is wrong too ("The plaintiffs in *Brown* were concerned with the marginalization and subjugation of black people. They said you can't consider race, but that's how race was being used.") (Liptak 2007: A24), and William T. Coleman ("It's dirty pool, to say that the people *Brown* was supposed to protect are the people it's now not going to protect.") ("Court Strikes Blow" 2007: 8A). And, of course, Thurgood Marshall. Maybe none of them really knew what *Brown* was about.

* * *

We do not know the elements of narrative truth. We know that the opinion in *Parents Involved* was entirely predictable. But that doesn't make it true. We know that the Court had the power to do what it did, and that the chief justice carefully aligned his opinion with prior decisions, and that the chief justice did what the president who appointed him wanted him to do, and did what the supporters of the president wanted him to do, and that the president was supported by a majority of the voters in the election preceding the chief justice's appointment. But none of that makes it true – any more than it is true that there are weapons of mass destruction in Iraq, or that Saddam Hussein was behind September 11, or that the science is equivocal on global warming.

But then again, it is not less true because two-thirds of Americans disapprove of the job the president is doing. And the opinion in *Parents Involved* is not rendered demonstrably untrue by the failure of the Court to ground it in the text of the Fourteenth Amendment, or the history of the Thirty-Ninth Congress, or the available evidence on the construction of race and inequality.

And yet – *Brown* seems true and *Parents Involved* seems not. We cannot say precisely what separates them, but we think it has something to do with suffering. And understanding. And, in the final analysis, love.

We need to learn, we think, the elements of narrative truth. Or our children will not believe us when we tell them that Ms. Casey really does not like Gabrielle the best.

* * *

Let us tell you a story about legal realism. The first legal realism was born of sociologically trained legal theorists, who criticized the formalist model of law as a collection of "paper rules," and the natural law concept of law as principles dictated by a "brooding omnipresence in the skies" (Llewellyn 1934: 210). These realists saw law as dynamic, judges as policy makers who were influenced by their own ideologies, and the primary task of legal academics as formulating a functional approach to law, one that would explain law according to its social purposes, rather than in terms of abstract concepts ("transcendental nonsense"; Cohen 1935).

The first legal realism had a number of descendants: the law and society movement, normative law and economics, and various critical theories. Now, at the turn of the twenty-first century, it has yielded a "new legal realism," one that weaves together a number of the philosophical strands from the first effort: the interplay of law, social science, and political analysis; skepticism about the prospects for formal rules to generate social change; and empirical investigations, using the methods of the social sciences, into a wide range of questions about the formation and impact of law.

Like the first legal realism, the new legal realism is acutely concerned with "law in action" – developing understandings of the role of law in relation to social hierarchies, the distributive consequences of law, and the prospects for law to bring about progressive social change (Gulati and Nielsen 2006: 797). It renews attention to the architecture of law (e.g., the public-private distinction) and to the effects of economic status on political rights (Balkin 1990: 381–2). It embraces a commitment to "bottom-up" research, which emphasizes examinations of "everyday experience" to assess "the impact of law on ordinary people's lives" (Erlanger et al. 2005: 340).

The new realism is also interdisciplinary in multiple ways. It encompasses greater engagement between legal theorists and social scientists, including conversations, critique, and collaboration. Social scientists – sociologists, anthropologists, social psychologists – are publishing in law reviews, law professors are producing empirical legal scholarship, and theorists in all disciplines are blogging and bringing the fruits of their research to a wide public audience. The empirical work is increasingly sophisticated, with complex quantitative studies using multiple regression analyses and Bayesian methods. Even the qualitative or interpretive work – ethnographic studies, microinstitutional analyses, and examinations of local cultural practices – is methodologically more refined (Rubin 1996).

The increased emphasis on empiricism includes not only a receptivity to social science methods in law but also a more nuanced understanding of interpenetrations between the disciplines, so that empirical work is more than just "the means of investigating questions formulated by lawyers" (Erlanger et al. 2005: 337). It also encompasses a more sophisticated use of quantitative methods, more refined empirical explorations of judicial ideology on voting behavior, the wide-scale use of rational choice theory and economic models to understand human decision making, greater attention to standpoint epistemology or situated knowledge in the legal systems of various cultures, and a reliance on experimental studies and other social science research by courts (Cross 1997; Farber 2001).

But empiricism seems not quite enough; in a sense, it proves its own limitations. To adequately describe legal decision making, it evolves; multivariate analysis must nearly be omnivariate – such, we have learned, is the importance of context.

As an instrument of persuasion, the knowledge generated by empirical works proves remarkably unstable; studies beget counterstudies, facts produce counterfacts, all in an endless cycle of skepticism. And then there are those things not easily quantified, not easily objectified, not easily reduced to a determinate essence: our aspirations, our motivations, the bounds – or boundlessness – of our comprehension and our compassion.

What we are left with is the words. It is a return of sorts – to rhetoric, to forms. But it is not classical rhetoric; it is not a revived formalism. The task is different now – as the realist movements, old and new, have each peeled away levels of naïveté. The modern student of narrative may begin and end with the words, but he or she knows now that not all the words are written.

Thus, the new realism also suggests an alternative path to empiricism, one that focuses more on the narrative dimensions of law. The original realists saw stories primarily as ethnographic accounts or case studies. Many focused on appellate decisions to understand legal doctrine; others understood the importance of examining trial-court decision making (Frank 1949). Karl Llewellyn once joined anthropologist E. Adamson Hoebel (1941) to undertake a project on case studies of law making and dispute resolution among the Cheyenne. Llewellyn spent just ten days among the Cheyenne, and "a photograph taken at the time shows Llewellyn and his wife seated in the back seat of an open convertible with elderly Indians being led up to him to be interviewed" (Conley and O'Barr 2004). Still, he recognized that for indigenous people, in the oral tradition, stories of individual cases were the foundations of their legal systems.

The new realists see a variety of dimensions to the narrative project. They see narrative as framework, as methodology, as evidence, as plural truths, and as a means of fundamentally reshaping legal doctrine.

They also tell stories. Beginning in the late 1970s, they have told parables, allegories, and real stories of their own experiences and those of their clients (Alfieri 1991; Bell 1987; Dworkin 1977; Williams 1991). These stories have raised awareness – of discrimination based on identity characteristics (race, gender, sexual orientation, disability), of unequal treatment based on class, of the absence of fair process based on power differentials. They have done more: they have changed the lens through which we view legal experiences. Stories insist on the importance of local knowledge and perspective; as such, they have been instrumental in incorporating the voices of outsiders – particularly of subordinated groups – whose narratives have been omitted in the development of law and legal theory.

The turn toward storytelling has fundamentally changed the way we think about legal theory, and law. Scholars like Richard Delgado and Catharine MacKinnon have demonstrated that judges' opinions in legal cases were merely stories too – they simply told the dominant narrative. Critical legal studies writers, feminist legal theorists, and critical race theorists thus confronted the "just-so" stories of the legal academy and told counterstories to challenge the "received wisdoms" (Delgado 1989: 2413).

Legal theorists soon began to recognize what historians and practicing lawyers had long known and what cognitive psychologists were just discovering – the extraordinary power of stories. Research in the social sciences shows that stories are the way people organize information and make sense of the world. Stories matter in law not only because they are the way people comprehend experiences, but because personal stories are such powerful tools for persuasion. They are rich with details and facts; they humanize, evoke empathy, and offer insights into other people's lives. For good lawyers, then, legal practice is a storytelling enterprise.

Trials have long been contests in storytelling, and now, stories are sifting into appellate litigation. As just one example, in the mid-1980s, the National Abortion Rights Action League began to submit an amicus brief in major Supreme Court abortion cases. Known as the "Voices Brief," this document was primarily a compilation of letters – narratives of women's reasons for having an abortion and experiences in trying to obtain one – intended to create some level of empathic understanding in members of the Court by allowing them to more directly hear women's voices. Today, appellate decisions, once relentlessly stripped of their human content, now address the stories of lived experience.

Even the ability to tell a story – to have one's day in court – has value. The expressive function of the legal process – the very heart of due process – is significant and often undervalued. People who have been wronged want to tell their stories, want to voice their pain. The opportunity to be heard in a formal tribunal that takes complaints seriously may give a victim a restored sense of control or a renewed sense of dignity. This is why the client-centered narrative work by Alfieri and others is so important – it makes sure that the story is the client's, not the lawyer's.

Narratives provide truths beyond the individual tellings. Because lived experiences have plural truths, stories offer multiple different perspectives and interpretations of events. Narratives thus offer an important type of qualitative research – they record personal experiences in varying cultural contexts and often provide a platform for survey research. Researchers are beginning to undertake ethnographic studies of participants in the legal system. For example, John M. Conley, an anthropologist and law professor, conducted interviews of lawyers in law firms to compare perceptions of racial and gender equity in law firms to diversity statistics. The combination of interviews and statistics revealed that lawyers felt resigned to the racial status quo, while law students lack incentives to change the racial dimensions of firms and feel powerless to do so (Conley 2006).

Stories have become the evidentiary foundation for some fundamental changes in law, particularly in the human rights arena. Stories from all over the world have documented human rights abuses: arbitrary detention, enslavement, forced labor, rape, torture, forced relocations, political executions, cultural genocide. Organizations like Human Rights Watch and Amnesty International gather victims' stories to illuminate these violations of rights. The Battered Mothers' Testimony Project collected the accounts of battered women about their degrading treatment in Massachusetts family court. "'Typically, these are the very voices that are muted or silenced by the government and society'" (Goodmark 2005: 723, 729). Law from the bottom up will demand even more specific attention to the particular situations of individuals – and that means their stories.

We are learning that narrative truths are vital to human existence. As generations age, the gathering and preservation of stories has taken on a particular urgency.

The projects to collect these narrative truths have ranged widely from the stories of comfort women in Asia to those of the stolen generations in Australia. The Department of Justice's Office of Special Investigations has preserved stories from Holocaust survivors to assist in the prosecution of Nazi war criminals. The Truth and Reconciliation Commission in South Africa helped a country transition from apartheid to democracy. The lesson is timeless – stories can do more than unearth agonizing truths, expose perpetrators, and document atrocities; they can turn toward understanding, toward forgiveness and love; they can begin to heal people, and even heal nations.

* * *

But if lawyers are to trade in stories – and if we are to take the lawyer's trade seriously – is it fair to ask that their stories be true? The "Voices Brief," after all, has yielded to the new reality of *Gonzales v. Carhart*: the teaching of a very different amicus brief, that women come to regret the choice to terminate a pregnancy. Which story do we believe? What stories are true?

The simplest answer – and, we suspect, the most common response – equates truth with persuasiveness: those stories are true that persuade. There is no end to the questions begged by this response – the whom's, how many's, how much's, for how long's, and so on – but we sense a more fundamental dilemma.

The line separating persuasion and coercion is surely a fine one when we speak of the law: the official narrative comes cloaked in an inherent – and perhaps necessary – veneer of truth. But official narratives can be faulty; official narratives can be false. And we – storytellers, and critics of stories – need a way to describe the faults, and the falsehoods. We need a way, then, to describe the truth, as a condition of – not merely the result of – persuasion.

Thus, the task of the modern storyteller, we think, is to renew the struggle for truth. It is a struggle that must recognize limits: that knowledge is culture bound; that the structural conditions on knowledge are barely known and perhaps unknowable; that truth must be contextual, and contingent, and personal. But it is simultaneously a struggle for transcendence – for truths to be found beyond these limits, if only because the limits must be, in the course of the search, momentarily suspended.

If law is to partake equally of science and art, we probably should insist that its art be genuine. "Language destroyed by irrational negation becomes lost in verbal delirium," wrote Camus; "subject to determinist ideology, it is summed up in the slogan." "Halfway between the two," he concluded, lies art. We should insist on more than verbal delirium, on more than slogan. We should insist on something that "uses reality and only reality with all its warmth and its blood, its passion and its outcries" but that simultaneously "adds something that transfigures reality" (Camus 1956: 273). We should insist on some reconciliation of the actual and aspirational, of the real and the ideal. We should insist on something that we can, without embarrassment, describe as the truth.

We do not know the criteria of narrative truth. We suspect that they will be found in those features of our lives that are distinctively – and universally – human. Precisely what those are, and how they are to be identified, we cannot say.

But we think the search is a worthy project – a necessary chapter, perhaps, in the story of American law.

WORKS CITED

Alfieri, Anthony V. "Reconstructive Poverty Law Practice: Learning Lessons of Client Narrative." *Yale L.J.* 100.7 (1991): 2107–47.

Balkin, J. M. "Some Realism about Pluralism: Legal Realist Approaches to the First Amendment." *Duke L.J.* 1990.3 (1990): 375–430.

Bell, Derrick. *And We Are Not Saved: The Elusive Quest for Racial Justice.* New York: Basic Books, 1987.

Camus, Albert. *The Rebel.* New York: Vintage, 1956.

Cohen, Felix S. "Transcendental Nonsense and the Functional Approach." *Colum. L. Rev.* 35.6 (1935): 809–47.

Conley, John M. "Tales of Diversity: Lawyers' Narratives of Racial Equity in Private Firms." *Law & Soc. Inquiry* 31.4 (2006): 831–53.

Conley, John M., and William M. O'Barr. "A Classic in Spite of Itself: The Cheyenne Way and the Case Method in Legal Anthropology." *Law & Soc. Inquiry* 29.1 (2004): 179–216.

"Court Strikes Blow to School Race Policies: Justices Used Brown Decision to Undo Its Spirit and Intent." *Star-Trib. (Minneapolis-St. Paul)*, July 2, 2007: 8A.

Cross, Frank B. "Political Science and the New Legal Realism: A Case of Unfortunate Interdisciplinary Ignorance." *Nw. U. L. Rev.* 92.1 (1997): 251–326.

Delgado, Richard. "Storytelling for Oppositionists and Others: A Plea for Narrative." *Mich. L. Rev.* 87.8 (1989): 2411–41.

Dworkin, Ronald. *Taking Rights Seriously.* Cambridge, MA: Harvard Univ. Press, 1977.

Erlanger, Howard, Bryant Garth, Jane Larson, Elizabeth Mertz, Victoria Nourse, and David Wilkins. "Is It Time for a New Legal Realism?" *Wis. L. Rev.* 2005.2 (2005): 335–63.

Farber, Daniel A. "Toward a New Legal Realism." *U. Chi. L. Rev.* 68.1 (2001): 279–303.

Frank, Jerome. *Courts on Trial: Myth and Reality in American Justice.* Princeton, NJ: Princeton Univ. Press, 1949.

Goodmark, Leigh. "Telling Stories, Saving Lives: The Battered Mothers' Testimony Project, Women's Narratives, and Court Reform." *Ariz. St. L.J.* 37.3 (2005): 709–57.

Gulati, Mitu, and Laura Beth Nielsen. "Introduction: A New Legal Realist Perspective on Employment Discrimination." *Law & Soc. Inquiry* 31.4 (2006): 797–800.

Liptak, Adam. "The Same Words, but Differing Views." *N.Y. Times*, June 29, 2007: A24.

Llewellyn, K. N. "On Philosophy in American Law." *U. Pa. L. Rev.* 82.3 (1934): 205–12.

Llewellyn, Karl N., and E. *Adamson Hoebel. The Cheyenne Way: Conflict and Case Law in Primitive Jurisprudence.* Norman: Univ. of Oklahoma Press, 1941.

Rubin, Edward L. "The New Legal Process, the Synthesis of Discourse, and the Microanalysis of Institutions." *Harv. L. Rev.* 109.6 (1996): 1393–1438.

Williams, Patricia J. *The Alchemy of Race and Rights.* Cambridge, MA: Harvard Univ. Press, 1991.

PART THREE. AREAS OF PHILOSOPHY AND THEIR RELATIONSHIP TO LAW

12 On Philosophy in American Law: Analytical Legal Philosophy

BRIAN H. BIX

THE RECEPTION OF ANALYTICAL LEGAL PHILOSOPHY

Analytical legal philosophy is the study of the nature of law, and the nature of legal concepts, through analysis – the breaking down to component parts, the search for necessary and sufficient conditions, or the rational reconstruction of a practice. It is connected to, or a subcategory of, the analytical tradition in philosophy generally, a tradition that has dominated English-language philosophy for the past century.[1]

In Britain, analytical legal philosophy is at the center of jurisprudence, a position it has held basically since John Austin's work in the early nineteenth century (e.g., Austin 1995). It is not accidental that most of the central work in analytical jurisprudence has been done by theorists teaching at British universities (e.g., Austin, H. L. A. Hart, Joseph Raz, and Neil MacCormick). In particular, modern English-language legal philosophy largely derives from the work of Hart (1968, 1982, 1983, 1994). In other countries, legal philosophy is often dominated by theories that derive from the work of another analytical legal philosopher (and another legal positivist), Hans Kelsen (e.g., 1992).

Matters have always been different on this side of the Atlantic. In the United States, analytical legal philosophy has been both consistently misunderstood and marginalized. For an American scholarly audience that tends to focus on practical questions – in particular, how should judges decide cases? And how should the Constitution be interpreted and applied? – the analytical questions about the basic nature of law and legal concepts seem out of place. American law students, when faced with analytical writers, tend to be perplexed as to why one would spend time inquiring about the nature of law if such investigations have no bottom-line implications for legal practice. And such misunderstandings or dismissals do not occur only among students; they have been common among legal scholars as well, with the legal realists of the early twentieth century mischaracterizing the analytical

[1] Analytical approaches to philosophy are generally contrasted with the Continental tradition, usually associated with more systemic thinkers like G. W. F. Hegel, though some commentators argue that the analytic-Continental distinction is misleading or overstated.

I am grateful to Matthew Adler, Francis J. Mootz III, Mark D. White, and an anonymous reviewer for their comments and suggestions on an earlier draft of this chapter.

legal theorists (seeing them as mere formalists; Sebok 1998: 20–47) just as badly as have contemporary law and economics analysts and critical theory advocates. Among contemporary American legal scholars, it is common for central analytical legal philosophy texts like H. L. A. Hart's (1994) *The Concept of Law* to be read as merely misguided instructions for judicial (or constitutional) reasoning.[2]

Despite the somewhat hostile reception analytical legal philosophy has had in the United States, American theorists have made important contributions. On the whole, this is both a very good time and a very difficult time for analytical legal philosophy in the United States. The positive news is the growing quality and sophistication of the product. If the analytical legal philosophy of one hundred years ago, or even forty years ago, was mostly reflections of lawyers with theoretical interests but little philosophical training, contemporary writing in the area is dominated by academics with doctorates in philosophy or comparable training and commitment, and the literature reflects this.

However, the growing sophistication of the debate within analytical jurisprudence,[3] and a corresponding demand for expertise among those taking part, has created its own obstacles for the role and reception of analytical legal philosophy in the United States. The problem is that the current level of debate in analytical legal philosophy requires a level of theoretical knowledge of the philosophical literature that few not already afflicted with a philosophy doctorate are likely to have, and few not already committed to working in the area will likely have the time or motivation to attain. To partake in the most important debates in the current literature, it is helpful – and perhaps necessary – to have a familiarity with conceptual analysis, natural kinds analysis, Wittgenstein's rule-following considerations, epistemological naturalism, the philosophical analysis of conventions and joint intentional activity, and many other philosophical topics. None of these is easy to develop fluency in over a weekend. It is perhaps not surprising that those who have taken the long, hard path to a careful understanding of a difficult thinker might be irritated when coming across the shoddy and misleading use of those same ideas by academics who display only a surface familiarity (see Leiter 1992). I think it is reasonable to ask scholars who invoke (say) Wittgenstein or Hegel or Kant or Foucault to do so knowledgeably. However, these are not theorists who can be quickly or easily mastered.

At the same time, much is lost if legal philosophy, narrowly understood, becomes a conversation confined to a handful of specially qualified scholars. The argument here is not that analytical philosophy needs to be accessible so that it can contribute directly to debates about legal reform. To the contrary, as already mentioned, I think such a view would reflect a common but quite unhelpful misunderstanding of analytical legal theory. However, there is a great and obvious loss if theories about the nature of law were to be cut off from input by thoughtful practitioners and

[2] Misunderstandings, to be sure, do not go in only one direction; it is equally common for European theorists to misinterpret American legal realism, law and economics, and contemporary critical theories.

[3] This in no way is to deny that there is a similar increase of expertise and specialization (and jargon) in other parts of American legal theory. It is just this universal increase in specialization that, unfortunately, decreases the possibility of discussions across disciplinary approaches.

theorists whose specialty or (inter)discipline was something other than advanced philosophy.

A related, if somewhat different, complaint regarding the discussion of famous analytical theorists in the legal literature is the tendency to display a famous theorist's name as an authority – as a conversation stopper. The message comes across as, "My position is supported by famous philosopher (or social theorist or literary critic or economist) X, and who are you, mere mortal, to question X's views!" Basically, what one has here are theorists hiding behind big names in philosophy, as if the mere mention of Wittgenstein or Kant or Aquinas should be sufficient to quiet all opposition.

The first problem with these sorts of articles is (as already discussed) that the author has often not done the work necessary to ground his or her reading of the great theorist's work, or to justify the application of that work to the legal topic in question (I am most familiar to such errors in the purported application of Ludwig Wittgenstein's later work to legal interpretation [Bix 2005], but I have heard of similar errors relating to many other theorists – from Hobbes to Kant to Heidegger and Habermas, and beyond).

Second, even if the article's argument does offer an accurate portrayal of, say, Wittgenstein's or Kant's or Foucault's views on the topic in question, the accuracy of the exegetical claim is no guarantee that the claim is correct in its assertions (e.g., about the nature of language, reality, or law). It is true that we should show proper humility and deference before the great figures in our field. However, all but the truest of true believers are willing to concede that even the likes of Wittgenstein or Kant (or Rawls or Raz) get it wrong on occasion. Ideas stand or fall on their own merits, and even the greatest philosophers make mistakes. The authors citing these grand figures need to do more work to ground the arguments they have borrowed or adapted.

It probably does not help matters that the current tenure criteria at many schools value quantity of output (number of articles, and preferably very long articles) rather than quality, and that the American legal academic culture generally (furthered by the madness of students editing the most prestigious journals, usually without the assistance of professorial peer review) tends to reward broad claims (and sometimes outlandish claims) rather than more modest and careful claims.

Most theories about the nature of law purport to have some connection with law as it is normally practiced and conventionally perceived. Legal realists like Karl Llewellyn (1934: 205) properly focused our attention on the connection between theory and "life-in-action." However, it is important to realize that there is an interest at least in many, if not all, people, to better understand the world around them. And while it might be that all understanding must have a connection to practical use, if only through a long chain of connections, in the short term, understanding for its own sake fulfills a real human need.

SELECTED TOPICS

The paradigmatic analytical jurisprudence topic is the discussion of the nature of law. If analytical legal philosophers still drag out the seemingly clichéd question,

What is law?, the compensation is that there are new twists to the analysis. Theorists are now more conscious of the underlying methodological questions: What justifies or grounds general or universal claims about the nature of law? How is it that we can even talk about law as a general category: is law a Platonic idea, a natural kind, a functional kind? Alternatively, can a general theory of law be grounded on a form of conceptual analysis that does not require controversial ontological claims (like a Platonic idea of law)?

The primary discussants in debates about the nature of law in the United States are followers of legal positivism and natural law theorists. Within legal positivism, there are some quite distinct approaches (all of which originated with theorists from outside the United States).

John Austin (1995, and, to some extent, Jeremy Bentham [1970]) proffered a command theory of law, equating law with the command of the sovereign. Austin refers to his project at one point as the "scientific" study of law (2002: 2:1107–8); in any event, it tries to reduce legal norms to a single common denominator, focusing on empirical claims that are in principle observable (e.g., who is in the habit of obeying whom, whether requests have been made, and whether the entity making a request has the willingness and ability to impose sanctions if the requests are not complied with). Frederick Schauer has developed a legal positivist theory with some ties to Austin's approach.

H. L. A. Hart (1994) brought a hermeneutic turn to analytical legal philosophy in general, and to legal positivism in particular. That is, he emphasized the importance of the participant's perspective. A theory of law is better, Hart argued, to the extent that it incorporated an "internal point of view," the perspective of a participant for whom legal rules give reasons for action. Hart focuses on the social facts and conventions that underlie the operation of the legal system. The difference between a norm and a habit is the social fact that those who accept the norm use it as a justification for their own actions, and a justification for criticisms of deviations from what the norm prescribes. At the level of a legal system, what divides legal norms from norms that are not part of the legal system under Hart's approach is a rule of recognition, whose criteria are in turn set by the facts of official behavior. American scholars prominent in the Hartian tradition of legal positivism include Jules L. Coleman, Matthew H. Kramer, David Lyons, Gerald J. Postema, Scott J. Shapiro, and Philip Soper.

Hans Kelsen (1992) brought a neo-Kantian approach to his pure theory of law, seeking the logic intrinsic to the normative system of law. Kelsen applied something like Kant's transcendental argument to law: his theory starts from the question, What follows from the fact that people sometimes treat the actions and words of other people (legal officials) as valid norms? Particular legal norms are part of chains of normative reasoning (e.g., the statute is valid because enacted by the legislature, the legislature gets its power from the Constitution, and so on). Thus, to assert the normative validity of an individual legal norm is implicitly to endorse the whole chain, including the foundational norm, upon which the chain is grounded. Kelsen referred to this foundational norm as the "Basic Norm" (*Grundnorm*) of the legal system (e.g., "one ought to do what is authorized by the historically first constitution"). American scholars working on Kelsenian legal positivism include Stanley L. Paulson and Michael Steven Green.

While traditional natural law theory itself is more of a moral, metatheoretical, and (at times and for some theorists) theological set of claims (and thus may not fit comfortably within the rubric of analytical philosophy), there has also been one line of argument that starts with natural law assumptions and offers analytical claims about the nature of law that compete with the claims of legal positivists. The best contemporary example of a natural law theory of the nature of law is given by the work of John Finnis (1980). Among the Americans working in the natural law tradition, and its application to theories of law, is Mark C. Murphy.

A second common focus for analytical legal scholars is the analysis of legal concepts. These theorists attempt to gain a more precise understanding of what is meant by (legal) rights, (legal) duties, causation, (legal) responsibility, and other legal concepts. This may be the part of the analytical legal philosophy that is least known and discussed by those outside the area (outsiders may make fun of debates about the question, What is law?, but that at least reflects some awareness of the discussions, even if it tends to be inaccurate as well as dismissive), but it may also be the part that has the most real-world impact. Case law debates about the nature of, for example, legal cause often show the influence of academic discussions (e.g., Wright 1985). And discussions at a more general level have also been influential: for example, Ronald Dworkin (1977: 153) on rights as trumps, the idea that rights are essentially claims that override consequentialist or majoritarian reasons, and the work by Wesley N. Hohfeld (1913, 1917) analyzing the way that judicial references to (legal) rights could be helpfully analyzed into either claim rights, powers, liberties, or immunities (with each having legal correlates and opposites).

A third focus is the so-called philosophical foundations of different areas of law (most commonly the traditional common law areas – like property, tort, and contract – but also extending to other doctrinal areas). These are generally efforts that partake equally of explanation and justification of existing doctrine – like much of legal advocacy and law school teaching, it is rational reconstruction, though at a fairly high or broad level. As the parallel with legal advocacy indicates, theories of doctrinal areas of law potentially have significant practical applications, possibly offering significant guidance to judges, especially when dealing with novel questions of law. The extent to which such theories in fact inform judicial decisions is less clear (and not easy to discern).

In theories of areas of law, it is common to find competing theories dividing roughly between consequentialist theories (usually efficiency based, affiliated with the economic analysis of law) on one side (e.g., Posner 2007, Shavell 2004), and some form of deontological theory on the other. Examples of deontological theories include corrective justice theories of tort law (e.g., Coleman 1992) and promise- and/or autonomy-based theories of contract law (e.g., Fried 1981). Important American figures in philosophical foundations include Jules L. Coleman and Gregory C. Keating (tort), Charles Fried and Jody S. Kraus (contract), Stephen Munzer, Gregory S. Alexander, and Laura S. Underkuffler (property), and Larry Alexander, Stephen J. Morse, and Michael S. Moore (criminal law).

On the whole, the connection between the analytical theories and legal practice is uncertain and controversial. And it is probably not to the benefit of either theorists or practitioners to overstate the connection, for it is just the easy assumption that all theories should or do have immediate normative implications that causes many American scholars (and law students) to misunderstanding or underappreciate analytical legal theory.

CONCLUSION

Analytical legal philosophy faces ongoing difficulties in the United States: already frequently misunderstood or marginalized, it must also learn to balance theoretical advances with accessibility. At the same time, it is an approach that has the advantages of a rich tradition as well as, in many ways, a bright future. The work being done by contemporary scholars seems very strong, building on what came before but bringing ever better analytical and normative tools to the task.

WORKS CITED

Austin, John. *Lectures on Jurisprudence; or, The Philosophy of Positive Law*, 2 vols., 4th ed. Rev. and ed. R. Campbell. 1879. *Reprint*, Bristol, UK: Thoemmes Press, 2002.

———. *The Province of Jurisprudence Determined*. 1832. Ed. Wilfrid E. Rumble. Cambridge: Cambridge Univ. Press, 1995.

Bentham, Jeremy. *Of Laws in General*. Ed. H. L. A. Hart. London: Athlone Press, 1970.

Bix, Brian H. "Cautions and Caveats for the Application of Wittgenstein to Legal Theory." In *Topics in Contemporary Philosophy*. Eds. Joseph Keim Campbell, Michael O'Rourke, and David Shier. Cambridge, MA: MIT Press, 2005, 217–29.

Coleman, Jules L. *Risks and Wrongs*. Cambridge: Cambridge Univ. Press, 1992.

Dworkin, Ronald. *Taking Rights Seriously*. Cambridge, MA: Harvard Univ. Press, 1977.

Finnis, John. *Natural Law and Natural Rights*. Oxford: Clarendon Press, 1980.

Fried, Charles. *Contract as Promise: A Theory of Contractual Obligation*. Cambridge, MA: Harvard Univ. Press, 1981.

Hart, H. L. A. *The Concept of Law*, rev. ed. Oxford: Clarendon Press, 1994.

———. *Essays on Bentham*. Oxford: Clarendon Press, 1982.

———. *Essays on Jurisprudence and Philosophy*. Oxford: Clarendon Press, 1983.

———. *Punishment and Responsibility: Essays in the Philosophy of Law*. Oxford: Clarendon Press, 1968.

Hohfeld, Wesley Newcomb. "Some Fundamental Legal Conceptions as Applied in Judicial Reasoning." *Yale L.J.* 23.1 (1913): 16–59.

———. "Fundamental Legal Conceptions as Applied in Judicial Reasoning." *Yale L.J.* 26.8 (1917): 710–70.

Kelsen, Hans. *An Introduction to the Problems of Legal Theory: A Translation of the First Edition of* Reine Rechtslehre *or Pure Theory of Law*. Eds. and trans. Bonnie Litschewski Paulson and Stanley L. Paulson. Oxford: Oxford Univ. Press, 1992.

Leiter, Brian. "Intellectual Voyeurism in Legal Scholarship." *Yale J.L. & Human.* 4.1 (1992): 79–104.

Llewellyn, K. N. "On Philosophy in American Law." *U. Pa. L. Rev.* 82.3 (1934): 205–12.

Posner, Richard A. *Economic Analysis of Law*, 7th ed. New York: Aspen Publishers, 2007.

Sebok, Anthony J. *Legal Positivism in American Jurisprudence.* Cambridge: Cambridge Univ. Press, 1998.

Shavell, Steven. *Foundations of Economic Analysis of Law.* Cambridge, MA: Harvard Univ. Press, 2004.

Wright, Richard W. "Causation in Tort Law." *Cal. L. Rev.* 73.6 (1985): 1735–1828.

13 Political Philosophy and Prosecutorial Power

AUSTIN SARAT AND CONNOR CLARKE

Much recent scholarship has been animated by the desire to understand the limits of law and how law figures its own limits. It has charted the gaps, fissures, and incompleteness of legality in a society whose political rhetoric stresses the depth and strength of our commitment to the rule of law. This work is enlivened and enriched when it is rooted in, or informed by, the perspectives of political philosophy.

Karl Llewellyn (1934: 205) was correct in identifying ways philosophy shapes legal action and noting that "[p]hilosophers' writings and law-men's doings meet rarely on the same level of discourse, and part of the game is to find out where they do, where they do not, and – if you can – the why of either." However, the relevance of philosophical perspectives to law was, and is, broader than Llewellyn acknowledged. His invitation to examine what he variously called "philosophy-in-action" or "implicit philosophy" so as to identify the "implicit" and "unthought" premises of legal action pointed to that broader relevance even if he did not himself pursue it (Llewellyn 1934: 206). In what follows we take up Llewellyn's invitation, using political philosophy to cast new light on the work of one kind of "law man" – prosecutors – and, in so doing, to chart another domain of what Sarat and Hussain (2004: 1311) have called "lawful lawlessness."

PERSPECTIVES ON PROSECUTORS

It is widely recognized that prosecutors have substantial discretion, but this acknowledgment is generally framed in the language of administration and points to their place in an executive bureaucracy (see, e.g., Davis 2001; Ely 2004; Loewenstein 2001). Theorists explain that prosecutors are granted very wide latitude to pursue their own strategies of law enforcement out of respect for the separation of powers, or to facilitate the prosecutor's ability to do substantive justice. Critics (see Jackson 1940; Vorenberg 1981) worry, however, that prosecutorial discretion can be a dangerously tyrannical power that poses a threat to justice, fairness, and the rule of law.

In our view, the decisions that prosecutors make involve something more than a straightforward exercise of discretion, something more than a bureaucratic phenomenon. Drawing on political philosophy, we want to alter the frame within which prosecutors are understood from the administrative to the political. Doing so will help us see that prosecutors participate in, and exemplify, the logic of sovereignty and its complex relationship to legality. In particular, it is the decision not to prosecute, in a case where there is probable cause to believe that a crime has been committed, that most vividly exemplifies this logic.

In this essay we trace the legal and theoretical connections between decisions not to prosecute and sovereign power. In particular, we draw on Carl Schmitt's (1985: 5) well-known definition of the sovereign as "he who decides on the exception" and its subsequent rearticulation by Giorgio Agamben (1998, 2005). Applying the work of Schmitt and Agamben suggests that prosecutors decide on the exception when they decline to bring charges when there is a legally sufficient basis for doing so, thus exempting individuals selectively from the reach of valid law.

Of course, not every refusal to prosecute is exceptional in the way that Schmitt and Agamben use the term. Some of those decisions result from predictions about the probability of success at trial based on reasons such as insufficient evidence, witness problems, and the like – all reasons that derive from legal norms. However, other decisions draw on the logic of the exception, resting as they do on criteria of desirability and appropriateness, as when prosecutors decline prosecution because they feel that a suspect is not morally culpable or because they believe that adequate alternatives to charging exist. In addition, prosecutors may decline to prosecute for policy reasons, as when they feel that their office is overwhelmed and it would be impractical to take a case, or when she believes that charging would make for bad press. More dramatically, they may decline to prosecute for no apparent reason and need provide no account of their decisions. The point is that none of these latter decisions is necessarily dictated by legal norms.

The lawless potential of prosecutorial discretion has been described by Mortimer Kadish and Sanford Kadish (1973: 81), who argue that the prosecutor is one of several official roles in which such departures from mandatory rules are justified, even commonplace; the prosecutor's discretionary power, they write, is "substantially uncontrolled." While we agree with their analysis, this way of framing prosecutorial decisions fails to identify the extent to which prosecutorial decisions engage the lawless logic of sovereignty. Those decisions are more than instances of discretion to disobey the law. Guided by the political philosophy of Schmitt and Agamben, we can see that prosecutors act in a sovereign manner by creating exceptions to the reach of valid law. While prosecutors are not sovereign in any simple sense, declining to prosecute an individual when there is probable cause exemplifies the logic of sovereignty in a constitutional democracy, and thereby exposes law's limit.

POLITICAL PHILOSOPHY, SOVEREIGNTY, AND PROSECUTORIAL POWER

For centuries political philosophers have emphasized the power to decide – be it the power to decide life and death or to decide something more banal – as a distinguishing feature of sovereign might. Traditionally this power has been linked with nothing more than expediency. Thus, Montesquieu (1989: 54) could write that the great advantage monarchies enjoyed over republics was that because the former were "conducted by a single person, the executive power is thereby enabled to act with greater expedition" – a word that reflects well the combination of daring and discretion the sovereign should employ. Linking a single, decisive individual with the health of the commonwealth, this argument reflects the most basic defense of executive discretion.

Even John Locke – a lover of the rule of law if there ever was one – treated executive discretion as something necessary for preserving the health of the political order. Far from contradicting his support for the rule of law, this power is, for Locke, simply obvious. Prerogative is "nothing but whatsoever shall be done manifestly for the good of the people, and establishing the government upon its true foundations is, and always will be, just prerogative" (Locke 1986: sec. 158).

In the political theories of Locke, Montesquieu, and others, the prosecutor has been portrayed as a kind of surrogate sovereign. This is certainly the case for Montesquieu, who, in the *Spirit of the Laws*, contrasts the Roman system of private prosecution with that of his own time, in an effort to show the superiority of the latter. "We have at present," he said, "an admirable law, namely, that by which the prince, who is established for the execution of the laws, appoints an officer in each court of judicature to prosecute all sorts of crimes in his name . . . [who] watches for the safety of the citizens; he proceeds in his office while they enjoy their quiet and ease" (Montesquieu 1949: 54).

Blackstone (1850) brings the connection between prosecution and sovereignty into even sharper focus. Like Locke, Blackstone defends executive discretion in broad terms (it is a "necessity in general") and elaborates its benefits. The king, says Blackstone, is "the *fountain of justice*," by which he means not the "author" or "origin" of the law, but rather its "distributor" (1850: 239): "He is not the spring, but the reservoir; from whence right and equity are conducted, by a thousand channels, to every individual" (1850: 265–6). Blackstone continues: "The original power of the judicature, by the fundamental principles of society, is lodged in the society at large; but as it would be impracticable to render complete justice to every individual by the people in their collective capacity, therefore every nation has committed that power to certain select magistrates, who, with more ease and expedition, can hear and determine complaints; and in England this authority has immemorially been exercised by the king or his substitutes" (1850: 267). This is important not only because the king has jurisdiction over these affairs, but because Blackstone regards the prosecutor as one of the king's "substitutes."

However, these classical accounts ultimately prove inadequate for dealing with the complexities that prosecutorial discretion and the decision not to prosecute raise for the rule of law. Decisions not to prosecute reveal situations in which law empowers someone to ignore or, in effect, overturn valid law, situations of lawful lawlessness. Agamben's recent development of Schmitt's political philosophy emphasizes this quality of sovereignty and therefore provides a more useful vehicle for examining the practice.

Schmitt's definition of the sovereign as "he who decides on the exception" springs from his recognition of the inability of norms to cover all exigencies, especially situations of state emergency. The great theorist of Weimar Germany tried to fully explicate the fraught relationship between law and decision, wherein the sovereign is he or she who stands both inside and outside the law, operating within and affecting a legal structure but not necessarily guided by legal norms. Schmitt insisted that sovereign decisions often depart from or overturn law and are not guided by it.

Recognition of this phenomenon – lawful lawlessness – leads to a consideration of sovereignty and the state of exception. For Schmitt, the exceptions that define sovereignty become most apparent in situations of emergency or extreme peril, where legal norms fail to prescribe the appropriate action. Because the "precise details of an emergency cannot be anticipated, nor can one spell out what may take place in such a case," situations of peril necessitate a sovereign decision. Indeed, Schmitt (1985: 6) continues, this is so even in a constitutional democracy, as the "most guidance the constitution can provide is to indicate *who* can act" in such a case. Thus, even the most robust system of legal constraints cannot avoid decisions on the exception. Even if the sovereign is granted power to act by law, the law cannot guide the subsequent actions that the sovereign takes.

By focusing on the inside-outside relationship of sovereign and norm, Schmitt advances well beyond previous accounts of sovereignty. Decisions on the exception – decisions concerning both when it exists and how to respond – are what he calls borderline concepts, a word that reflects the fact that decisions on the exception exist at the very border of the law. While a sovereign "stands outside the normally valid legal system, he nevertheless belongs to it, for it is he who must decide whether the constitution needs to be suspended in its entirety" (Schmitt 1985: 7).

Schmitt's more ambitious claim is that sovereign decisions form the basis of every legal order because legal norms are not self-realizing. For theory to become reality, a decision must be made – a decision that cannot, in turn, spring solely from a legal norm. That the legal idea cannot translate itself independently is, moreover, "evident from the fact that it says nothing about who should apply it" (Schmitt 1985: 7). Thus, Schmitt concludes, "In every transformation" – from legal idea to actual law – "there is present an *auctoritatis interposition*," or a "distinctive determination of which individual person or which concrete body can assume such an authority [that] cannot to be derived from the more legal quality of the maxim" (31). "Ascription," Schmitt contends, "is not achieved with the aid of a norm; it happens the other way around" – that is, by a sovereign decision that, in its very lawlessness, affirms the existence of law (33).

Agamben (1998: 3) has extended Schmitt's thesis by drawing on the biopolitics of Michel Foucault, arguing that bare life increasingly is included in the "mechanisms and calculations of state power." Agamben agrees with Foucault that "the politicization of bare life as such – constitutes the decisive event of modernity and signals a radical transformation of the political-philosophical categories of classical thought" (4). Is there, Agamben wonders, a unitary center around which biopower takes shape?

Agamben's answer is yes, and it leads him back to a Schmittian conception of sovereignty. Indeed, he maintains that the "inclusion of bare life in the political realm constitutes the original – if concealed – nucleus of sovereign power"

(Agamben 1998: 6). As with Schmitt, the state of exception, a state that both constitutes and threatens the political order, is the work of a sovereign who "is, at the same time, outside and inside the juridical order." His power exists within a legal order, yet is not legally controlled and as a result he marks "the limit . . . of the juridical order" (Agamben 1998: 15). Sovereign decisions reside at the zone of irreducible indistinction mentioned previously, a place where law bleeds into lawless fact, and vice versa. "The state of exception," Agamben (2005: 4) writes, "is not a special kind of law (like the law of war); rather, insofar as it is a suspension of the juridical order itself, it defines law's threshold or limit."

Agamben suggests that the essence of sovereign prerogative is its embodiment of the power to decide on an exception and remove a subject from the purview of regular law. Prosecutorial power, of course, does not generally deal in terms of imminent peril or collapse. And yet the two are not entirely dissimilar, as neither can be fully subsumed by the rule of law. As Schmitt repeatedly emphasizes, situations of danger can never be exhaustively anticipated or codified in advance, and thus the suspension of law that it requires has to be the result of a conscious decision. Here, Schmitt (1985: 13) says, "resides the essence of the state's sovereignty, which must be juridically defined correctly, not as the monopoly to coerce or to rule, but as the monopoly to decide." Sovereignty cannot, of course, live without the concept of norm that it subtends and is parasitical upon, but that only highlights its agonistic relation to the rule of law.

The exception is, as Agamben (1998: 17–18) puts it, "a kind of exclusion," and he says that "What is excluded from the general rule is an individual case. . . . [W]hat is excluded . . . is not, on account of being excluded, absolutely without relation to the rule. On the contrary, what is excluded in the exception maintains itself in relation to the rule in the form of the rule's suspension. *The rule applies to the exception in no longer applying, in withdrawing from it.*" Acts of sovereignty, like a prosecutor who refuses to indict even when there is probable cause, create exceptions, exclusions, but as Agamben (1998: 18) notes, the exception does not "subtract itself from the rule; rather the rule, suspending itself, gives rise to the exception and, maintaining itself in relation to the exception, first constitutes itself as a rule." Decisions of prosecutors are quintessentially sovereign acts in that they are authorized by law as moments when officials can decide who shall be removed from the purview of the law, but they are not themselves subject to legal review or remedy. They mark the boundaries of the rule of law even as they do work that law requires.

Our contention is that Schmitt and Agamben help us see that decisions not to prosecute constitute decisions on the exception and move us from the domain of administration to politics. Even Justice Scalia (*Davis v. United States* 1994: 452) acknowledges that the "[e]xecutive has the power (whether or not it has the right) effectively to nullify some provisions of the law by the failure to prosecute – the exercise of so-called prosecutorial discretion." It is this ability to make exceptions – in effect to nullify the law – that partakes of sovereign prerogative. The courts recognize and accept this power in their consistent refusal to second-guess prosecutorial decision making, thereby legally authorizing this decision making that operates without formal legal restraint.

One might question our analogy between the state of exception and decisions not to prosecute, asking if states of exception must involve (or have the potential to involve) the entire legal order. While Schmitt (1985: 12) makes reference to the "unlimited authority" of the sovereign, which means "the suspension of the entire existing order," both Schmitt and Agamben also suggest that states of exception can be either "total or partial" (Agamben 2005: 3) or can occur "in general or in a specific case" (Schmitt 1985: 12). Because decisions not to prosecute always occur in specific, individual cases, we believe that it is best to call them a fragment of sovereignty.

Although those decisions are not made with the sense of emergency or imminent danger that Schmitt and Agamben often invoke when discussing decisions on the exception, the effect – a decision within the legal framework that is unbound by legal rules – is the same. Despite vast differences in scale, decisions not to prosecute implicate foundational questions about the relationship between norms and exceptions, and the limits of the law.

We say this despite what may seem like another obvious difference between decisions not to prosecute and other legal exceptions. In the former case (one might argue) no exception to a legal rule is actually being decided, because it has not yet been determined (e.g., as it would by a trial) whether or not a legal norm actually applies. However, the key issue is not whether some other official or institution would subsequently determine whether the norm applies in a particular case – that is, whether the person being excepted from prosecution would ultimately be found innocent or guilty. Courts do not consider the strength or weakness of the prosecutor's potential case in upholding his or her exercise of discretion. Furthermore, because the prosecutor is under no obligation to even provide a reason for his decision not to prosecute, it makes no difference to judges whether the decision is made for reasons of evidence or equity or for no reason at all.

And yet decisions not to prosecute are notable for how routine, even banal, they are. It is hard to overstate the frequency, consistency, and familiarity with which such decisions occur. Indeed, there must be thousands, if not tens of thousands, of such decisions each year – truly decisions on the exception that have become a norm. This stands in sharp contrast to the descriptions of the state of exception by Schmitt and Agamben. From the very opening pages of *Political Theology*, sovereign decisions on the exception are almost by definition atypical. "The definition of sovereignty," Schmitt (1985: 5) says, must "be associated with a borderline case and not with routine." Later Schmitt's dismissal of all things routine is even more pronounced: "A jurisprudence concerned with ordering day-to-day questions," he says, "has practically no interest in the concept of sovereignty" (12). In *Homo Sacer*, the normalcy of the exception is discussed in relation to the internment camp, which, for Agamben (1998: 43), is the "biopolitical paradigm of the modern." In *State of Exception*, the focus is both more local and modern: Guantánamo. Indeed, from Agamben's perspective, the state of exception appears as a threshold of indeterminacy between democracy and absolutism. The more exceptional we become, the more we slide away from democracy and toward authoritarian modes of governance.

This formulation is, by our lights, overly schematic. Here we follow Connolly (2006: 143) in noting that "the very formalism" of Agamben's analysis damages his attempt to negotiate the paradox of sovereignty. This formalism extends to the consequences of emergency decisions. Do all decisions on the exception really lead inevitably to the concentration camp? We suggest that the decision not to prosecute is one of many examples in which this is not the case, involving an exercise of a fragment of sovereignty.

While we acknowledge that the decision not to prosecute does not fit precisely into the framework of sovereignty that Agamben and Schmitt discuss, it is more at home there than it is when thought of as nothing more than discretion within an administrative bureaucracy. Their philosophical work highlights that prosecutorial power involves something more than a perquisite designed to do no more than shore up the rule of law and something less than the rare and sweeping grandeur of emergency powers – a sovereignty that can suspend the entire legal order when the situation beckons. The power is legally approved but unchecked, legally exceptional and yet almost totally commonplace. It has the flavor of two worlds but resides completely in neither.

CONCLUSION

By bringing political philosophy to bear on the seemingly mundane features of legal practice, we open new ways of seeing those practices and provide more complete accounts of what legal actors do, even when those actors would not see or describe their work in philosophical terms. Political philosophy helps give meaning to everyday legal action and to make sense of that action in ways that connect it to broad and significant questions about the nature and limits of law itself. Thus, it has an important role to play in legal scholarship even when it has not "been established in the habits and attitudes of any person," even when it does not "affect or deflect the current of... [the] times" (Llewellyn 1934: 206).

Political philosophy helps us understand ways that sovereignty troubles the rule of law by being at once prior to it and yet a product of it. Fragments of sovereignty in a constitutional democracy, like the power of prosecutors, exist in a legal borderland, where ideas of principled predictability and meaningful constraints on officials meet their limits. This suggests that the boundaries of legality are less stable and secure, less clear, certain, and chartable, than we are willing to admit in our everyday practices.

Redescribing prosecutorial power through the lens of philosophical accounts of sovereignty shows that the rule of law is replete with gaps, fissures, and failures, places where law runs up against sovereign prerogative. Doing so reminds us that in many places (e.g., jury decisions not to impose the death penalty, gubernatorial clemency decisions) law runs out, law gives way, law authorizes the exercise of a power that it cannot regulate. Political philosophy thus may contribute greatly in helping us live in a more enlightened and critical relationship to law. While Llewellyn was right to examine the way philosophy becomes law, the agenda of philosophy and its relevance to legal thinking was, and remains, much broader than the role he described in his essay.

WORKS CITED

Agamben, Giorgio. *Homo Sacer: Sovereign Power and Bare Life.* Stanford, CA: Stanford Univ. Press, 1998.

———. *State of Exception.* Chicago: Univ. of Chicago Press, 2005.

Blackstone, William. *Commentaries on the Laws of England.* New York: Harper, 1850.

Connolly, William. "The Ethos of Sovereignty." In *Law and the Sacred.* Eds. Austin Sarat, Lawrence Douglas, and Martha Umphrey. Palo Alto, CA: Stanford Univ. Press, 2006.

Davis, Angela J. "The American Prosecutor: Independence, Power, and the Threat of Tyranny." *Iowa L. Rev.* 86.2 (2001): 393–465.

Davis v. United States, 512 U.S. 452 (1994).

Ely, Amie N. "Prosecutorial Discretion as an Ethical Necessity: The Ashcroft Memorandum's Curtailment of the Prosecutor's Duty to 'Seek Justice.'" *Cornell L. Rev.* 90.1 (2004): 237–78.

Jackson, Robert H. "The Federal Prosecutor." *J. Am. Judicature Soc'y* 24 (June, 1940): 18–20.

Kadish, Mortimer, and Sanford Kadish. *Discretion to Disobey.* Palo Alto, CA: Stanford Univ. Press, 1973.

Llewellyn, Karl. "On Philosophy in American Law," *U. Pa. L. Rev.* 82.3 (1934): 205–12.

Locke, John. *The Second Treatise on Civil Government.* Amherst, NY: Prometheus Books, 1986.

Loewenstein, Andrew B. "Judicial Review and the Limits of Prosecutorial Discretion." *Am. Crim. L. Rev.* 38.2 (2001): 351–72.

Montesquieu, Baron de. *The Spirit of the Laws.* New York: Hafner Publishing, 1949.

Sarat, Austin, and Nasser Hussain. "On Lawful Lawlessness: George Ryan and the Rhetoric of Sparing Life." *Stan. L. Rev.* 56.5 (2004): 1307–44.

Schmitt, Carl. *Political Theology.* Chicago: Univ. of Chicago Press, 1985.

Vorenberg, James "Decent Restraint of Prosecutorial Power." *Harv. L. Rev.* 94.7 (1981): 1521–73.

14 On (Moral) Philosophy and American Legal Scholarship

MATTHEW D. ADLER

Why isn't contemporary moral philosophy more influential in contemporary U.S. legal scholarship? I am a legal scholar who tries to stay current with the academic literature on moral philosophy and to bring its insights to bear on legal issues. I have, for some time, been puzzled by the paucity of fellow travelers. A thought piece for a book on philosophy and American law seems to be an appropriate forum for me to ventilate a bit on the question. My focus here will be U.S. legal scholarship (and I'll henceforth generally drop the adjective *U.S.*, which will be assumed in what follows).

I take it that many legal scholars have a general familiarity with moral philosophy, not just classical work (Bentham, Hobbes, Locke) but also famous modern work. They have read, or at least have heard of, the work of Robert Nozick, Derek Parfit, and John Rawls, and they aren't surprised by terms like *consequentialism*, *veil of ignorance*, *difference principle*, or *side-constraint*. But why aren't there more legal scholars who make it a point to remain well-versed in current developments in moral philosophy? Academic moral philosophers, housed in university philosophy departments, continue to work in the philosophical traditions to which Nozick, Parfit, and Rawls so notably contributed. Why do so few legal scholars try to stay abreast of that work?

The reader might question the question's premise. "How do you know, Adler, that there aren't many legal academics who read the current issues of *Ethics*, *Philosophy and Public Affairs*, and similar journals and draw upon this literature in their own work?" Well, I don't know for sure. But I read a lot of law review articles (in large part because of years of forced service on appointments committees!) and my firm sense is that major figures in contemporary moral philosophy, such as Larry Temkin, Thomas Hurka, Frances Kamm, or T. M. Scanlon (an illustrative rather than exhaustive list) and major recent issues, such as the debate about prioritarian conceptions of equality, rarely surface in contemporary legal scholarship.

But maybe my memory is bad, or I read too quickly, so I did a little checking.[1] A search in Westlaw's journals and law reviews database yields thirty-one hits for the search term *prioritarian* or *prioritarianism*; forty for Larry Temkin; thirty-nine for

[1] All the search numbers that follow are from a search I performed on November 30, 2007.

Thanks to Brian Bix and Dennis Patterson for comments.

Thomas Hurka; eighty-nine for Frances Kamm; and one hundred for T. M. Scanlon together with *What We Owe to Each Other* (Scanlon's book on contractarianism).[2] By comparison, John Rawls gets 5,387 hits, a huge number, which is in the range of the most-cited legal scholars.[3]

So if it is true that relatively few legal academics try to stay abreast of academic work in moral philosophy, and (a fortiori) that even fewer self-define as law-and-moral-philosophy scholars, why is that? The answer can't be that legal scholars have no appetite for cutting-edge work in other disciplines. It's easy to think of counterexamples. Behavioral law and economics, also known as law and psychology, is now booming. This body of legal scholarship is well versed in the research of Amos Tversky and Daniel Kahneman and their successors about prospect theory and heuristics and biases. (Amos Tversky gets 1,330 hits in the Westlaw search, and Daniel Kahneman 1,745). Many of the papers presented at the large American Law and Economics Association conference every year are steeped in one or another subfield of contemporary economics. An increasing number of these involve sophisticated econometrics – a central focus of the new conference on empirical legal studies. Positive political theory (PPT) is an increasingly popular methodology in public law scholarship: PPT scholars use the tools of game theory and spatial models, developed by economists and political scientists, to think about the functioning of courts, agencies, Congress, and the president. Law and history is hot these days, particularly in constitutional law, one of my areas of interest. There are now a substantial number of scholars at law schools doing original work in legal history, and many more (I would guess) who are pretty well read in the field. Law and sociology also seem to be flourishing – witness the size of the annual Law and Society conference.

In short, these are boom days for interdisciplinary legal scholarship – with some exceptions. The field of law and moral philosophy is not the only exception – that law and literature is another – but it is an exception, and it is the one that puzzles me.

It might be objected that, as a nonpractitioner of the booming "law-and" methodologies described two paragraphs previously, I am overly impressed by their claims to sophistication. Perhaps the legal scholars who style themselves behavioral law and economists don't really know much about what's going on *right now* in cognitive psychology. Perhaps the legal econometricians are using outdated tools. It is surely true that interdisciplinary work by legal scholars has generally lagged relative to the fields that the scholars are trying to bring to bear. A new idea, result, finding, or method enters history, psychology, sociology, economics, econometrics, or political science; *x* years later, with *x* greater than 0, it enters legal scholarship. But my claim was not that many more legal scholars are fully up to

[2] I put this in the search term for Scanlon so as to screen out law review articles in which Scanlon is cited for his earlier, noncontractarian work, such as his well-known 1972 article on freedom of expression.

[3] I searched on the names of the ten most-cited legal scholars on a list compiled by Brian Leiter, posted at http://www.leiterrankings.com/faculty/2002faculty_impact_cites.shtml. Cass Sunstein receives more than 10,000 hits; Laurence Tribe, 9,149; Richard Epstein, 7,497; Ronald Dworkin, 7,127; Mark Tushnet, 6,910; Bruce Ackerman, 5,379; Bill Eskridge, 5,320; Daniel Farber, 5,166; John Ely, 5,111; and Akhil Amar, 4,644.

date in fields such as history, psychology, economics, and sociology than in moral philosophy. The claim, rather, is that there are many more legal scholars who try to stay up to date in these disciplines than try to stay up to date in moral philosophy.

So – to sharpen the puzzle – what's curious is the comparatively low degree of interest among legal scholars in academic work in moral philosophy compared to the interest in a number of other academic fields in the arts and sciences.

A partial explanation, perhaps, is the towering-figure effect. Perhaps another discipline generates excitement and interest among legal academics only when a truly major, paradigm-shifting figure emerges in that discipline: a Tversky/Kahneman. But the towering-figure claim, thus stated, is untrue. It is not a necessary condition for a substantial number of legal scholars to be interested in another academic field, with potential relevance to law, that a towering figure has recently reshaped the field. As far as I'm aware, there's no figure in economics, history, political science, or sociology, within the past generation or even the past two generations, who has had anything like the influence within those fields that Tversky and Kahneman have had in psychology. It may be true that the emergence of a towering figure in another academic field, of potential relevance to law, is a sufficient condition for substantial attention to that field by legal scholars. That is to say, the psychological regularity *R* that predicts legal-scholarly interest in another academic field has a disjunctive form: the emergence of a towering figure or condition c2 or condition c3 or condition c4 and so on. Regularity *R* is consistent both with Rawls's large influence in legal scholarship (Rawls is a towering figure if there ever was) and with the current vibrancy of law and economics, law and history, law and political science, and law and sociology. But, because regularity *R* has the disjunctive form – with c2, c3, c4, and so on, mere placeholders for whatever explains the vibrancy of these fields but would not predict vibrancy in law and moral philosophy – the puzzle remains.

The puzzle, as I further implicitly sharpened it in the preceding paragraph, is the fact that contemporary legal scholars are particularly engaged by certain academic literatures and not by academic moral philosophy, even though academic moral philosophy – like these other literatures – has potential relevance to law. But it might be suggested here that straight or first-order moral philosophy doesn't really have that much relevance to law.[4] Legal scholars haven't mined this literature for the same reason they haven't mined academic work in physics or chemistry.

The most sophisticated variant of this suggestion runs as follows: Much legal scholarship is normative. Many legal scholars are interested in determining what judges or legislators ought to do. And scholarship in moral philosophy is also normative. Moral philosophers are interested in defending, criticizing, or elaborating

[4] By *first-order*, I mean to draw the fairly standard distinction between the second-order enterprises of metaethics (which is about whether moral facts exist and, if so, what the nature of such facts is) and moral epistemology and the (first-order) enterprise of (1) defending or criticizing some claim about what morally ought to be done, or (2) explaining the relationships between different claims about what morally ought to be done, for example, showing that rule consequentialism collapses to act consequentialism, without outright defending or criticizing some such claim. Obviously, the distinction between first-order and second-order has lots of fuzziness. I make the distinction here because I find the absence of legal-scholarly attention to metaethics and moral epistemology less puzzling than the absence of attention to first-order work.

different views about what ought to be done, such as utilitarianism, nonutilitarian consequentialism, contractarianism, and so forth. But these are different kinds of oughts. Legal scholars are interested in legal normativity. They are interested in what judges, legislators, and other legal actors have legal reason to do. Moral philosophers, by contrast, are interested in moral normativity. They are interested in what actors generally have moral reason to do. Legal and moral normativity are distinct. Someone can have legal reason to perform an action that he or she lacks moral reason to perform, and vice versa.

And the suggestion continues: There is a body of legal scholarship that is both interested in normativity and philosophically sophisticated. This is jurisprudence, a well-defined field of legal scholarship since H. L. A. Hart and Ronald Dworkin, with continuing work (in the United States) by figures such as Larry Alexander, Brian Bix, Jules Coleman, Mark Greenberg, Heidi Hurd, Brian Leiter, Stephen Perry, Fred Schauer, Scott Shapiro, Jeremy Waldron, and others. This work focuses on explicating the concept of law and on clarifying the relationship between law and morality – for example, discussing whether law has moral authority, or whether law can incorporate moral norms (the issue at dispute between exclusive and inclusive positivists). And it does draw on contemporary philosophy where relevant – for example, building on the work of the philosopher Michael Bratman about the nature of collective intentions, or on recent developments in the philosophy of language. But this work is fundamentally about legal normativity, and it talks about moral normativity only where it bears on legal normativity. To expect legal scholars to regularly draw from straight, first-order, moral philosophy is naive – just as it would be naive to expect legal scholars to regularly draw from the philosophy of aesthetics, on the silly grounds that because legal scholars are interested in the good and the right, and aesthetic philosophers also are, they should have loads to say to one another. Aesthetics is about what's artistically good and right, and legal scholarship about what's legally good and right.

But I don't think the suggestion works. Rawls, at least in *A Theory of Justice*, was engaged in first-order moral philosophy – first-order philosophy about an aspect of morality, namely, justice – as much as any contemporary moral philosopher explicating, defending, or criticizing consequentialism, contractarianism, virtue ethics, or deontology. Further, what is morally good or right is of general interest to legal actors – much more so than, for example, what is artistically good or right. What does "of interest" mean? Well, let's say that many legal actors are partly motivated, or at least claim to be partly motivated, by moral considerations, not just legal considerations. This includes not merely civil disobedients – who are motivated to act morally, in the teeth of legal reasons – but legal actors who believe, often quite plausibly, that they have legal discretion. For example, the legislator considering the enactment of a statute presumably quite often believes that there are multiple courses of action available to him or her, all of which are legally permissible under applicable law (the U.S. Constitution in the case of members of Congress and state constitutions for state legislators). In this case, the legislator chooses among the different possible options (or claims to thus choose) with reference to the public interest – which is just a less fancy term for moral reasons, or at least a subset of moral reasons (consequentialist ones). Some of the options the legislator may well claim to be impermissible as a matter of rights (not just legal rights, but moral rights, such as the moral rights of privacy, free expression, or property ownership). A similar story could be sketched for regulators and, to some extent, judges.

In short, morality actually figures into – or at least is actually claimed to figure into – the motivational set of many legal actors. It may be possible to have a legal system in which actors rarely make reference to moral considerations, but that system is not ours. Relatedly, there is in fact plenty of legal scholarship that argues that some actor ought to do something, where the *ought* is best understood as a moral ought and not (or at least not just) a legal ought. Consider the vast corpus of law and economics scholarship claiming that legislators or regulators ought to enact some statute or regulation, or that judges ought to issue some doctrine, because it is Pareto efficient. Surely law and economics scholars are not laboring under the illusion that judges and legislators have a general, background legal obligation to undertake Pareto-efficient courses of action. Rather, the moral goodness or rightness of a Pareto-efficient choice is taken by economists as wholly uncontroversial, and Pareto efficiency is used as a moral criterion by which to morally evaluate candidate statutes, regulations, and doctrines.

Perhaps the paucity of legal-scholarly attention to current moral philosophy is explained not by the irrelevance of moral philosophy generally to law but by the fact that contemporary moral philosophy is in the doldrums. ALEA has lots of papers drawing on contemporary economics because economics is thriving. Ditto for history, cognitive psychology, and so on. But contemporary moral philosophy has not made much progress in the past decade or two. Contractarianism has not advanced much beyond Rawls. Deontology has not advanced much beyond Nozick. Consequentialism has not advanced much beyond Parfit.

There may well be a perception among legal scholars that academic moral philosophy hasn't made much progress since the 1970s and 1980s. But the perception, I suggest, is inaccurate. Academic moral philosophers continue to generate important new insights and results, and the perception that they haven't (if there is one) is just part and parcel of the inattention to this literature that needs explaining.

What important insights and results am I thinking of? I am thinking, above all, of the contemporary philosophical scholarship about equality: not just the seminal work in the 1980s by Dworkin on equality and responsibility, and the seminal work by Sen on "equality of what," but more recent work, within the past two decades. Much of this work centers on the distinction between egalitarianism and prioritarianism, introduced into moral philosophy by Parfit and Temkin in the early 1990s. Is equality a matter of comparing how individuals fare, relative to one another, or rather of giving extra moral weight to increases in the well-being or resources of individuals who are badly off in absolute terms? This is, I believe, an absolutely fundamental question, about the nature of equality, which moral philosophers are now rigorously and illuminatingly discussing. A related body of work centers on the Pareto principle: can actors have prima facie or all-things-considered moral reason to make everyone worse off? A yet more recent offshoot of the prioritarianism and egalitarianism literature distinguishes between prioritarianism and sufficientism. At the same time, the literature continues to work through the vital issues of integrating equality and responsibility and deciding what the currency for equality is (e.g., resources, capabilities, midfare, well-being).

Three observations intensify the puzzle. One is that this literature is about equality, a topic of long-standing interest to legal scholars, not just in the areas of constitutional law and antidiscrimination law but in other areas of legal scholarship too (e.g., tax policy, environmental law, family law, health law). A second is that it addresses the Pareto principle, of even more general legal-scholarly interest. A third is that there is much interaction between this literature and recent work in social choice theory. The social-choice writing about equality tends to be published in journals like *Social Choice and Welfare* rather than *Ethics*, to be more mathematically formal, and to be written by scholars who are housed in economics rather than philosophy departments. But the very same range of subjects is addressed; the social-choice theorists writing about equality are often well versed in, and draw upon, the philosophical scholarship, and vice versa.[5]

The social-choice literature "looks" like some of the other fields of economics that are influential in law (at least in using formal mathematical language, and in often equating individual well-being with preference satisfaction and using utility theory to analyze preferences). And the literature is normative: it is interested in making formal deductions about appropriate policy choice or about the measurement of policy impacts from normative axioms. Yet my sense is that this literature – both the equality subfield and other subfields – has had little impact on legal scholars. Marc Fleurbaey, an important figure in contemporary social choice theory, who is the paradigm of a scholar who is interested in equality and working at the intersection of social choice and moral philosophy, receives only ten (!) hits in Westlaw.

Perhaps the answer (or a partial answer) is that the recent, illuminating work in moral philosophy (as well as the whole field of social choice) will hold little interest for nonconsequentialists. There is a tradition, in the United States, of philosophically sophisticated work by legal scholars that draws on moral philosophy. I am thinking, in particular, of scholarship about the content of private law and criminal law. Michael Moore's scholarship in criminal law would be exemplary. But this work overwhelmingly tends to take a nonconsequentialist perspective. Unless the contemporary philosophical literature has made substantial progress in deontology, contractarianism, or some other variant of nonconsequentialism, why be surprised that legal scholars aren't reading it?

But I think contemporary moral philosophy does continue to advance our understanding of nonconsequentialism. Think, for example, of Hurka's work on virtue ethics, Kamm's work on deontology, or Scanlon's work on contractarianism, and the responses by other philosophers to this work. (There was a reason, earlier, why I mentioned Hurka, Kamm, and Scanlon along with Temkin.) And even if it were true that academic moral philosophy is currently in the doldrums

[5] For a good sense of the two literatures, and the interaction between them, see the articles and papers posted on the Equality Exchange Web site, at http://mora.rente.nhh.no/projects/EqualityExchange/.

with respect to the explication of nonconsequentialist rather than consequentialist moral views, that would at best partly explain the absence of legal-scholarly attention to contemporary moral philosophy (namely, by explaining the inattention by legal scholars who reject consequentialism). To complete the explanation, we'd need to say that there aren't many legal scholars who both are sympathetic to consequentialism and have a taste for philosophy. But this is hardly an explanation (given that there are straight philosophers who have both characteristics)!

Anyway, the whole premise of this discussion, namely, that the vibrant recent philosophical and social-choice literature on equality is consequentialist, is wrong. Certainly many in the literature are not welfarists: the whole point of the equality-of-what debate, about whether equality's currency is well-being, capabilities, resources, and so on, is to debate (not take for granted) the significance of welfare facts to morality. Nor is it necessarily consequentialist in the sense of taking the good to be prior to the right, or taking moral requirements to be derivative from an agent-neutral ranking of outcomes. Some of the contributors are consequentialists; others are not.

So we are left with a puzzle. Many, probably most, legal scholars have normative interests. By virtue of these interests, many legal scholars have read and cited – and not just that but, I believe, genuinely engaged – the work of some twentieth-century moral philosophers, above all John Rawls. Many legal scholars have interdisciplinary tastes. Many legal scholars with interdisciplinary tastes are well versed in other literatures, on an ongoing basis. Few legal scholars are well versed in academic moral philosophy, on an ongoing basis. Academic moral philosophy is doing fine, and it is flourishing with respect to topics at the core of normative legal scholarship: equality and Paretianism.

I don't have a solution to the puzzle. I do think – and this should be clear – that the U.S. legal academy's neglect of contemporary moral philosophy is a real pity.

* * *

Finally, let me respond to an important comment raised by a reader of the first draft of this chapter. The reader notes that I focus exclusively on Anglo-American philosophy and that I don't mention Rorty or Habermas, who are cited often in the law reviews.

Indeed, I did focus on Anglo-American moral philosophy, which is my area of expertise. (*Anglo-American* is a crude shorthand, given the important work of contemporary European academic philosophers and economists in this tradition, such as Serge-Christophe Kolm, Marc Fleurbaey, Philippe van Parijs, Wlodek Rabinowicz, or Bertil Tungodden; but I'll acquiesce in the term here.) And, indeed, Rorty is cited 1,246 times in a Westlaw search, and Habermas 2,548 times.[6] But, notwithstanding the high citation rate of world-famous philosophical figures like Rorty and Habermas (as a crude shorthand, let's call them continental philosophers) and Rawls (working within Anglo-American philosophy), the puzzle remains that there are major figures in current academic moral philosophy (I used Temkin, Hurka, Kamm, and Scanlon as paradigms) who are barely cited.

[6] Search performed on June 2, 2008.

Are the counterparts of Temkin, Hurka, Kamm, and Scanlon within Continental philosophy – important academic figures, but less visible than a Rorty or Habermas – influential and cited by legal scholars? Given time constraints, and my lack of expertise in contemporary continental philosophy, I haven't attempted to investigate this question. Even if the answer to this question is yes, the puzzle I raise here remains. Despite the active state, and relevance for legal scholarship, of a large and important branch of contemporary academic philosophy, namely, Anglo-American moral philosophy, the legal academy generally ignores it.

15 The Aretaic Turn in American Philosophy of Law

LAWRENCE B. SOLUM

American philosophy of law has begun to make what has been called the aretaic turn. What is the aretaic turn in normative legal theory? This question has both a positive and a negative answer. Begin with the negative – the aretaic turn is a turn away from the domination of normative legal theory by consequentialist and deontological paradigms, including normative law and economics and Dworkin's theory of law as integrity. In other words, the aretaic turn rejects the dominant traditions in contemporary theorizing about the ends of law.

A more illuminating description of the aretaic turn can begin with a definition. The word to express virtue or excellence in classical Greek was *arête*, from which we derive the English word *aretaic*, of, or pertaining to, excellence or virtue. Thus, the aretaic turn is a turn toward a virtue-centered theory of law, to which we can give the name *virtue jurisprudence*. Virtue jurisprudence offers a rich and fruitful account of the nature, means, and ends of law that simultaneously dissolves old problems and poses a new set of challenges for legal theorists. A good place to start our investigation of the aretaic turn in the philosophy of law is with a statement of problems it attempts to address.

TWO ANTINOMIES: RIGHTS VERSUS CONSEQUENCES AND FORMALISM VERSUS REALISM

Contemporary legal theory is characterized by two antinomies: the antinomy of rights and consequences and the antinomy of realism and formalism. Each antinomy captures a persistent controversy in contemporary legal theory that has proved resistant to resolution (or even clarification) through the practice of reasoned argument.

The antinomy of rights and consequences is the legal form of the modern philosophical debate between consequentialists and deontologists. In the legal academy, the flag of consequentialism is borne by the normative law and economics movement. An especially prominent and trenchant example is found in *Fairness versus Welfare*, a monumental law review article and later book by Louis Kaplow and Steven Shavell (2002) of Harvard Law School, but normative law and economics has a long and distinguished pedigree, prominently including work by Ronald Coase, Robert Cooter, Frank Easterbrook, Richard Posner, and many others.

If the flag of consequentialism is borne by normative law and economics, then surely the most prominent standard-bearer for a rights-based approach to normative legal theory is Ronald Dworkin. Dworkin's theory, law as integrity, emphasizes the idea that the parties have preexisting rights that oblige judges to decide cases on the basis of principle rather than policy. Of course, Dworkin is only one of many who carry the flag for deontology in the legal academy. Deontological approaches are associated with such prominent legal theorists as Randy Barnett, Jules Coleman, James Fleming, Michael Moore, and countless others.

When I describe the lay of the jurisprudential landscape as an antinomy of rights and consequences, I mean to make a bold assertion about the state of debate between the partisans of consequence and the advocates of rights. This debate does not seem to be progressing toward a conclusion; instead, we seem to be in a state of perpetual conflict (at best) or mutual disengagement (at worst).

Let me explain. On the one hand, there is considerable evidence for the proposition that normative legal theory is fragmenting. Normative law and economics have sufficient momentum so that it is institutionally feasible to proceed as if there were no deontological critique of the moral foundations of welfarism. Likewise, deontologists can debate among themselves, with, for example, egalitarians and libertarians arguing for the own preferred version of rights-based normative legal theory. Genuine dialogue is rare. Genuine progress is even rarer. Kaplow and Shavell's *Fairness versus Welfare* certainly reignited the debate between the partisans of consequence and the advocates of rights, but I do not think it can fairly be said that much progress was made. Kaplow and Shavell's critics declared victory, but the normative law and economics movement proceeded as if nothing had happened.

If the antinomy of rights and consequences is characterized by perpetual warfare or mutual disengagement between two more or less equally matched forces, the antinomy of realism and formalism is reflected in a more fractured and less crystalline pattern of legal discourse. We can remind ourselves of the dialectic with a sweeping historical survey: the original legal realist movement of the 1920s and 1930s gave way to the law and process synthesis of the 1950s and 1960s, which in turn was challenged by the indeterminacy thesis advanced by critical legal studies (CLS) in the 1980s. And CLS gave way to a blistering critique of implausible claims about radical indeterminacy in the 1990s, only to see realist cynicism reach a new zenith in the wake of the U.S. Supreme Court's decision in *Bush v. Gore.*

Contemporary legal theory is of two minds about realism and formalism. The practitioners of legal theory have incorporated the standard realist moves into the conceptual toolbox. Who hasn't written an article or taught a class in which one shows that a formal legal distinction masks decision making that is really driven by other considerations – ideology, morality, politics, policy, economics, or something else? We are all realists. But legal formalism is surprisingly resilient to attempts to declare its demise. Once formalism is rescued from the realist caricature of a self-contained system of pure deduction, it is hard to deny that (1) there are easy cases, and (2) while the law may underdetermine judicial decision making, it is rarely (or never) radically indeterminate. And neoformalism, in various forms, is on the rise. Originalism, textualism, and plain meaning – these are the watchwords of the neoformalists, a group that makes up in prominence and attention what it may lack in numerosity.

In summary, contemporary legal theory can be characterized as at an impasse or stuck in a rut. The two antinomies correspond to the sticking points, the theoretical junctures beyond which contemporary legal theory seems unable to move.

THE ARETAIC TURN IN LEGAL THEORY

There is a striking parallel between the state of contemporary legal theory after the turn of the millennium and the situation of modern moral philosophy in 1958, when Elizabeth Anscombe wrote her famous essay *Modern Moral Philosophy*. Modern moral philosophy, Anscombe argued, has involved a competition between two great families of moral theories, consequentialism and deontology. Both views face severe difficulties and each provides a powerful critique of the other. Consequentialism has the advantage of providing a method that, in principle, is capable of resolving moral disputes, but it purchases its discriminatory power by leaving no room for inviolable human rights and independent consideration of fairness. Deontology has the disadvantage of an uncertain method, and at least sometimes seems to exclude consideration of consequences that seem either relevant to or dispositive of the choice that must be made. How are we to overcome this aporia? Anscombe (1958: 40) famously suggested that after consequentialism and deontology had been exhausted, moral philosophy "might remain to look for 'norms' in human virtues." This suggestion was one important impetus for the aretaic turn in moral philosophy.

And what of the state of contemporary legal theory? Most readers will recognize the eerie parallels between twenty-first-century legal scholarship and Anscombe's sketch of the predicament of modern moral philosophy. The two antinomies of contemporary legal theory capture persistent controversies that have proved resistant to resolution (or even clarification) through the practice of reasoned argument. In the less theoretical corners of the legal academy, many believe that legal scholars choose their position with respect to these antinomies on the basis of an existential leap as opposed to reasoned argument. Even in the pages of learned journals and in the introduction to learned monographs, readers may limn the contours of a struggle where rhetorical flourish and name-calling take the place of careful scholarly analysis.

Anscombe's suggestion was one of many factors leading to renewed interest in Aristotle's moral philosophy and the development of contemporary virtue ethics. Important early work was done by Philippa Foot, Peter Geach, and others. More recently, major contributions have been made by Julia Annas, Rosalind Hursthouse, Nancy Sherman, Michael Slote, Christine Swanton, and many, many others. Aristotle viewed his ethical theory as continuous in an important way with his biology. Just as a biologist might ask about the characteristics of a well-functioning antelope or lion, so Aristotle's ethics can be seen as asking the question, What are the characteristics of a well-functioning human? And his politics extends this question to, What are the characteristics of a well-functioning community of humans? Aristotle's naturalism poses many questions for our assessment of his theory, but one of those questions is this: because we now reject much of what Aristotle had to say about human biology and psychology, doesn't this undermine his account of the virtues? I am not going to answer that question, because contemporary virtue ethics provides a way for the project of virtue jurisprudence to avoid it. In a sense, the point of contemporary virtue ethics is to ground our understanding of the virtues in contemporary biology and psychology. One important agenda of contemporary virtue ethics is to develop an account of the virtues that is consistent with modern science. And this grounding may entail some important divergence between contemporary theories and Aristotle's account.

Just as moral philosophy has made the aretaic turn, so, too, contemporary legal theory has begun to turn to virtue jurisprudence, the name we can give to an aretaic or virtue-centered theory of law. For virtue jurisprudence, the final end of law is not to maximize preference satisfaction or to protect some set of rights and privileges: the final end of law is to promote human flourishing – to enable humans to lead excellent lives. The central thesis of virtue jurisprudence can be summarized as follows: the fundamental concepts of legal philosophy should not be welfare, efficiency, autonomy, or equality; the fundamental notions of legal theory should be virtue and excellence.

THE JUDICIAL VIRTUES

General virtue jurisprudence would include at least the following: (1) an aretaic theory of legislation, in other words, a virtue-centered account of the ends of law, (2) an aretaic theory of the role of law in the virtue of justice, and (3) an aretaic theory of adjudication; that is, a virtue-centered account of the proper resolution of legal disputes. Special virtue jurisprudence would offer virtue-centered theories of particular areas of law such as torts (found in recent work by Heidi Li Feldman) or criminal law (found in the work of Kyron Huigens and the critique offered by Antony Duff). On this occasion, we can use a virtue-centered theory of judging as illustrative of the content of virtue jurisprudence. An aretaic theory of adjudication begins with the judicial virtues – the qualities of mind and will that are constitutive of excellent judging.

There is disagreement about the qualities that make for good judging, but before we discuss the controversial judicial virtues, we can quickly survey those judicial virtues and vices on which there is likely to be widespread agreement. One judicial vice on which there is likely to be near-universal agreement is corruption; incorruptibility is surely a judicial virtue. Cowardly judges will be disposed to render decisions based on fear of physical danger or social pressure; we can agree that courage is a judicial virtue. Judges are likely to find themselves in situations where a hot temper could produce intemperate actions. In the face of provocation, a judge with an anger-management problem may fly off the handle and misapply the law. Aristotle identified *proates* or "good temper" as the corrective virtue for the vice of bad temper.

Can anyone doubt that stupidity is a judicial vice? Judging is the kind of task that sometimes requires extraordinary intelligence. Both law and facts can be complex. Only a judge with intelligence will be able to sort out the complexities of the rule against perpetuities or penetrate the mysteries of a complex statute. But more than intelligence is required. A truly excellent judge must also be learned in the law, because one cannot start from scratch in each and every case and because there is at least some truth to the notion that the law is a seamless web. To put these same points the other way round: stupid and ignorant judges will be error prone, likely to misunderstand and misstate the law, and unlikely to make findings of fact that are correct.

One advantage of a theory of judicial excellence is that it reveals a large zone of agreement. For all practical purposes, we can agree that judges should be incorruptible, courageous, good tempered, and smart. But these (mostly uncontested) virtues do not tell the whole story about judicial excellence. Even if we agree in our judgments about who the very worst judges are – the corrupt, ill-tempered, cowardly, lazy, incompetent, and stupid ones – there are strong and persistent disagreements about who the best judges are. The partisans of Lord Coke may deride the accomplishments of Lord Mansfield; the admirers of Justice Breyer may be among the critics of Justice Scalia.

Disagreements about judicial excellence are typically rooted in two interrelated disagreements about the nature of judicial virtue. The first disagreement is about the nature of the virtue of justice. The second disagreement concerns the role of equity and practical wisdom. On the one hand, some disagreements about judicial excellence turn out to be disagreements about and within conceptions of the virtue of justice – qualities that some call justice, others see as unjust. On the other hand, other controversies hang on differences in the understanding of the role of practical wisdom in judging: some believe that wise judges will range far from the rules in the name of equity, while others believe that equity should be tightly constrained by the rule of law.

THE VIRTUE OF JUSTICE

An excellent judge is just; a judge who lacks the virtue of justice has a serious defect. At this level of abstraction, the virtue of justice is likely to be the object of widespread agreement. But what does the virtue of justice require? In this section, I will examine two different conceptions of the virtue of justice: justice as lawfulness and justice as fairness.

The fairness conception of the virtue of justice begins with the premise that the just and the lawful are (or should be) separate and distinct. Therefore, humans with the virtue of justice will act fairly even when the lawful result would be otherwise. This does not mean that a judge with the virtue of justice as fairness would disregard the law entirely. The existence of legal norms will frequently give rise to considerations of fairness that will transform the moral landscape, creating salient reasons of fairness that motivate a judge who is fair to act in accord with the law.

Nonetheless, the fairness conception faces a formidable objection because of the role that private judgment plays for judges who are disposed to act on the basis of their own sense of fairness. This objection is based on a distinction between two questions about fairness – which I shall call first-order and second-order questions of fairness. A first-order question of fairness is simply the question, Which action is fair given the circumstances? A second-order question of fairness concerns whose judgment about first-order questions will be taken as authoritative.

The fairness conception implicitly requires judges to exercise private judgment about first-order questions of fairness. In exercising that judgment, the judge may conclude that expectations generated by reasonable reliance on the law provide reasons of fairness. Because each judge makes a private judgment about the all-things-considered fairness of following the law in each case, these judgments can (and we expect they will) differ with the political, moral, religious, and ideological views of the particular judge. As a result, the outcome of disputes will be systematically unpredictable – varying ex post with the assignment of judges with particular political views. This leads to the further consequence that the law would be unable to perform the function of coordinating behavior, creating stable expectations, and constraining arbitrary or self-interested actions by officials. How bad this would be is a matter of dispute. A Hobbesian answer to this question is "very bad indeed"; a Lockean answer is that reliance on private judgment leads to serious inconvenience.

If the fairness conception of the virtue of justice is unsatisfactory, is there an alternative? In the *Nicomachean Ethics*, Aristotle suggests an alternative understanding of justice as lawfulness, but to understand Aristotle's view, we need to take a look at the Greek word *nomos*, which is usually translated as "law." For the ancient Greeks, nomos had a broader meaning than does *law* in contemporary English – incorporating widely shared and deeply held social norms. A judge who has the virtue of justice as lawfulness internalizes the *nomoi*. Rather than rely on their own private, first-order judgments of fairness as the basis for the resolution of disputes, such judges rely on the law – understood as both the positive law and the widely shared and deeply held social norms of the community.

For this reason, there are good reasons to doubt that the fairness conception can offer a satisfying account of the virtue of justice. A view of justice must take into account the distinctions between first- and second-order judgments and between public and private judgments. Once these distinctions are introduced, the need for second-order agreement on a public standard of judgment becomes clear. The lawfulness conception of the virtue of justice answers to this need; the fairness conception does not.

THE VIRTUE OF PRACTICAL WISDOM

The virtue of justice may not be exhausted by the lawfulness conception. Even if we concede that in ordinary cases justice requires adherence to the law, the question remains whether there are extraordinary cases – cases in which excellent judges would depart from the law (or, to put it differently, decide that the law does not really apply). Even if first-order private judgment cannot do the work of filling in the content of a general conception of the virtue of justice, that does not necessarily imply that the judge's sense of fairness has no role to play. One reason we might doubt the adequacy of the lawfulness conception as the whole story about the virtue of justice flows from the fact that the positive law is cast in the form of abstract and general rules; such rules may lead to results that are unfair in those particular cases that do not fit the pattern contemplated by the formulation of the rule. If lawfulness were the whole story about the virtue of justice, then an excellent judge would apply the rule "come hell and high water" even if the rule led to consequences that were absurd or manifestly unjust. But this implication of the lawfulness conception seems odd and unsatisfactory.

Does the excellent judge apply the rules in a rigid and mechanical way? Or does a virtuous judge correct the rigidity of the lawfulness conception with equity? The classic discussion of these questions is provided by Aristotle in book 5, chapter 10, of the *Nicomachean Ethics*, in which he articulates his theory of *epieikeia*, which is usually translated as "equity" but can also be translated as "fair-mindedness." Judges with the virtue of equity do not apply the law in a rigid or mechanical fashion; they are fair minded and sensitive to the spirit or functional purposes of the law.

But as we have already seen, there is a problem with supplementing the lawfulness conception of the virtue of justice with the notion of equity. Once first-order private judgments about fairness are admitted to have the power to override the second-order judgment to rely on the public judgments embodied in the law, the question becomes one of how the role of private judgment can be constrained. Without constraint, private judgment threatens to swallow public judgment, and we are on a slippery slope that threatens to transform the lawfulness conception into the fairness conception.

The trick is to constrain equity while preserving its corrective role. To put the point metaphorically, we need an account of equity that enables us to navigate the slope while providing sufficient traction to avoid slipping or sliding. An Aristotelian account of the virtue of equity gives us three points of traction. The first point of traction is provided by the distinction between the equitable correction of law's generality and the substitution of private first-order judgments for the *nomoi*. Equity is not doing what the judge believes is fair when that conflicts with the law; rather, equity is doing what the spirit of the law requires, when the expression of the role fails to capture its point or purpose in a particular factual context. The second point of traction is provided by the virtue of justice itself. A judge who is *nomimos* simply isn't tempted to use equity to avoid the constraining force of the law. A *nomimos* has internalized the normative force of the law; such a judge wants to act in accord with the animating purposes of the system of social norms and positive law.

The third point of traction is provided by Aristotle's understanding of the intellectual virtue of practical wisdom or *phronesis* – think of the quality that we describe as good judgment or common sense. A judge with virtue of practical wisdom, a *phronimos*, has the ability to perceive the salient features of particular situations. In the context of judging, we can use Llewellyn's (1996: 59–61, 121–57, 206–8) phrase "situation sense," or by way of analogy to the phrase "moral vision," we can say that a sense of justice requires legal vision, the ability to size up a case and discern which aspects are legally important. The *phronimos* can do equity because he or she grasps the point of legal rules and discerns the legally and morally salient features of particular fact situations.

CONCLUSION

Virtue jurisprudence suggests that the standard for correct adjudication is the virtuous judge as defined by a full account of judicial excellence. Such an account would include the uncontested virtues of incorruptibility, sobriety, courage, good temper, and intelligence, as well as the contested and controversial virtues of justice and practical wisdom. Virtue jurisprudence provides a neo-Aristotelian account of the just and wise judge as *nomimos* (lawful) and *phronimos* (having legal vision).

Does the aretaic turn in American philosophy of law offer a resolution to the two antinomies of contemporary legal theory? With respect to the antinomy of rights and consequences, the strategy of virtue jurisprudence is precisely analogous to that which virtue ethics offers in moral philosophy. Virtue jurisprudence rejects both consequentialism and deontology as comprehensive conceptions of the good and the right, and replaces them with a virtue-centered account. But a focus on virtue does not entail the elimination of either rights or consequences. Rather, the strategy of virtue jurisprudence is similar to the strategy that legal pragmatists offer: a virtuous judge will give both consequences and rights their due with the organizing and reconciling work done by the virtues of justice and practical wisdom. With respect to the antinomy of realism and formalism, virtue jurisprudence recognizes the real tension between formal rules and realization of the functional purposes of the law. Once again, the key to reconciliation is found in an account of the judicial virtues of justice and practical wisdom. The *phronimos* can do equity without substituting private judgment for the public reasons of the law precisely because he or she is *nomimos* – someone who grasps and internalizes the functional purposes of the widely shared and deeply held norms of his or her community.

WORKS CITED

Anscombe, Elizabeth. "Modern Moral Philosophy." In *Virtue Ethics: Oxford Readings in Philosophy*. Eds. Roger Crisp & Michael Slote. Oxford: Oxford Univ. Press, 1997, 26–44.

Kaplow, Louis, and Stephen Shavell. *Fairness versus Welfare*. Cambridge, MA: Harvard Univ. Press, 2002.

Llewellyn, Karl. *The Common Law Tradition*. Buffalo, NY: William S. Hein, 1996.

16 On Continental Philosophy in American Jurisprudence

ADAM THURSCHWELL

What is it that Karl Llewellyn is asking for in "On Philosophy in American Law"? (He is clearly asking for something: he tells us that he has been "impatient" – his "wattles grow red" – waiting for a response.) Here is one way of reading the essay: it registers a complaint (that received jurisprudential accounts of American law provide an inconsistent hodgepodge of theories rather than a unifying panoramic synthesis), proffers an analysis and solution (realism), and concludes with an invitation for the reader to join the ranks of the enlightened few (the realists, whose thought "is a wedge that is opening up the future behavior of the guild" [Llewellyn 1934: 212]). That solution has turned out to be a resounding success, as the "the future behavior of the guild" has indeed fallen in line with Llewellyn's hopes and predictions. It has become a chestnut that "we are all Realists now." Meanwhile, in the legal academy – Llewellyn's initial target audience – realism's scientistic offspring, law and economics and rational choice theory, along with various related species of neopragmatism, have assumed a dominant position among the various competing general theories of law.

This interpretation of Llewellyn's essay and its aftermath seems to me inarguable, if banal. Other readings are also possible, however, and I will attempt one such alternative here, a reading that suggests that Llewellyn's demand has not yet been fulfilled and that it therefore retains something of the critical edge that it had in 1934. Indeed, the main problem with the conventional reading (and the source of its banality) is precisely the absence of this critical edge. To read Llewellyn's essay as an historical success story is, paradoxically, to relegate it as an historical artifact – to see in it nothing more than an anticipation of the present state of affairs. Its argument is all too familiar (we are all realists now), and it only tells us things we already know and confirms us in practices (both theoretical and practical) that we already take for granted. Why read it today? Didn't Llewellyn get what he wanted?

My thesis is that if we read the essay against the grain of this conventional historical reception, we can regain the essay's critical potential. In particular, it seems to me that what Llewellyn was calling for – although he could not have known it at the time because the term had not yet been coined – was not just more realism in American law, but more Continental philosophy in American jurisprudence. Or to be more precise, we can read the essay as *saying* one thing – "realism answers the felt needs of the moment" – and *doing* another, a "doing" that implicitly embraces Continental-philosophical modes of thought. In his own words, even while advancing realism as the conscious articulation of the "implicit philosophy, ... those premises, albeit inarticulate and in fact unthought, which yet make coherence out of a multiplicity of single ways of doing," the essay itself is a particular "way ... of doing that comport[s] with some one philosophy and not another." That "some one philosophy" – "albeit inarticulate and in fact unthought" in the essay itself – with which Llewellyn's argument comports is the (broadly speaking) Continental-philosophical approach to jurisprudence. To close the circle, my further thesis is that it is a Continental-philosophical approach that best responds to the felt needs of American jurisprudence today, whether or not American jurisprudence is conscious of those needs (Llewellyn 1934: 206).

That thesis will appear absurd to anyone even passingly familiar with current Anglo-American legal philosophy. Indeed, the title of this essay may appear as something of an oxymoron. Under almost any definition, there is virtually no Continental philosophy in American jurisprudence today, especially if the term is taken in its usual professional-disciplinary sense of the traditions of post-Kantian thought that, beginning with Hegel, rejected Kant's rigid dualism and its related binary oppositions – between subject and object, freedom and necessity, the forms of thought and the content of empirical experience, facts and norms, and so on – and insisted on the continuing relevance of properly philosophical modes of thought (Kant's speculative reason) to all of human historical experience. (There are other ways of defining Continental philosophy, but that is the sense in which I will use it here.)

The absence of these modes of thinking from American jurisprudence is rooted in the larger divide that has separated Continental philosophy from the dominant traditions of Anglo-American philosophy since the early twentieth century. This is not the place to recount how that separation occurred; the story is complex (and, it should be said, the separation has been far from total). Nor will I attempt any synoptic account of the (widely divergent) schools that make up the Continental tradition, beyond identifying some characteristic and significant themes that I will extract from Llewellyn's essay. Suffice it to say that I think Simon Critchley is essentially correct when he characterizes the distinction between Continental and Anglo-American philosophy as the distinction between a traditional philosophical concern with the broader questions of human life – a concern that goes back at least as far as Socrates' claim that the unexamined life is not worth living – and a more modern concern, rooted in the natural sciences, with establishing the certainty of our theoretical knowledge of the world (Critchley 2001: 1–11).

Within the professional-disciplinary context of Anglo-American academic philosophy, Continental-philosophical schools have tended to be treated with suspicion, incomprehension, or outright dismissal, and the American legal academy has generally followed suit. Outside of Benjamin Cardozo School of Law – the one American law school with a tradition of sponsoring scholarship based in the Continental traditions – there is very little to suggest that Continental philosophy has had much influence at all in the legal academy. Even the critical legal studies movement, the only recent school of American legal thought to have cited Continental sources with any regularity, appears to have confirmed the irrelevance of

Continental philosophy by its demise. In the law journals one can still find an occasional citation to contemporary figures like Jacques Derrida or Giorgio Agamben, but one finds almost no discussion of these thinkers' writings on law or politics (which are abundant), or the writings of more established figures in the tradition like Hegel, Marx, Nietzsche, Gadamer, or Heidegger, to name only the best known.

It is against this background that I find Llewellyn's essay relevant to American jurisprudence today. As noted previously, the essay is a call for a new philosophy of law, one that must meet certain very ambitious criteria. First, it must have sufficient explanatory power to comprehend the entire history of American law up to that point ("It is due our student that cases with dates ranging from 1780 to 1930 should be given some chart of the sweep, on which they can be plotted."). Of course, historical explanation can take many forms, including notions of causation drawn from the physical sciences. Llewellyn, however, will have none of that: "I have never felt satisfied with the mere listing and description of our apparently inconsistent jurisprudential trends in the latter [nineteenth century]. It is not enough to know what they were and whence they came. We must see why men adopted them, and above all, *how* they all fitted into the single picture." Let us pause to appreciate the breathtaking demand that Llewellyn has just registered. An adequate philosophy of law must be (1) historical in the sense of explaining the sequence of jurisprudential trends and cases; (2) internal, in the sense of taking into account not just the occurrence of events but the underlying motivations of the actors in the historical drama; and (3) total in two discrete senses – first, in comprehending the entire sweep of American legal history, and second, in providing one unifying, synoptic theory, the "single picture" into which the sweep of American legal history must "fit" (Llewellyn 1934: 205 n.∗).

At issue for Llewellyn is the series of implicit philosophies – unconscious forms of thought, "those premises, albeit inarticulate and in fact unthought, which yet make coherence out of a multiplicity single ways of doing" – concretely embodied in the history of American law as it has been practiced, "done," and "lived," and not as it has been written about or theorized by legal philosophers (who, with the exception of some contemporaries, Llewellyn interprets as doing no more than "giving fortunate expression" to those "living currents" of their time). Llewellyn's demand is that we no longer settle for treating this series of philosophies-in-action as an "inconsistent hodgepodge" but that we reduce it in thought to a "single picture" capacious enough to comprehend the entire series as a meaningful totality in which the motivating realities of the historical actors in each period are given their due, but their own explanations of their motivations – whether natural law, right reason, or a positive system of precedent – are dismissed as ideology. (Llewellyn 1934: 206).

Anyone familiar with Hegel's philosophy of history will recognize in the account so far a rather precise description of its contours. For Hegel, history was a sequence of embodied forms of consciousness captured in the habits and attitudes of the community (which he called its *Sittlichkeit*, or "ethical life"). This sequence was no inconsistent hodgepodge, moreover, but a unified and meaningful totality – albeit a temporally extended totality – understood as the concrete manifestation of what Hegel called reason (or spirit, *Geist*) developing itself over time. Reason, for Hegel, was not (as it is for us late moderns) a characteristic of an individual mind. Rather, it was a supraindividual principle that operated through but behind the backs of (in a manner "inarticulate and in fact unthought"), the passions, thoughts, and feelings that motivated individual historical actors' conduct (Hegel's [1980: 89] expression for this was "the cunning of Reason"). Of course Hegel's field was world history and not American legal history. Nevertheless, the structural parallel with Llewellyn's history of American law is striking – and let us not forget that for Hegel the final historical form assumed by reason was the state, its laws, and its institutions. In short, for Hegel, reason provided the single picture that Llewellyn was looking for, the one implicit philosophy that could "yet make a coherence out of a multiplicity of single ways of doing."

Llewellyn's essay is thus a quasi-Hegelian exercise in historical interpretation, in which he reinterprets first the natural law philosophy of the founders and then the positivism of the Gilded Age as ideological products of the underlying social needs of the moment. For Llewellyn, in other words, it is not Reason or Spirit but "social need" that constitutes the implicit philosophy that guides individuals on the stage of legal history, regardless of their own citations to "Right Reason" or the formal dictates of positive precedent as the explanation for their actions. This functional understanding of law – the notion that it is best understood in terms of its role in mediating and serving social needs – is so familiar today as to appear banal. In that sense, Llewellyn's overarching "implicit philosophy" (Llewellyn 1934: 206) has not only become dominant; it has become explicit. The predominance of social need has risen to the level of active consciousness and has thus itself become, in our enlightened modern age, the philosophy that is citable by individual historical actors in legal opinions and arguments (and law review articles) as the basis for action.

Of course, we should not forget that the natural lawyers of the founding era held similar beliefs about the overarching explanatory power of "Right Reason," as did the lawyers of the late nineteenth century about formalism and positive precedent. And, we should note – perhaps with even more trepidation – that that is also what Hegel believed about his own metaphysical philosophy of spirit. In his view, the emergence of the modern legal state signaled the fact that Spirit had manifested itself in its final form, and thus, by necessary implication, that his own philosophy of Spirit was the becoming-explicit of what had theretofore been only an "implicit philosophy" (Llewellyn 1934: 206) of the social order. The sheer fact of these historical precedents perhaps ought to cause us to wonder whether our Realism (understood broadly to include the related schools mentioned earlier) will, or should, suffer the same fate that has befallen the intellectual hubris of these earlier schools.

That said, there is one important respect in which Llewellyn's conception of philosophy differs from Hegel's, an even more important difference than his substitution of social need for Spirit. (Karl Marx, by way of example, similarly substituted a certain concept of social need – class interest – for Spirit in the Hegelian philosophy of history without fundamentally changing its structure.) Although he emphasized the implicit nature of most philosophy, Llewellyn (1934: 206) also insisted on the possibility, however rare, of the conscious invention of new philosophies, and – even more important for my purposes – that such new philosophies may have important social and political consequences: "I shall urge that the inventor of a new philosophy, or of a creative adaptation of some ancient one to current needs, may with luck affect or deflect the current of his times. There is a certain – or better, an uncertain – leeway within which the individual contributes to the shaping of society" (Llewellyn 1934: 206).

Despite the caution of Llewellyn's formulation, the notion that philosophizing could have any practical impact on its historical moment – as Marx put it, could change the world as well as interpret it – is one that Hegel could never have accepted. He explicitly rejected the idea that philosophy could give "instruction as to what the world ought to be," because "[a]s the thought of the world, it appears only when actuality is already there cut and dried after its process of formation has been completed" (Hegel 1952: 12–13).

Llewellyn's cautious faith in the possibility that an individual thinker can affect the course of history, despite the Hegelian nature of his conception of history and philosophy, places him squarely in the camp of post-Hegelian thinkers who remain respectful of the Hegelian legacy – that is, those thinkers who, taking Hegel's critique of Kant's dualisms with absolute seriousness, nevertheless reject his ultimate reconciliation of those dualisms in the metaphysical teleology and determinism of Absolute Spirit. That camp includes the traditions of contemporary Continental philosophy, including those Continental philosophers who have written specifically on law and politics. But it also includes philosophical traditions that are much closer to Llewellyn's (and our own) Realism. With regard to American pragmatism, for example – one of the pillars of the realist movement, according to Llewellyn (1934: 212) – Richard Rorty (1982: 16) has referred to "John Dewey's 'naturalized' version of Hegelian historicism," a characterization that accurately captures both pragmatism's acceptance of Hegel's historically situated conception of reason and its rejection of his metaphysics. The jurisprudential problem shared by these post-Hegelian Continental traditions and American pragmatism – a problem that is at the same time political and ethical – is the problem of freedom: how to articulate a notion of meaningful historical action that does not presuppose Kant's dualism of the free, noumenal subject and its heteronomous, phenomenal historical circumstances.

Llewellyn insists that philosophical writers can be both free actors and embedded in their history: that they can be "heralds of the future" even while remaining "products of their times." How can these two notions be reconciled? He is very clear about the mechanism of this reconciliation, a mechanism that is deeply Hegelian. It is by bringing to consciousness felt needs that were previously present but unconscious that the "inventor of a new philosophy . . . may, with luck, affect or deflect the current of his times." "A lone man, by his formulations, may indeed make felt a need of which no one had been conscious before" (Llewellyn 1934: 206). In this way – and again in good Hegelian fashion – even the inventor's freedom is itself in a real sense not the writer's own but a "product of its times."

The challenge left to us by Llewellyn's essay, it seems to me, is thus whether our current legal philosophy-in-action and its dominant conscious articulations continue to respond to the "felt needs" of our time, or whether there are needs that, although felt, can be articulated only in some other philosophical vocabulary. In considering this question, we might take some guidance from Llewellyn (1934: 211–12), who warned against a certain deafness to the marginalized and oppressed as the "most important" reason the legal-philosophy-in-action of his time had "fallen hopelessly behind the times." And, in considering the merits of such a "new philosophy," we might also keep in mind just how "hopelessly unorthodox" (Llewellyn 1934: 212) the views of Holmes, Pound, and Llewellyn himself appeared in their own time.

I cannot, obviously, engage here in a systematic critique of the currently dominant American jurisprudential schools from this perspective. Nevertheless, it seems to me that in their various mixes of ahistoricism, incipient formalism (sometimes mathematical formalism), and unthinking positivism (whether in the reliance on unanalyzed notions of interest or fundamental value), the dominant schools of American jurisprudence bear a family resemblance to the formalist, positivist, and natural law philosophies that Llewellyn criticized seventy-five years ago. Nor can I defend in a systematic fashion the proposition that Continental modes of philosophizing hold out some better hope for articulating the yet-unarticulated felt needs of our philosophical moment (beyond the preceding attempt to suggest the fruitfulness of a Hegelian reading of a founder of the Realist movement). By way of concluding, I will instead offer a prolegomenon to such a systematic account that begins with a concrete example of a current jurisprudential problem, one that (it seems to me) suggests how Continental approaches might better serve the "felt needs" of American jurisprudence.

That example is the problem of affirmative action, which has proved difficult to justify in traditionally liberal-philosophical terms. The problem has been that deontological approaches to right inevitably seem to falter when it comes to explaining why individuals with stronger merit-based claims to a particular benefit should be passed over in favor of others with less strong claims, particularly when the criterion for favoritism is based on race or some other (typically invidious) basis for discrimination (Sandel 1998: 135–47). Even if one accepts the utilitarian value of these programs, the apparent violation of individual claimants' formal right to equal treatment under law – again, particularly when the criterion of favoritism is as historically suspect as race – seems to run up against the liberal principle that individual rights remain inviolate even in the face of arguments for the greater good of the community. Thus, conservative opponents of affirmative action have been able to turn the liberal language of formal individual right against the liberals who seek to remedy social ills.

In response, Michael Sandel (1998: 143) and others have argued that what is needed is a different conception of the rights-bearing subject, one that views the subject not as an atomic individual but a "participant in a common identity": "we may come to regard ourselves... less as individualized subjects with certain things in common, and more as members of a wider (but still determinate) subjectivity, less as 'others' and more as participants in a common identity." Understood in this way, the failure to obtain a particular benefit may come to be seen as a gain for the individual claimant rather than a loss insofar as the larger community benefits, not because of a utilitarian sacrifice of the individual but because the individual is inseparable from the community of which he or she is a part.

As Sandel's argument suggests, affirmative action constitutes one front in the larger battle played out in the so-called liberalism-communitarianism debates of the past twenty years. The revolving-door nature of these debates is, arguably, a function of their essentially ahistorical character, because positions that begin from incompatible views of the deontological constitution of the legal subject (individual and autonomous, or socially constituted and decentered?) are doomed to talk past one another. What if instead, however, the autonomous liberal-legal subject of right was itself an historical achievement and not a metaphysical (or postmetaphysical, for that matter) postulate of liberal philosophy? If it turned out that the dominant normative role of the subject's autonomy and abstract right in developed liberal legal systems was itself the end point of a social-historical development, then a bridge conceivably could be built between the liberal and communitarian positions in the debates. In the context of affirmative action, it would become plausible to argue that it is proper and legitimate to judge affirmative action remedies by substantive and historically grounded criteria rather than by strictly formal conceptions of equality, because the notion of formal equality is itself a substantive and historical "product of its times," to use Llewellyn's expression.

Sandel's account gets halfway there by emphasizing the communitarian nature of the subject of right, but it was Hegel who first offered a full-blown history of the modern subject that based formal right on a concrete historical narrative. For Hegel, the individual's self-conscious understanding of him- or herself as possessing an intrinsic dignity and freedom that stands apart from his or her social role (e.g., as slave, peasant, aristocrat, landowner) cannot be understood apart from the historical development of social and legal institutions that gave this new concept of autonomy its meaning and effect. Without claiming that this historicized view can by itself decide particular cases, I do suggest that it provides rich justification for supplementing (or superseding) arguments on affirmative action based on formal right with socially grounded and substantive arguments based on histories of racial exclusion, and on the inconsistencies of those exclusionary histories with the larger history of equality and freedom that underwrites the formal right position.

Such a historicized account of formal right is difficult to square with those currently dominant interpretations of our realism that explicitly or implicitly posit the autonomy of the subject, like the Law and Economics and rational choice schools, but it is fully compatible with at least one intellectual wellspring of Realism, American pragmatism, which (as I observed earlier) begins with a naturalized Hegelian view of philosophy and history. From the legal-philosophical point of view, however, what remains problematic in pragmatism is precisely its insistence on naturalized explanation, as to naturalize an explanations is to rob it of its justificatory power – it collapses the "ought" into the "is." Pragmatism rejects the metaphysical underpinning of Hegel's philosophy of history, but for Hegel it was only that metaphysical underpinning that guaranteed the normative force of the really existing doctrines and institutions of the modern legal system. Thus, having rejected both the metaphysical autonomy of the Kantian rational subject and Hegel's suprasubjective rational metaphysics, pragmatic philosophy is left with the continuing question of how to articulate a notion of rationality with enough genuinely normative force that one can rationally justify or criticize our existing legal system.

That question, it seems to me, is the one that defines the most pressing dilemma currently facing legal philosophy, and the one that highlights the most fundamental deficiency in "our Realism" of whatever stripe. It undergirds the crisis of legitimacy that has left legal thinkers groping for values – wealth maximization, original intent, or what have you – that can supply the authoritative ethical force that once inhered the legal tradition itself. One solution to this crisis is to decide that no such post-Hegelian rationality is available, and thus that, absent any governing rationality, law is simply politics carried on by other means. That was the conclusion reached by the irrationalist strand of the American critical legal studies movement, for example (a conclusion that – at least to the extent that it relied on Continental philosophical sources – was unwarranted [Thurschwell 2006]). Today's Realists purport to reject that conclusion, arguing that some calculus of social interest, individual preference, and/or wealth maximization can still issue in legitimate normative evaluations of doctrine that can guide legal practice.

Nevertheless, it seems to me that the "implicit philosophy" of our current Realism is one that precludes the possibility of *philosophically* justifying any fundamental change in our deeply flawed political-legal status quo. At least that is the case if one accepts Hegel's and Llewellyn's insight that the individual subject is not autonomous but rather a product of his or her times. Having substituted social interest (or its social-choice correlates) for the emphatic principle of rationality that gave metaphysical philosophies of law their critical bite, Realists can no longer see, as a philosophical matter, past the positivity of today's realities – embodied in the particular social interests and subjective preferences coughed up by our present juridical-socio-economic arrangements – to potential tomorrows in which these arrangements have themselves been fundamentally transformed. In Llewellyn's expression (1934:211–2), they no longer have "ears for words that betoken . . . change in an existing order." Given the profound injustice of so much of our existing order, that limitation of philosophical vision has itself become unjustifiable.

Contemporary Continental philosophical approaches to law and politics respond to this situation in a different way, one that avoids the incipient historical positivism of our latter-day Realism. Beginning with the abstract fact of our finitude and historical situatedness rather than the particular interests and values of our present historical situation, they find a source of ethical impetus for change in the condition of historical finitude itself. It is impossible to generalize about the conclusions reached by these thinkers, because they range from a reaffirmation of the value of legal tradition (Hans-Georg Gadamer), to neo-anarchist rejections of law and the state form *in toto* (Giorgio Agamben), to an insistence that traditions themselves, including the legal tradition, contain resources for their own fundamental reform and radical transformation (Jacques Derrida). What all of these thinkers share, however, is a simultaneous respect for the inevitably historical character of thought and action and a recognition of the plight of history's victims – they have "ears for words that betoken . . . change in an existing order." In very different ways, they all elevate that ethical concern to philosophical status, and thereby provide some hope that, in Llewellyn's (1934: 206) words, "the inventor of a new philosophy, or of a creative adaptation of some ancient one to current needs, may with luck affect or deflect the current of his times." "Hopelessly unorthodox" (212) though they undoubtedly are, at least from the perspective of the American legal academy, these approaches offer a compelling response to the "felt needs" (206) of our jurisprudence that we ignore at our own expense.

WORKS CITED

Critchley, Simon. *Continental Philosophy: A Very Short Introduction.* New York: Oxford Univ. Press, 2001.

Hegel, G. W. F. *Lectures on the Philosophy of World History: Introduction.* Cambridge: Cambridge Univ. Press, 1980.

———. *The Philosophy of Right.* Oxford: Oxford Univ. Press, 1952.

Llewellyn, K. N. "On Philosophy in American Law." *U. Pa. L. Rev.* 82.3 (1934): 205–12.

Rorty, Richard. "World Well Lost." In *Consequences of Pragmatism (Essays: 1972–1980)* Minneapolis: Univ. of Minnesota Press, 1982: 3–18.

Sandel, Michael. *Liberalism and the Limits of Justice*, 2d ed. Cambridge: Cambridge Univ. Press, 1998.

Thurschwell, Adam. "Critical Legal Studies." In *A Dictionary of Continental Philosophy.* Ed. John Protevi. New Haven, CT: Yale Univ. Press, 2006: 112–4.

17 Psychoanalysis as the Jurisprudence of Freedom

JEANNE L. SCHROEDER AND DAVID GRAY CARLSON

What is the future of legal philosophy? No doubt it has many. But we are betting that jurisprudence will gravitate towards freedom. Freedom, the attribute of the human subject, has largely been absent from legal philosophy. This is a lack that psychoanalytic jurisprudence aims to correct.

THE PSYCHOANALYTIC SUBJECT

All liberal theories start with some intuition of the free, autonomous individual. In contrast, psychoanalysis views the subject's definition as *the* problem of philosophy.

For psychoanalysis, as reformulated by Jacques Lacan, personality and freedom cannot exist in any empirical or hypothetical state of nature because nature is unfree – bound by ironclad laws of cause and effect. Personality and freedom are artificial creations – hard-won achievements. Subjectivity – the capacity to bear duties and rights – is a stage in this struggle.

What then is the subject? As David Hume argued, the subject is not an affirmative substance but a unity of the memory of perceptions. As such it is not the perceptions but a negativity, the force holding them together. Negativity by its nature cannot be perceived directly, only inferred from what has vanished. Lacan expresses this through his symbol $: the barred or split subject. In Simon Critchley's (2007: 11) formulation the subject is not an individual but a "dividual."

DYNAMIC JURISPRUDENCE

Because of its negativity, subjectivity is the active principle – the capacity for freedom as spontaneity. Freedom must, however, be given positive existence. This can be done only through law. Subjectivity is a living, breathing contradiction. Its introduction into jurisprudence makes the latter dynamic. In comparison, competing jurisprudences are static in nature. For them, law is a finite, fixed set for which freedom is either the enemy or irrelevant.

For utilitarianism, freedom threatens the possibility of social policy. Policy requires the behavior of those subjected to law to be predictable – manipulable through reward and punishment. Values become preferences; rationality, ends-means reasoning. Utilitarianism degrades the human subject to animality (Badiou

2002: 10–11). The individual is enslaved by inclination (pathology). To Richard Posner (1992: 17) it is no solecism to speak of a rational frog. But freedom, to psychoanalysis, is precisely the uncaused. As Kant (1900: 18) emphasized, freedom is the stumbling block on which all empiricism, including utilitarianism, founders.

Positivism is also a static jurisprudence. In positivism, the subject's condition improves, rising to irrelevance. Positivism's project is description. The observing subject adds nothing to the object it apperceives. Once law is described, positivism can't speak to law's normative worth because law and morality are conceived as separate.

THE SYMBOLIC AND SEXUALITY

Psychoanalysis challenges the ontology of certitude of utilitarianism and positivism. Lacan locates law in the social realm called the symbolic. The symbolic, like the subject, is in a constant state of contradiction and, therefore, dynamic. This is a hard truth to bear. The two ways of confronting it are denial and acceptance. The former is the masculine; the latter, the feminine position.

These Lacanian terms do not refer to anatomically male and female people. Rather, they name two positions that one can take with respect to completeness and openness, commensurability and incommensurability, metaphor and metonymy. Empirically, anatomical males might be more likely to be drawn to the masculine position than females, and vice versa. It is, however, impossible for anyone to be purely man or woman – each position requires the other.

In developing these terms, Lacan upends traditional stereotypes. The masculine is not the norm, with the feminine as exception. Subjectivity is characteristically feminine; men are, in effect, failed women. Moreover, the feminine is the active principle. The masculine is passive.

The masculine position is liberal individuality: man imagines both he and law are, or could form, correlative and complete wholes. This is masculine because the individual claims to "have the phallus." Here, *phallus* does not refer to male anatomy but is the signifier for subjectivity. By claiming to have subjectivity, man suppresses negativity and fantasizes he has an affirmative, fixed self. Man is passive because – like H. L. A. Hart's officials – he seeks to be completely constrained by law. But, subjectivity is not a fixed thing – in Lacanian terms, it does not exist in the rigorous way that Hegel defines existence. If subjectivity could be so captured, it would not be free.

The feminine position of being the phallus is completely diverse from the masculine. Woman accepts that no one could have the phallus because subjectivity is a process, a doing not a being. In Lacanian terms, it is an insistence as opposed to an existence. Woman embodies the phallus (subjectivity) by acting.

The feminine and masculine are not opposites, like yin and yang. If they were, they could fit together harmoniously. Subjectivity and the symbolic would be closed and whole. This is masculine fantasy. Rather, the sexes are fundamentally inconsistent. There is no sexual rapport – sexuality is an impasse. Woman is not whole. Subjectivity can not be wholly circumscribed within law – some aspect of personality escapes. This does not mean that masculinity is the legalistic aspect of personality, adopting an ethic of justice as opposed to a feminine one of care. This different voice theory adopts this masculine yin-yang fantasy. Although not wholly within the symbolic, woman "is *not* not at all there. She is there in full. But there is something more" (Lacan 1998: 74). She partially escapes law because law is not closed. Law, like woman, is not whole.

The sexual impasse is not limited to the nonrelation of masculine and feminine people but characterizes the entire symbolic order. Consequently, law is different from morality, but the two – like the sexes – are not opposites and can never be separated. Each depends on the other even as each is incompatible with the other.

Psychoanalysis offers a possibility of authentic feminist jurisprudence. Mainstream feminist legal theory can't get beyond yin-yang essentialism, either extolling the stereotypical feminine different voice or exalting masculine power as a program for empirical women. In contrast, psychoanalysis presents sexual difference as a tension within subjectivity and law, a becoming that can never close.

DISCOURSES

Psychoanalytic feminism depends upon, and therefore can not abolish, the masculine to the feminine. The masculine fantasy of commensuration is the condition for the possibility of meaning and communication. Accordingly, psychoanalysis sees at least four discourses of the symbolic – two masculine and two feminine.

The first masculine discourse is that of the master, which we identify with positivism. Lacan's master's discourse is inspired by Hegel's master-slave dialectic. In this discourse, law is obeyed not because it is just but just because it is law. Law exists, H. L. A. Hart says, when officials taking the internal position recognize laws as rules to be obeyed. The official, like Hegel's slave, does not obey out of fear. Rather, the official takes on the masculine position and tries to erase "his" personal discretion so that law alone can enjoy sole sovereign sway and masterdom. This is a necessary, but insufficient, element of law's reality.

Lacan agrees that, in the master's positivistic discourse, law must be divorced from morality, understood as "the ought." The official applies the rule recognized as law regardless of what it should be. Consequently, the master and law are idiotic. They do not deserve their position because of wisdom, morality, or any other reason. The master rules because the slave recognizes the master's status. Similarly, the official obeys the law because he or she recognizes its status through an appropriate rule. Of course, any empirical master might be wise, and any positive law just, but this is accidental. Any justification for mastery makes it contingent, not absolute.

This leaves an absence – a gap. Why should the master be master? Why should law be law?

Into this gap rushes the second masculine discourse – the university's. Unlike the master, the university claims to deserve its privileged position because of superior knowledge. Despite its name, this discourse is not limited to universities (indeed, true science requires the feminine discourses). The university's discourse refers generally to the concept of expertise.

Experts seek to justify the law's rule. They seek to fill the gap left by the master's discourse by discovering law's purpose. Experts might sometimes criticize an existing legal regime, suggesting utilitarian reform. But nevertheless experts justify a rule – if not the current master, then some other master yet to be. Experts apologize either for what positive law is or what it should be. Utilitarians supposedly consult the preferences of society's members to determine collective goals – such as maximized welfare or wealth. They then propose legal programs to cause those subjected to law to act in a way calculated to achieve this goal. Law is no longer idiotic but rationalized and justified. However, this is at the expense of the freedom of any specific subject whose own desire is subordinated to the collectivity.

This being said, psychoanalysis is the critic, not the enemy, of the two masculine discourses of law. Hart's concept of law as rules is a necessary moment in all legal regimes. One cannot have a functioning society if officials can choose to disobey laws with which they disagree. Nor does it oppose expertise or collectivity. The subject is intersubjective – only coming into being through symbolic relations. To be a part of society requires one to subordinate oneself to society's collective goals, thereby compromising one's radical freedom.

The complaint of the feminine position is not that the masculine exists, but that it represses law's feminine moment that is the very condition of its possibility. Consequently, Lacan supplements the masculine discourses with the feminine analyst's and hysteric's discourse. We are in the process of applying these to law, identifying the former with counseling and interpretation and the latter with representation and criticism. We leave these for another day.

MORALITY

Positivism preaches that law and morality (i.e., content) are not necessarily connected. Psychoanalysis – and utilitarianism – insists the opposite is true. Rather, they require each other. This reflects the sexual impasse.

What positive law reports as its finding (law and morality are not necessarily connected) is in fact its aspiration, its program – its "ought," as it were. Positive law strives to banish morality. It aspires to replace it with legality. Radical freedom (Kantian autonomy) is sublime and monstrous. Legality is a relief; it permits pathological indulgence without moral qualm. But positive law can never succeed in its program of banishing morality. Ultimately, empirical subjects must make judgments about the law.

Law is revealed through Kant's notion of autonomy – the very heart of morality. Judgment (interpretation generally) requires the judge to suppress his or her heteronomy and assume the autonomous position so that whatever the judge recognizes is indeed the law and not some subjective fantasy.

Interpretation requires a free and spontaneous act – a feminine moment of jouissance. It just occurs. The fact of reason is a crucial, and controversial, aspect of Kant's thought. To simplify, reason itself can not be identified by reason. Reason turned on itself yields antinomy. Like facts, reason confronts us as being both external and internal to our subjectivity.

After the act of interpretation, the actor retroactively tells a story to explain the decision so that the act seems reasoned *ex ante*. Lacan says that truth has the structure of fiction. This does not mean that there is no truth or that this after-the-fact narration is necessarily untrue. Quite the contrary, psychoanalysis suggests that rational acts are possible but the whole truth is unknowable. Acts are overdetermined. There is no way to know whether rationality or irrationality – autonomy or heteronomy – really caused the act. Psychoanalysis calls this the ethics of the real (Zupančič 2000: 143). Any attempt to recognize the truth, any interpretation, requires the subject's active participation. To interpret is to tell a story. That the story is true is within the realm of the possible.

The logic of interpretation is to be distinguished from deduction and induction. C. S. Peirce, following Aristotle, called it abduction – the proposing of informed hypotheses. Although the subject has reason to believe that his or her abductions are true, the fact that he or she abduces is no guarantor of its truth. Judging reflects the parallax of the sexual impasse. Our feminine side reminds us of limitation, that all interpretations are subjective and falsifiable. Our masculine side reminds us that time is running out. The judge does not have the leisure of the theory class. The judge must eventually take the leap of faith, pretend to have the phallus, and decide the case. The judge is both masculinely passive, obeying the law's rules, and femininely active in imposing "her" own judgment.

This view of interpretation suggests that there can be no rule of recognition, as Hart asserts, only Dworkin's shock of recognition. Legal reasoning is the retroactive narrative designed to convince others (and one's own self) that the act of interpretation is a genuine and true objective interpretation. It acts as a constraint, but a post hoc one. It enables us to adopt or disavow our past acts. Kant thought that an autonomous, noumenal moment of personality was hidden under our pathological, empirical selves. To Lacan, this is the masculine fantasy. Yet although the (masculine) autonomous position is imaginary, it is necessary. Subjectivity and law are revealed to be in tension in the dynamics of interpretation.

RIGHT

Psychoanalysis seeks an uneasy reconciliation between law and freedom. Not wishing to reinvent the wheel of philosophy, it relies on German idealist philosophy. The task begins with Kant's destructive jurisprudence of duty. Kant's freedom is a negative freedom, in which all constraints are obliterated. Kantian freedom is spontaneity – the subject's capacity to act purely out of duty to a moral law he or she self-legislates. In order to do so, the subject must, therefore, erase all heteronomy – become masculine. Heteronomy is everything other than autonomy including the very things that utilitarianism and positivism exalt – natural inclination and positive law. Inclinations, emotions, and compulsions from positive law are all pathological content that must be eliminated in the name of freedom. Freedom requires each individual to be an end in him- or herself, not the means to the ends of another. What is left standing is the free, autonomous individual. And whatever this individual does is guaranteed to be universally valid for all autonomous individuals.

Kant's individual would be a pure noumenon, stripped of phenomena. Hegel and Lacan, however, completely reject all notions of transcendence. There can be nothing that is not embodied, no noumenon beyond phenomena. Nothing is potential unless it is actualized in the empirical world. Action is the proof of being. The free Kantian (masculine) individual is, from Hegel's perspective, a mere potentiality, not an actuality. Freedom can be actualized not by eliminating heteronomy but by embracing it.

In Hegel's philosophy of right, the autonomous (masculine) individual makes his freedom actual by advancing to higher stages of personality – by becoming feminine. The most primitive stage is what Hegel calls abstract right. Logically, subjectivity turns out to be intersubjectivity. One becomes a subject by being recognized as such by another subject. Hegel identifies the most primitive intersubjectivity as property and contract. Thus, law is the medium by which freedom actualizes itself through the creation of subjectivity.

Subjectivity can be bestowed only by another subject's recognition. However, there are no subjects in the state of nature, only other abstract individuals. Consequently, to achieve subjectivity each individual must first help other individuals to achieve the status of subjectivity. The individual does this by deciding to recognize other people as subjects entitled to be recognized – as having rights. Consequently, Hegel reconciles liberalism's concern with rights and the Kantian concern with moral duty. As in Kant, an individual cannot actualize freedom by claiming rights for oneself but by recognizing one's duty to the other. However, Hegel, anticipating Hohfeld's legal correlatives, understands that a duty can only be understood in terms of rights owed to others. The alchemy of the psychoanalytic approach to law is that abstract right both achieves the goals of making another person into a subject and allowing the other subject to recognize (thereby creating) the first as a subject.

To have intersubjective relations, one must first become recognizable – to others and to oneself. However, the Kantian individual, stripped of heteronomy, has no distinguishing characteristics. The individual can differentiate herself through private property: the regime of possession, enjoyment, and alienation of external things.

Property standing alone, however, is a wrong, not a right. Property is aggressive. Property claims are asserted against other people. Property only becomes a right when consummated in contract. In contract, the first protosubject recognizes the other as owning an object of property. The first person offers the other one object (a thing, a promise, money, whatever) in exchange for another. In doing so, the first recognizes the other as a distinguishable subject who has the right to accept or reject the offer. If the other subject accepts the offer, he or she simultaneously also recognizes the first as a distinguishable subject having the ability to take free action.

Kantian negative freedom was no freedom at all. Positive freedom is bestowed, through contract, by the other. No one actualizes freedom alone. So, if Kant has a philosophy of duty, Hegel has a philosophy of right. In this account, freedom requires a moment of unfreedom. Although, Hegel's (2002: 69) is famously a philosophy of right, he insists that only the basest people claim rights for themselves.

Once again, psychoanalysis promises no permanent reconciliation. The intersubjectivity of psychoanalysis is not reciprocal in the sense of mirror image. To claim a right from another is to treat the other as a means to one's own ends and, therefore, not free. One can grant rights and recognize duties to others only in the hope that they might reciprocate. This is why private law is a primitive form of love – in love the lover sees in the beloved more than he or she is and thereby helps the beloved become more than he or she once was. When reciprocated the beloved changes places, becoming a lover who also raises the beloved up to a new capacity. Similarly, in private law, the first individual turns the second into a subject by granting him or her the rights of a subject. If the contract is accepted, the subject returns the favor by bestowing on the first individual the rights of a subject. Each momentarily recognizes the other as the means to the other's own ends when they come to an agreement on one specific end (exchange).

Law is, therefore, revealed as the stuff subjectivity is made of – and vice versa. But, in this vision, law is not narrowly defined as the command of the sovereign that the official with the internal perspective recognizes. For this reason, psychoanalysis relaxes the distinction between law and other normative systems – they are all part and parcel of the intersubjective realm of the symbolic. Indeed, psychoanalysis identifies language itself as the ultimate normative system. In language the subject positivizes him- or herself. Yet this most intimate part of the private subject is highly public. That which is most ourselves – our personality, our subjectivity – is dependent on that which is outside of ourselves: other persons and the law itself. The subject is inherently split between private and public, between the feminine and masculine. In Lacan's neologism, subjectivity is not intimate but "extimate" (Miller 1994: 74).

The subject is unable to do without law, but the law is equally unable to do without the subject. Lacan says the subject is split, castrated, and barred. But it follows from this that law is also the barred other because law has precisely the same constitution as the subject. If the subject is castrated and incomplete, so is law.

In fact, legal interpretation constitutes one subject observing and recognizing another subject, each depending on the other for its completion. Psychoanalysis takes seriously the notion of loving the law. The subject has, in Dworkin's terms, a duty to make the law the best it can be, and in this activity the subject will recognize itself in the law.

POLICY

We conclude by addressing the all-important question, What is the cash value of this line of inquiry? The answer is that psychoanalysis yields personal freedom, not determinate answers. The return on investment can be appraised by considering the psychoanalytic critique of romanticism – the idea that somehow there is a natural subject distorted by law. Romanticism emphasizes the pain of desire. It supposes that this pain is caused; something is to blame for it. And that something is, of course, law. "Legal interpretation takes place in a field of pain and death," the arch-romantic Robert Cover (1986: 1601) once wrote. Romanticism promises to get back in touch with the authentic subject that feels no pain. Psychoanalysis views this as false autobiography.

The romantic dreams of authenticity – yearns to be masculine, an individual, undivided, integral, and undesiring. The romantic wants to recover the phallus. But the speculative position argues that the individual is only a potentiality that can have no empirical existence. To exercise actual freedom, and to relate to others, is to become feminine, a "dividual," a barred subject, split between her own idiosyncratic desires and the demands of others.

There is no subject preceding law. Liberalism's masculine individual is revealed to be a retroactively generated hypothesis – a fantasy in the psychoanalytic sense. There never was a time in which we were whole and complete (had the phallus). We do not desire because law has taken something away from us. Desire is our very constitution. The subject is the very product of law. Yet the subject is not wholly in the law. Beneath the law is nothing but an absence – the negative unity that holds the positive law together. For this reason, psychoanalysis is not antilaw, as romanticism thoroughly is.

So, the end result of psychoanalysis is the acceptance of the fact that no law or policy can ever sate unquenchable subjective desire. Consequently, Lacan (1986: 319) argues that the only ethic psychoanalysis can suggest is "do not give way with respect to your desire." Of course, the empirical people who practice psychoanalytic jurisprudence have political opinions, but they have given up the notion that philosophy can play any very useful role in the microethical issues with which politics concerns itself. Psychoanalysis leaves the task of suggesting policy – the quotidian bread and butter of the American academic scene – to the experts of the university's discourse.

Hegel (2002: 23) insisted that philosophy comes too late to give advice on concrete issues – "the owl of Minerva begins its flight only with the onset of dusk." Speculative philosophy's presupposition is that the legal subject is the personification of freedom. The two feminine discourses of the analyst and hysteric can only interpret and critique the law from the perspective of the desire of the subject subjected to the law. Or more accurately, the subject is nothing and, therefore, free. The consequence of this lesson is that philosophy cannot tell us what we must do. We are doomed to make up our own minds.

WORKS CITED

Badiou, Alain. *An Essay on the Understanding of Evil.* Trans. Peter Hallward. New York: Verso, 2002.

Cover, Robert M. "Violence and the Word." *Yale L.J.* 95.1 (1986): 1601–30.

Critchley, Simon. *Infinitely Demanding: Ethics of Commitment, Politics of Resistance.* London: Verso, 2007.

Hegel, G. W. F. *Elements of the Philosophy of Right.* Ed. Allen W. Wood. Trans. H. B. Nisbet. Cambridge: Cambridge Univ. Press, 2002.

Kant, Immanuel. *The Critique of Practical Reason.* Trans. T. K. Abbott. Amherst, MA: Prometheus Books, 1996.

Lacan, Jacques. *The Seminar of Jacques Lacan: Book VII: The Ethics of Psychoanalysis.* Ed. Jacques-Alain Miller. Trans. Dennis Porter. New York: W. W. Norton, 1986.

———. *The Seminar of Jacques Lacan. Book XX: Encore, on Feminine Sexuality, the Limits of Love and Knowledge*. Ed. Jacques-Alain Miller. Trans. Bruce Fink. New York: W. W. Norton, 1998.

Miller, Jacques-Alain. "Extimité." Trans. Francoise Massardier-Kenney. In *Lacanian Theory of Discourse: Subject, Structure, and Society*. Ed. Mark Bracher et al. New York: New York Univ. Press, 1994.

Posner, Richard A. *Economic Analysis of Law*, 5th ed. New York: Aspen Press, 1992.

Zupančič, Alenka. *Ethics of the Real*. London: Verso, 2000.

PART FOUR. PHILOSOPHICAL EXAMINATIONS OF LEGAL ISSUES

18 Law as Premise

FRANK I. MICHELMAN

Suppose we are passing legal judgment on the conduct of another. We want, therefore, to know what the law requires and permits of actors in the other's position in the case at hand. We don't know yet, so we shall have to conduct some sort of inquiry to find out. It happens that we are already dead certain about what morality permits and requires of the other in this case (setting aside whatever general moral obligation or pressure there may be to conform to the law as the law). What part, if any, does our prelegal moral knowledge (so to call it) play in our inquiry into the regulative content of the situationally applicable law?

A possible answer, in some ways quite appealing, is "none at all." Legal content, we might then say, is whatever authorized lawmakers decide to make it. Authorized lawmakers may or may not have conformed the applicable law for this case to the applicable moral permissions and requirements. If they did not, the product of their law-making activity is no less *the law* than if they had. If we wish to follow the law, our task is to find out what they did; never mind what morality would have had them do. Law is one thing, morality is another.

Contentious as this strict separationist view may be in some quarters, it nevertheless infiltrates almost everyone's thought about what it means to find and follow the law. But *making* the law is something else entirely. Among those who hold that it lies within the capacity of lawmakers to disregard morality in making law, only all-out skeptics or nihilists about morality will deny that it equally lies within their capacity to take morality into account. Suppose we set aside all-out moral skepticism or nihilism. Questions then remain about possible inferential flows from the lawmaker's beliefs about the applicable moral considerations to the lawmaker's conclusions regarding what the law is to be, or conversely (the point I am driving toward), from beliefs about the existing state of legal affairs to conclusions regarding morally required or permitted courses of action, given the legal facts. Retaining the view that law is one thing and morality another, we can still believe that a known truth about the one can have a bearing on what we ought to decide or conclude about the other.

At least that is so when the one is morality and the other is law. Pondering inferential flows between morality and law, we tend to make morality the polestar, the unguided guide. Morality is what it is, requires what it requires, and the question is whether law and legal practice will shape up accordingly. No doubt that question – of shaping law to fit morality – can be quite controversial, depending on how it is framed. Only total skeptics about morality could deny that legal officials ought to act in their official capacities as morality would have them do. But even the stoutest moral true believer may deny that morality requires or even permits judicial officials to strive to make the law be moral (as opposed to taking the law as they find it), and indeed can even join those who say similarly for other branches of government – that their job is to further the national interest, or perhaps that they will best serve the public if they simply follow the dictates of personal self-interest (keeping within the lawful ambits of their offices). But still that usually is the general form of the question – whether and how law might follow from morality, not how morality might follow from law.

Are the positions ever reversed? Do moral conclusions ever flow from legal givens, so that law comes first and morality follows? Do states of law ever figure as contingencies on which moral conclusions turn, so that you don't know what morality requires until you know the state of legal affairs? That is my question.

Of course the answer is bound to be yes in any society in which law is capable of serving as a guide to social coordination for mutual gain. In such a society, law's arbitrary choice for driving on the left will be a decisive datum for the driver's moral code. But that is a trivial point. Here we consider a more intriguing way in which moral conclusions might turn on legal contingencies. Prior legal-institutional facts might serve as a sustaining cause for belief in a certain non–self-evident moral conclusion, which conclusion is directed to the moral criticism of law itself (to distinguish these cases from the trivial, side-of-the-road sort of case).

Consider the case of rights, and particularly socioeconomic rights. Both in morals and in law, rights are warrants for demands. To attribute to someone a right to *X* – where *X* is an act or state of affairs falling under a certain description – is to imbue that person with a warrant of some kind, moral or legal, for demanding *X*. Thus, the expression "socioeconomic rights" apparently envisions demands for a certain class of social outcomes pertaining to the right holders – as a first approximation, that the holders should at no time lack access to levels deemed adequate of subsistence, housing, health and health care, education, and safety, or to the means of providing the same (e.g., through available, remunerated work) for themselves and their dependents. These are demands, then, that some agent or agents shall so exert themselves that the targets are as likely as possible to be hit.

Never mind how many questions I have just begged. With one important exception – that being the question of which agents bear what duties correlative to socioeconomic rights – they are all collateral to the claim I now advance, to wit: the least controversial, most widely appealing case in morality for giving legal force to socioeconomic rights – say, by including socioeconomic guarantees in a constitutional bill of rights – is one that abstains from claims about moral rights and obligations as they might arise in conditions of no law or in a state of nature. In this respect, socioeconomic rights appear to differ from legal rights protecting against assault, theft, and the like. Debates over the morally proper scope of such garden-variety legal rights typically reach back to prelegal, moral rights and obligations as the source of a demand upon lawmakers to do the correspondingly right thing. The least controversial moral case for installing socioeconomic rights in a country's laws – what I shall later call the "political" case – does not proceed in that way. It rather starts from the historical contingency that law exists in the country. It makes that fact a premise in the argument, thus bypassing speculation about moral duties to aid under prelegal conditions. One might think here of Ronald Dworkin's (1977: 93) well-known model of "background" (moral) rights as a motivating source for "institutional" (legal) rights. Some such background rights, I mean to point out, may be found to depend for their existence on a prior institutional fact, a fact of legal ordering in that country, and so would not arise at all in prelegal nature.

Suppose it is somewhere (as in sec. 26[1] of the Constitution of South Africa) declared that "everyone has the right to have access to adequate housing." Those are vague terms, but assume that defensible answers to questionable cases can be extracted from them, so that the declaration specifies completely the scope of the right whose existence it posits. The declaration might posit the existence of either a moral right or a legal right. If it posits a legal right, then it most probably (for reasons we shall glimpse) intends a constitutional-legal right, an imposition by constitutional lawmakers on a country's ordinary lawmakers of a continuing legal obligation to see to the actual, effective implementation of the right. We easily understand the distinction between moral and legal rights. Moral rights refer to demands that hold regardless of what any law may have to say. Legal rights refer to demands warranted by positive law – demands whose nonfulfillment will thus presumably attract at least the condemnatory judgments of legal officials and also, in what we may regard as the normal case, will beget some sort of remedial intervention by a court of law. On this view, there can perfectly possibly be a moral right to housing but no legal right to it – in which case the law may seem to be at least prima facie morally deficient. Conversely, there can be a legal right, even a constitutional-legal right, to housing but no moral right to it (aside from any general moral duty there may be to comply with the law) – in which case the law establishing the legal right is either morally optional or, as some libertarians would have it, morally faulty. At any rate, either sort of right, moral or legal, can be found to exist or not without any finding or implication that the other sort exists or not.

That is all at the analytical level of probing for the right's existence, in morals or in law. On a prescriptive level, the separation seems not to be so clean and the two sorts of rights propositions seem no longer to stand on an equal footing. The existence or nonexistence of a legal right to housing is commonly thought to tell us nothing – certainly nothing conclusive – about whether a moral right to housing lies in the background. (The law, we commonly think, can be morally off base.) But the converse does not hold, for it seems that to posit a moral right to housing is tantamount to declaring that there ought to be a legal right to housing, at least presumptively to the point at which morally weighty justification is required for the absence of the legal right. Recognition of the moral right's existence implies a prima facie justified demand for the right's installation in law, but there is no converse inference from the existence of the legal right to a justified demand for the moral right's recognition. (The very fact that some particular lawmakers have seen fit to establish the right in law might figure for some as probative testimony to the moral right's existence – why otherwise would they do it? – but that would be controversial and anyway is a different question.) Thus, on the prescriptive level, the moral right dominates or leads the constitutional-legal right; the moral right comes first and the legal right follows.

Such is the intuitive common view, and it suffuses advocacy on behalf of constitutional-legal establishment of socioeconomic rights. For how, in fact, do we typically advocate for such establishment or defend the idea against criticism? We start, and feel we must start, by making the moral case for socioeconomic assurances. If the moral case fails, we feel, the case for constitutional-legal establishment fails a fortiori, because there are widely conceded, special institutional worries – about overextension of the judiciary and undue encroachment on democratic self-government – that attend upon the recognition of a constitutional-legal right to, say, housing that simply do not pertain to recognition of a moral right to housing. The moral case for recognition can provide a platform for public complaint against a sitting government's failure to fulfill the right it vindicates without raising the institutional worries attendant upon a constitutional-legal right.

I think this view is basically correct. It hews to an important sense in which the priority of morality to law stands beyond any possible doubt – that being the same as the sense in which law but not morality is a politically decidable matter. The existence or not of a constitutional-legal right to this or that is a question for some law-making process to resolve; if the process answers no, then no it is. (Thus, Ronald Dworkin [1996: 36] denies that American constitutional law as it stands contains socioeconomic guarantees while "wishing" for moral reasons that it did.) Moral rights, by contrast, are what they are regardless of what any person, body, or political process may say or do about them. No constitutional or other law-making process – no political decision – can decree away a moral right that otherwise would exist.

Is that correct? No doubt moral rights can be contingent on political choices – indeed, I aim here to show how a moral right to socioeconomic assurances might be thought contingent on a prior political choice for legal ordering – but the point here is that moral rights are not freely decidable by political choices. Any moral right against infringement of a registered, proprietary patent must be contingent on prior legislative enactment of a proprietary patent registration system. Regardless of whatever background moral obligation there might be to enact such a system into law, it is plain that without the actuality of such an enactment there can be no registered patents and hence no rights against infringements of them. A right to legislation of a patent system is one thing, a right against infringement of a patent is another thing, and it would be a bad mistake to confuse the two in practice – say, by ostracizing someone for patent infringement where no system of patent registration exists.[1] Once given the enactment of such a system, however, the possible attachment to patents registered under it of a general, background

[1] I claim nothing either way about the existence of a general, preinstitutional moral duty to refrain from nonpermitted copying of your neighbor's techniques. That moral question plainly is distinct from the one about a general, postinstitutional moral duty to respect a registered patent as property. One can answer no to the first question but yes to the second. I say simply that you can't convict a person of the latter sort of immorality in the absence of an institutionalized patent system.

moral duty to respect property rights is no longer a matter of political choice or decision. Lawmakers cannot control the moral consequences of the legislative choices they make – except, of course, by modifying those choices. Morality is in that way prior to law.

I raise here no question about that way of thinking. What I do wish to block is any thought that the moral issues surrounding socioeconomic rights are necessarily prior to law in the sense that the moral issues would or could exist in the form they do were certain legal-institutional contingencies not as they are. I want to show that indeed, in this instance, in the sight of many, law precedes morality in the sense that in the absence of law – of legal ordering, of a legal system – what otherwise would figure as a decisive moral case for socioeconomic assurances would be greatly weakened, if it would not collapse altogether. What many will find to be the decisive moral argument for establishing socioeconomic rights in the law is immediately anchored, not in some morality-prior-to-law, but in what we might call, in a bit of a twist on Lon Fuller, the morality *of law*. The case I have in mind takes as given the main, contingent facts of legal ordering in our societies and goes on from there. In saying this, I do not mean just that there (obviously) is no point, in law's absence, in building a moral case for recognition of some right in the law. I mean that contingencies of legal ordering serve as a premise, or call it a sustaining cause for belief, in a certain argument for a moral right to housing, from which the case for instigation of a legal right is then supposed to depend.

Application of the line of thought I have in mind is not necessarily limited to socioeconomic rights; it may be extended also to so-called first-generation or garden-variety legal rights. It is, however, not nearly so crucial to the defense of latter as of the former.

Take a first-generation right, the existence and extent of which, as a legal right, is currently contested in various countries: a right to be secure in one's home and other off-public sites against journalistic and other privately conducted electronic and photographic snooping. We have no trouble conceiving how this might exist as a moral right without existing as a legal right. The case, then, would simply be that everyone stands under a correlative moral duty to refrain from spying on others in their homes, regardless of whether violations beget any legal-institutional response. If the law is in fact nonresponsive, we may judge it to be morally out of whack for that reason, but the law's default would be no impeachment of the moral standard by which we judged it faulty.

Nor, accordingly, would the total absence of a legal system be any impeachment of the existence of moral rights tout court or of the personal moral duties correlative to them. In the absence of a legal system, everyone might stand under a moral duty to collaborate actively in the establishment of a morally suitable one – Kant (1999: 114–15, sec. 42) thinks so – but failure in the prosecution of any such morally mandated joint venture would not release anyone from whatever personal moral duty there may be not to spy on others in their homes. (Compare the effect of absence of a patent registration law on personal duties not to infringe patents.) People can have homes in the absence of a legal system, just as they can and do have bodies (but not patents). Moral rights against unprovoked physical assault do not lapse in the notional absence of a legal system, nor do the moral duties correlative to such rights, and neither would the duties correlative to moral rights (if there are such moral rights) against being spied on in one's home. As a general proposition, the existence of a legal system seems not to be a sustaining cause for anyone's belief in the existence of moral duties correlative to those moral rights that correspond to garden-variety legal rights – or, hence, for belief in the existence of those moral rights.

Does the same hold for rights to housing or other socioeconomic rights? There is at least some reason to conclude that it does not. A key question here is, Which agents bear what duties correlative to such rights? To say that everyone has a moral right to have access to housing is to say that some agent or class of agents stands under obligation to try (at least) to see that everyone does have it, or that the obligation is shared out in some away among agents or agent classes. Now, it would be extremely morally contentious to attribute the entire load of obligation to any or every individual person. It is one thing to debate whether you or I stand under a moral duty to take in overnight in subzero weather the homeless person who fetches up at our doorstep. It is a very different and hugely more contentious thing to suggest that you or I stand under a moral duty to sell everything we have, and mortgage everything we may ever have, to have every poor person housed, especially when others who could are not helping out at all.

Charles Fried (1978: 118–31) and, more recently and elaborately, Liam Murphy (2000) have shown convincingly this difference in contentiousness. They have not, however, as some libertarians do, gone on to conclude that there can be no moral right to housing, or any individual moral duties pertaining to such a right. There happens to exist among us an agent – the government – capable of imposing a fair and workable distribution among citizens of the burdens connected to fulfillment of the right. It is not bizarre to claim that the government is morally bound to do just that, or that citizens are morally bound to press it to do so and to pay unresistingly the taxes required for fulfillment of the government's obligation. I suggested previously that any legal right to housing would likely be a public law or constitutional-legal right, and now we see one of the reasons why. And of course the duties and duty-bound agents incident to a public law right to housing are all creatures of law and legal contingency: the state, its citizens, its programs, taxes, taxpayers – all of them creatures of law, inconceivable in law's absence. If so, then to speak of a moral right to housing where there is no law is an order of magnitude more contentious than to speak of a moral right not to be assaulted or spied upon where there is no law. Arranging for a fair distribution of correlative burdens seems not to be a troublesome issue with the latter sort of rights, as it is with socioeconomic rights (Murphy 2000: 74–5, 94–7). That is one way in which the notional absence of a legal system can seriously impede the moral case for socioeconomic rights: if no law, then no government on which plausibly to place a duty correlative to such rights or through which to seek and ensure a fair sharing by everyone of the attendant burdens.

Some maintain that everyone stands morally liable for his or her fair share, regardless of what others may do (Murphy, 2000). If that is the correct moral position (a question we need not here engage), then the need for government and law to ground a background moral right to housing, which can serve to motivate installation of such a right into law, to that extent falls away. That position, however, seems destined for controversy that will not soon abate. The day seems distant when nearly everyone will stand convinced that they carry any share at all of a state-of-nature obligation of aid to distant strangers whose needs they have not proximately and culpably caused. How do might one answer those who doubt? There seems at least a chance of doing so effectively by presenting a political-moral case for inclusion of socioeconomic guarantees in our country's constitutional law – a case adducing facts of social cooperation in the form of legal ordering, and the demands for general compliance with the laws that a legally ordered society directs to everyone in sight. This political case seems much likelier to persuade doubters than to offend or repel those who stand already convinced without it. That is why I call it the least controversial, most widely appealing case available for including socioeconomic rights in constitutional law, where of course their fulfillment will, as intended, burden taxpayers at large.

All legal systems are, at bottom, practices of social cooperation, dependent for survival on the persistence in society of general compliance with the laws and legal interpretations that issue from the practice. They thus all present the question of political justification or legitimacy, the need to supply a moral warrant for demands for general compliance with laws produced by nonconsensual means, directed against individual members of a population of presumptively free and equal people. In the political-liberal formulation of John Rawls (1996: 137, 217), political imposition of this legalistic sort is justified when it is aimed at support of laws issuing from a constitutional regime that everyone who is both rationally self-interested and socially reasonable may be expected to endorse. To meet the test of rational acceptability to every reasonable person, a law-making system has to include a principle or guarantee affecting every topic for which a rational person, responding reasonably, would demand a guarantee as a condition of willing support for the system as a whole. It may well seem that we cannot reasonably call on everyone, as reasonable but also as rational, to submit their fates to the tender mercies of a democratic-majoritarian law-making system without also committing our society, from the start, to run itself in ways designed to constitute and sustain every person as a competent and respected contributor to political exchange and contestation and furthermore to social and economic life at large. And that quite arguably means that social rights guarantees of some kind must compose an essential part of the constitutional law of any country committed to a broadly speaking liberal political morality.

That has been an extremely abbreviated summation of how a Rawlsian political-moral case (as we may call it) would go. This moral case may possibly be decisive for many who otherwise would stand outside the fold of those who see some compelling moral reason to establish socioeconomic rights in constitutional law. Nor does acceptance of the case drive out of the fold anyone who stands already convinced without it. (Acceptance need not commit anyone to the view that morally warranted concern for the needs of others flows "entirely" from "concerns with legitimate governance" [Murphy, 1998: 273, 277]). The political-moral case thus stands as an example of how a philosophically excogitated, background moral right, understood to prescribe for law still to be determined, can itself depend on prior determinations of law. But even regarding that modest suggestion, we need to be careful.

If we are disposed to affirm the existence, wherever there is legal ordering, of individual duties to support socioeconomic guarantees in constitutional law, and if we also are disposed to accept Kant's claim of the existence at all times of moral duties on everyone to support and sustain systems of legal ordering, then we cannot deny the existence in prelegal nature of a background moral duty respecting socioeconomic guarantees. For we then would be conceding the existence in nature of a moral duty to do a thing (collaborate in establishing and sustaining a legal order), the doing of which either triggers or strongly reinforces moral duties respecting socioeconomic guarantees. It nevertheless remains true that the political-moral case for including socioeconomic rights in constitutional law depends on supposed prior facts of legal ordering, in a way that the moral case for garden-variety legal rights is not usually thought to do.

Just as no right against patent infringement can arise so long as the putative moral duty to enact a patent system into law remains unperformed, so the political-moral argument for the legal establishment of socioeconomic rights takes wing only if and where the putative moral duty to maintain a legal system is actually performed. More to the point, the political-moral argument is not dependent on the existence of any moral duty of the latter kind. The conclusion applies to us as long as we engage actively in sustaining a legal order, whether or not we are morally obliged to do so. In fact, it applies to us even if, on some superanarchist view, our engagement in legal ordering is against the dictates of morality – granting that the application would then be a conclusion from moral theorizing under nonideal conditions.

WORKS CITED

Dworkin, Ronald. *Freedom's Law.* Cambridge, MA: Harvard Univ. Press, 1996.

———. *Taking Rights Seriously.* Cambridge, MA: Harvard Univ. Press, 1977.

Fried, Charles. *Right and Wrong.* Cambridge, MA: Harvard Univ. Press, 1978.

Kant, Immanuel. *The Metaphysical Elements of Justice*, 2d ed. Trans. John Ladd. 1797. Reprint, Indianapolis: Hackett, 1999.

Murphy, Liam. "Institutions and the Demands of Justice." *Philosophy and Public Affairs* 27.4 (1998): 251–91.

———. *Moral Demands in Ideal Theory.* Oxford: Oxford Univ. Press, 2000.

Rawls, John. *Political Liberalism.* New York: Columbia Univ. Press, 1996 (paper ed.).

19 Doing Justice to Justice: Paul Ricoeur

DAVID H. FISHER

What has law's justice to do with revenge, or revenge justice with law? Traditional readings of Aeschylus's *Oresteia* see the trilogy as marking the early triumph of the rule of law over revenge-driven violence personified as Furies (*Erinyes*). Thanks to the persuasive wisdom of Athena in establishing the first dicastic court, these savage beings are transformed into Eumenides – "kindly ones" – and installed in a place of honor beneath the Areopagus from whence they will serve as guardians of *dike* (justice). A closer reading suggests another darker possibility: that revenge violence continues to reside at the heart of the very institution that claims to have tamed it. In Athens, litigants often used the court system as a means to continue blood feuds (Cohen 1995). And through the ages law has been used as an instrument of torment, as demonstrated by Shylock's effort in the *Merchant of Venice* to use civil law against Antonio's flesh to right his shame suffered at the hands and mouth of Antonio. The Furies, far from being tamed or banished, continue to reside at the heart of law. For Paul Ricoeur, these archaic symbols of revenge violence give rise to his thinking about justice that bears fruit in his final works.

Ricoeur (1992: 197) suggests that the "*just* faces in two directions: towards the *good*, with respect to which it marks the extension of interpersonal relationships to institutions; and toward the *legal*, the judicial system conferring upon the law coherence and the right of constraint." Before law there are the Furies:

> The furies are at home
> in the mirror; it is their address.
> Even the clearest water,
> if deep enough can drown.
>
> Never think to surprise them.
> Your face approaching ever
> so friendly is the white flag
> they ignore. There is no truce
>
> with the furies. A mirror's temperature
> is always at zero. It is ice
> in the veins. Its camera
> is an X-ray. It is a chalice

held out to you in
silent communion, where gaspingly
you partake of a shifting
identity never your own.
(Thomas 1995: 31)

Ricoeur knows that "there is no truce with the Furies"; those archaic representations of binary opposition demanding blood for blood. Law's understanding of their claims, in the search for a "state of peace,"[1] requires establishing the agon of a trial, a space of discourse governed by formal norms and procedures that creates the necessary but not sufficient condition for justice: "just distance" between violence undergone and desires for revenge.

In his preface to *The Just*, Ricoeur (2000: ix) states that he has "undertaken, over the past few years, to do justice to the question of right and law, to do justice to justice." Given oppositions in legal theory between natural law and variants of postpositivism such as law and economics, critical legal studies, or feminist jurisprudence,[2] Ricoeur's late work on justice opens up "unthought possibilities for the telling of law and saying of justice" (Constable 2005: 178). His voice is informed by appreciation of differences between Continental and analytic approaches to philosophy and between Continental and Anglo-American understandings of law, and his analysis of links among violence, vengeance, and justice at the origins of law suggests a way to deal with the Furies. His discussion of preunderstandings embedded in Rawls's procedural conception of justice (and Habermas's discourse ethics) further shows the need to ground deontological norms in a combination of teleological desire and wisdom informed by tragedy and the work of memory.

Ricoeur depicts law's origins as a social response to desires for retaliation following unwarranted violence, desires that, if not checked, lead to interminable cycles of revenge. This point of departure invites critical comparison with Derrida's (1992) reading of law's violence. But where Derrida sees the deconstruction of binaries into aporia as justice, for Ricoeur (1992: 352) the ethical premise of law as an institution is recognition of "oneself as being enjoined to live well with and for others in just institutions." If just institutions provide a possibility for life together, law's promise allows more: the possibility of recognition of fault followed by rehabilitation, restoration to civic life for the condemned (Ricoeur 2000: 133–45), and perhaps – beyond justice – for forgiveness capable of "unbinding the agent from the act," a restoration of the capacity for acting.[3] Pardon cannot be substituted for

[1] Ricoeur (2005: 219–25) describes characteristics of a "state of peace" in relation to models based on *philia*, *eros*, and *agape*, asking whether we "can build a bridge between the poetics of agape and the prose of justice, between the hymn and the formal rule?" (224). His response develops in a discussion of gift similar to Derrida's discussion of gift in *The Gift of Death* and elsewhere.

[2] As well as binary oppositions in the social imaginary of the contemporary public sphere.

[3] Ricoeur (2004: 474) does not adopt a naive or idealistic view of the law: "While one of the functions of the trial is to substitute discourse for violence, it is a fact that everyone does not have the same access to the arms of discussion. There are those who are excluded from speech, who, dragged before the courts . . . can view their appearance in court as one more instance of what they experience on a daily basis as institutional violence."

justice, but this "unbinding would mark the inscription, in the field of horizontal disparity between power and act, of the vertical disparity between the great height of forgiveness and the abyss of guilt" (Ricoeur 2004: 490).

In *Reflections on the Just* Ricoeur states that, having focused on the relation between justice as a moral rule and as an institution in *The Just*, he now sees "the just" as the connecting thread running through his entire later work. The just – *to dikaion* – should be seen "in terms of two different relations: a horizontal relation having to do with the threefold relation of the self, neighbors, and others, and a vertical relation having to do with the hierarchical model of the good, the obligatory and the fitting" (Ricoeur 2007: 5).

Ricoeur's work on justice is a continuation of his ethics. In *Oneself as Another*, he argues for the priority of ethics over morality (i.e., for the priority of Aristotle's ethical aim to live well over a Kantian ethic of obligation), for the necessity of passing the ethical aim through the sieve of the moral norm, and finally for the legitimacy of moving from the norm to the aim when conflicts arise in practice (i.e., *phronesis* in both Gadamerian and Aristotelian senses). Primary capacities required to achieve the aim of living well – the capacities to speak, to act, to narrate, and to impute – are potentials developed in care with and for others. Conditions for care ("solicitude") find their formal expression in moral norms of obligation.[4] Moral norms sometimes conflict, causing "impasses in practice," as a result of the one-sidedness of moral principles confronted with complexity. "In the conflicts to which morality gives rise, only recourse to the ethical ground against which morality stands out can give rise [in turn] to the wisdom of judgment in situation. From tragic *phronein* to practical *phronesis*" (Ricoeur 1992: 249).

Ricoeur (1998: 120) begins his account of justice giving priority to a sense of injustice: "in Plato and in Aristotle the word *adikos* (unjust) always comes before the work *dikaïosunè* (justice): perhaps that is indeed the way we initially enter into the problem of justice, through the feeling of injustice, for the feeling that there are unjust and apportionments." "The just" is first of all an object of desire, of a lack, of a wish (Ricoeur 2000: xv); a wish to retaliate with violence against unjust violation and achieve the "satisfaction" of revenge.[5] "The sense of injustice," he claims, "is not simply more poignant but more perspicacious than the sense of justice.... [P]eople have a clearer vision of what is missing in human relations that of the right way to organize them" (Ricoeur 1992: 198).

It is impossible to do justice to Ricoeur's final reflections on forgiveness and justice here. Instead, I focus on his understanding of relationships among violence, vengeance, and justice, and then on his response to Rawls's contractualist procedure with a "deontology without a transcendental foundation" (Ricoeur 2000: 39), to illustrate some of the possibilities in Ricoeur's thinking on justice, ethics, and law.

[4] This raises a political and legal question: "how, in a democratic society, we can connect the horizontal axis of wanting to live together with the vertical axis that Weber calls the axis of domination[?]" (Ricoeur 2007: 22).

[5] Although as William Ian Miller (2006: 157) remarks, "If there were a perfect satisfaction, we expect that it would put an end to matters. But we do not even know how to envisage perfection: what our anger wants may not be what our hate wants."

BEGINNING WITH INJUSTICE: VIOLENCE, VENGEANCE, AND JUSTICE

"At bottom justice is opposed not just to violence per se . . . but to that simulation of justice constituted by vengeance, the act of procuring justice by oneself" (Ricoeur 2000: 131). Violence includes the initial wrongdoing that provokes indignation, the state monopoly on violence that attempts to channel desires for vengeance, and "the resurgence of vengeance at the heart of exercising of the act of justice. The sentence makes someone suffer. It adds suffering to suffering, and thus places the stamp of violence on a speech act that claims to state the law" (Ricoeur 2007: 38). What initial indignation in the face of injustice lacks is distance between the protagonists. If endless chains of vengeance are to be halted, a "just distance" must be constructed between claim and counterclaim. This requires "mediation of an institution capable of incarnating the third person," armed with coercive powers moderated by establishment of a corpus of written law (Ricoeur 2007: xx).[6]

Ricoeur (2007: 227–8) insists that lawfulness arises from indignant responses to injustice. The origin of legal justice is an affirmation of the respect owed to persons: "*legality* appears to sum up the moral vision of the world," and "the principle legacy of ethics to morality lies in the very idea of the *just,* which looks both ways: in the direction of the 'good' as the extension of solicitude to 'each one' of the faceless members of society; and in the direction of the 'legal,' to such a degree does the prestige of justice appear to dissolve into that of positive law."[7]

A basic premise of Ricoeur's search for reflective equilibrium between a sense of injustice and resolution of conflict in specific situations is respect, described as self-esteem filtered through moral norm. He draws on Thomas Nagel's (1991) argument that every life counts and none is more important than any other (Ricoeur 2000: 150; 2007: 66–7). Respect, as understood by Ricoeur (2007: 83), is based on the paradox of autonomy as both a presupposition and a goal to attain, as "a condition of possibility and a task." Respect is directed toward a capable human being – and Ricoeur juxtaposes human capacities with vulnerabilities. Capacities include the ability to speak, to act, to "gather one's own life into an intelligible narrative," and the *imputation* – the capacity to "answer *for* my acts . . . to be taken as having been their actual author" (Ricoeur 2007: 82). Vulnerabilities include an inability to speak (both speech defects and lack of voice in a public forum); a lack of narrative identity or singularity of personal identity; and a lack of connection with a symbolic order, which is the "very site of the strongest connection between

[6] While expressing agreement with Kant and Hegel that "sanction restores the law" and that "pardon cannot be substituted for justice" (Ricoeur 2000: 137; 2004: 473), in his final works Ricoeur (2005: 220) discusses the limitations on the closure that can be achieved through juridical processes: "Justice does not exhaust the question of putting an end to the dispute begun by violence and reopened by vengeance. . . . If ending the dispute is the first criterion for a state of peace, justice fails the test." This perspective leads to extended reflection on collective violence, its impact in cultural memory, and the possibility of "unbinding the agent from his act" in a context shaped by memory and mourning.

[7] Beginning with a sense of injustice rather than a normal model of justice is a point of departure shared with Judith Shklar (1990: 47, 87), who argues that "[n]o theory of either justice or injustice can be complete if it does not take account of the subjective sense of injustice and the sentiments that make us cry out for revenge, and that "[t]o have no idea of what it means to be treated unjustly is to have no more knowledge, no moral life."

self and norm" (Ricoeur 2007: 85). Law's role, in relation to these capacities and vulnerabilities, involves the role of a third person in "holding at a distance . . . the facts in the case to be judged" and a "just distance between the victim and the offender" (Ricoeur 2007: 89).

To appreciate the nuances of Ricoeur's understanding of capacity-based respect, it may be helpful to consider Peter French's defense of "virtues of vengeance." French rejects the premise of equal moral worth as well as the ideal of distance between violence suffered and retaliation in return. "People have unequal moral merit and thereby unequal moral worth. The virtues of vengeance are founded in that inequality. . . . [T]here is an unbridgeable moral chasm between people who regularly do wicked deeds and those who typically do good deeds. . . . People who do evil . . . from the moral point of view should be targeted for penalties that are painful to them" (French 2001: 89, 187). French finds unpersuasive "the notion that concern about spiraling cycles of vengeance provoked the impersonal institutionalization of punishment[,] . . . the greater fear would have been of all sorts of wrongdoers practicing their transgressions with impunity due to the economic rationality and cowardice of the general populace" (110). French's views are similar to more broadly instrumental ideas of law as a tool to be used to achieve whatever ends are sought. "Instrumentalism . . . entails only means-ends reasoning. Once an end has been decided upon, law can be used in any way possible to advance the designated end, without limit. . . . The legitimacy of law then rides on the rightness of the end the law is utilized to advance. . . . The 'torture memo' offers a supreme example" (Tamanaha 2006: 219).

Ricoeur would disagree with French's empirical claims about the social costs and benefits of revenge, his normative claims about unequal worth, and the more general instrumentalist notion of law as a normless tool. Ricoeur's position reflects cultural difference as well as difference in anthropology. Where French assumes a typically American, individualistic account of identity based on a combination of Locke, Machiavelli, and Nozick, and some contemporary legal instrumentalists assume a Schmittian understanding of the political as a space conflict between friend and enemy, Ricoeur (1998: 52–62; 2005: 212–16) argues throughout his work for an intersubjective, interactive understanding of personal identity with strong affinities to the work of Charles Taylor and Axel Honneth (see Honneth 1996; Taylor 1989, 1994).

Contrasting Ricoeur's view with "virtues of vengeance" and instrumentalist perspectives on law underlines the impact of his early work on Freud's death drive (Ricoeur 1970), of his subsequent working through of the "Hegelian temptation" (Ricoeur 1988: 202–6; 1991: 200–4), and points toward in his final exploration of too much and too little memory in *Memory, History, Forgetting* (Ricoeur 2004). In that work he demonstrates the long-term social, political, and cultural costs of satisfying desires for revenge. Such desires are fostered by a manipulated memory of historical events, turning the events remembered into symbolic wounds. These wounds then become sites within cultural memory for a compulsion to repeat cycles of revenge. Advocates of revenge believe their wounds can be healed only by ensuring that the wrongdoer suffers an equivalent or greater amount of pain, while advocates of law as a normless tool for advancing goals believe reconciliation to be an impossible fantasy. But there is never enough pain given to erase traumatized memory – and rejecting the possibility of reconciliation licenses acts of cruelty and rage that can only initiate new cycles of revenge.

Against the background of an intersubjective anthropology of human capacities and the burdens of unresolved cultural legacies, Ricoeur (2000: 139) insists that legal "sanction will have reached its goal . . . only if the penalty is, if not accepted, at least understood by the one who undergoes it. . . . If sanction must have a future . . . must it not be that . . . the accused knows himself to be recognized at least as a reasonable, responsible being, that is, as the author of his acts?" While the procedural rules of the trial process "constitute an advance in justice over the spirit of vengeance . . . the punishment as a type of penalty opens the way to the spirit of vengeance, in spite of the fact that it came about through . . . trial process, because the trial process in no way completely suppressed or abolished the spirit of vengeance" (Ricoeur 2007: 229).

ARISTOTLE AVEC KANT: RICOEUR ON RAWLS

The range of alternatives for law's legitimacy in the post–World War II environment – positivism, realism, utilitarianism, and natural law – were among the stimuli for John Rawls's development of a contractarian version of deontology. Ricoeur's (2000: 37) primary questions for Rawls are whether a deontological approach to moral philosophy can be logically joined with a purely contractualist procedure, and whether contractualism can "substitute a procedural approach for every attempt to ground justice on some prior convictions concerning the good?" His response is based on a combination of Aristotelian *phronesis* and an understanding of judgment shaped by Kant's *Critique of Judgment*. While Ricoeur (2000: 39) agrees with Rawls' rejection of utilitarianism's "sacrificial principle that is equivalent to legitimating the strategy of the scapegoat," he argues that Rawls's *A Theory of Justice* constitutes an indirect plea for an ethical foundation for the concept of justice" (38). Rawls' entire effort, according to Ricoeur, "turns on the demonstration that, for the utilitarian hypothesis, the one holding the least favored position is a sacrificial victim, whereas the conception of justice he [Rawls] defends is the only one to make this person [the victim] an equal partner" (49).

Ricoeur's (2000: 50) claim is that Rawls' procedural conception of justice "at best provides a rationalization of a sense of justice that is always presupposed." The order that prevails through *A Theory of Justice* is circular, not lexical, and Rawls's procedural definition of justice does not constitute an independent theory but "rests on the preunderstanding that allows us to define and interpret the two principles of justice" (51). Rawls's "considered convictions" sums up this preunderstanding, which includes an understanding of injustice based on equality. Reviewing Rawls's modification of his position following *A Theory of Justice*, Ricoeur claims that while Rawls's subsequent attempt to ensure stability in circumstances of pluralism is more aware of the contingent historical and sociological backgrounds than is his earlier work, he still requires a preunderstanding of people as free and equal sufficient to support the notion of an overlapping consensus, a notion that is Rawls's not-entirely-satisfactory answer to "the problematic of domination which, in continental Europe at least, has largely occupied the scene of political philosophy from Hegel to Max Weber and Carl Schmitt" (Ricoeur 2000: 74).

Ricoeur (2007: 232) does not dismiss the search for universal principles, but it is an open question "whether we can formulate on the ethical juridical, and social planes universal principles that are valid independently of persons, communities, and cultures which are able to apply them, without any limitation having to do with the particular circumstances of their application." Ricoeur's answer is a guarded yes.

The aim to live well with and for others in just institutions begins with face-to-face reciprocity, where solicitude is widely supported in many cultures. But my other is not just the person who appears to me through his or her face, but everyone defined through his or her social role. While it may be possible to take a generalized willingness to live together as a universal fact, "as soon as we qualify it by the wish for just institutions, we place ourselves at a level where the universal is inextricably intermingled with the contextual" (Ricoeur 2007: 235). Spaces for conflict in society exist, and conflict is often expressed in terms of violence and vengeance. While formal rules of procedure may limit the extent of violence, there are also limits to the ability of a Kantian – or neo-Kantian Rawlsian or Habermasian – attempt to legitimate these rules with norms of autonomy. These limits lead Ricoeur to the notion of practical wisdom: "Why add such a third dimension to ethics and morality? If it is the fact of conflict and more fundamentally the fact of violence that forces us to pass from an ethics of the good life to a morality of obligation and interdiction, it is what we can call the tragic aspect of action that leads us to complete these formal principles of a universal ethics by rules of application concerning historical-cultural contexts" (242).

As example of tragic action, Ricoeur (2007: 242) includes conflict of duties such as those in Sophocles' *Antigone* and cases in which the complexity of social relations multiply situations in which "a moral or legal rule enters into conflict with concern for the care of individual persons." Rawls is said to be incapable of dealing with tragic aspects of action: "It is above all in the juridical domain that the necessity of a properly creative application is required" (Ricoeur 2007: 246).

What is law's role in facilitating movement from desire to live well with others, through the sieve of moral norms, to just institutions where practical wisdom can determine conflict – and create possible conditions for states of peace? In our binary social and political world, a world imagined through the lens of Carl Schmitt's sterile concept of the political as conflict between friends and enemies – "feminazis" versus "Neanderthals", "radical Islamicist terrorists" versus "neoconservative Christian fundamentalists" – the terms of abuse are as endless as the imaginations that produce them are stupid and shallow.

Meditating on a century of lies and horror in Europe, Ricoeur understood all too well where the binary logic of Manichaean thinking leads: blindness, followed by killing fields and ovens. By temperament a mediating thinker, his alternative to the death drive's compulsion to repeat seeking vengeance – and to deconstruction's dissolutions of oppositions as justice – has some affinities with Heidegger's exposition of difference in *Identity and Difference* but is better characterized as a post-Hegelian movement toward reconciliation through recognition. *Gelassenheit* from false or manipulated memory was, for Ricoeur, reached only through a difficult process of memory, recognition, and the work of mourning that might, in turn, open onto possibilities of pardon, gift, and release. "A society cannot be continually angry with itself. . . . Poetry knows that the political rests on forgetting the unforgettable, 'that never formulated oxymoron'" (Ricoeur 2005: 501). So did Paul Ricoeur.

WORKS CITED

Cohen, David. *Law, Violence and Community in Classical Athens.* Cambridge: Cambridge Univ. Press, 1995.

Constable, Marianne. *Just Silences: The Limits and Possibilities of Modern Law.* Princeton, NJ: Princeton Univ. Press, 2005.

Derrida, Jacques. "Force of Law: The 'Mystical Foundation of Authority.'" In *Deconstruction and the Possibility of Justice.* Eds. Drucilla Cornell, Michel Rosenfeld, and David Gray Carlson. New York: Routledge, 1992: 3–67.

French, Peter. *The Virtues of Vengeance.* Lawrence: Univ. Press of Kansas, 2001.

Honneth, Axel. *The Struggle for Recognition: The Moral Grammar of Social Conflicts.* Cambridge, MA: MIT Press, 1996.

Miller, William Ian. *Eye for Eye.* Cambridge: Cambridge Univ. Press, 2006.

Nagel, Thomas. *Equality and Partiality.* New York: Oxford Univ. Press, 1991.

Rawls, John. *A Theory of Justice.* Cambridge, MA: Harvard Univ. Press, 1971.

Ricoeur, Paul. *The Course of Recognition.* Trans. David Pellauer. Cambridge, MA: Harvard Univ. Press, 2005.

———. *Critique and Conviction: Conversations with François Azouvi and Marc de Launay.* Trans. Kathleen Blamey. New York: Columbia Univ. Press, 1998.

———. *Freud and Philosophy: An Essay on Interpretation.* Trans. Denis Savage. New Haven, CT: Yale Univ. Press, 1970.

———. *From Text to Action: Essays in Hermeneutics II.* Trans. Kathleen Blamey and John B. Thompson. Evanston, IL: Northwestern Univ. Press, 1991.

———. *The Just.* Trans. David Pellauer. Chicago: Univ. of Chicago Press, 2000.

———. *Memory, History, Forgetting.* Trans. Kathleen Blamey and David Pellauer. Chicago: Univ. of Chicago Press, 2004.

———. *Oneself as Another.* Trans. Kathleen Blamey. Chicago: Univ. of Chicago Press, 1992.

———. *Reflections on the Just.* Trans. David Pellauer. Chicago: Univ. of Chicago Press, 2007.

———. *Time and Narrative*, 3 vols. Trans. Kathleen McLaughlin and David Pellauer. Chicago: Univ. of Chicago Press, 1983–8.

Shklar, Judith. *Faces of Injustice.* New Haven, CT: Yale Univ. Press, 1990.

Tamanaha, Brian Z. *Law as a Means to an End: Threat to the Rule of Law.* New York: Cambridge Univ. Press, 2006.

Taylor, Charles. "The Politics of Recognition." In *Multiculturalism: Examining the Politics of Recognition.* Ed. Amy Gutmann. Princeton, NJ: Princeton Univ. Press, 1994: 25–73.

———. *Sources of the Self: The Making of Modern Identity.* Cambridge, MA: Harvard Univ. Press, 1989.

Thomas R. S. *No Truce With The Furies.* Bloodaxe Books, Tarset 1995. © Kunjana Thomas 2001.

20 Love Is All You Need: Freedom of Thought versus Freedom of Action

EUGENE GARVER

Why should we give greater freedom to thought, speech, and expression than to actions? Speech can cause as much harm as action, and yet just because speech causes damage is not by itself a sufficient reason to prevent it. If I persuade large numbers of people that condoms don't work, and they then don't use them, I cause harm but would be guilty of no crime. If I infiltrate a condom factory and reset the machines so that the condoms' failure rate increases to match the claims that condoms don't work, I not only do harm but also can be prosecuted for the injuries I cause to others. Hume (1816: 48) refers to the "paradoxical principle and salutary practice of toleration"; I would like to strengthen the practice by making its principle appear as paradoxical as it should.[1]

A great deal of political and moral theory of the past three hundred years has been devoted to supplying new understandings of fundamental moral and political ideas once their original religious underpinnings are no longer credible. Thus Mill (1977, 217) begins *On Liberty* by distinguishing his subject, civil and political liberty, from "so-called 'freedom of the will.'" By his time, free will had become a metaphysical fiction no longer connected to sin, grace, and salvation, but it left in its train live, practical issues about civil and political freedom. The separation of power over thought and expression from power over actions originated in the battle for freedom of religious conscience. The philosophical issue facing law today is whether the distinction between thought and action, and the greater deference we extend to thought and speech as opposed to actions, is coherent independent of its religious origin.

If my salvation depends on my beliefs, and not on my actions, then my thoughts have an incomparable importance to me that makes state interference otiose. Once personal salvation drops out of the picture, though, many of my actions can be more important to me and more closely tied to my personal identity than any beliefs I might have: the "real" me is located in making money by driving competitors out of business, while religion is just a hobby. Given the choice, I would prefer to give

[1] Whether freedom of speech is identical to freedom of thought is a disputed question that I cannot consider in detail here. For purposes of this essay, I will assume, with Spinoza and Mill, that they are the same.

up religious freedom in exchange for keeping the freedom to defeat others through sharp business practices (see, e.g., Carter 1987).

Making the thought-action or speech-action distinction crucial means that in litigation everything turns on whether a given act is classified as speech or action, yet it is hard to say why that classification should matter so much once the religious sense of freedom of conscience disappears. Putting up tents across from the White House as an act of protest is allowed but as places to live they will be torn down. Disrupting traffic is a nuisance or a protest. Nude dancing either is a nuisance or expresses an idea, in which case it no longer counts as a nuisance (see, generally, Bollinger 2002). I want to see if there are good grounds for placing such a heavy reliance on this distinction between thinking and acting (Bollinger 1986: 10). Justifications that words don't wound – that speech has no effects on others, or that state coercion of opinion doesn't work, that the actions of others have no effects on speech – are not ultimately credible. The variety of attempts at justifying the First Amendment protection of freedom of speech presupposes a difference between freedom of thought and freedom of action. I want to ask why we treat thought and action so differently.

Take away the religious arguments for freedom of conscience, and it might seem that we can make a simple practical argument for freedom of thought. One might think that protecting freedom of thought leads to an increased scope for freedom of action, as Mill's single principle would have it. Therefore freedom of thought can be justified, not because thinking for oneself and saying what one thinks to others are themselves good things, but because they lead to the good thing of a greater realm of personal freedom of action. Unfortunately, that argument is too good to be true, and there are counterexamples that force us to do better. As Kant (1990: 85) puts it in *What Is Enlightenment?*: "[a]rgue as much as you want and about what you want, but obey!" Freedom of thought and speech is consistent with significant limitations on freedom of action. Indeed, in thinkers like Spinoza and Kant, protecting freedom of thought can lead to greater restrictions on freedom of action. "A lesser degree of civil freedom gives intellectual freedom enough room to expand to its fullest extent" (Kant 1990: 85).

SOCRATES ON THOUGHTS HARMING MORE THAN ACTIONS

Instead of trying to produce yet another justification for treating thoughts and actions differently, I want to use a Platonic example to highlight its puzzles. Plato lives in a world without a distinction between public and private, without any connection between freedom of thought and discussion and freedom of religion and conscience. If freedom of thought is a value in such a world, it certainly is not because of its connection to individual salvation. In the *Gorgias*, Plato turns upside down (481c) all the difficulties with freedom of thought and the thought-action distinction, and his arguments can serve as a thought experiment that help us see what is special about freedom of thought and expression. Callicles warns Socrates that his unworldly, naive behavior makes him easy prey to anyone who wants to master him, in law courts or elsewhere (484d–484e). Callicles thinks that Socrates' confession of vulnerability to assaults by others refutes his way of life. But Socrates outrageously claims that being tortured, jailed, exiled, or put to death cannot harm the good person (521b5–521b6, see *Apology* at 41d1). Only being corrupted can do harm, and the better you are, the harder it is for you to be corrupted. The better you are, the more you are invulnerable to harm. The only way anyone can be harmed is by being made worse, less virtuous, and more vicious. We can take the care of our souls seriously if we become indifferent to the cares of the body, to wealth, reputation, and personal security.

In a complete reversal of both his contemporaries and liberal democracy, Socrates maintains that only thoughts can cause harm, or good, and that we should be indifferent to others' actions, because they can't harm us. I can be harmed only by coming to have worse opinions, not by being impoverished or physically assaulted. Of course, Socrates says, it is a bad thing to be physically harmed by someone, but not as bad as doing the harming. It is less bad to be the victim of injustice than to commit it. Callicles is right that Socrates turns the moral world upside down. My initial question was why thought and expression should be more protected than actions. According to Socrates, thought and expression are more dangerous than action.

The first thing to notice about Socrates' thesis is that its practical consequences are ambiguous. The fact that only thoughts can do harm is not, Socrates argues in the *Apology*, a reason for the state to limit freedom of thought and discussion, but a reason to turn our attention and care from other people's actions to their opinions. If the unexamined life is not worth living, then each must have the freedom to examine his or her life for him- or herself. But that same fact that only thoughts can harm is the reason that the ideal state of the *Republic* takes opinions seriously enough that most of its laws concern education, and not the security of person and property that is central to other legal schemes. Just as people who make wealth central to people's lives can either infer that the state must keep its hands off of wealth-making activities, or that the state has a duty to regulate those activities, so making the truth of one's opinions central to life can either lead to freedom of thought or to its complete regulation.

The religious, and especially Protestant, origins of contemporary freedom of conscience have made the inference from thought's importance to its freedom smoother than it would otherwise be. Freedom of thought does not follow from the fact that only thoughts can harm, that only thoughts count. If the individual's thoughts and opinions are of ultimate value, it is equally possible to infer either to freedom or to complete control over thoughts to ensure that we all have the right ones. Plato draws both conclusions. Historically, both tolerance and imposed uniformity of belief followed from the thesis that one's faith is of ultimate importance.

Second, paradoxical as his thesis is, at least Socrates offers reasons why other people's actions cannot harm us, as the only true harm is making us worse, and no one else's actions can do that to us. We today have a harder time explaining why the thoughts and words of others shouldn't be subject to regulation, because they so obviously can do harm, and in ways that go beyond the obvious exceptions to freedom of speech such as fighting words or defamation. Because of this trouble, modern arguments about freedom of thought are divided into two incompatible lines of thought, first protecting free speech because conscience is so important to me, and second because my opinions and beliefs are so unimportant to you. That is the contemporary equivalent of Socrates' paradox. Today I care only about your actions, while you – at least according to the theory of the First Amendment – care most about your thoughts. I am indifferent to your thoughts, and so I can tolerate them. As Jefferson (1984: 285) put it, "It does me no harm for my neighbor to say that there are no gods or twenty gods; it neither picks my pocket nor breaks my leg." I don't protect freedom of speech because of its importance to him but because of its unimportance to me. Indifference has been the greatest historical force for freedom of thought. Indifference is the emotional counterpart to the skepticism that has also been a force in the cause of freedom.

But whenever freedom of thought is secure, it works to distinguish itself from skepticism and indifference. For good reason. Indifference can be insulting or a patronizing appreciation of the exotic. Thus the attitude of the Supreme Court toward the Old Order Amish in *Yoder* (1972). Indifference may be better than persecution, but once I've been left alone through indifference, I want more: I not only want to be able to speak but also want you to listen to me.[2] Therefore Socrates in the *Apology* rejects any outcome short of the citizens of Athens listening seriously to his questioning.

Therefore the great paradox of freedom of thought, a paradox that does not apply to freedom of action. Thoughts deserve protection both because of their supreme importance to me and because they are of no consequence to anyone else. Indifference answers only one question about freedom of thought. It justifies your allowing me to express divergent and disturbing ideas. But the argument from indifference says nothing about why I should want freedom of thought for myself, only why others shouldn't be bothered by it. It goes against a lot of evidence simply to postulate a universal desire for freedom of thought, even if everyone should reasonably be supposed to want to act as he or she likes.

Here, then, is a difference between thought and action. Kant (1990: 83) begins *What Is Enlightenment?* thus: "Enlightenment is man's emergence from his self-imposed immaturity. Immaturity is the inability to use one's understanding without guidance from another. This immaturity is self-imposed when its cause lies not in lack of understanding, but in lack of resolve and courage to use it without guidance from another." If I need to believe for myself in order for salvation, the need to think for myself is obvious. But take that need away, and it isn't clear why I shouldn't "have a book to serve as my understanding, a pastor to serve as my conscience, a physician to determine my diet for me." Why I should want freedom of action might be obvious, but why I should want freedom of thought and speech is not. Socrates frames his ideas paradoxically because not everyone sees freedom of belief and expression as valuable.

Indifference is correlative with the freedom to be left alone. But there is another side to the freedom of thought and discussion, for which indifference is not enough.

[2] Hence Mill argues in *On Liberty* not only that my thought and expression should be free from coercion but also that my freedom of thought is in everyone else's interest.

Such freedom is enough for the liberty of thought and discussion when conceived as a matter of self-development. This is negative and private freedom. But there is another side to the freedom of thought and discussion for which indifference is not enough. Freedom of thought and discussion, unlike freedom of action, leads to the discovery of truth, the other side of "man as a progressive being" that, for Mill, replaces salvation as the justification for liberty of thought and discussion. Negative liberty, Mill (1977: 288) says, "acknowledges no right to any freedom whatever, except perhaps to that of holding opinions in secret, without ever disclosing them." Freedom of thought not only allows you to speak as you like but also allows me to listen and talk to you. Freedom of thought creates a public in a way different from freedom of action. Because I think of my opinions as true, I want others to agree with me. Because I want my opinions to be true, Mill thinks, we want to listen to others.

If the purpose of freedom of thought is individual salvation, then you can be indifferent to what is most valuable to me. If its purpose is more communal, whether self-governance or even the salvation or stability of the community, then you cannot be so indifferent. Freedom of conscience and political freedom might be at odds, far from freedom of thought leading to freedom of actions. As the dissenter in *Yoder* (1972) and the majority in *Mozert* (1988) argued, exercising religious freedom might prevent people from developing the faculties needed to exercise civic freedom. Negative liberty is not enough to escape the paradox that my thought and speech is important to me and indifferent to you.

Returning to the *Gorgias*, we see a third consequence of Socrates' paradox that gets us closer to the paradox that my opinions and words are crucial to me and not to you. By the usual standards of harm and injustice, Socrates has argued that the good person cannot be injured. However, when it comes to his own actions toward others, the good person will observe those conventional standards of what counts as harm. He won't take others' property, enslave them, or physically harm them (e.g., *Apology* 32a6–32a7, 33a1–33a3; *Crito* 48d1–48d5; *Gorgias* 522b9–522c1). When it comes to being affected, Socrates turns the thought-action distinction upside down, but when it comes to affecting others, Socrates lives by conventional morality. Socrates' career of speaking is offensive and consistently violates decorum, but his actions are completely conventional in relying on the traditional sense of harm that he denies applies to himself. Thoughts violate convention; we follow arguments wherever they lead, but actions and justice must be conventional. If the problem with freedom of thought understood as toleration is always to avoid the idea that the reason for allowing freedom of thought is indifference, Socrates faces the parallel problem. If actions don't wound, I don't care what others do to me. But I still have to care about what I do toward others and they should care about what they do to me, even though they can't harm me.

We can see a trace of Socratic reasoning in contemporary thought. Arguing that other people's actions cannot harm me and therefore I shouldn't care about them makes things too easy for Socrates. Socrates, like everyone else, does not want to be a victim or assault or theft. He just thinks that defending oneself against such threats diverts one's attention from what matters most, defending the soul. Socrates' paradox impels him to take two distinct lines toward the usual ideas of injury, both that the good man is invulnerable and that we should train ourselves to become indifferent to those harms. It is similar today. We need the equivalent of both Socrates' lines of argument to see how other people's thoughts and speech can be crucial to them and unimportant to us. Of course other people's thoughts and words can harm me. The noise that passes for political argument today makes it harder to hear thoughtful opinion and to respond appropriately. Other people's thoughts can damage not only my thinking but my acting as well. Being attentive to those assaults on my mind diverts attention from what matters most, freedom of action. I decrease my own freedom of action by caring about those assaults on my judgment.

There is a further parallel between Socrates' indifference to physical harm and modern indifference to the harms caused by thought and expression. Physical attacks in Socrates' case and offensive expression in our case are in things that are by nature indifferent, possessing no power to harm. We and Socrates make a policy decision, and an emotional decision, not to be affected. We decide that they are by nature indifferent. The fact that Socrates' behavior seems so incredible to Callicles – he keeps asking whether Socrates is serious or not – is a reminder that this decision is not an easy or quick one, but takes a lifetime of effort. Socrates gives a reason we should make that decision – you can't be attentive both to your own thoughts about how to live and to what other people do to you and think about you. Modern understandings of free speech have to give reasons not to be offended by speech we think is wrong.

Most people, in Plato's time and ours, think that having the right thoughts is easy, as all one has to do is look around and think like everyone else (e.g., *Meno* 914c–992e), but right acting is hard and might need expert teaching and the power to overcome emotions. Socrates instead maintains that right action is easy – simply do what is conventionally just – but right thought takes all one's efforts. Today, everyone wants to act freely, but not everyone wants to think freely, let alone let others do so. I learn that the best way of exercising my own freedom of thought and expression is by letting others do the same.

TOLERATION AND LOVE

My gesture at *Yoder* suggests some of the difficulties with the idea that those things that are most important to you can be indifferent to me, and how I can be simultaneously deeply concerned, yet in another sense indifferent. It is possible to be indifferent to something without trivializing it in two different ways. The usual legal response would be that the law recognizes that there are things that are important to you and indifferent to me. Those things are, exactly, your property. If you own something, it follows that I have to keep my hands off it – negative liberty and the freedom of conscience associated with it. Without a metaphysical freedom of the will or a religious idea of an inviolable conscience, justifying freedom of speech and expression in this way is, as I've argued, difficult. But Plato suggests another, more interesting, way to address the paradox of something being protected because of its importance to you and its lack of importance to me.

Love is the way to think about something being central to one person and indifferent to another, and indifferent in the right way.[3] Objects of love are different both from objects of desire and from objects of reason. Desire and reason are both universal: either I share your reasons or I judge you to be irrational. Either I share your desires or I take you to be perverted. But love, compared to other desires, is both particular and objective. If I declare something lovable, I impute to it a value beyond just the fact that I love it. Objects of love can be personal, and private in that sense, but at the same time make a claim to objectivity and impersonality, in the sense that it isn't simply beautiful to me but beautiful and lovable. Santayana called beauty "pleasure objectified." I need not share your love to acknowledge it. In some cases I acknowledge your love by not sharing it.[4] The problem with freedom of thought, then, is that we have to treat the thoughts of others differently from how we treat our own thoughts: the mere fact that you think something can give me a reason to act, while the fact that I think something doesn't count for me at all; I only have a reason to act if I think my opinions are true.[5] Love and beauty are a way of understanding others' thoughts as central to them yet still indifferent to me. Our attitudes toward love and beauty are a way to understand others' thoughts as central to them, yet still indifferent to me. I can understand that you love someone without myself loving her. In that case, I can even be indifferent to her charms exactly because you think she is beautiful, without thinking of her as your property. That is the policy decision I described earlier, deciding to be indifferent. The challenge love offers is to avoid both indifference and jealousy or desire. Indifference, then, means not skepticism but withholding the usual judgments and emotions; Kant's term *disinterest* in the *Critique of Judgment* better

[3] Socrates begins his discussion with Callicles by noting that each of them have two loves, Socrates for Alkibiades and philosophy, Callicles for Demos and the Athenian people (*demos*). They both, Socrates says, are willing to agree with anything their beloved says. At least for Callicles, this means becoming a flatterer, not a friend, as he will shift what he says as his beloved changes what it says. He doesn't care what the beloved says; whatever it is, he will agree. When faced with love, then, he has no convictions of his own. He cares only about what the beloved wants, and is indifferent towards himself. How to love becomes more complicated as the dialogue proceeds.

[4] "Unlike friendship, which involves other-regarding actions we are ourselves disposed to perform, justice primarily concerns other-regarding actions that we are disposed to demand from others" (Yack 1993: 41). I elsewhere discuss one aspect of Plato's distinguishing love from desire and reason in (Garver 2006). Love, as distinct from desire and reason, is thus related to the Christian idea of the will (see Kahn 2005) and to the Greek idea of *thumos* (see Mansfield 1996).

[5]

> We rely on our answer to the question not because it is our view, but because it is, as we believe, true. If our reply to the question of the significance of disagreement is that we should refrain from this action or that because it is controversial, i.e., because others believe it to be wrong, or unfair, or unwise, then we refrain from that action not because the views of those others are true, but simply because they are held by them, because they are their views, be they true or false. To the extent that that is our answer we give other people's views a weight which we do not give our own. Or, to be more precise, we give the fact that other people hold whatever views they have some weight, whereas we give none to the fact that we hold any view.... There is an asymmetry here between the role that my beliefs and those of others play in my reasoning. Giving weight to the view of others is not treating them the same way I treat myself. It is giving them, i.e., their views, greater weight than the weight I give myself. (Raz 1998: 27–8)

captures this idea than indifference. Plato is the great philosopher of love, and love proves the model for freedom of thought.

Thinking about freedom of thought in terms of love has explanatory power. It is silly to claim that offensive thought and expression do no harm. The presence of happy atheists in our midst shakes my faith in a just God. My pleasures of smoking are diminished, or maybe enhanced, by your censure; in any case the meaning of not going to church or of smoking will be transformed because of the thoughts of others. Not to be offended, not to be harmed by other people's thoughts, speech, and action based on those thoughts, is a decision.

The Supreme Court's claim that there is no such thing as a false idea functions in the same way (*Gertz v. Robert Welch* 1974). Of course there are false ideas. But a policy decision makes the truth and falsity ideas irrelevant to their protection, just as Socrates' commitment to the life of reason makes him indifferent to physical threats and harms. Because she is your wife, I artificially and deliberately separate beauty from its usual associations with desire. I am not offended at your disgusting and deviant behavior because I recognize it as a function of sincere belief. It is because it is important to you that I can understand it in a disinterested way, without having to agree or disagree. If I thought instead that you are engaging in that same disgusting and deviant behavior out of laziness or immorality, then I would have no reason not to be offended. Friendship and love do not come into play here.

This kind of disinterest makes it possible to connect the tolerance essential to free speech with friendship. I can appreciate beauty without its usual emotional correlate in desire, and so I can understand your thoughts without the usual correlation to understanding, namely, assent. The difficulty of such an emotional and imaginative attitude is precisely the ethical challenge of toleration: it is easy to agree with someone with the same opinion, or to refute, reject, and fight against someone who thinks differently. To live together with someone one recognizes as different is at the core a difficult ethical challenge.

Ultimately, we are left with the research project of finding forms of friendship that can make sense in American society today, with its size, its impersonal administration of justice, and its diversity, without pining for a face-to-face community instead. Then we can take freedom of thought for what it is. Without thinking about friendship as a model for free speech, we are left with a model of freedom of conscience designed to protect religious belief and yet now applied to protecting the free choices of consumers in a free market. I hope that this historical excursion allows us to do better.

Why, finally, should thought be treated differently from action, in the absence of religion or metaphysics? The surprising answer, implicit in the *Gorgias*, is that actions are more private than thoughts! Actions are private unless they harm others. But you have an interest in my thoughts you don't have in my actions, because my thoughts can lead to your moral development. Others should care more about my thoughts than my actions. We saw that in Plato this care could take the form either as it does in the *Republic*, of a larger role for the state in education and in prohibiting seditious ideas, or as in the *Gorgias* and the *Apology*, greater freedom for each to think for him- or herself and to say what he or she thinks. It is because my words are more your business than my actions that you have greater reason for resentment and offense but at the same time greater reason for restraint.

WORKS CITED

Bollinger, Lee C. *The Tolerant Society: Freedom of Speech and Extremist Speech in America.* Oxford: Oxford Univ. Press, 1986.

Bollinger, Lee C., and Geoffrey Stone, eds. *Eternally Vigilant: Free Speech in the Modern Era.* Chicago: Univ. of Chicago Press, 2002.

Carter, Stephen L. "Evolutionism, Creationism, and Teaching Religion as a Hobby." *Duke L.J.* 1987.6 (1987): 977–96.

Garver, Eugene. *Confronting Aristotle's Ethics: Ancient and Modern Morality.* Chicago: Univ. of Chicago Press, 2006.

Gertz v. Robert Welch, Inc., 418 U.S. 323 (1974).

Hume, David. *History of England.* London: J. Hatchard, 1816.

Jefferson, Thomas. "Notes on the State of Virginia," in Thomas Jefferson, *Writings*, Merrill D. Peterson, ed. New York: Library of America, 1984.

Kahn, Paul W. *Putting Liberalism in Its Place.* Princeton, NJ: Princeton Univ. Press, 2005.

Kant, Immanuel. *What Is Enlightenment?* 2d rev. ed. Trans. Lewis White Beck. 1784. Reprint, New York: Macmillan, 1990.

Mansfield, Harvey. *Machiavelli's Virtue.* Chicago: Univ. of Chicago Press, 1996.

Mill, John Stuart. "On Liberty." In *Collected Works*, vol. 18. Ed. John M. Robson. 1859 (4th ed. 1869). London: Routledge and Kegan Paul, 1977.

Mozert v. Hawkins County Public Schools, 484 U.S. 1066 (1988).

Raz, Joseph. "Disagreement in Politics." *Am. J. Juris.* 43 (1998): 25–52.

Wisconsin v. Yoder, 406 U.S. 205 (1972).

Yack, Bernard. *Problems of a Political Animal: Community, Justice, and Conflict in Aristotelian Political Thought.* Berkeley: Univ. of California Press, 1993.

21 Legal Philosophy over the Next Century (While We Wait for the Personal Rocket Transportation We Were Promised)

R. GEORGE WRIGHT

Prediction poses special difficulties, as those of us who were once confidently promised personalized rocket transportation can attest. Some predictions can be left vague, and thus conveniently reinterpretable or indefinitely deferrable. But real predictions are falsifiable, sometimes even within the compass of the predictor's own professional career. Appreciating this awkward possibility, we often succumb to the temptation to limit our predictions to mere extrapolation. Predicting only incremental change along preexisting lines may be less interesting than predicting sharp discontinuities, path dependencies, random walks, catastrophes, chaotic swirls, tipping points, symmetry breaks, cascades, emergent properties, butterfly effects, or exponential acceleration. The payoff for mere extrapolationism is in seeming levelheaded and judicious.

One crucial problem with the strategy of extrapolationism, though, is that current trends often go south surprisingly quickly. And over the truly long haul, even betting on a normally sure thing, such as increasing entropy, will at some point have no future. Most established trends in legal philosophy, it is fair to guess, will unravel long before entropy halts its advance.

Legal philosophers recognize all of this. Asked to depict likely scenarios for legal philosophy over the century hence, most would resist the temptation to limn merely a contest among, say, recognizable descendents of today's inclusive legal positivists, exclusive legal positivists, and a smattering of broadly described natural law theorists. Even if that were indeed the single most likely scenario among many alternatives, it seems too unlikely to place many chips on.

One further problem with predicting continuity is that a century of legal philosophy will require perhaps four or five successive generations of recruitment. Exacting oaths of doctrinal fidelity from one's own direct successors is of little help. If legal philosophers are indeed still debating merely the recognizable descendents of today's issues decades from now, they will by then have trouble attracting the best and brightest potential successors to the field.

So, predicting basically more of the same in legal philosophy seems on balance unappealing. But isn't there more to be said on the role of continuities even in areas of real intellectual progress? Aren't there recurrent themes and categories within legal and other sorts of philosophies, and even in other academic disciplines? There are indeed certain ways to draw academic distinctions that seem in literal terms to crop up repeatedly across time in different contexts. Perhaps noticing such generic, reusable distinctions might give us a better handle on the terms of future debates within legal philosophy.

We could call these terms standard metadistinctions. Examples are not hard to think of. Inclusive versus exclusive, as noted earlier, may qualify. Or, relatedly, don't adjectival distinctions such as between hard and soft versions of whatever is under discussion tend to recurrently arise? Internalist versus externalist? Mixed versus pure? Methodological versus substantive? Normative versus descriptive? Absolutist versus presumptivist? A focus on rules versus a focus on individual discretion? Distinctions among negative, positive, triadic, integrative, and holistic versions of various sorts of concepts and categories commonly recur as well. Or perhaps nearly any given subject, taken at the metaphysical, epistemological, and pragmatic levels. The persistent reappearance in new contexts of these metadistinctions may also help account for the observation that, in legal and other philosophies, every imaginable particular position on the matrix of all possibilities will eventually be staked out and endorsed.

To predict that something we have today only in undifferentiated form will eventually be split along some such axes above is not to commit the fallacy of merely assuming continuity. The preceding metadistinctions have proved their adaptive fitness by attaching themselves to more than one underlying host concept over time. Jointly or separately, they could be applied rather mechanically to any as-yet-undifferentiated concepts. But the mechanical quality of predicting the emergence of, say, a hard and soft version of some as-yet-unitary legal philosophical notion of course seems uninspired.

A slightly better strategy – still rather mechanical, but less obviously so – would be to make predictions that are safe because they crucially depend on what are called observer selection effects. Cosmologically, for example, we obviously wouldn't be here to observe anything specific at all if we didn't have underlying conditions conducive to the existence of observers such as us. So, equally clearly, no theory that implies anything incompatible with our current existence as observers can possibly be right.

We can make a little headway as prognosticators, then, by making predictions that imply the existence of future legal philosophers interested in our predictions, but that are not overly ambitious beyond that. And this approach actually does seem to have a certain potential value. To survive into the indefinite future as a significant discipline, for example, legal philosophy must claim for itself at least some more or less distinctive emphasis. But for the sake of its own significance, legal philosophy must also broaden the scope of its inquiry into areas it shares with other academic disciplines. If there is nothing distinctive about legal philosophy even as a matter of emphasis, its recognition by outsiders as a distinct academic discipline might eventually be jeopardized. But if legal philosophy, on the other hand, focuses excessively on what is most narrowly central to legal philosophy, the interest value of legal philosophy to potential recruits might fall below the level needed for disciplinary viability. Legal philosophers do not want to answer to Tolstoy's description of the historians, providing answers to questions that no one has asked.

Another way to almost effortlessly generate sensible predictions is to notice a number of at least minimally independent phenomena, all tending in the same general direction, and to then bet that not all of these phenomena will entirely run their course before the predictions are to be scored. Here is one possible application. For some time now, moral and related sorts of philosophy have, among a large number of mainstream academics, been on what we might informally call one sort or another of weight-reduction program. These related trends have long been obvious enough, which cuts against the boldness of any predictions based on them but adds to the short-term creditworthiness of any such predictions as well.

The phrase "weight-reduction program" is meant here as a neutral portmanteau, encompassing various philosophical schools, phenomena, and terms. The idea is to encompass terms such as *nihilism* and *skepticism*, *noncognitivism*, *emotivism*, *subjectivism*, *projectivism*, *expressivism*, *quasi-realism*, *irrealism*, *antirealism*, *fictionalism*, *error theory*, some forms of *relativism*, *extreme contextualism*, *conventionalism*, *constructivism*, and *pragmatism*, along with *minimalism*, *deflationism*, various forms of *reductionism*, and finally, a disposition to incredulity before all metanarratives. As well, there is some related tendency, among those still minimally adhering to the belief that some moral responses can be objectively better than some other moral responses, to define basic terms, including *sanctity*, the *sacred*, and the *inviolable*, along with metaethical objectivity itself, in similarly weight-reduced terms.

Some of these approaches overlap or even coincide with one another. This reduces their mutual independence. To the extent, though, that some are mutually independent, the weight-reduction program in one form or another is likely to affect legal philosophy for some time, even after other approaches listed here have become spent forces. It is not unprecedented for a school of thought to continue to exert influence in a related discipline, even after it has passed its peak of influence in its own home territory. A school that originated in epistemology may fade there but not elsewhere. We dare not count solely on this lag-time effect, however. On the other hand, even if all the approaches listed here really derive from some single broader attitude or phenomenon, we might well then ask how fast anyone realistically expects that broader underlying single attitude or phenomenon to itself be turned around. It is difficult to quickly turn around all of a dozen separate and diverse small boats. It is also difficult to quickly turn around a single massive ocean liner.

It is also possible, on the other hand, that whatever legal philosophers think about objectivity within the law itself could actually come to push back against, or at least redirect, the entire broad weight-reduction program, on the basis of legal philosophers' generalizing their insights into the idea of objectivity in the specific narrow legal context. This is possible but speculative, and to this point evidently not the way to bet prudently.

Beyond moral philosophy and related areas, there seems no reason legal philosophy could not also be linked in the future with literally any academic discipline, traditional or emerging, from the hard and soft sciences through any or all of the humanities. Legal philosophy has already embarked upon such a course in a number of areas. Over the past thirty years or so, legal philosophy has famously turned outward toward economics and feminism and cultural theory, and inward toward the philosophy of particular curricular or doctrinal legal subjects, beyond the staples of causation, responsibility, moral luck in the law, defenses and excuses, crime as offense or harm, and theories of punishment.

In particular, there is much more to be said about what will or should happen if policy makers and the public gradually become convinced that free will as commonly envisioned is either a sustainable illusion or an unsustainable illusion. This work will take us far beyond criminal and civil responsibility, into the quality of life itself, as all the influence of the old illusions are on some theories presumed to gradually fade. Whether traditional ideas of free will are genuinely abandonable is, of course, at the moment controversial. Assuming especially that we can genuinely dispense with traditional ideas of free will, the resultant depth and dignity of our lives would then be controversial.

All this has already been widely broached, and so can hardly count as the basis of an interesting prediction. Another rhetorical technique, though, is to merely dress up an already-developing phenomenon in the futurized language of prediction. We can thus safely predict that conflicts and compatibilities between various forms of liberty and equality will be an important focus of legal philosophy of the applied sort over the next couple of decades. This is really a matter of current observation and irresistible momentum, and thus it makes for a fairly safe prediction. Unless we choose to redefine the terms, interesting conflicts between some forms of liberty and equality are not all going away anytime soon.

Only slightly more venturesomely, we can safely predict a (continuing) interest in the legal philosophy associated with what we might call the technical or artificial enhancement of people and their basic capabilities. We explore this further below. Over the next century, there will likely arise many more or less independent ways to valuably enhance or upgrade the human person. They likely won't all technically fail, be out of the price range of even the rich, cause disastrous side effects for the consumer, be effectively legally suppressed, or be rejected by all consumers and self-improvers, let alone by those who want an advantage for their children.

Before exploring such issues further, though, we should note that in a very loosely similar way, it is also fairly safe to say that legal philosophical issues of climate change and global warming and their redistributive effects will likely not disappear over the next half century. Too many different things, currently substantially against the odds, would all have to break right for global warming to be halted at the current level. The philosophy of international law will thereby inevitably be implicated. Relatedly, we also have the conjunction of fairly stable long-term global demographic trends; global immigration issues; important international economic markets in labor; the blurring of distinctions among war, crime, and rebellion; and the vicissitudes, if not the fragmentation, of classical national sovereignty. The increasing significance of the philosophy of international law thus becomes less a matter of interesting prediction and more of mere casual newspaper reading.

In particular, the philosophy of the law of war, arms control, and armed conflict deserves attention, especially if we want recognizable legal philosophers to exist in a hundred years. Common sense and the rudiments of evolutionary theory suggest that there are really only two general kinds of stable, and therefore likely, global civilizations. First are those civilizations simply lacking the capacity to destroy themselves and their habitat. Second are those civilizations that have through one means or another made civilization- or species-habitat–destroying conflict exceedingly unlikely even over the long term.

As of the present, our global civilization unhappily fits neatly into neither of these two stable scenarios. We might as well predict that legal philosophy will over the next century play a role in the global adoption of the only solution practically open, the preceding second course. If such a course is in fact not adopted, it seems unlikely that there will long remain a community of legal philosophers to notice our predictions. The only way for us to embarrass ourselves in the eyes of the actual future philosophers is by falsely predicting global disaster. The only way for us to gain any future public credit, however undeservedly, is by correctly predicting the avoidance of global disaster.

Another likely bet, as introduced briefly earlier, has to do with legal philosophy as applied to the phenomenon of the technical enhancement of persons. This broad problem directly implicates philosophical concerns such as forms of equality, forms of liberty and consent, the moral limits of markets, solidarity and community, desert and moral luck, relationships between generations, international equity, and even the dignity of the person.

Just as important for our predictive purposes, the general problem of the artificial enhancement of people is apparently unlikely to dissipate. The sheer range and variety of independent – if perhaps combinable – advanced techniques looming ahead practically ensures the future reality of the problem, in rather the same way that a well-diversified investment portfolio practically ensures against winding up with no financial assets.

First, though, let us set aside some preliminary objections. It is true that artificial human enhancement techniques, such as, historically, a set of the *Encyclopaedia Britannica* for a child's private use, have long been available and have been differentially available on the basis of economic class inequalities. Future enhancements, however, will in some cases likely be crucially different. Internalizing the *Encyclopaedia Britannica* has always also required motivation and sustained effort, and the payoff has often been rather modest. This will likely not be true of all future enhancement technologies, and this is only the very start of the differences.

It is also certainly possible to argue that the dividing line between artificially enhancing persons and engaging in novel forms of therapeutic medicine – enhancement versus therapy – is itself artificial, socially constructed, and easily contestable. We can call orthodontics, human-growth-hormone injections, cosmetic surgery, germ-line genetic modification, or the replacement of one's blood cells by five hundred trillion nanobots either therapy or enhancement. We should not, however, deny the reality of their consequences, which may differ substantially.

Doubtless some future technical means to human enhancement will run up against unanticipated and insuperable obstacles, including cost. Perhaps some technologies that seem impractical today will benefit from breakthroughs tomorrow. But for all of the apparently powerful techniques of human enhancement, at various stages of development, to fail to have an impact seems unlikely. No single crucial vulnerability seems, as far as we can tell, to be shared across the board by all the potential technologies.

This current uncertainty does not mean, however, that legal philosophers should not think and write about such issues until the effects of the techniques have been demonstrated. If legal philosophers wait, they will often wind up either ratifying whatever the markets, legal or illegal, decree, or engaging in mere rationalizing or hand-wringing. If legal philosophers do or do not want to see the unimpeded development of such techniques, perhaps as subsidized or taxed in various ways, there is no reason not to begin saying so now.

Finally, consider in particular not only future generations of pharmaceuticals and upgradable connective brain implants but also the long-term prospect of various sorts of inheritable genetic enhancements, perhaps in connection with other techniques we have not even collectively envisioned. Again, the unanticipated problems and limitations associated with genetic or any other technologies may be even greater than those we already know of. Genetic reductionism is bad science and ineffective technology. Relatively rarely does any single gene by itself control one's future in a positive way. Tinkering with even a single gene, though, may have unpleasant and unpredicted side effects. The first safe and practical version of any such technique to hit the consumer market, like any other innovation, may come to seem clunky, crude, and limited, and it may even impair crucial future updates.

Genetic enhancements, particularly those associated with the brain or with general health, disease avoidance, and disease appearance are nonetheless likely to call for legal philosophers' attention over the coming decades. Alone or in combination with other enhancement techniques, they could, depending on prices and other cultural considerations, generate an increasing absolute and relative gap between groups of people. Advantages in more than one respect might reinforce one another and cumulate in unprecedented ways. Such a gap might turn, over time, into a gulf or even into an unbridgeable chasm. Almost every important dimension of applied legal philosophy would at some point be pressed into service.

It is comforting to imagine that, like the unit cost of computing power, the unit cost of all sorts of technical enhancements may start out unaffordably high except to the rich, but that the costs will drop so sharply that, perhaps with government subsidies, the most crucial enhancements in the most sophisticated versions will become realistically available to the poor – of the nation and of the world – before the rich can speed permanently ahead of the curve, consigning rough equality of human capacity to the dustbin of history.

This optimistic scenario is certainly a real possibility. In a spirit of humility and open inquiry, we can hardly rule it out. Let us consider as well, however, the possibility that even small advantages and small lag times between early and late adopters may in some cases translate into dramatic and increasing differences in capacities. Let us bear in mind as well that in a competitive employment market, any significant differences between two classes of applicants may lead to dramatic hiring and employment disparities, and in our cases, perhaps eventually to nearly zero class mobility. In the absence of an enlightened social and legal response, something like a permanent caste system could eventually result, with or without the occasional suppressed or bought-off rebellion.

Along the way, there are also crucial issues of voluntariness and freedom of choice, and of meaningful consent and proxy consent for one's family and descendents into the future. Issues of various sorts of luck, desert, effort, unenforceability, responsibility, and reward, and the moral and legal limits to all of these elements may be starkly presented as well.

Presumably, we want to respect the decisions of those who can afford important enhancements but who nevertheless choose not to adopt them. Would it make any difference whether the decision not to enhance were made on the basis of some intelligible principle, some distinctive religious tenet, a reasonable fear, or on sheer superstition and demonstrable misunderstanding? What if parents must choose today for their minor offspring in some way that is practically irrevocable? Should parents be allowed to, in effect, rule out anything but a permanent Huxleyan Delta status for their minor children, and indirectly for all succeeding generations of their progeny? May we instead try to authoritatively envision what the minor children, under some specified circumstances, would reasonably prefer?

Consider as well the position of parents who can afford crucial enhancements for their children and who opt in favor of those enhancements, but only from a sense of defensive necessity. The parents might even consider the enhancements to be literally dehumanizing. They may fear an unbridgeable chasm between the enhanced and the unenhanced, to the moral prejudice of all. Yet the parents opt for the enhancements, lest their children's futures be starkly limited.

Many parents could find themselves in this position. Dramatic prisoner's dilemma problems could thus arise. Issues of freedom and constraint in general would abound. By way of a very minimal parallel, some contemporary parents would prefer to inculcate what they see as strong moral virtues in their children but fear that the children would pay too high a price in personal exploitation. How, if at all, and on what philosophical basis should governments specially intervene in our far more extreme circumstances?

We often distinguish between a bad outcome that resulted, fairly, from a genuinely free but risky choice, and a bad outcome that resulted from brute bad luck. We sometimes claim as well to distinguish between outcomes that resulted merely from our natural or native endowments and outcomes that also reflect some otherwise unaccounted-for distinctive effort or painstakingly developed talent on our part. Some of us may distinguish between those with healthy ambition and those who seem merely to lack ambition, despite their talent. We may distinguish between the person and the person's circumstances. Perhaps even more awkwardly, we may try, however naively, to distinguish between the natural and the social, with the latter including law, economics, and politics. In other contexts, we may try to distinguish between the personal and the political. The very constituents of our bodies are, we often think, not merely our property or exchangeable components but aspects of who we are.

Whatever the integrity and usefulness of these distinctions, they all tend to unravel in the enhancement context under discussion. Legal philosophy over the next century cannot ignore these substantive issues. Will there be much difference in our advanced enhancement context between, on the one hand, fair equality of opportunity and, on the other hand, more substantive or outcome-based measures of equality? What, in any of our future enhancement cases, does the equal protection of the laws require? What would be the proper rate of intergenerational savings and investment, with the likelihood that the next generation may be dramatically more capable and productive than its predecessor?

What, in addition, will become of the idea of the community and of the common well-being? Or even of broad empathy and universal identification? What would our current ideas of a social discount rate suggest? Do those who cannot afford to or who choose not to keep up in the enhancement arms race still have a dignified place? Can they also be called genuinely free? Analogies to voluntarily separate Amish-type communities might be comforting, but they are entirely inapt.

Even if we can come to terms with our own local unenhanced persons, however, we still face the problem of almost entire nations and cultures unable to keep pace with their richer and now acceleratingly enhanced international peers. Legally requiring that no one be enhanced until all can, with or without subsidy, would be hopelessly unenforceable. Is it then the obligation of the enhanced to make life as pleasant and as dignified as possible for those across the globe who cannot afford enhancement? Is that also the end of their obligations in this regard? Would that also be the demise of the age-old human dream of universal solidarity, and of universal egalitarian brotherhood and sisterhood? Would the idea of human progress and of the human itself fracture and disintegrate?

Or, returning to our earlier metaethical concerns, should any of this really matter, independent of our adopted interests, attitudes, and preferences? Suppose that all relevant policy makers over the next century became thoroughly imbued with the weight-reduction programs, such that every trace of any aspiration to moral objectivity disappeared. Would that make any practical difference in how those policy makers then addressed any of the issues raised by the dramatic technical enhancement of some people's basic capabilities?

22 Atmospherics: Abortion Law and Philosophy

ANITA L. ALLEN

> Respect for human life finds an ultimate expression in the bond of love the mother has for her child.
>
> (*Gonzales* 2007: 1634)

> From the positivists the realists take the insistence on concrete data. . . . The profession at large still shows, at times, the influence of the natural law.
>
> (Llewellyn 1934: 212)

> While we find no reliable data to measure the phenomenon, it seems unexceptionable to conclude some women come to regret their choice to abort the infant life they once created and sustained. . . . Severe depression and loss of esteem can follow.
>
> (*Gonzales* 2007: 1634)

> Police officers with cadaver-sniffing dogs, shovels and a backhoe dug in the backyard of a home Monday where the bodies of four infants have been found since last week. The police say the infants belong to Christy L. Freeman, 37, a taxi company owner and mother of four. Ms. Freeman has been charged with murder in the death of one of the infants, a male fetus in the 26th week of gestation found in a vanity under a bathroom sink.
>
> ("Bodies" 2007: A15)

In 1934, Karl N. Llewellyn published a lively essay trumpeting the dawn of legal realism, "On Philosophy in American Law." The charm of his defective little piece is its style and audacity. A philosopher might be seduced into reading Llewellyn's essay by its title; but one soon learns that by *philosophy* Llewellyn only meant *atmosphere.* His concerns were the "general approaches" taken by practitioners, who may not even be aware of having general approaches. Llewellyn paired an anemic concept of philosophy with a pumped-up conception of law. Llewellyn's law included anything that reflects the "ways of the law guild at large" – the ways of judges, legislators, regulators, and enforcers (Llewellyn 1934: 206).

Whether atmospherics conform to coherent sets of theoretical ideas of the sort a Richard Posner or Ronald Dworkin might defend was not Llewellyn's question.

Yet he credited intellectual judges and scholars, especially Oliver Wendell Holmes, Roscoe Pound, and Benjamin Cardozo, with roles in making the embrace of realism headier than a law guild's unconscious groping for solutions (Llewellyn 1934: 210–12). A story could be told (but not here) about academic philosophy's contributions to American law. Contemporary philosophers have modestly contributed logical and conceptual clarity; economists and statisticians may have contributed more.

Llewellyn argued that the legal philosophies implicit in American legal practice had been natural law, positivism, and realism, each adopted in response to felt needs of a time. We must reckon with many other implicit "philosophies" to understand the workings of the law guild, not the least of which has been racism. Others, maternalism and paternalism, my foci here, persist in American law, despite women's progress toward equality. Both maternalism and paternalism were strikingly present in a recent decision of the U.S. Supreme Court, *Gonzales v. Carhart* (2007), which upheld the federal Partial-Birth Abortion Ban Act.

PHILOSOPHIES OF LAW

Natural law, Llewellyn said, was adopted in response to the needs of a new nation lacking precedents of its own and short on hospitality for the tradition of British law. Unashamed reliance upon "right reason" was an expression of the founding generation's self-confidence and rebellion against British rule (Llewellyn 1934: 206–7). Like natural law, racism and maternalism and paternalism were conceptual needs of a newly independent federation of slaveholding patriots intent on dominating the swatches of North America grabbed from the Native Americans. White women, slaves, and indigenous Americans did not immediately benefit from the atmospherics of divinely inspired natural law. The original constitution defined nonwhites out of full citizenship and overlooked women altogether.[1]

Positivism bloomed in the late nineteenth century, Llewellyn argued. Capitalist industrialism called for pragmatic law making, especially within private law. Positivism legitimates rules put into place by the sovereign. Stressing allegiance to rules and precedent, positivism fostered stability more than justice. Natural law had been unkind to the powerless and positivism was, too. Complemented by racism, raw "buccaneer" self-interest, as Llewellyn called it, spelled major trouble. For example, West Coast towns and cities passed laws to eliminate the competition from their Chinese immigrant communities – laws prohibiting laundries built of wood and carrying things on poles. The Chinese were rounded up and their property confiscated or burned. In principle, legal positivism is a two-way street. Indeed, some Chinese immigrants who sued for restitution under positive law theories of tort and contract won (Pfaelzer 2008). Although the letter of law strictly applied sometimes helps the little guys, power will manipulate law to serve the interests of power. Positivism in the air may help explain *Plessy v. Ferguson*. The Supreme

[1] See art. 1, sec. 2: "Representatives and direct taxes shall be apportioned among the several states which may be included within this union, according to their respective numbers, which shall be determined by adding to the whole number of free persons, including those bound to service for a term of years, and excluding Indians not taxed, three fifths of all other Persons."

Court read the law of equal protection ungenerously, so as virtually to reenslave southern African Americans through demeaning segregation.

According to Llewellyn, realism evolved in response to the needs of the twentieth century. The little guys organized and flexed muscle. Popular movements – labor, farmworkers, and small business among them – demanded policies of protection and reform. The gospel of realism teaches that law is an instrument of power that can be educated with hard fact and marshaled through politics for social improvement and a more complete democracy. From its cynical (Holmes) and ethical (Pound) variants, and its sociological roots, realism emerged (with the help of Cardozo) to enable the legal system to solicit "more exact knowledge" for policy making (Llewellyn 1934: 212). Realism suits us as a nation of pragmatists compelled to govern the powerful and the powerless alike, Llewellyn contended. In 1934 realism had found "yet little echo among judges"; nonetheless, it came into its own as Llewellyn (1934: 212) predicted because it was "much closer than any others to the actual behavior of the better bar." The realist atmospheric survives in progressive legal theory and mainstream legal practice. But positivism is a vital sibling and natural law is good for an occasional cameo.

NEGLECTED PHILOSOPHIES: BEYOND THE BIG THREE

The big three philosophies – natural law, positivism, and realism – have never exhausted the atmospherics of American law. It is implausible to reduce to only three all of the philosophies immanent in the ways of the law guild. Moralism, for example, was evident in Anthony Comstock's legal innovations targeting pornography, contraception, and abortion. Llewellyn neglected the challenge to moralistic paternalism embodied both by Margaret Sanger's battle against Comstock-era laws and the successful reform movement for women's suffrage. Outside the shadows, there are no women in Llewellyn's story of American legal philosophy, not even when he describes the push for democratizing reforms in the early twentieth century. Maternalism and paternalism are major atmospherics, especially noteworthy for the injustice they have done, and continue to do. Women are dragged down by the law's implicit paternalism (its tendency to control the lives of individuals, nominally for their own good) and maternalism (its assumption that bearing children and caring for others is the natural and optimal role of women).

In *Gonzales v. Carhart* the U.S. Supreme Court upheld a federal abortion prohibition. Congress enacted the Partial-Birth Abortion Ban Act, signed into law by President George W. Bush in 2003. Under the ban, physicians can be punished for knowingly performing an abortion using techniques labeled *partial-birth abortion.* Congress was attempting to bring an end to a class of procedures that second- and third-trimester abortion providers sometimes term *D&X* (short for "dilation and extraction") or *intact D&E* (short for "intact dilation and evacuation").[2] Written by Justice Anthony Kennedy, the majority opinion in *Gonzales* is mired in the atmospherics of maternalism and paternalism. Justice Kennedy's maternalism and paternalism do not countenance the possibility that a sane and ethical woman

[2] See generally. http://www.guttmacher.org/statecenter/spibs/spib_BPBA.pdf.

could knowingly approve the destruction of her living fetus once it has been coaxed halfway through her cervix.

The Partial-Birth Abortion Ban Act criminalizes abortions in which a living viable or living nonviable fetus is killed after its head or abdomen passes from the womb through the cervix. The Act includes an exception for abortions necessary to save the lives of pregnant women, but there is no exception for women's health. Abortion rights advocacy groups went to court to oppose the partial-birth ban.[3] They feared the act would set the nation on a slippery slope toward the recriminalization of most abortions. They also feared that authorities could interpret the act to prohibit medically safe best practices. The act's opponents maintained before the Supreme Court that the act was unconstitutionally vague, like the Nebraska law the Court had struck down a few years earlier in *Stenberg v. Carhart.* Opponents further argued that by proscribing medically safe and popular D&E abortions of nonviable fetuses and by not including a maternal health exception, the act imposed an "undue burden" on the woman's right to choose, in violation of *Planned Parenthood v. Casey* (1992: 839).

Since *Roe v. Wade*, women in the United States have enjoyed a right against categorical criminalization of medically safe abortions. At least one million women in the United States obtain surgical or medical abortions each year from professional health-care providers. Typical abortions are $300 surgical abortions obtained in the first trimester of pregnancy. Most surgical abortions involve inserting a device through the woman's cervix and suctioning the contents of the uterus. In a medical abortion a woman who is one to two months pregnant ingests prescribed drugs (usually methotrexate and mifepristone) that cause her fetus to be expelled from her body over a period of days in a manner akin to a natural spontaneous miscarriage.

The essential holding of *Roe v. Wade* was affirmed in 1992 in *Planned Parenthood v. Casey.* But *Casey* also held that government can establish abortion restrictions, including waiting periods, that do not "unduly burden" the right to elect abortion. Even before *Casey*, the Court had concluded that states and the federal government can express through their laws and policies a preference for childbearing over abortion (see *Webster* and *Rust*). States may assert an interest in protecting the life from the moment of conception and may regulate abortion in the interest of women's health. Abortion privacy is being replaced by abortion paternalism.

The *Gonzales* Court held 5–4 that the Partial-Birth Abortion Ban Act is constitutionally valid. Justice Kennedy reasoned first that the act is not unconstitutionally vague because "[d]octors performing D&E will know that if they do not deliver a living fetus to an anatomical landmark they will not face criminal liability" (*Gonzales*: 1628). Second, the act is not unduly burdensome because it does not prohibit most or all abortions and cannot be read to do so. The act proscribes only those D&E abortions performed both intentionally (not accidentally) and by killing an intact fetus whose head (or abdomen) has been delivered past the cervix. Justice Kennedy acknowledged that *Casey* upheld *Roe.* Yet under the holding of

[3] *Gonzales v. Carhart* and *Gonzales v. Planned Parenthood* were joined as *Gonzales v. Carhart.* See *Gonzales v. Carhart,* 127 S. Ct. 1610 (2007).

Casey (878), "[r]egulations which do no more than create a structural mechanism by which the State, or the parent or guardian of a minor, may express profound respect for the life of the unborn are permitted, if they are not a substantial obstacle to the woman's exercise of the right to choose." Justice Kennedy further argued that the act does not require a health exception because there are alternatives to the banned procedure. The Court noted that the act bans neither an injection to induce vaginal expulsion of a nonviable living fetus nor surgery to remove the nonviable fetus.

PATERNALISM AND MATERNALISM

Kennedy's opinion is striking for the extent of its paternalism and maternalism. According to the justice, "Respect for human life finds an ultimate expression in the bond of love the mother has for her child" (*Gonzales*: 1634). Might respect for human life find another ultimate expression in deference governments show toward the morally autonomous decisions adult women and their partners make about their own lives and families? Kennedy takes the ascribed bond of love to explain why women must surely go a little crazy after an abortion, and especially a partial-birth abortion.

Kennedy had no hard data to support his maternalist assumptions. But in a superficially realist spirit of adjudication guided by data, Kennedy provided two medical professionals' descriptions of partial-birth abortion. The first was a clinical account of the abortionist's technique:

> The doctor, often guided by ultrasound, inserts grasping forceps through the woman's cervix and into the uterus to grab the fetus. The doctor grips a fetal part with the forceps and pulls it... through the cervix and vagina.... The friction causes the fetus to tear apart. For example, a leg might be ripped off the fetus as it is pulled through the cervix and out of the woman.... Once the fetus has been evacuated, the placenta and any remaining fetal material are suctioned or scraped out of the uterus. The doctor examines the different parts to ensure the entire fetal body has been removed. (*Gonzales*: 1621)

The second account of abortion was a more feminine narrative, appropriately sincere and tenderhearted. He quoted a nurse who witnessed a procedure to abort a twenty-six-week old "baby" performed by a Dr. W. Martin Haskell:

> Dr. Haskell went in with forceps and grabbed the baby's legs and pulled them down into the birth canal. Then he delivered the baby's body and the arms – everything but the head. The doctor kept the head right inside the uterus.... The baby's little fingers were clasping and unclasping, and his little feet were kicking. Then the doctor stuck the scissors in the back of his head, and the baby's arms jerked out, like a startle reaction, like a flinch, like a baby does when he thinks he is going to fall. The doctor opened up the scissors, stuck a high-powered suction tube into the opening, and sucked the baby's brains out. Now the baby went completely limp.... He cut the umbilical cord and delivered the placenta. He threw the baby in a pan, along with the placenta and the instruments he had just used. (*Gonzales*: 1622)

Justice Kennedy was working on emotions as much as offering facts. He was inviting readers to share his belief that the intact D&E or D&X procedures on living fetuses are ghoulish, something a true mother would recoil at discovering her physician had done to her unborn "child." In Kennedy's words: "The State has an interest in ensuring so grave a choice is well informed. It is self-evident that a mother who comes to regret her choice to abort must struggle with grief more anguished and sorrow more profound when she learns, only after the event, what she once did not know: that she allowed a doctor to pierce the skull and vacuum the fast-developing brain of her unborn child, a child assuming the human form" (*Gonzales*: 1634). Justice Kennedy knows that mothers voluntarily seek out physicians to fatally abort their children. Yet he wants to believe they are naturally tender on matters relating to children. Kennedy surmises that mothers would likely be disturbed by partial-birth abortion and unwilling to consent to the D&X procedure if properly disclosed by a physician. There are many reasons to doubt this assumption. First of all, a woman whose belly is swollen with a pregnancy knows what lies therein (namely, a living human form), and she knows that there are only a limited number of ways to remove it. When abortion was illegal, a desperate woman might insert coat hangers and knitting needles through her own cervix to kill her fetus. She might fling herself down flights of stairs toward the same end. Women understand basic anatomy and are grateful that modern physicians can safely do what they themselves cannot safely do on their own. Women generally understand, I would submit, that after the first trimester of pregnancy, the body of a fetus has to be physically removed or made to come out on its own through a small opening. Women know that physicians do not use laser beams to neatly and painlessly vaporize the unwanted unborn.

Second, a woman might rationally believe that the D&X procedure is the best and safest procedure available for the termination of a pregnancy she believes is vitally important to herself or loved ones. This belief may override any tendency toward squeamishness. A woman may regard a partial-birth abortion as a lesser of two evils, if an evil at all. Women's morality of killing as applied to abortion is like men's morality of killing applied to war – subtle and contextual.

Third, women are not especially squeamish about surgical procedures. Women elect cosmetic procedures on their own bodies that are extremely risky, invasive, and gruesome to witness and describe. Women authorize invasive heart, brain, and transplant surgeries on their children, disabled spouses, and elderly parents when they believe removing the top of a skull, sawing open a sternum, or taking out a liver is the best option. Women are accustomed to blood and tissue exiting their vaginas, as part of the menses. Some women prefer untidy, painful drawn-out medical abortions despite the requirement that they examine bloody discharge from their own bodies to look for the expelled embryo.

It is not the culture of medicine for physicians to be as explicit with patients as they are with one another. Still, health-care consumers appreciate fully informed consent. Many people, male and female, who discover that their consent to a medical procedure was not fully informed are angry or unhappy. The common law validates these reactions by recognizing that a procedure performed without informed consent is battery and medical negligence. We do not ordinarily think that we should ban elective or medically necessary surgical procedures because they could potentially be performed without fully informed consent. We typically demand fully informed consent instead. Yet Justice Kennedy seemed to reason that the possibility that physicians will not spell out the details of the D&X abortion technique is a reason to ban the technique altogether.

GINSBURG'S DISSENT

She – Justice Ruth Bader Ginsburg, a mother and the sole woman on the Supreme Court after the retirement of Justice Sandra Day O'Connor – could see through Kennedy's analysis. She recognized Kennedy's maternalism and paternalism for what they are. "This way of thinking," she wrote in an animated dissent, "reflects ancient notions about women's place in the family and under the Constitution – ideas that have long since been discredited." She appropriately cited the discredited *Muller v. Oregon* (422–3), which upheld "protective" legislation imposing work-hour limitations on women in view of the supposed "physical structure and a proper discharge of her maternal funct[ion]." Ginsburg also cited the infamous *Bradwell v. State*, in which the Supreme Court upheld an Illinois statute denying women the right to practice law. Citing (his conception of) natural law, Justice Bradley concurred in *Bradwell* (141): "Man is, or should be, woman's protector and defender. The natural and proper timidity and delicacy which belongs to the female sex evidently unfits it for many of the occupations of civil life.... The paramount destiny and mission of woman are to fulfil[l] the noble and benign offices of wife and mother."

Bradwell rather than *Casey* is the real precedent for Justice Kennedy's analysis in *Gonzales*. Justice Kennedy was sadly out of step with the times and with court decisions of recent decades that disallow "archaic and overbroad generalizations... such as assumptions as to [women's] dependency" (*Califano*: 207) and "overbroad generalizations" about the "talents, capacities, or preferences" of women that "have... impeded... women's progress toward full citizenship stature throughout our Nation's history" (*United States v. Virginia*: 543n12). Kennedy seemed to miss the egalitarian strand of *Casey*, which he repeatedly cited to support restrictions on abortion. Justice Ginsburg made the point: "Though today's majority may regard women's feelings on the matter as 'self-evident,' this Court has repeatedly confirmed that '[t]he destiny of the woman must be shaped... on her own conception of her spiritual imperatives and her place in society.' Casey, 505 U.S., at 852. See also id., at 877 (plurality opinion) ('[M]eans chosen by the State to further the interest in potential life must be calculated to inform the woman's free choice, not hinder it.')" (*Gonzales*: 1650). Kennedy set aside realism's call for progressive reforms and scientific data in favor of natural law's self-evident metaphysic of true womanhood. Maternalism and paternalism demand unselfish motherhood and, for women, the guidance of male superiors. It is notable that the Partial-Birth Abortion Ban Act criminalizes the conduct of abortionists but not of their female patients who are presumed to be uninformed or misinformed and therefore innocent. But women seeking abortions are probably no less informed that women seeking other medical procedures. They should not be presumed victims of cruel-minded clinicians wielding scissors of destruction. They should get no free pass from complicity and responsibility.

COMPETENCE AND CARE

Paternalism insults pregnant women, who make life-shaping choices every day. Women decide whether to place senile parents in a nursing home and pull the plug on their life support. Women decide whether to authorize experimental surgery for their children and whether to prefer mastectomy to lumpectomy for themselves. Lawmakers should not suppose that special paternalistic intervention is needed in the abortion context that is not needed elsewhere when important decisions must be made. Where are all the guardians of women's safety when they are being sold risky variable-rate mortgages?

Today, American society seems prepared to presume women's competence to run their own lives and to run for president, but abortion opponents rush to assume that women's psychological health must be in jeopardy if they abort. True women must naturally regret abortions, find them depressing. Women must therefore be discouraged from abortion, led to alternatives like horses to water. Ginsburg's dissent in *Gonzales* broke through all the tired, twisted nineteenth-century nonsense of women's health.

Of course a small minority of women bent on terminating the lives of their fetuses may well need paternalistic intervention. Women with mental illnesses, for example, may be unable to manage pregnancy on their own. A thirty-seven-year old businesswoman with four living children, Christy Freeman, hid four dead fetuses on her property. Freeman may have intentionally caused four separate stillborn births. Or maybe products of natural miscarriages were a kind of fetish for her disjointed maternalism. The four corpses were discovered after Freeman, covered with bruises and showing signs of having given birth, appeared at a hospital near her Ocean City, Maryland, home without a baby. Police discovered a recently deceased twenty-six-week old male fetus in Freeman's home wrapped in a towel under her bathroom vanity, another in her Winnebago, and two others wrapped in plastic in a trunk. Freeman was charged with the murder of the recently deceased male fetus, although she "told police she had delivered a deformed baby, which she called 'gloopity glop,' and that she had flushed the fetus down the toilet. According to the charging documents, though, the baby was a 'viable fetus/infant,' with hands, feet and facial features" ("Investigators").

A minority of women need to be protected from self-harm and cruelty. We can reject maternalism and paternalism in abortion law without denying this reality. Some unfortunate women like Christy Freeman need serious help making choices and coping with the consequences of their choices, but the Court should not water down *Roe v. Wade* on their account.

WORKS CITED

"Bodies of 4 Infants Found at Maryland Home." *New York Times*, July 31, 2007, A15.

Bradwell v. State, 16 Wall. 130 (1873).

Califano v. Goldfarb, 430 U.S. 199 (1977).
Gonzales v. Carhart, 127 S. Ct. 1610 (2007).
Hodgson v. Minnesota, 497 U.S. 417 (1990).
"Investigators Work to Tie Dead Fetuses to Taxi Driver." http:www.wbalttv.com/news/13788193/detail.html (July 31, 2007).
Llewellyn, Karl. "On Philosophy in American Law." *U. Pa. L. Rev.* 82.3 (1934): 205–12.
Muller v. Oregon, 208 U.S. 412 (1908).
Partial-Birth Abortion Ban X, Pub. L. No. 108-105, H.R. 760, sec. 3, 18 U.S.C. 1531.
Pfaelzer, Jean. *Driven Out: The Forgotten War against Chinese Americans.* New York: Random House, 2008.
Planned Parenthood v. Casey, 505 U.S. 833 (1992).
Planned Parenthood of Central Missouri v. Danforth, 428 U.S. 52 (1976).
Plessy v. Ferguson, 163 U.S. 537 (1896).
Roe v. Wade, 410 U.S. 113 (1973).
Rust v. Sullivan, 500 U.S. 173 (1991).
Stenberg v. Carhart, 530 U.S. 914 (2000).
United States v. Virginia, 518 U.S. 515 (1996).
Webster v. Reproductive Health Services, 492 U.S. 490 (1989).

PART FIVE. LAW, RHETORIC, AND PRACTICE THEORY

23 Foundationalism and Ground Truth in American Legal Philosophy: Classical Rhetoric, Realism, and Pragmatism

EILEEN A. SCALLEN

One of the visual clichés in modern newscasts is a clip of a hapless reporter standing in the midst of a hurricane, blizzard, flood, or other natural disaster. I am sure I am not alone in wondering, "What is that idiot doing out there?" It turns out this is a melodramatic representation of a standard concept in meteorology, known as "ground truth." Ground truth is provided by professional or volunteer spotters who are in a position to observe and report weather conditions as they are being experienced on – well – the ground. Although modern meteorology uses a wide range of sophisticated remote sensing technology, "[o]nly a spotter can see a tornado" (McAuliffe 2007). Ground truth is also used in cartography and military operations, where even high-definition remote sensing devices, including satellite imagery and aerial photographs, can provide misleading or inaccurate information unless compared with and connected to observed conditions on the earth. In the military and international law contexts, ground truth is used in opposition to other kinds of truth, such as "legal truth" (Warren 1996: 50) or "paper truth" (Cárdenas 2004: 1343). In each of these cases, the use of generalized or abstract knowledge is balanced with contextual, firsthand observation and reporting: ground truth.

Advocates of ground truth suggest that it is often more accurate than the abstraction it validates. Yet ground truth makes no claim of perfection. Ground truth can be dead wrong; a spotter can miss the funnel cloud or mischaracterize the condition (e.g., categorizing sleet as hail). To use a different example, remote sensing technology and ground intelligence can report the existence of weapons of mass destruction at a particular location. But, shortly thereafter, no such weapons are found. Yet no one suggests abandoning the concept of ground truth in meteorology or intelligence gathering. Ground truth is integral to these fields. This essay suggests that ground truth is also essential to the philosophy and practice of American law – whether we like it or not.

And some of us do not like it, stressing instead the need to reach "the ground truth" (Park and Saks 2006: 977). However, finding *the* ground truth should not be confused with using ground truth. The use of the definite article says it all. Ground truth is one source of information, just as the abstraction it illuminates is one source of information. Good intelligence gathering or meteorology demands both kinds of information. In contrast, a demand for *the* ground truth reveals a foundationalist belief in a singular, objective, and universal truth. Consequently, foundationalists, whether in religion, science, philosophy, or law, commonly present us with this false dilemma: take the path to *the* ground truth or take the path to the place where anything at all can pass for truth (radical relativism) or where there is no truth at all (radical skepticism).

Law is particularly susceptible to foundationalist calls for the ground truth. Recent controversy over the admissibility of scientific and social science evidence at trial reflects this dilemma. Some writers suggest that expert testimony based on any basis other than empirically tested hypotheses should be dismissed as "junk science" (Huber 1991). Others have suggested that evidence scholarship can be "dangerous" when it examines issues other than increasing the accuracy of verdicts, such as the social, economic, or political implications of evidence law (Park and Saks 2006: 1028, 1030). Finally, although no one seriously disputes the need for application of strict empirical testing for questions of natural science, conflicts arise over the admissibility of clinically based expert testimony, including syndrome evidence (Slobogin 2007: 6). Such evidence is often used to make legal decisions about criminal mental states, such as premeditation or intent, but is highly controversial. This is not surprising, for these questions are among the most difficult, if not impossible, to subject to rigorous controlled testing. States of mind are not reflections of objective reality – criminal prosecutions focus on the mental state at the time of the crime. Thus, Christopher Slobogin (2007: 44) argues that, "although ascertaining objective truth might be possible with respect to acts, *narrative thinking* dominates attempts to reconstruct mental state" (emphasis in original). Such expert testimony offered at trial – the ground zero of the adversary system – can be denigrated by claims that it amounts only to "suppositional" tales of intent, told by would-be Dostoyevskian novelists (Faigman 1989: 1073–7). However, Slobogin and others argue that certain clinically based expert testimony can provide useful context and perspective for decision making, including decisions made by lay jurors whose life experience is far different from that of the defendant on trial.

Despite objections from foundationalists, the use of ground truth is alive and well in American law. In this essay, I trace the conflict between foundationalism and ground truth from one of its earliest manifestations in classical rhetoric to its more recent appearances in American legal philosophy in realism and pragmatism. I argue that the use of ground truth is not a defect of reasoning but rather enriches our decision making. Decision making that uses ground truth does not require us to abandon good science or empirical research. Hypothesis testing and valid deductive reasoning are invaluable for producing certain conclusions. But humans do not live by certainty – or even statistically significant confidence levels – alone. The problem with foundationalism is not that it advocates the use of deductive reasoning and empirical studies. Foundationalism is the fetishizing of deductive reasoning and empirical studies. Foundationalism thus demeans the diversity and richness of inductive reasoning based on context and experience – ground truth (i.e., unless ground truth can lead to a testable hypothesis).

FOUNDATIONALISM AND GROUND TRUTH IN CLASSICAL RHETORIC

Plato and his student Aristotle have dominated the legal academy's view of classical rhetoric. Yet there is a different branch of classical rhetoric, scorned or – even worse – ignored by legal scholars. What to call this line of thought is debatable. Some of its practitioners – from Isocrates in ancient Greece to Cicero in ancient Rome – called it philosophy, which makes it sound rather respectable. Others, such as Plato and Aristotle, damned it as sophistry. We might dismiss the choice of labels as mere rhetoric, but the ability of language to create images and frames of reference that have the power to shape human political, legal, and moral theory is hard to deny.

Rhetoric, the study of argumentation and persuasion, was vital in ancient Greece because of its particular political and legal structures. Participation in Greek political and legal systems was restricted to particular members of society, free men. But Greeks were not allowed to speak to the legislature through lobbyists or to juries through lawyers. Some Greeks responded by hiring speechwriters to script their arguments. Others sought out education to help them become better advocates. One school was Plato's Academy, which immortalized the Socratic dialogue, a process through which the student could be disabused of false beliefs by a skilled interrogator, until only *the* ground truth remained. Plato, an Athenian aristocrat who was suspicious of Athenian democracy, distinguished his school of philosophy from the schools of the Sophists. Because Plato believed in divine and absolute truth, he found some Sophists, such as Protagoras and Gorgias, particularly offensive for their relativism or skepticism. In addition to being a radical skeptic, Gorgias was obsessed with the structure and sound of language, teaching complex alliteration and stylistic excess. As a result, he was especially easy to parody in Plato's dialogues.

The problem with Plato's portrait of the Sophists is that he paints all of them with this same oversimplified brush. In fact, there were significant differences among the individuals whom Plato labels as Sophists. The best way to illustrate this is to describe Plato's competitor Isocrates, who Plato called a Sophist but who considered himself a philosopher and attempted to distinguish himself from the other Sophists. Many of the Sophists were itinerant teachers, taking their shows on the road and accepting any student who could pay their fees. Moreover, some of these Sophists focused narrowly on specific tricks of argumentation. In this sense, these Sophists were more akin to today's continuing legal education presenters who promise to teach their students to dazzle any jury in ten easy steps.

In contrast to these Sophists, Isocrates founded a permanent school of higher education in Athens and selected students with an aptitude for education, not just anyone who paid the tuition. Most important, the concept of rhetoric at the heart of Isocrates' school required broad and rigorous study in a variety of subjects. Today we might call it a liberal arts curriculum, requiring the study of philosophy, science, mathematics, literature, history, and communication. Unlike other Sophists, however, Isocrates did not believe that moral excellence or virtue could be taught or transferred from teacher to student. Instead, his notion of practical wisdom emphasized the development of a student's own moral character through encouragement and inspiration.

Isocrates, however, aligned with the Sophists on the nature of moral principles and truth. For Plato, these unchanging, universal, and absolute concepts existed independent of humans. Isocrates, however, directed his students away from formal and abstract notions of truth and morality toward specific contemporary and historical problems. For Isocrates, natural ability plus the rigorous study of practical political, social, scientific, and legal problems produced an educated citizen who could exercise his best judgment in service to the community: "For since it is not in the nature of man to attain a science by the possession of which we can know positively what we should do or what we should say... I hold that man to be wise who is able by his powers of conjecture to arrive generally at the best course" (Isocrates 1929: 271). Like other Sophists, Isocrates viewed the human world as unclear and uncertain but accessible and manageable through language, which is why the study of argumentation and persuasion was so important to the education of the citizen-lawyer (Foss, Foss, and Trapp 2001: 3).

The school of Isocrates lasted for more than fifty years, and it was there where he trained as many as one hundred students at a time, many of whom became leaders of Athens and other parts of ancient Greece. The Romans Cicero and Quintilian built on the teaching of Isocrates. These Romans were practicing lawyers as well as philosophers who emphasized the use of ground truth in court and in the legislature. Indeed, Cicero lamented the dominance of the foundationalist treatment of law: "The followers of Socrates cut connection with the practicing lawyers and detached them from the common title of philosophy, although the old masters had intended there to be a marvelously close alliance between oratory and philosophy" (Cicero 1959: 59). The influence of Isocrates went far beyond the Roman Empire, eventually reaching America in its formative years. Because of the lack of formal law schools in the American colonies, Isocrates, Cicero, and Quintilian served as the "law professors" of America's earliest lawyers and prominent citizens: John Adams, Alexander Hamilton, and James Madison (Richard 1994). The leaders of America's revolution certainly valued intellectual and moral principle and unalienable rights; they were not against theory. But they also understood the dangers of foundationalism, the limits of theory, and the value of ground truth in a democracy.

FOUNDATIONALISM AND GROUND TRUTH IN AMERICAN LEGAL REALISM

The role of ground truth in American legal philosophy resurfaced in the early twentieth century. As with the conflict between the schools of Plato and Isocrates in ancient Athens, American legal realism arose in contrast with a foundationalist view of American law, commonly called legal formalism. Adherents of legal formalism, which reigned in American jurisprudence for a good part of the nineteenth century, argued that law was an objective, universal, and absolute concept. As a result, law could be discovered, collected, and organized in discrete subjects such as contracts, torts, or property. Most important, law should be applied to the facts of a case by a process of pure deductive reasoning.

As with the Sophists, it is difficult to find one brand of legal realism. The realists, which included distinguished legal scholars such as Felix Cohen, Jerome Frank, Karl Llewellyn, and Max Radin, reflected a wide range of views. At one end of the spectrum was Jerome Frank's radical skepticism about judicial decision making, arguing that judges decided cases on the basis of their particular personal biases or beliefs and then justified them with whatever legal rules support the conclusion. As in the case of the Sophists, this portrait of radical skepticism has become the image of legal realism, perhaps because of its dramatic and unsettling quality. However, other realists were far less skeptical but tried to use insights and empirical studies from psychology, sociology, and political science to understand judicial decision making.

Brian Leiter (1997: 275–6) has argued that despite their considerable differences, all legal realists subscribed to at least one "core claim" about adjudication: "in deciding cases, judges respond primarily to the stimulus of the facts." Or, phrased in terms of this essay, all legal realists respected ground truth. Yet there were differences in approach to ground truth. For example, N. E. H. Hull (1997: 313) contrasts Roscoe Pound's attempt to study the Chinese criminal justice system with Karl Llewellyn's study of the Cheyenne legal system: "Pound drafted and wished to impose a Western-style social science survey on provincial officials; Llewellyn listened to local 'law-men' and tried to see the world through their eyes. Pound wanted to generalize through extensive comparison and categorization; Llewellyn wanted to particularize through the stories of individual cases." Although many realists, including Llewellyn, approved of the surge in empirical studies in the social sciences, Llewellyn was not convinced that the scientific approach could produce by itself "a whole view of anything" (Twining 1973: 513). The appellate judge, argued Llewellyn, made decisions by applying a "situation-sense." Others also stressed that a judge's professional and social experiences provided a frame of reference, or "type situation" (Radin 1925: 358), from which the judge would view the facts of particular case and that had a profound impact on the outcome of the case. Both notions of situation-sense and type situation rest on concepts of ground truth – the value of individual experience and context.

Although he never used the phrase "ground truth," Llewellyn contended that there were two kinds of truth in law – testable and nontestable. The lawyer's work rested on both, but "[a]ll practical judgments must of necessity move on such *working* bases: One seeks *enough* significant 'facts,' accurately *enough*, with a measure *sufficiently* explored as to likely consequence as to be a worthwhile 'best' move into the confessedly uncertain future" (Twining 1973: 515, emphasis in original). It is hard to miss the echo of Isocrates in Llewellyn's view of the place of ground truth in law.

FOUNDATIONALISM, LEGAL PRAGMATISM (AMERICAN AND OTHER VARIETIES)

As the title of this section suggests, categories of thought become more complex as American legal philosophy matures. Certainly pragmatism goes by many names, such as *neopragmatism*, *practical legal studies*, *practical reason*, *practical wisdom*, and *skepticism*. And within each label, one finds a range of views that undermines the identity of a school of thought. What follows here is an attempt to describe the various approaches in a way that is pragmatic – in the sense of comprehensible – and to show the significance of ground truth to each.

Neopragmatism is the most recent brand of pragmatism. Its best known advocates are Richard Rorty, Richard J. Bernstein, and Hilary Putnam. Neopragmatists build on the work of the earlier American pragmatism of John Dewey, William James, and Charles Peirce. The link between legal realism and the older version of pragmatism is apparent in Justice Oliver Wendell Holmes, who some have labeled a realist (Posner 1988: 287) and others have labeled a pragmatist (Grey 1989: 793).

However, neopragmatists distinguish themselves from earlier pragmatists in two ways. First, neopragmatists "talk about language instead of experience or mind or consciousness, as the old Pragmatists did. Second, we have all read Kuhn, Hanson, Toulmin, and Feyerabend, and have thereby become suspicious of the term 'scientific method'" (Rorty 1990: 813). In this respect, the neopragmatists also differ from the early legal realists, who were fascinated with the psyche and the possibilities of the empirical method and the social sciences, but who (with the notable exception of Llewellyn) did not question the limits of empiricism.

Although both old pragmatism and neopragmatism are responses to foundationalism, I would add another difference. Some neopragmatists, such as Margaret Jane Radin (1990: 1708–11), have stressed the importance of critical self-consciousness. Although the early pragmatists emphasized the psychological and context-dependent dimensions of decision making, they did not seem to be as open about their own contexts, such as their own biases, attitudes, and values. In contrast, some neopragmatists tend to be more autobiographical in their theoretical writing, sharing their ground truth as narratives. But this has provoked criticism that such writers are mere storytellers, not legal scholars, and that ground truth cannot accurately be generalized (Farber and Sherry: 95–117).

Recent scholarship reemphasizes ground truth and the value of sophisticated use of legal empirical studies, seeking a new legal realism (Macauley 2005). Brian Leiter and Ron Allen introduced to evidence law the philosophical concept of naturalized epistemology, which moderates any move toward abstraction with high-quality empirical studies but acknowledges that not all evidence rules are susceptible to such studies (Allen and Leiter 2001: 1498). Similarly, the philosophical notions of relative plausibility and inference to best explanation or abduction attempt to use ground truth to find a path through the horns of the dilemma of foundationalism and radical skepticism or relativism.

But the tension between foundationalism and the desire to use ground truth in law continues. One area of contention is eyewitness identification (Levenson 2008: 279n). One could view the testimony of an eyewitness to a crime as the paradigm of ground truth. Here, no theory is required; guilt or innocence is established by the witness, who testifies on the basis of his or her firsthand sensory information to answer the question, Who done it? But those who work in the criminal justice system know there are well-documented and numerous examples of false or mistaken eyewitness identifications. And yet courts are reticent to admit expert testimony about the problems with eyewitness testimony because such expert opinion is often based on testing that is not sufficiently reliable in the eyes of the judges excluding it. Interestingly, one of the major flaws cited about these studies is the lack of ground truth – knowledge of actual innocence or guilt of the alleged perpetrator (Ross and Malpass 2008: 17, 19). The conundrum of expert opinion on the flaws with eyewitness testimony thus presents the classic dilemma – we must have *the* ground truth (foundationalist objective, universal truth) so we conclude that we cannot use ground truth (partial, imperfect, contextual, contingent truth) to provide the decision maker with information about the strength and weaknesses of other evidence. But, in our adversarial system, we often cannot know the ground truth, such as where there is no physical evidence or where the ultimate issue in the trial is a question of mental state, such as intent or premeditation. The circularity of the argument is maddening.

The way out of this circular path is to recognize that trials are not always about finding *the* ground truth, because it may never be capable of being known with any degree of certainty. However, trials are always about using ground truth to reach a reasonable decision under circumstances of uncertainty. Both an eye witness identification and expert testimony about the problems with eyewitness identification may be imperfect or flawed but still make useful contributions to a conclusion about "who done it." Excluding one or the other type of evidence does not protect the system or its participants – it only impoverishes the resources of the decision maker who must make a decision on a question of fact that is inherently unclear (for if it was clear, we would not need a trial).

At the bottom of the tension between foundationalists and advocates of ground truth is an attitude toward the decision maker, particularly where that decision maker is a juror. Those who argue that only *the* ground truth is acceptable as expert testimony do not respect juries – because they are not sophisticated, not trustworthy, not intelligent, or not educated. Those who are willing to use ground truth know that juries will make mistakes; juries may come to conclusions that ultimately can be proved (perhaps objectively) wrong in hindsight. But those who are willing to consider ground truth know that jurors – or other decision makers – who inform their reasoning solely with evidence that is believed to be the ground truth may also be proved wrong. The difference between the two positions is that those willing to use ground truth sometimes see the injustice of abstract principles when applied to concrete situations that are more complex than the theory presupposes. The resultant expanded perspective may generate new propositions about justice, some of which can be subject to controlled experiments and some of which cannot – but that are no less worthy of respect.

CONCLUSION

William Twining (1973: 3–4), in his masterful book on the legal realists and Llewellyn, observed that the story of American legal philosophy can be seen as an effort to respond to several problems: (1) adapting the English common law to the conditions of the New World; (2) interpreting the expansive language of the Constitution and Bill of Rights as the country evolved; (3) validating the existence of a unified common law in a growing, heterogeneous federation of independent states; (4) adapting the law to the dramatic industrial revolution of the late nineteenth century; and (5) coping with the increased quantity and complexity of law arising from legislation, administrative regulation, and decisional law.

Just as Twining refined and built on observations by Max Rheinstein, I wish to add another dimension to Twining's list of forces that have shaped the story of American legal philosophy: the expansion of the legal profession in the mid- to late-twentieth century, as barriers to law school and the legal profession began to weaken for women and minorities of all kinds – religious, racial, ethnic, and sexual. Not surprisingly, confronted by foundationalist claims of neutrality and objectivity of law, a few of these new legal scholars and lawyers turned to the kind of radical skepticism and radical relativism that Plato reviled 2,500 years earlier. But as with legal realism and legal pragmatism, it would be erroneous to reduce critical feminist, Marxist, race, or queer theory to a one-size-fits-all destabilizing force (although, as Plato knew, it is easier to discredit and dismiss one's opponents that way). The beauty of American legal philosophy is that as new ground truth emerges a range of responses develop – from the most skeptical and relativist to the moderate and practical.

Yet it is easy to grow weary of the conflict between foundationalists and ground truth. In fact, some legal scholars contend that it is impossible for anyone to be a faithful foundationalist, opining that now "we are all realists" (Green 2005: 1917), or "every conscientious judge and scholar . . . in any of the supposed camps, is a pragmatist in the broadest sense" (Smith 1990: 827). But ground truth proves these conclusions are not true. Legislators, judges, regulators, law professors, and lawyers still regularly rely on foundationalist claims based on natural law, tradition, natural science, or religion. Such claims offer clarity and certainty, so reassuring and alluring in unsettling times – when steel and concrete skyscrapers or bridges crumble into dust or when strange new families (with two dads and children with different-colored skin) move in down the block.

The lessons of classical rhetoric, realism, and pragmatism, and their progeny are important. We need not be skewered by Plato's false dilemma; to embrace the value of ground truth is not to become a radical relativist or skeptic. Ground truth is real; it can be reported and counted (although sometimes imperfectly). One can often (though not always) generalize from ground truth and empirically test it. The very nature of ground truth is that it is relatively stable, even if it does shift with additional experience and discovery. Most of these shifts in the earth below us are subtle, detected only by specialists who study them with sensitive instruments.

Sometimes, however, there are earthquakes (Kuhn 1970). But these major upheavals do not have to end in chaos and anarchy. Although building on bedrock may be better than building on landfill, there are limited amounts of bedrock. Where bedrock is not available, seismologists have shown that buildings with rigidity suffer more severe damage in earthquakes than buildings with some give or flexibility in their construction (Langenbach 1989).

Obviously, my notion of ground is operating as a metaphor here, as is the concept of ground truth, and that is intentional. Human understanding is shaped by associating the intangible with the material – hence our attraction to metaphor, which transforms the abstract into the concrete. It is no accident that battles between foundationalism and ground truth in American legal philosophy also have been fought over the role of rhetoric: is it a conduit of absolute truth, the tool of deceit and manipulation, or something else? We keep asking these questions because humans have only language (whether verbal or nonverbal) to express our ground truth.

Classical legal rhetoric, realism, and pragmatism have a surprisingly strong lineage to one another. Some might yawn at the banality of such an observation, but the tension between foundationalist truth and ground truth has persisted in Western culture for more than 2,500 years. At times, that tension has erupted into war – both cultural and martial. However, if we can stop fetishizing foundationalist claims (e.g., democracy is an unqualified good for any culture, any time; the only worthwhile expert testimony or scholarship is that which is based on empirically testable theories) and take ground truth more seriously, we might avoid some of the inevitable injustice resulting from such conflicts.

WORKS CITED

Allen, Ronald J., and Brian Leiter. "Naturalized Epistemology and the Law of Evidence." *Va. L. Rev.* 87.8 (2001): 1491–550.

Cárdenas, Emilio J. "The United Nations Security Council's Quest for Effectiveness." *Mich. J.* Int'l L. 25.4 (2004): 1341–8.

Cicero, Marcus Tullius. *De Oratore: Book III* in *Cicero; On the Orator, Book III On Fate, Stoic Paradoxes, Divisions of Oratory.* Trans. H. Rackam. Cambridge MA: Oxford Univ. Press, 1959, pp. 3–185.

Faigman, David L. "To Have and Have Not: Assessing the Value of Social Science to the Law as Science and Policy." *Emory L.J.* 38.4 (1989): 1005–95.

Farber, Daniel A., and Suzanna Sherry. *Beyond All Reason: The Radical Assault on Truth in American Law.* New York: Oxford Univ. Press: 1997.

Foss, Sonja K., Karen A. Foss, and Robert Trapp. *Contemporary Perspectives on Rhetoric,* 3d ed. New York: Waveland Press, 2001.

Green, Michael Steven. "Legal Realism as Theory of Law." *Wm. & Mary L. Rev.* 46.6 (2005): 1915–2000.

Grey, Thomas C. "Holmes and Legal Pragmatism." *Stan. L. Rev.* 41.4 (1989): 787–870.

Huber, Peter W. *Galileo's Revenge: Junk Science in the Courtroom.* New York: Basic Books, 1991.

Hull, N. E. H. *Roscoe Pound and Karl Llewellyn: Searching for an American Jurisprudence.* Chicago: Univ. of Chicago Press, 1997.

Isocrates, "Antidosis," in *Isocrates,* vol. 2. Trans. George Norlin. Cambridge, MA: Harvard Univ. Press, 1929, 185–365.

Kuhn, Thomas S. *The Structure of Scientific Revolutions,* 2d ed. Chicago: Univ. of Chicago Press, 1970.

Langenbach, Randolph. "Bricks, Mortar, and Earthquakes; Historic Preservation vs. Earthquake Safety." *Apt Bulletin,* 21.3–4 (1989): 30–43.

Leiter, Brian. "Rethinking Legal Realism: Toward a Naturalized Jurisprudence." *Tex. L. Rev.* 76.2 (1997): 267–315.

Levenson, Laurie L. "Courtroom Demeanor: The Theater of the Courtroom." *Minn. L. Rev.* 92.3 (2008): 573–633.

Macaulay, Stewart. "The New Versus the Old Legal Realism: 'Things Ain't What They Used to Be.'" *Wis. L. Rev.* 2005.2 (2005): 365–403.

McAuliffe, Bill. "Weather Spotters Stay in Front of Storms' Siren Call." *Minneapolis Star Tribune,* Aug. 22, 2007, A1 (quoting John Wetter, Skywarn operations coordinator, National Weather Service Office, Chanhassen, Minnesota).

Park, Roger C., and Michael J. Saks. "Evidence Scholarship Reconsidered: Results of the Interdisciplinary Turn." *B.C. L. Rev.* 47.4 (2006): 949–1031.

Posner, Richard A. *Law and Literature: A Misunderstood Relation.* Cambridge, MA: Harvard Univ. Press, 1988.

Radin, Margaret Jane. "The Pragmatist and the Feminist." *S. Cal. L. Rev.* 63.6 (1990): 1699–726.

Radin, Max. "The Theory of Judicial Decision: Or How Judges Think." *A.B.A. J.* 11.6 (1925): 357–62.

Richard, Carl J. *The Founders and the Classics: Greece, Rome, and the American Enlightenment.* Cambridge, MA: Harvard Univ. Press, 1994.

Rorty, Richard. "The Banality of Pragmatism and the Poetry of Justice." *S. Cal. L. Rev.* 63.6 (1990): 1811–19.

Ross, Stephen J., and Roy S. Malpass. "Moving Forward: Response to Studying Eye Witness Identifications in the Field." *Law & Hum. Behav.* 32.1 (2008): 16–20.

Slobogin, Christopher. *Proving the Unprovable: The Role of Law, Science and Speculation in Adjudicating Culpability and Dangerousness.* New York: Oxford Univ. Press, 2007.

Smith, Steven D. "The Pursuit of Pragmatism." *Yale L.J.* 100.2 (1990): 409–49.

Twining, William. *Karl Llewellyn and the Realist Movement.* London: Weidenfeld and Nicolson, 1973.

Warren, Marc L. "Operational Law: A Concept Matures." *Mil. L. Rev.* 152.1 (1996): 33–73.

24 The Irrelevance of Contemporary Academic Philosophy for Law: Recovering the Rhetorical Tradition

FRANCIS J. MOOTZ III

Can we hope for justice in this world? Plato thought not. In the *Republic*, he suggests that justice can be achieved only if the philosophers rule, but also that philosophers cannot simultaneously rule the many and remain in the sunlight of true knowledge. They must return to the cave. Leo Strauss famously interprets Plato as arguing that the philosopher in the cave must speak esoterically because if he speaks plainly his wisdom will be misunderstood, leading the prisoners to attack the one who opens this dangerous line of thinking. After all, the philosopher "returning from divine contemplations to the petty miseries of men cuts a sorry figure and appears most ridiculous, if, while still blinking through the gloom, and before he has become sufficiently accustomed to the environing darkness, he is compelled in courtrooms or elsewhere to contend about the shadows of justice" (Plato 1930: 517d–517e). What, then, can be said about striving to create a just world? Plato leaves us with the *Laws*, in which three tradition-bound men discuss politics in light of real-world practical constraints. Law is our resignation in the face of the impossible demands of justice; it is not just unphilosophical; it is antiphilosophical.

Against this backdrop, is it realistic to believe that today's philosophers will provide our divided world with the roadmap to just social relations? Can philosophy reveal that we are living in the shadows and shed light on our imprisoned predicament? Dare we hope for salvation to emerge from the cadre of Ph.D. philosophers who teach in our universities and colleges, or have they descended back into the cave so far that they only vaguely recall the blinding light that captivated them in their youth? These questions, of course, suggest their own answers.

PHILOSOPHY

Philosophy no longer is a way of life for members of a community seeking to determine what the good life entails. Today, philosophy designates a department of the modern research university, a technical discipline whose members vie for

I dedicate this essay to the memory of William Hardman Poteat, formerly chair of the Department of Religion at Duke University, who served as a wonderful role model for me by living the life of a philosopher in the real world. Poteat exemplified what he termed our "mindbodily" presence; his presence will be missed by many.

prestige and glory in the shadowy world of academe. This is not to say that philosophers are disqualified by their profession from active participation in the communal effort to define justice, but it is to suggest that being a professional philosopher is no better preparation for this task than is being a literature professor, artist, or medical doctor.

Academic philosophers are quick to point out that the ugly machinery of law ignores the painstaking philosophical clarification of pertinent concepts such as responsibility, culpability, and intent. This is a hollow indictment, however, because they inevitably fail to establish that conceptual confusions in law have important negative consequences that can be identified and corrected only through philosophical analysis. A woefully tangled mess of cases has attempted to define an intentional act for purposes of insurance coverage, and there can be no doubt that this area of law always benefits from careful analysis. Can a philosophical exegesis of the concepts of intention and causation assist lawyers and judges in a manner that is uniquely philosophical?

Philosophers tend not to think so. Applied philosophy is a ghetto that the philosophical Brahmins are loath to enter. It is enough simply to establish that judges and lawyers do not deal with concepts like intentionality with the precision of philosophers, and it is better not to struggle to bring philosophical precision to bear on specific legal problems, which are inherently normative and contextual rather than analytical and conceptual. An intentional act for purposes of insurance coverage is different from an intentional act for purposes of criminal law, tort law, or the expression of moral opprobrium by the community toward the actor. Clarifying the polysemic concept of intentional act is a philosophical challenge that is important and difficult, but any potential payoff with regard to specific legal dilemmas is both unlikely and rather beside the point. Once you've basked in the sunlight, it is difficult to go grubbing around in the earth again.

Perhaps the most dramatic illustration that law is a speluncean adventure occurred when Ronald Dworkin, John Rawls, Robert Nozick, and other moral philosophers submitted an amicus brief to the U.S. Supreme Court regarding the asserted constitutional right to assisted suicide. The Philosopher's Brief, as it was named when published in *The New York Review of Books*, began by admitting that the Court was not being asked to make a moral or ethical judgment but rather to determine the scope of the constitutional principle of liberty that guarantees individual self-determination (Dworkin 1997). The elegant and persuasive argument elided various philosophical debates in which the authors might otherwise have engaged, and instead made an argument for what justice demands under our constitutional system in a manner not altogether different in kind from an ordinary legal argument (although, thankfully, they did not cloak their arguments with endless case citations and overblown claims of inevitability and univocity).

The philosopher-lawyer H. L. A. Hart brought rigor to legal theory, but this is not the same as connecting the disciplines of philosophy and law. Analytic legal philosophy strives to rise above the everyday struggles within a legal system to focus on the conceptual structure that existing legal practices imply. Just as a philosopher of aesthetics wouldn't attempt to tell a painter how to paint, philosophers of law in this vein don't attempt to tell parties how to engage in legal practice.

The Hart-Fuller debate and the Hart-Dworkin debate, as interesting as they may be, do not connect with legal practice in a unique and directive manner.

Some philosophers embrace an even more hermetic posture. Friedrich Nietzsche famously acknowledged that he would be a posthumous philosopher because his contemporaries were incapable of seeing the light. There appears to be no reason for the philosopher to return to the cave, where, still blinded by the light of true knowledge, he or she is unable to relate to prisoners who live among the shadows. Heidegger (2002: 61) suggests that the murder of the philosopher returning from the light is a metaphor of the poisoning of philosophy that occurs when the philosopher abandons the quest for truth as the unconcealedness of beings in favor of the search for truth as the correct framing of propositions about the shadows. Heidegger's elitist reading of Plato's elitism leads him to conclude that the philosopher is destined to rescue only a few prisoners by force, but only if he ignores the "obligatory cave-chatter" of the sophist-philosophers of the cave. "He does not liberate by conversing with the cave-dwellers in the language, and with the aims and intentions, of the cave, but by laying hold of them violently and dragging them away. He does not try to persuade the cave-dwellers by reference to norms, grounds and proofs. In that way, as Plato says, he would only make himself laughable" (Heidegger 2002: 62). Heidegger, like Nietzsche before him, considered academic philosophers to be cave dwellers who could not be saved, and he almost certainly would characterize philosophers of law who work even indirectly with the shadows in the same manner. For Heidegger, academic philosophy is the enemy of thinking.

LAW

If philosophers generally do not seek to engage law on the ground, it is equally true that lawyers generally do not seek such engagement. Llewellyn's sentiments on this score are particularly revealing. Although he taught jurisprudence and was engaged in the preeminent theoretical disputes of his day, academic philosophy offended Llewellyn's realist sensibilities (Twining 1985: 93, 173). He embraced a notion of philosophy that was pragmatic and instrumental: relevant legal philosophy just is the set of concepts and heuristics that facilitate the everyday work of the legal system, whereas elitist academic posturing is of no consequence. Llewellyn attempted to understand the play of shadows on the wall, and he saw no point in musing about the light of philosophy that was outside the scope of the concerns of people making their way through life in the cave. Moreover, he regarded philosophy as a follower rather than a leader; philosophy gains traction by answering a felt need within society by permitting us to render dynamic social trends coherent. He argued that legal realism was a helpful way of thinking about law whose time had come rather than a dictate to change the legal system in a particular manner. The very name *legal realism* denoted an effort to develop concepts that match what already exists so as to serve present needs.

It is easy to indict the vast majority of lawyers and judges, and not a few law professors, for an anti-intellectual approach to their profession. If a jurisprudential giant like Llewellyn took such a dim view of academic philosophy, it is safe to assume that most contemporary legal actors would be even more skeptical. It is not that they necessarily are uninterested in philosophy, but only that philosophy is irrelevant to their day-to-day activities as lawyers. This in no way suggests that philosophy is a frivolous enterprise. Philosophy is hard work, and professional philosophers earn their pay. The question is whether contemporary academic philosophy is able to, wishes to, or should speak directly to the troubling issues that pervade our legal system. Llewellyn, like Plato, thought not.

THEORY-PRACTICE

We might explain the lack of a relationship between philosophy and law by characterizing it as a feature of the unavoidable chasm between theory and practice, grudgingly conceding that philosophers philosophize and lawyers lawyer. But this facile answer ignores the inevitable slippage between the two activities. Philosophers must talk about something. However ill-informed or removed from reality their knowledge of law and legal practice, it forms part of the basis for philosophizing about social and political experience. The merit of contemporary legal positivism is its attempt to engage with legal practice to the greatest degree possible before ascending back toward the light of conceptual clarity. Similarly, lawyers inevitably utilize philosophy in their work, however poorly. Great legal arguments and decisions have crisp analysis, conceptual clarity, and normative force. We would never confuse legal practice with philosophy, but it is not possible to make a difficult legal argument without confronting the great issues of legal philosophy. To repeat the old saw, there is nothing so practical as a good theory, and nothing that calls for theoretical reflection so much as a difficult practical problem.

The contemporary divide between academic philosophy and legal practice is neither absolute nor unavoidable. At the height of natural law philosophy there was an organic connection between the work of ecclesiastical courts and the theologians. The question is whether such a bond can be reforged between the academic philosophy of the modern research university and the vast bureaucratic machinery of the legal system. If the goal is a robust relationship between philosophy and law, then both disciplines will have to adjust their orientation and find common ground. Llewellyn suggested, in an unnoticed and almost unnoticeable manner, that this common ground is the ancient art of rhetoric.

Llewellyn is well known for his series of lectures to entering law students beginning in 1929 and eventually published in 1951 as *The Bramble Bush*. In the acknowledgments and afterword he bemoaned his failure to deal with the role of the rhetorical arts in the lawyer's craft, arguing that this would have done much to blunt his critics' accusation that he was a nihilist. His castigation of the elite law schools for their slavish adherence to the theoretical dogmatism of the case method suggested an uncompromising antiphilosophical stance, but Llewellyn's point was to argue that we must develop a broader theoretical appreciation of law that remains connected to practice. He emphasized that the craft of law "cries out for the development and teaching of its theory, as it does also for study by *doing* in light of that theory" (Llewellyn 1981: 185). He named the needed theory

"Spokesmanship," and he derived it from the theories first developed in Greece as "Rhetoric–in essence: the effective techniques of persuasion" (Llewellyn 1981: 185). Spokesmanship calls for a theoretical-practical inquiry intended to equip lawyers for the rhetorical challenges of their profession. Counseling clients is an important feature of spokesmanship no less than arguing a case, and this art cannot be reduced to simple rules for communicating doctrine because it involves theoretical development of, and argumentation about, contested principles (Llewellyn 1981: 185).

Llewellyn's suggestive reflections in 1951 were presaged in "On Philosophy in American Law." Before proceeding to take the reader on a dizzying ride through the tides of American jurisprudence, Llewellyn delivered the following tease in his customary florid prose:

> "One system of precedent" we may have, but it works in forty different ways. Some day, someone will help the second year student orient himself. Nor does anyone bother to present to him the difference between logic and persuasion, nor what a man facing old courts is to do with a new vocabulary; in a word, the game, in framing an argument, of diagnosing the peculiar presuppositions of the hearers. I think the second year student is entitled to feel himself aggrieved. Meanwhile, while we wait upon the treading of the Angel, there is rushing in that calls for doing. Here is a start. (Llewellyn 1934: 205n*)

This was Llewellyn's call for a theory of the practice of spokesmanship, but the essay that follows answers this call only obliquely and in an unsatisfying manner. In the afterword to *The Bramble Bush* he rediscovered this focus and attempted to recast his life's work in this way, but he did so only suggestively. Forging a productive relationship between philosophy and law today requires embracing Llewellyn's intuition and developing it with vigor. Doing so challenges the self-understanding of large segments of both philosophy and law, but it is precisely these self-understandings that have promoted the current state of relative nonengagement.

LAW, HERMENEUTICS, AND RHETORIC

The sharp distinction between philosophy and law occurred when both disciplines built insular guilds that employed distinctive vocabularies to distinguish themselves from rhetoric. Rhetoric was part of the trivium at the core of classical education, and it is the point at which philosophical thinking and legal practice naturally, and inevitably, join. By fleeing rhetoric, we severed the connection between philosophy and law.

Modern Western philosophy emerged in ancient Greece, in part, by painting the rhetoricians with a broad brush as opportunistic Sophists concerned only with achieving success with jurors rather than devoting themselves to the pursuit of knowledge. Rhetoric was tied inextricably to the law courts and politics of the day, and so the philosophers regarded the teachers of rhetoric with great suspicion. Plato cast the die and, Aristotle's moderate approach to rhetoric notwithstanding, philosophy successfully marginalized rhetoric and sent it packing to departments of communication studies. Two thousand years later Vico lamented that the emerging critical philosophy of Descartes sought to erase the rhetorical tradition altogether, destroying an essential feature of liberal education that was particularly important for statesmen and lawyers. Vico (1990: 41) summarizes:

> [W]hosoever intends to devote his efforts, not to physics or mechanics, but to a political career, whether as a civil servant or as a member of the legal profession or of the judiciary, a political speaker or a pulpit orator, should not waste too much time, in his adolescence, on those subjects which are taught by abstract geometry. Let him instead, cultivate his mind with an ingenious method; let him study topics and defend both sides of a controversy, be it on nature, man, or politics, in a freer and brighter style of expression. Let him not spurn reasons that wear a semblance of probability and verisimilitude. Let our efforts not be directed towards achieving superiority over the Ancients merely in the field of science, while they surpass us in wisdom; let us not be merely more exact and more true than the Ancients, while allowing them to be more eloquent than we are; let us equal the Ancients in the fields of wisdom and eloquence as we excel them in the domain of science.

Vico's call fell on deaf ears. Even he must have known that it was too late to avoid philosophy's excision of rhetoric, and therefore its excision of law.

Lawyers pursued their own parochial concerns by sundering the legal system from rhetoric and securing it on one or another (supposed) bedrock such as natural right or economic rationality. The legal guild had no desire to embrace the endless discussions of the philosophers, and even less to embrace the potentially deconstructive effects of the rhetoricians. As law schools became fixtures of the modern research university and the training of lawyers was severed from practical apprenticeships, legal scholars sought a distinctive and stable method that could secure law from the hurly-burly of civil life and constitute a suitable object for their analysis. It was against this unfortunate concerted effort that Llewellyn registered his lament on behalf of the aggrieved second-year law student, a lament that remains unanswered.

Recuperating ancient rhetoric should not be confused with an antiquarian interest in oratorical style. I use the term *rhetoric* to refer to both a practical activity and a self-referential theoretical consideration of that activity; philosophical argumentation is a form of rhetoric despite its protests to the contrary. Today, the study of rhetoric is informed by an important, though still marginalized, strand of contemporary philosophical inquiry. Philosophical hermeneutics provides an ontological account of the social nature of understanding that girds rhetorical activity. Rhetorical analysis moves from this ontology to political engagement, revealing the entwinement of theory and practice. The recent effort to link rhetoric and hermeneutics (Hyde 1979; Jost 1997; Mootz 2006; Schrag 1992) follows from the insight that there is a lived truth that is not captured by the circumscribed rationalism of modernity, and that within a social practice such as law one can adopt a theoretical comportment that clarifies and influences the practice of interpretation and persuasion by participating in, rather than sitting in judgment on, hermeneutical discernment and rhetorical elaboration.

Hermeneutics and rhetoric experienced a revival with the publication of two seminal works: Chaïm Perelman and Lucie Olbrechts-Tyteca's *The New Rhetoric* (1958) and Hans-Georg Gadamer's *Truth and Method* (1960). Perelman argued that justice is a "confused notion" that can be developed only in the course of responding to the practical demands of political action in a manner informed by reasonable beliefs that arise from rhetorical exchanges. Following Aristotle, he famously distinguished the rational (subject to demonstration) from the reasonable (subject to persuasion), and he cited legal practice as a prominent example of the latter. Gadamer explained his ontology of understanding by analogizing to the playful give-and-take of a conversation in which each participant is drawn out of her prejudiced horizon to some degree and they experience a fusion of horizons. Also drawing from Aristotle, Gadamer argued that this experience of human understanding is no less legitimate or important than scientific demonstration, and he too placed great weight on the example of law.

The modern age has disastrously equated knowledge with the logical foundations of modern science and has characterized nonscientific discourse as merely aesthetics or hortatory moralizing. The development of a rhetorical hermeneutics stresses the independent significance of what we can call "rhetorical knowledge" (Mootz 2006; compare with Scott 1977). Rhetorical knowledge cannot be subsumed under the model of rational thinking according to logical dictates because it arises within a historically situated social encounter that is irremediably dynamic and contingent. (Of course, this is true also of methodologically secured knowledge, but in this context we can indulge the Cartesian fantasy that solitary reflection generated the critical tradition against which Vico struggled). Legal practice is an exemplary site of rhetorical knowledge, and so it is by returning to rhetoric that law and philosophy might reconnect in a vital manner.

We can begin the recuperation of rhetorical knowledge by reading Plato against the grain of the tradition that seeks to find a systematic-propositional Platonist philosophy embedded in his work. Gadamer (1992: 71) believed that the Platonic dialogues reveal that it "is more important to find the words which convince the other than those which can be demonstrated in their truth, once and for all" (see, generally, Gadamer 1980). Gadamer drew heavily from Aristotle's practical philosophy, but he regarded Aristotle's achievement as a systematization that was possible only in the wake of Plato's dialectical exploration of Socratic dialogue as a living rhetorical experience (Sullivan 1989: 87–117) As Gilles Deleuze (1990: 256) later asked, "Was it not Plato himself who pointed out the direction for the reversal of Platonism?"

Recent work carries Gadamer's insight forward and develops an understanding of Plato's philosophy that supports the significance of rhetorical knowledge (see, generally, Gonzalez 1998). Although Plato argues for the superiority of philosophy over sophistic, Marina McCoy (2008) suggests that Plato recognizes that both are rooted in rhetoric and cannot be distinguished from each other in a definitive manner. Socrates employs practical reasoning and emotion in his conversations, and he understands that an apt argument is determined only in the context. McCoy contends that Plato's argument for the superiority of philosophy is rooted in the virtue of the philosopher and his willingness to put himself at risk in rhetorical exchange.

> If the dramatic and poetic elements of Plato's dialogues are closely intertwined with the arguments given in the dialogues (and not merely decoratively designed to make them more alluring or easier to understand), then one cannot distinguish between philosophy and rhetoric by claiming that the philosopher offers rational arguments free of rhetoric while the rhetorician merely tries to persuade.... The task of separating the sophist from the philosopher becomes all the more interesting since Plato does not reject the use of rhetoric or see it as entirely separable from philosophy but rather views philosophy and good rhetoric as mutually interdependent.
>
> ....
>
> ... Plato's central means of defending philosophy against these non-philosophers is not to give a definition of philosophy but instead to make a series of claims about *who the philosopher is* (his character) and *what he does* (his practice). (McCoy 2008: 16–18)

The philosopher, then, just is the individual who engages in "good" rhetoric for the right reasons.

Returning to the allegory of the cave, we can construe the puppeteers casting shadows as Sophists who understand that the shadows are illusions and yet are willing to deceive the prisoners (McCoy 2008: 129–31). In contrast, the philosopher strives to learn the truth and cares about his or her dialogue partners as truth-seeking individuals rather than viewing them as objects to be manipulated (McCoy 2008: 133). Francisco Gonzalez identifies three characteristics of the knowledge that Socrates seeks through dialogue: "(1) it is 'knowledge how' in the sense that it is instantiated by the very way in which Socrates conducts the inquiry...; (2) it is 'self-knowledge' in the sense that its 'object' is not completely external to the knower...; (3) it is 'nonpropositional knowledge' in the sense that its theoretical 'context' cannot be expressed in propositions/definitions (thus the inevitable *aporia*)" (Gonzalez 1998: 61). Socrates seeks rhetorical knowledge rather than propositional philosophical knowledge. We can seek no more than rhetorical knowledge in law; indeed, Gadamer and Perelman both claimed that legal reasoning exemplified the form of knowledge that might be achieved through philosophical dialogue.

Reading Plato in this manner reveals the necessarily rhetorical character of inquiry but also the need to be wary of sophistry. Rhetoric produces ideology and knowledge: it is both a technical art that can be abused and an openness to the world that decenters the pretense of individual self-possession. By understanding how rhetoric produces knowledge within certain social and institutional settings we might foster the "good" rhetoric of the philosopher without having to endorse the Platonist's misguided faith in the forms that can be seen in the sunlight of timeless knowledge. Rhetorical knowledge is a practical accomplishment that neither achieves apodictic certitude nor collapses into a relativistic irrationalism; this is enough to sustain legal practice as a reasonable – even if not thoroughly rationalized – activity.

Using rhetorical knowledge as a polestar, philosophers and lawyers can avoid the theory-practice quandary by not severing the two at the outset. At the most practical level, the concept of rhetorical knowledge will guide investigations of how the legal system fosters reasonable resolutions of controversy, examining how understanding and persuasion work in myriad contexts, from client interviews to appellate argumentation. At the most theoretical level, the concept of rhetorical knowledge will guide an investigation of the ontology of understanding and persuasion, not by identifying a fixed human nature but rather by illuminating the unfolding hermeneutical-rhetorical character of human understanding in which the investigation itself participates.

The merging of the philosophical traditions of hermeneutics and rhetoric provides the basis for understanding the rhetorical character of knowledge that is achieved in legal practice. Rhetorical knowledge is an incredibly rich starting point for thinking about legal practice and legal theory, stretching back to the pre-Socratics and Roman jurisprudence, and carrying forward today in a variety of work in both philosophy and law. Mining this vein of thinking promises to bring together philosophers and lawyers who currently bump into each other in the darkness of the cave, hardly pausing to take real notice of one another.

WORKS CITED

Deleuze, Gilles. *The Logic of Sense*. Ed. Constantin V. Boundas. Trans. Mark Lester with Charles Stivale. New York: Columbia Univ. Press, 1990.

Dworkin, Ronald et al. "Assisted Suicide: The Philosopher's Brief." *The New York Review of Books* 44.5 (March 27, 1997): 41–7.

Gadamer, Hans-Georg. "Writing and the Living Voice." In *Hans-Georg Gadamer on Education, Poetry, and History: Applied Hermeneutics*. Eds. Dieter Misgeld and Graeme Nicholson. Trans. Lawrence Schmidt and Monica Reuss. Albany: State Univ. of New York Press, 1992, 63–71 (interviews conducted in 1983 and 1986).

———. *Truth and Method*, 2d rev. ed. Trans. Joel Weinsheimer and Donald G. Marshall. 1960. Reprint, New York: Crossroad, 1989.

———. *Dialogue and Dialectic: Eight Hermeneutical Studies on Plato*. Trans. P. Christopher Smith. New Haven, CT: Yale Univ. Press, 1980.

Gonzalez, Francisco. *Dialectic and Dialogue: Plato's Practice of Philosophical Inquiry*. Evanston, IL: Northwestern Univ. Press, 1998.

Heidegger, Martin. *The Essence of Truth*. Trans. Ted Sadler. New York: Continuum, 2002 (1931–2 lectures).

Hyde, Michael J., and Craig R. Smith. "Hermeneutics and Rhetoric: A Seen but Unobserved Relationship." *Q. J. of Speech* 65.4 (1979): 347–63.

Jost, Walter, and Michael J. Hyde, eds. *Rhetoric and Hermeneutics in Our Time: A Reader*. New Haven, CT: Yale Univ. Press, 1997.

Llewellyn, Karl N. *The Bramble Bush*. Dobbs Ferry, NY: Oceana, 1981 (1929–30 lectures originally published in 1951).

———. "On Philosophy in American Law." *U. Pa. L. Rev.* 82.3 (1934): 205–12.

McCoy, Marina. *Plato on the Rhetoric of Philosophers and Sophists*. Cambridge: Cambridge Univ. Press, 2008.

Mootz, Francis J., III. *Rhetorical Knowledge in Legal Practice and Critical Legal Theory*. Tuscaloosa: Univ. of Alabama Press, 2006.

Perelman, Chaïm, and Lucie Olbrechts-Tyteca. *The New Rhetoric: A Treatise on Argumentation.* Trans. John Wilkinson and Purcell Weaver. 1958. Reprint, Notre Dame, IN: Univ. of Notre Dame Press, 1969.

Plato. *Republic.* Trans. Paul Shorey. Cambridge, MA: Harvard Univ. Press, 1930.

Schrag, Calvin O. *The Resources of Rationality: A Response to the Postmodern Challenge.* Bloomington: Indiana Univ. Press, 1992.

Scott, Robert L. "On Viewing Rhetoric as Epistemic: Ten Years Later." *Cent. States Speech J.* 27.4 (1977): 258–66.

Sullivan, Robert R. *Political Hermeneutics: The Early Thinking of Hans-Georg Gadamer.* University Park: Pennsylvania State Univ. Press, 1989.

Twining, William. *Karl Llewellyn and the Realist Movement.* 1973. Reprint, Norman: Univ. of Oklahoma Press, 1985.

Vico, Giambattista. *On the Study Methods of Our Time.* Trans. Elio Gianturco. 1965 (translation published), 1609. Reprint, Ithaca, NY: Cornell Univ. Press, 1990.

25 Dicta

PETER GOODRICH

> I should like to raise a query, however, whether the distinction taken between *dictum* and *obiter dictum* really corresponds to any definite usage of the legal profession. Most lawyers, I think, regard *dictum* as the elliptical equivalent of *obiter dictum.*
>
> (Fuller 1934a: 551)

Even by his own count or criteria, "On Philosophy in American Law" (PAL) must reckon low on the list of Llewellyn's notable literary efforts (Fuller 1934b: 435). It is a short and unprepossessing article, an occasional paper that seems hurriedly written, slight in content, and significantly lacking in the author's usual stylistic flair. It is sketchy in tone, low on humor, free of polemic, and rather parochial in its references. Ostensibly focused on philosophy in American law, it in fact has nothing explicit to say about philosophy or philosophers. More than that, the law that is discussed by way of a few grand generalizations is far removed from the doctrine or guild talk that represents the practice that the realist wishes to describe, teach, and possibly also affect. To this we can add that, since its publication, the article appears to have slipped rapidly into the obscurity of the stacks. It was not reprinted in Llewellyn's collected essays and has seldom been referenced, let alone revived. It is something of an enigma, a marginal piece, a symptomatic exercise and as such should be addressed through its incidents, its rhetorical figures, its dicta, its asterisk footnote, and other asides.

Published at what can be viewed as the midpoint of Llewellyn's career, after his major statements on legal realism and close to the height of his fame, PAL is on the surface a synoptic piece that offers an overview of the absence of philosophy from the practice of American law. He is quite explicit on this. His theme is not "the changing array of verbalized philosophies." He is not concerned with "the philosophers themselves, with whom indeed my acquaintance is but scanty" (Llewellyn 1934: 206). More interesting and productive than addressing philosophies and philosophers, and despite his chosen title, Llewellyn wishes to excavate and address implicit philosophy, tacit theories, ways of acting in the world. In fact he puts it very strongly, the object of analysis is the "inarticulate," the "unthought," the less than conscious – in a word, the nonphilosophical. Consistent with that method, seeking to read the paper in a manner that is at least close to its own allusive form, in this brief essay I will attempt to extract the implicit thesis, the less-than-conscious argument, the persistently buried proposition that PAL secretes between its lines. It is that hidden message, I will argue, that most directly affects legal theory now.

Start at a distance. Writing in the same volume of the *University of Pennsylvania Law Review*, Lon Fuller, then a professor at Duke Law School, addresses Llewellyn's work at length. Borrowing an analogy from the German free law exponent Herman Kantorowicz, Fuller argues that modern judges torture legal doctrine much as medieval judges tortured individuals. The evidence produced by torture, namely, confessions, has now been ruled out and in the future the torture of doctrine – by fictions, analogies, theories – will also slip into desuetude: "The millennium when it arrives, will bring not only a humanitarian reform of our treatment of legal doctrine, but also, I feel sure, a greater certainty in the prediction of judicial decision" (Fuller 1934b: 435). Unwittingly perhaps, and inaccurate though the prediction has transpired to be of the actual millennium, Fuller well captures the two implicit faces of Llewellyn's project in PAL. As with Janus, one face looks forward and one looks back; one looks to the public sphere of action and one to the private realm of motive and tacit determination. The former is putatively scientific and concerns prediction, certainty, the future; the latter is humanistic and addresses the past as prologue, history as motor and cause of human action. Each in their turn.

The larger point to be made is that Llewellyn's primary focus in PAL is on legal history, the humanistic endeavor of collating and interpreting the textual past, the record of precedent, as also of biography and scholarly enterprise. There is reference to the passage toward the academicization of law, the trend toward school law, but the key to the patterns and positions adopted lies rather in the humanistic quality of the history, and specifically the accounting of affect and motive. The humanist model of history views the textual past as a correspondence between a community of friends and across generations. Books are letters within the humanist family; they are how a scholar lives on and knowledge as *communis opinio* survives. The friends, the brotherhood, the fraternity of lawyers relay the narrative of their community, of their belonging and of the rupture that founded their sect or religion or polity. The brothers did not arrive ex nihilo, and so despite the seemingly transnational character of humanism, it always bears its local imaginary, its religious and national tradition. Thus English common law was a community that purported to found itself through its difference from and antagonism toward continental (Roman) law. Unsurprisingly the American lawyers also needed their enemies and that is precisely where Llewellyn (1934: 207) starts: "England was hated." He goes on to point out that English precedent was in fact rapidly adopted as American precedent, that the enemy was internalized, but the key lies in the recognition that at the origin of the U.S. legal system lay an affective antinomy, an emotive topos, an ambivalent relation to its paternity and hence a conflicted sense of identity. It grew from political struggle, was embroiled in assertions of national uniqueness, and developed on the back of ideological incitements.

To offer the statement "England was hated" as an explanation of the early recourse to natural law within the American system is surprising. Not to put too fine a point on it, the attribution of motive suggests a vehement affective root that drives the judicial decisions. Emotion, heat, passion, clearly suggest polemical and rhetorical, political and partisan, motives underlying and dictating decisions. It is only fair to state further that hate of the English is not very specific and that hate itself, the antirrhetic or denunciatory tone of nationalistic polemic does not dictate any specific outcomes. Indeed Llewellyn points out that the judges ended up following the English precedents but effectively pretended they were their own. The denunciatory animus of the nascent legal profession was not a matter of substance but was necessary rather to bonding, to banding together as a new *communis opinio* of a putatively unique American law. It was necessary to the establishment of a custom prior to custom, an *ius commune* inherent in the local and novel jurisdiction. The hatred, in other words, was political, proprietary, and strongly polemical. It was also, by placement and period, foundational and constitutive of ethos and practice. More than that, if vehement emotion, here a denunciatory hatred of the prior sovereign and regime, founds the community and order of law, it seems plausible to suppose that this fundamental fissure will live on. The emotion that subtends the system will likely govern the order, the vehemence that marks its origin, if untreated – which is to say, if unaddressed – will repeat itself, and at the very least reappear in subsequent instances of structural shift or identity challenge to lawyers and law. As Renaissance lawyers liked to put it, the origin is *instar omnium* – it is worth all (Selden 1614: C.4.b.). From the first, just to make the point explicit, all else derives, all honor and dignity, office and role, modus vivendi and style of practice.

Certainly for lawyers, the origin lives on, acts as precedent, deserves to be followed, and this we might add simply by virtue of its priority, its firstness, unless of course and exceptionally it is overruled. There is little sign of that in American law, and so it is a safe bet that such passion, rebellion, or hatred will appear again, and again. Llewellyn (1934: 211) gives a further example in relation to the turn of the twentieth century: "the emotional revolt of laborers, farmers and small business men . . . worked its way up into the thinking of the intellectuals." Leave aside the ethereal drift, workers below and intellectuals above, but acknowledge that the *syneciosis*, the coupling of causes, treats revolt as organic to legal change. First, the revolt against Anglican law and Englishness, and then latterly the revolt against *das Capital* and its attendant legal positivism or law by financial position. In both instances it was less than total in effect. The object rebelled against was internalized, made the rebels' own. Negation rules. Again, however, what is important analytically is that the *syneciosis* is emotive; it marks revolt, irreverence, heat as sources of legal argument and, over time, of systemic change.

Emotion is not ethics. Neither vehemence nor polemic constitute philosophy. The passage of emotion, the transmission of feelings of hate or revolt into judicial legislation raises questions that are both broader and more intransigent than those that legal philosophy traditionally addresses. There is no question that as with his polemics against casebooks and law teaching, so too with his assessment of jurisprudence, Llewellyn passionately desired an opening of the boundaries of philosophy, a broader conversation, with participants in the guild, on the bench and in the academy. Dialogue was to cross the boundaries of specialization, ivory tower and court practice, contemplation and action. First, however, motive. He was evidently himself emotional, here meaning impetuous, frustrated, vociferous, and at times angry. Consider the asterisk footnote, attached to the title of the article, where the dual thesis is stated *in nuce* and the full gamut of the author's emotions are on unguarded display.

The asterisk footnote now tends to play the role of listing institutional benefactors, influential colleagues, student assistants, and the circumstances surrounding the production of the article. It is largely a listing of names, patrons, and gratulants. The older and rarer asterisk footnote was more likely to comment, converse, and indicate the motive for the intervention. Instance and exemplar: "I feel my wattles grow red as I recall the shock with which, as a dyed-in-the-wool commercial lawyer, I met property phases of mortgage law which left me gasping" (Llewellyn 1934: 205n*). Wattles growing red is a synechdoche, part for whole, red face, or more accurately crimson gorge, for the totality, the body enraged, for anger. It is a euphemism of sorts but also a signal of vehemence and revolt at the incoherence of precedent. What, after all, are wattles? There are two possible root meanings. The first and more humanistic, and hence here more relevant, is from the Anglo-Saxon *watla*, meaning sticks or rods used in bundles to make walls or thatch (Nowell 1952). The Latin equivalent is *tegulae*, meaning tiles but in either instance the figurative meaning is of throat, neck, or face becoming red with embarrassment, shock, and rage. That the reference to rods and sticks twined together also has phallic connotations and is suggestive of desire, tumescence, ardor, also bears a mention with respect both to what the humanist lawyer desires and also as to how it is to be divined and reproduced.

The alternate root of *wattle*, is a Middle English metathesis from *watel*, meaning a pack, a knapsack, or wallet or envelope. The envelope, the skin, the purse grows heated and red. Again the color is a sign with complicated references. Visible blood, according to Aristotle, is always a sign of a wound, and here a blushing harm. The engorged gorge speaks volumes without speaking at all. More than that, and with a view to the desire for science, certainty, and prediction that PAL also evinces, it has to be noticed that wallet or purse have both sexual and (related) economic connotations. That the purse or wallet grows red again suggests desire, an invaginated want, but it equally connotes a warming of the wallet, the implication of money and wealth, or for lawyers, fees and the protracted payments available through caviling over distinctions, ambiguities, opacities, and other undecidables. The purse will pull the strings, the wallet instigate the (in)action, or simplest of all, money will talk. The implication is that the economic will determine, and, if so, then law and economics will be the future science of legal prediction, the source of the certainties that Lon Fuller believed the new millennium should bring.

If the red wattles are signs of a malaise or impatience, it is initially with the paucity of philosophies that rarely meet on the same plane of discourse as that of law. It is a frustration with the absence of the "great man" (Llewellyn 1934: 205n*), but more concretely and immediately still, it is with the failure of legal education. Llewellyn's wattles grow red because students are not given an adequate education in law and specifically they are not given a clear view of the "difference in 'feel' and tendency" of decisions in different substantive domains of law and in different epochs. Law students are given no feel for what is going on, the down and dirty of negotiation, advocacy, and judgment. They aren't taught how to read, nobody bothers to give them the humanistic techniques, the philological or historical tools, the hermeneutic and rhetorical acumen that alone will bridge the gap between classroom and lifeworld. And then, last words, ultimatum: "Nor does anyone bother to present to [the student] the difference between logic and persuasion, nor what a man facing old courts is to do with a new vocabulary" (Llewellyn 1934: 205n*). The student lacks the techniques needed to frame arguments, to diagnose audiences, to distinguish vocabularies and topics, or viscerally to affect his hearers. In short, the pretense of reason, the inculcation of a logic that would at best work only in the confines of contemplative philosophical speculation, incapacitates the law student. They need rhetoric. They need life experience. They need the tools of persuasion, the animus of argument, the feel of events. Without these, lacking skills, the student will have little access to the reality of law, the playing of the game, the winners and losers in the visceral struggles that litter the arena of legality and its enforcement.

Moving then to our modernity, the contemporary state of philosophy in American law, the two propositions implicit in PAL can be formulated prospectively. They have significant current resonance and ample unfulfilled promise. First, the emotive and, technically, figurative style of Llewellyn's argument. The implicit thesis is a proposal and exemplification of the importance of rhetoric as the proper study of law. Philosophy and philosophers seldom if ever engage with law understood as professional practice and the event of judgment. Thus the importance of rhetoric as the discipline that bridges the worlds of theory and application, education, and practice. The implicit argument is humanistic in that rhetoric was the humanist's primary discipline and the curricula manuals on "speaking justly in civil matters" were the first legal textbooks (Quintilian 2002: bk. 2, chap. 15). To this can be added two correlative points. Rhetoric precisely studies affect in argument, oratorical effects, the performative dimensions of advocacy, persuasion all told. It is the study of motive, presentation, and delivery – ethos, pathos, logos – and as such recognizes the emotive dimension of all argument and specifically that of the discourses used by practitioners of the *ars bablativa*, or art of chattering. How are clients to be communicated with, professional colleagues convinced or manipulated, juries persuaded, and judges prevailed upon without the inventions of rhetoric and its arts of elocution? The answer according to Llewellyn is "poorly," indeed not well at all. Rhetoric is crucial and yet everywhere Llewellyn sees mere casuistry, declamation, or simple corruption of speech.

The argument in favor of rhetoric, in support of taking dicta seriously, is best understood as humanistic in a second sense as well. As against philosophy, which endeavors to escape the world of action in favor of the purity of legal formulae, rhetoric is a discipline gauged to engagement, open to circumstance and event. The subsidiary, yet crucial, implicit feature of Llewellyn's observations in PAL is a shift away from philosophy, the technical, hermetic, and dry discipline derived from Aristotle's logic, to a much broader and more open conception of theory. Llewellyn refers to life philosophy with which we would now talk of theory and theoretical perspectives upon law. Rhetoric is theory in the sense both of framing the practice of law and in that of opening the educational transmission of legality to the wealth of humanism, the disciplines, the plethora of knowledges. Rhetoric is an organizational principle, a technique for finding (*inventio*), ordering (*narratio*), and delivering (*elocutio*) persuasive arguments, effective speeches. Lawyers as rhetors use the commonplaces or topics of their discipline to understand practice, to formulate arguments, to persuade and move to action. The topics, and the briefest glance at early legal treatises can substantiate this and more, include philology, history, geography, ethics, morals, philosophy, and religion. Now we would likely add the psychological disciplines, economics, linguistics, and film studies. Be that as it may, theory as implicitly proposed by Llewellyn undoes the closure of law and opens the ground for the interdisciplinary studies that now form the bulk of academic law, the substance of theory, the stuff of scholarship.

The second feature of the shift to theory lies in a leveling of the discipline of law. Theory is not a professional specialization; it has no proprietary stakes, and it confers little by way of status. It belongs to no single discipline and has only a marginal purchase within the institution. It is everywhere and nowhere. In the realist's usage, we are all theorists because theory is organic to intellectual activity; it is the self-reflection of a discipline, the self-consciousness of practice, critical doubt as to its ends. The legal theorist as organic intellectual is in this sense engaged in linking the topics of law to the disciplines that can aid in elaborating them. He or she is committed to discourse, dialogue, conversation with the usages and communities from which law stems and upon which it is applied. Theory is here first hermeneutic and second rhetorical; it seeks to understand and then relay. It is organic in the sense that no one is excluded; it is, in Llewellyn's nice coinage, life-in-action; it is the discourse of doing, and in sum it is law as a way of life.

The focus on rhetoric and with it on passion and action as the dimensions of discourse most relevant to theory suggests not only engagement but also realism as to how law is made. Fuller suggested that Llewellyn was unusually concerned with the predictive character of scholarship. The millennium, you will recollect, not only lays down the tools of doctrinal torture but will also have made prediction of judicial action much easier. Certainty will replace discord among the precedents. The realists wished to predict, to prophesy outcomes, and their avenue to this was scholarly scrutiny of the context and process of judicial decision making, as well as recourse to empirical science so as effectively to study the patterns of law in action. Law and society, which offers empirical studies of law application and enforcement, is one derivative of Llewellyn's proposal, while law and economics adds a specialist patina to prediction while generally aligning itself with school law or speculative cerebration rarely touching upon the same level of discourse as that of lawyers in practice (Goodrich 2007).

The more obvious point is that contemporary legal theory has followed in the open path that Llewellyn implicitly proposed. It has slowly added a series of conjunctives. Law and the humanities, and the social sciences, and cultural studies have slowly and tenuously made their way into the margins of the discipline. The plethora of conjunctions, of *ands*, ran loosely from Marxist sociology of law to critical legal studies to feminism and critical race theory on the left, and from analytic philosophy of language to law and economics on the right. In between, in the liberal humanist space of scholarly solace or academic confrontation the conjunctions range from law and literature to deconstruction, hermeneutics, semiotics, psychoanalysis, film, and aesthetics linked or juxtaposed to law. In admittedly varying forms, yet in the oldest of humanist traditions, the contemporary humanistic jurist endeavors to understand both the métier of legal intervention and the practices upon which it has an impact. Such is the reason for scholarship that extends beyond the strict guild talk or jargon of law and equally explains why philosophy narrowly defined did not appeal to Llewellyn any more than it does to contemporary legal theorists.

Reading between the lines, through the figures or dicta of his text, I have suggested that we return to Llewellyn, even to PAL, because contemporary legal theory stands more or less in the space that he opened up. What Llewellyn presents in his argument against philosophy and in favor of theory, in his implicit notion of the organic legal intellectual, in his call for rhetoric, for action, is prescient of where theory stands now. Put it like this, for simplicity and convenience. Law and economics has solved the quest for prediction except that what is predicted seldom crosses paths with what happens. Rational actors in a perfect market infrequently encounter law in action and even if they do it will almost always be ex post facto, after the event. We are left with a still-nascent humanism, a plethora of disciplines contributing to law. Law and economics are among these, but over the longer term this will be in a relatively minor key, as relates to moments of actual intervention in extant markets. For the rest of the curriculum, for the syllabus of practice, the project remains that which Llewellyn spelled out. How can we teach a rhetoric of law, a mode of scholarly conversation that bridges the gap between academy and court, between school law and law office, between declamation and the oratory of negotiation and adversarial advocacy?

Two final observations, last words, envoi. Contemporary theory stands at a crossroads. Circa 1934 and circa 2008, legal theory has lost its law. Stick with today, and it is all theory, all economics or aesthetics, limited to theorists and their names. Llewellyn suggested recourse to rhetoric, to the study of modes of dialog, because democratic conversation – *communis opinio iuris* as it used to be called, "custome and conversation . . . usuall and ordinarie speech" (Doderidge 1634), the animadversions that pass among the various sects of lawyers – is the starting place of common law. How do we study that, the formal and more often informal, the licit and illicit, the tacit and implicit, the impassioned and undisclosed? The answer is equally implicit. Fuller in the epigraph to this essay criticizes Llewellyn for distinguishing different types of dicta. I will end by suggesting that Llewellyn made the distinction for good reason. He was intrigued by dicta; he saw dicta as the source of legal scholarship, as the primary subject of juristic analysis. A legal dictum is never simply a dictum. As rhetoric lengthily teaches, it is an *ipse dixit*, an authoritative statement, a pronouncement, veridical speech, a figure, an illocutionary act, speech by position, an image, and more. The dicta change over time. *Rationes* become dicta, and dicta become *regulae*. Formulate it as a realist aphorism: real lawyers don't rest with *rationes.* It is all dicta in differing degrees. And perhaps for that reason the next phase of theory will have a novel name: the "dictists," meaning jurists, scholars, humanists open to the plenitude of legal speech.

WORKS CITED

Doderidge, Sir John, *The English Lawyer.* London: Assignes of I. More, 1631. Reprint, Clark, NJ: Lawbook Exchange, 2005.

Fuller, L. L., "Book Reviews." *U. Pa. L. Rev.* 82.5 (1934a): 551–3 (reviewing Karl Llewellyn, *Präjudizienrecht und Rechtsprechung in Amerika.* Leipzig: Verlag von Theodor Weicher, 1933).

———. "American Legal Realism." *U. Pa. L. Rev.* 82.5 (1934b): 429–62.

Goodrich, Peter. "The New Casuistry." *Critical Inquiry* 33.4 (2007): 673–709.

Llewellyn, Karl. "On Philosophy in American Law." *U. Pa. L. Rev.* 82.3 (1934): 205–12.

Nowell, Laurence. *Vocabularium Saxonicum.* Ed. Albert Mackwardt. Ann Arbor: Univ. of Michigan Press, 1952.

Quintilian, *The Orator's Education (Institutio oratoria).* Ed. and Trans. Donald A. Russell. Cambridge, MA: Harvard Univ. Press, 2002.

Selden, John, *Titles of Honor*, 3d ed. London: E. Tyler and R. Holt, 1672. Reprint, Clark, NJ: Lawbook Exchange, 2006.

26 Recent and Future Concepts of Law: From Conceptual Analysis to a Practice Theory of Law

DENNIS PATTERSON

General jurisprudence is the study of the most general features of law. The tradition of analytic jurisprudence – one that spans from Hobbes to Coleman – has exhibited a sustained focus on identifying the constitutive features of law. For some time, this question has been framed as the search for the essential or necessary features of the concept of law. But a look at the tradition reveals that this is only one of a number of ways of looking at law from a similar vantage point. That vantage point or perspective focuses on the structure of law. For a variety of reasons, this focus is changing and a new question is emerging.

This essay is written at a time when the field of analytic jurisprudence is in a state of flux. For the past several decades, debate has centered on evaluating and responding to Ronald Dworkin's critiques of positivism. While there are (and no doubt will continue to be) philosophers with an interest in these questions, discussion in the field is moving to other topics. One of these topics is the focus of this essay.

Stated in general terms, my interest lies in explicating the idea of law as a certain sort of practice. The idea of law as a practice is intuitively obvious. Law is an iterative enterprise in which practitioners make claims over time in forms that repeat themselves, albeit in sometimes unfamiliar ways. A feature of law's iterative character is that the practice is conducted in concert with others. In a sense, practitioners of law are together in the enterprise. What does it mean to say that law is something we do together?

John Austin's view of the nature of law dominated jurisprudential thinking from the nineteenth to well into the twentieth century. Famously, Austin regarded a law as an order backed by threat of sanction for noncompliance. One important, additional factor was that the threat issued from a sovereign. Taken together, these elements became the so-called command theory of law.

The view met its end in a work that is still regarded as the most important work of legal theory in the Anglo-American tradition, H. L. A. Hart's *The Concept of Law* (1994). Hart argued that Austin's account of the nature of law fails because of Austin's failure to successfully marry threats and sovereignty. That is, Hart exposed the weakness in Austin's picture of law when he asked the question of whether there was any substantive difference between the order of a gunman and that of a sovereign. Seeing none, Hart concluded that Austin's account of the nature of law failed to tell us what it was about a legal system that made it law and not a normative system of another sort. Having demolished Austin's picture of law, Hart had to replace it with an alternative.

Before describing Hart's accomplishment in *Concept*, it is necessary to comment on the nature of his project. Hart was deeply attracted to the professional philosophy of his day, especially the approach to philosophy exhibited in the work of J. L. Austin (Lacey 2004: 112–51). While Hart had an interest in the work of other philosophers, especially Wittgenstein, Hart was his own man philosophically. Finally, Hart self-described *Concept* as, among other things, a work in "descriptive sociology" (Hart 1994: v). With these disparate elements in view, what was Hart's project?

One way to answer this question is to ask whether Hart was doing conceptual analysis. In the late 1950s, it was quite fashionable philosophically to conceive of philosophy as an armchair exercise devoted to the search for the necessary and sufficient conditions for application of a concept. Thus, when one did philosophy of law with a view to conceptual analysis, one asked after the necessary and sufficient conditions for the concept of law. Was this what Hart had in mind when he wrote *Concept*? There can be little doubt that this question will likely never receive a definitive answer, for there exists evidence for more than one answer to the question. Thus, instead of trying to characterize what Hart did, I will describe his project and the contours of the position he advanced.

Law, Hart argued, is a matter of rules; rules of various kinds, to be sure. But the nerve of law was rules. So-called "modern" legal systems were composed of primary and secondary rules. The regime of secondary rules was of vital importance, because it was in the realm of secondary rules that one found the rules for introducing, amending, and repealing primary rules (e.g., the law of torts and criminal law). Most important, the so-called master secondary rule – the rule of recognition – was the means by which primary rules were identified as rules of law. The rule of recognition, Hart (1994: 97) argued, provided both citizen and legal official alike with "authoritative criteria for identifying primary rules of obligation." Hart was quick to point out that in modern legal systems, the rule of recognition might be quite complex: in short, there might well be multiple sources of law. Owing to its complexity, the rule of recognition of virtually any modern legal system is likely to be so complex that it warrants characterization as a practice. Further, Hart indicated quite clearly that the rule of recognition was ultimate in the chain of validity: the rule was, itself, neither valid nor invalid. Rather, it was simply "accepted" (Hart 1994: 105–6).

So far, I have described only one of the two principal parts of *Concept*. After describing the core features of a municipal legal system, Hart then turned his attention to adjudication. The seventh chapter of *Concept* introduces themes and questions that remain central to the discussion of Hart's jurisprudence. In terms we would recognize today, Hart begins with questions of rule following. While Hart treats problems of rule following from the point of view of both precedent and legislation, he takes an approach that we would instantly recognize as informed by Wittgenstein's problem of rule following discussed in *Philosophical Investigations*.

Famously, Hart introduces the concept of discretion as the nerve of his account of interpretation. Although Hart (1994: 132) has some harsh things to say about rule skepticism, he concedes that "a large and important field is left open for the exercise of discretion by the courts and other officials." Of course, the role of discretion in Hart's position became a central focus of debate. In *Concept*, Hart limits his discussion of discretion to two aspects: policy implications and the particulars of individual cases. From the vantage point of the present, Hart's discussion of discretion is simple and unsophisticated. In fact, Hart's entire discussion of adjudication is of largely historical interest.

Let us return to the question asked earlier; that is, how to characterize Hart's project in *Concept*? In describing the contours of a municipal legal system, Hart clearly saw himself as doing abstract work. True, he did say that *Concept* might possibly be described as a work in "descriptive sociology" (Hart 1994: vii). Whatever one makes of this comment, it is clear that Hart's primary concern was with what he termed *analysis*. Hart came to jurisprudence with only the command theory in view. There was something deeply wrong with this view, and Hart spends a fair amount of time in *Concept* getting clear about the shortcomings of the command theory and what a proper view of the essential features of law would look like.

RAZ, AUTHORITY, AND CONCEPTUAL ANALYSIS

Contemporary legal positivists divide themselves into two camps. The division is driven by differing conceptions of the relationship between law and moral standards. So-called inclusive positivists maintain that legal systems may be worthy of the name *legal* even though they explicitly incorporate moral standards into law. By contrast, so-called exclusive positivists maintain that no norm can be legal in nature if it incorporates moral notions into the criteria of legal validity. The debate between these two positivist camps has come down a central claim about the nature of law. The burden of proof would seem to lie with the hard positivists, for it is they who are making the strongest claim about the concept of law. The claim is one that sounds in necessity; that is, for a norm to be legal, it must possess certain essential features. The most compelling argument for the hard positivist view comes from Joseph Raz, specifically his account of law's authority.

Raz's account of authority is an essential feature of his view of the nature of law. He maintains that the law necessarily claims to be a genuine and not merely de facto authority. And for law to fulfill the mediating role that it claims for itself, on Raz's view, the law must issue dictates that can be readily understood and acted upon. More specifically, people need to be able to grasp legal norms (i.e., identify those norms as valid) independently of their identification and consideration of the (dependent) reasons for those norms. It is for this reason that Raz's position can be characterized as exclusive legal positivism.

Exclusive legal positivists insist that the content of law must come from social sources alone. Raz (1994: 211) articulates the sources thesis as follows: "All law is source based. A law is source-based if its existence and content can be identified by reference to social facts alone, without resort to any evaluative argument."

Although some read him as making a moral argument (Perry 2001), I think it more accurate to read Raz as making a conceptual or metaphysical claim about the nature of law. In this regard, Raz (2005, 2006) himself has been somewhat equivocal on the matter, sometimes speaking of "the" concept of authority, "our" concept of authority, or more recently, "concept(s) of authority."

The problem with Raz's position is that he makes no arguments directly in support of his claims for necessity. This is no small omission, for the success of Raz's account of law's authority depends upon the strength of his claim that the concept of law is special in that its meaning is not (solely) a function of linguistic usage and, further, that the content of the concept is (at least in part) dictated by something other than conventions for the use of the word.

I believe that Raz needs to answer the question of the nature of law with an account of concepts. To answer the question of the nature of law, we need to know what sort of concept law is. Once we have identified what kind of concept law is, we can move toward answering what sort of conceptual analysis is necessary for a concept like law. In short, an account of concepts is a necessary preliminary to answering the question, What is the nature of law?

The conventional metaphysical wisdom is that concepts divide up into at least two categories: natural kind concepts and artifactual kinds. Natural kind concepts are those whose essence is dictated by a microstructural element, such as atomic formula or DNA. Artifactual kinds are the product of human invention. These social constructs are the stuff of John Searle's (1995: 31–52) "Institutional Facts": their existence depends upon our attitudes or intentions. Where does Raz's account of the nature of law fall into this divide? It is not at all clear.

On the one hand, Raz (2005: 328), says this about the nature of law: "A theory consists of necessary truths, for only necessary truths about the law reveal the nature of law." But Raz (2005: 331) also maintains that "[i]n large measure what we study when we study the nature of law is the nature of our own self-understanding." It is difficult to see how necessary truths can arise out of the self-understanding of participants in a practice. Raz seems to want an account of the nature of law that identifies necessary truths at the same time it identifies something seemingly contingent about law (i.e., our self-understanding of it). Putting together necessity and contingency seems to me to be the next step in the development of exclusive legal positivism. Until Raz accomplishes this task, his claims for law's authority are unconvincing.

DWORKINIAN CONSTRUCTIVISM

Dworkin's jurisprudence is both a criticism of and an alternative to all forms of positivism. It is conventional wisdom that positivists believe that the content of law can be identified by a conventional practice Hart dubbed "the rule of recognition." For positivists, the content of law – or the answer to the question, What is the law in this jurisdiction? – is amenable to a descriptive report. Dworkin flatly denies this. In fact, for Dworkin, it is never possible to merely report the state of law on any but the simplest of legal questions because the concept of law is infinitely controversial.

Dworkin's interpretive account of law is grounded in the idea that to understand the concept of law one has to identify the point or purpose of law. Because the point or purpose of law is inherently controversial, no account of the law can be (purely) descriptive. For any such account will always depend upon a controversial thesis about the point of law, which thesis will drive the selection of some features of the practice and not others. Hence, all accounts of law are necessarily constructive in that their focus on some features of the practice and not others is a matter of selection driven by a prior choice of normative framework (i.e., an account of the point of law).

Dworkin's (1986: 190) argument about the need to discern the point of law is driven by his more basic assertion that any conception of law "must explain how what it takes to be law provides a general justification for the exercise of coercive power by the state." Hart (1994: 239–40) has never agreed with this characterization of jurisprudence. Some read Dworkin as asking a different question than Hart and thus agree with Hart that Dworkin and he are engaged in fundamentally different projects (Leiter 2003). This is an uncharitable if not incorrect reading of Dworkin. It is uncharitable in that it fails to take Dworkin's criticism seriously. Dworkin is arguing that Hart assumes away a problem Dworkin maintains is fundamental to any account of law. In other words, Dworkin argues that Hart misunderstands a central feature of his own (i.e., Hart's) account of law. This is not to suggest that Dworkin is correct in his critique of Hart. Rather, it is to suggest that Dworkin has a point, albeit a controversial one.

If we take Dworkin seriously, the question is whether he is correct in his claims for the inherently controversial nature of the concept of law. To answer this question, Dworkin needs to advance arguments about the nature of concepts or, at least, some account of why the concept of law is special. Alas, he supplies no arguments to sustain his controversial assertion. The burden of proof clearly lies with Dworkin. When Hart explicates the rule of recognition, he is providing an account of how participants in the practice of law understand judgments of validity. In providing his account of this practice, the measure of Hart's work is accuracy: does Hart's description account for what participants in the practice take to be the central features of validity conditions for law? Dworkin's critique has to be read to claim that even if Hart's account is an accurate sociological account of what participants in the practice take themselves to be doing, that account is not necessarily correct from the point of view of law as it is properly understood.

It seems that, at bottom, Dworkin's debate with Hart is one about the meaning of concepts. Hart says that the meaning of law (its extension) is fixed by what participants in the practice take the concept to mean. Dworkin denies that the way participants understand themselves exhausts the meaning of the concepts they employ. Dworkin (and, interestingly, Raz) maintain that law is a concept the content of which is (in part) dictated by something other than conventional understanding. How do we understand this?

TWO APPROACHES TO PRACTICE

Hart and Dworkin disagree about the role of practice in theory. For Dworkin, practice is material that is taken up by a theory. It is fuel or content. For Hart, practice is the product of history and cannot be theorized. The rule of recognition cannot be theoretically justified because it is a product of history and circumstance.

Dworkin cannot abide this quietism. In terms that are all too familiar, it can be said that Dworkin (2006: 170) privileges theory over practice. For Hart, it is always practice that is primary.

Dworkin clearly believes that theory is the preferred route to a better understanding of the practice of law. As others have argued, this claim is wildly implausible (Leiter 2007). Dworkin is ultimately not interested in an account of law as we find it (in practice). Rather, his project is devoted to providing us with an ideal conception of law, the merits of which are not discernible by the degree to which the theorizing illuminates the practice to which it is purportedly directed.

By contrast, Hart explores the social dimensions of legal practice, rooting his positivism in the critical, reflective attitudes of institutional participants in law. As mentioned earlier, the principal elements of Hart's account are the concepts of primary and secondary rules, the internal point of view, and, most importantly, the rule of recognition. Through the use of the rule of recognition, lawyers and nonlawyers alike are able to identify legal norms and, in that way, decide what the law is on any given question.

There can be little doubt that Hart provides the contours of a practice-theory approach to law. By "practice theory," I mean an account of law that answers the question, What is the law in this jurisdiction with respect to *x*? by looking at how participants in the practice decide the state of the law. Hart gave us only the barest essentials in outlining the rule of recognition. To be sure, he made it clear that rule of recognition is a practice, one that lies at the heart of Hart's account of law as a practice of special social rules. But what do we mean when we say that law is a practice, albeit one of a special sort? For an answer to that question, let us turn to the literature on practices.

PRACTICE THEORY

When theorizing a human activity, one of the most fundamental questions is locating the vantage point from which to start the endeavor. Consider the philosophy of mind. Cognitive naturalists of a variety of orientations (Fodor, Chomsky, Searle, the Churchlands, and Dennett) argue that problems of mind and consciousness are best explained by investigation of the inner theater of mind or brain. For them, philosophy of mind is a matter of theorizing the relationship between mental activity and our efforts to represent reality outside the mind. By contrast, nonnaturalists like Sellars, Davidson, McDowell, and Brandom follow Wittgenstein in seeing mind not as a thing or a place but as an array of social skills and activities. For the nonnaturalists, practices are the places where the mind is on display. An account of the skills necessary to participate in practices are the nonnaturalists' account of mind. Importantly, the nonnaturalists can theorize mind as found in practices without resorting to the inner theater that preoccupies the naturalists.

As a point of philosophical focus, practice theory ranges across a wide variety of social activities and philosophical specialties. From medicine to money and especially philosophy of science, practice theory has garnered sustained attention from philosophers, anthropologists, and sociologists. As Joseph Rouse

(2007a) explains in his recent overview of practice theory, the role of language in social practices has been a particular focus of attention for philosophers. One prominent example that has made its way into the legal literature (Canale and Tuzet 2007) is Robert Brandom's (1994) inferentialist account of the normativity of practices. Like other nonnaturalists, Brandom is keen to provide an account of normativity in practices that locates the explanatory power of the account in linguistic utterances or exchanges between participants in discursive practices.

Brandom's discussion of regulism provides an entree into the problem of normativity and its role in practices. To be clear, what we are after is an account of norms that illuminates the connection between norms and reasons. Along the way, I will have things to say about naturalism and intentionality, just to name two related topics. But the central focus is the role of normativity in practices.

When is a performance correct? In virtue of what is it true to say, "She did it right"? Brandom (1994: 18–19) begins his answer by reminding us that for Kant, "what makes a performance correct or not is its relation to some explicit rule." But what is the Kantian conception of performance in accordance with an explicit rule? Brandom (1994: 20) answers: "to assess correctness is always to make at least implicit reference to a rule or principle that *determines* what is correct by explicitly *saying* so." The rule and nothing but the rule determines what counts as correct in following the rule. The norm sets out its own standards of correctness. There is nothing between the rule and what counts as complying with it.

In a move that is now common, Brandom uses Wittgenstein's regress argument to show the shortcomings of the Kantian regulist account of norms. According to Brandom (1994: 23), Wittgenstein's regress argument is his "master argument for the appropriateness of the pragmatist rather than the regulist/intellectualist, order of explanation." On a pragmatist conception of norms, a conception of correctness of performance is implicit in practice. Practice is the ground of normativity for practice is the means by which the regress argument is answered and the problems of regulism avoided (Patterson 1996: 151–82).

But what account of practice is appropriate? Rouse has recently added depth to Brandom's arguments in ways that may prove useful to legal philosophers. As Brandom argues, "being in a practice" is all about mutual accountability. Maintenance of a practice is achieved through iteration of performances that require mutual accountability on the part of participants in the practice. But how is this achieved? Rouse (2007b: 48) suggests this as a test: "a performance belongs to a practice if it is appropriate to hold it accountable as a correct or incorrect performance of that practice." Fleshing out this general conception of accountability is the first step to developing a convincing account of the normativity of practices.

We demarcate practices from one another by the "ways in which constitutive performances bear on one another" (Rouse 2007b: 49). So, performances respond to one another through correction, praise, explication, and drawing inferences. Brandom's own account of normativity as "deontic scorekeeping" is but one example of how this notion of a practice as an interactive field of performance can be explicated.

NORMATIVITY AND THE PRACTICE OF LAW

The goal of any practice account of law has to be making sense of the practice as an ongoing, iterative, and most important, common activity. In providing an account of normativity, it is crucial that any account of law as a practice illuminates precisely how participants can be said to perform in a common world. What is it that makes the world common? And when participants disagree about their purportedly common world, how are such disagreements framed and adjudicated?

In what remains the definitive critique of Dworkinian interpretivism, Gerald Postema (1987) provided the first detailed outline of a practice theory of law. The best place to approach practice theory is through explication of what Postema calls "the common world." What joins lawyers together in a common practice? Is it their beliefs, propositional attitudes, intentionality, forms of argument, or consensus in judgment? One or all of these candidates is likely efficacious as a ground of any analysis of law as a practice.

Second, there is the question of consensus. Do participants share a practice if they share only questions about the nature of the practice? Dworkin famously argues that mere questions alone (e.g., about the grounds of law) suffice to bring performers together in the same practice. Postema makes a strong case for the proposition that disagreement is possible only against the background of deep shared commitments. His argument is persuasive but it is just a start.

An effective account of law as a practice will answer the interpretivist question about the grounds of law. As Postema argues convincingly, the unity and coherence of law do not depend on a structure of rules or a regime of principles. What, then, does this unity consist in? The answer to this question is for another day.

WORKS CITED

Brandom, Robert. *Making It Explicit: Reasoning, Representing, and Discursive Commitment.* Cambridge, MA: Harvard Univ. Press, 1994.

Canale, Damiano, and Giovanni Tuzet. "On Legal Inferentialism: Toward a Pragmatics of Semantic Content in Legal Interpretation." *Ratio Juris* 20.1 (2007): 32–44.

Dworkin, Ronald. *Justice in Robes.* Cambridge, MA: Belknap Press, 2006.

———. *Law's Empire.* Cambridge, MA: Belknap Press, 1986.

Hart, Herbert L. A. *The Concept of Law,* 2d ed. Oxford: Clarendon Press, 1994.

Lacey, Nicola. *The Nightmare and the Noble Dream: A Life of H. L. A. Hart.* Oxford: Oxford Univ. Press, 2004.

Leiter, Brian. "Beyond the Hart/Dworkin Debate: The Methodology Problem in Jurisprudence." *Am. J. Juris.* 48.1 (2003): 17–51.

———. "Book Review." *J. Legal Ed.* 56.4 (2007) (reviewing Dworkin 2006 and Scott Hershovitz, ed., *Exploring Law's Empire: The Jurisprudence of Ronald Dworkin,* 2006): 675–81.

Patterson, Dennis. *Law and Truth.* New York: Oxford Univ. Press, 1996.

Perry, Stephen R. "Hart's Methodological Positivism." In *Hart's Postscript.* Ed. Jules L. Coleman. New York: Oxford Univ. Press, 2001, 311–54.

Postema, Gerald. "'Protestant' Interpretation and Social Practice." *Law & Phil.* 6.3 (1987): 283–319.

Raz, Joseph. "Can There Be a Theory of Law?" In *The Blackwell Guide to the Philosophy of Law and Legal Theory.* Eds. Martin Golding and William Edmundson. Oxford: Blackwell Publishing, 2005, 324–42.

______. *Ethics in the Public Domain.* Oxford: Clarendon Univ. Press, 1994.

______. "The Problem of Authority: Revisiting the Service Conception." *Minn. L. Rev.* 90.4 (2006): 1003–44.

Rouse, Joseph. "Practice Theory." In *Philosophy of Anthropology and Sociology.* Eds. Stephen P. Turner and Mark W. Risjord. Amsterdam: North-Holland Elsevier, 2007a: 639–82.

______. "Social Practices and Normativity." *Phil. Soc. Sciences* 37.1 (2007): 46–56.

Searle, John R. *The Construction of Social Reality.* New York: Free Press, 1995.

27 The Tasks of a Philosophy of Law

ROBERT P. BURNS

> Out of the conjunction of activities and men around the law-jobs there arise the crafts of law and so the craftsmen. Advocacy, counseling, judging, lawmaking, administering – these are major groupings of the law-crafts. . . . At the present juncture, the fresh study of these crafts and of the manner of their best doing is one of the major needs of jurisprudence.
>
> (Llewellyn 1941: 188)

A principal task of a philosophy of law at this time is to provide a constructive account of legal practices that reveals how and when they achieve valid results. An adequate philosophy of law will thus understand the law as much more than legal doctrine, the law of rules. Such a philosophy will bring a radical empiricism to bear on the actual practices in which lawyers engage while interviewing, counseling, engaging in pretrial practices, mediating, trying cases, writing briefs, and arguing appeals, and in which judges engage in deciding their cases and justifying their decisions. It will rely on thick description and linguistic phenomenology. It will seek to identify how the best of those practices persuades their audiences of what true law in particular cases really is.

Thus the line between philosophy and legal anthropology will blur. This is something that Clifford Geertz (2000) has already seen occurring in the various forms of phenomenology and pragmatism that have characterized twentieth-century philosophy. In order both to interpret legal practices and to justify them, philosophy will embrace Geertz's (1979: 239) notion that we must engage in "a continuous dialectical tacking between the most local of local detail and the most global of global structures in such a way to bring both into view simultaneously." To identify the ideals situated within legal practices that can support valid results, we must proceed hermeneutically. Just as lawyers' and judges' practices are persuasive because of the overall plausibility of the accounts they provide, philosophers will seek to convince others of the account they give at the "metalevel" by the "overall plausibility of the interpretation they give" (Taylor 1975: 218). Those accounts will be interpretations of practices that are themselves interpretations of events. We will succeed "by the mutual support of many considerations, over everything fitting together into one coherent view" (Rawls 1971: 579). Philosophy will retain an aspiration toward normativity that anthropology generally doesn't and that Rawls' notion of reflective equilibrium attempted to express. Philosophy will thus have an idealizing element and will portray legal practices in their best light, but will look more to the situated ideals embedded in legal practices than to higher-order principles identified by the theorist for the sources of that light.

This means that the line between a philosophy of law and rhetorical studies will also blur. Philosophy will continue to seek the helpful clarity which the analytic tradition offers but will appreciate more deeply that conceptual analysis resolves rather few issues in the philosophy of law. Achieving conceptual clarity will not resolve the ultimate question of which account of law is the most comprehensive, accurate, and fruitful. Philosophy will also move further from an attempt to achieve foundational truths or first principles from which substantive deductions can occur and that serve as criteria for what law is or what justice is. Philosophy will generally accept Rawls's implicit abandonment of that enterprise in his later work for the explication of the ideals that are already situated in our considered judgments of justice.

Those ideals will be implicit in the persuasive practices of lawyers and judges. They are likely to be plural just as the languages of trials are plural (Burns 1999). Philosophical methods or styles that are themselves many voiced are likely to be fairest to a justice which is itself conflict (Hampshire 2000); that is, the determination through rhetorical practices of tensions that are actually constitutive of our social world. An adequate philosophy of law will hear the voices of thick description of legal practices, of legal doctrine, of quantitative social science, and of normative social theory. Philosophy will not homogenize those voices into a single-voiced theory but can arrange them and interpret them in a way that yields insight as it fulfills its traditional task to "think the concrete" or "think what we do." The insight into legal practices that arises from this effort will thus not parallel scientific knowledge but will be a form of reflective judgment, where "a particular issue is forced into the open that it may show itself from all sides, in every possible perspective, until it is flooded and made transparent by the full light of human comprehension" (Arendt 1968: 242). The philosopher who understands legal practices will not create a scientific theory, but will "find a footing" or find his or her "way around" (Dreyfus 1980: 12).

Part of the task of a philosophy of law will be to map the "language regions" within the legal world (Pitkin 1972: 140–9) and interpret the significance of the different uses of language from region to region. A related task will be to identify the appropriate modes of social ordering with each of those regions, to show the links between linguistic practices, modes of social ordering, and different forms of life within society. This effort will also have a dialectical structure, tacking between what we actually do and say in various legal contexts and the social theory that shows those practices in their best light. Philosophers will be more attentive than other scholars to the question of, Where do we stand? when we make such normative claims. On the epistemological side, there will be no Archimedean point, but one account may still be better than another. On the institutional side, "[o]ur task is less to create constantly new forms of life than to creatively renew actual forms by taking advantage of their internal multiplicity and tensions and their frictions with one another" (Kolb 1986: 259). We will thus be interested in identifying the appropriate place for politics, economics, morality, and fraternity in law and of law in politics, economics, morality, and fraternity. We will also continue to explore what we may call the social meaning of rule-based and equitable decision making in particular cases, how they intersect in legal practices, what social function each serves, and the social spheres within which each is appropriate and why.

Philosophy will have two tasks, one interpretive and the other critical. (Aristotle's *Nicomachean Ethics* has sometimes been called a hermeneutics of Athenian life.) Philosophers will provide an account of how multivoiced rhetorical methods can actually converge on a just resolution of a legally situated human event. A philosophy of legal rhetoric will describe, justify, and articulate any limits on rhetorical methods in law. Part of that work will be to show the way in which the constraints on advocacy can function to overcome sophistry and elevate judgment.

This will require qualifying the propositional model of truth that is dominant in legal academia and articulating notions of truth as disclosure. Philosophy will articulate how legal practices may disclose practical truths. Those truths will not be fully representational but will consist of a concrete grasp of facts, norms, and possibilities for action. Philosophy will have to be exquisitely sensitive to the real ideals embedded in current practices, to develop the kind of sensibility usually possessed by a novelist or the best of historians and to show how those practices can be criticized. There will be a number of different strategies here. The question of their relative explanatory power and fruitfulness cannot be determined a priori, only by working out their implications and evaluating their results.

But Geertz spoke not only of the local of local detail but also of the most global of global structures. The philosophy of law will be open to social and political theorizing well beyond the rather scholastic limitations jurisprudence has imposed on itself out of fear of transgressing the disciplinary bounds between itself and political theory or social theory. In particular, legal philosophy will set for itself the task of articulating an ultimately normative theory of social spheres. This will allow us to determine what is appropriately a legal issue and how the moral and political realms bear of those issues. Such a general social theory can be only a likely story. Such a theoretical account will be placed in dialectical tension with an anthropological account of legal practices described earlier. Purely conceptual disputes about what law is will recede as philosophers come to understand that the different issues surrounding that question cannot be solved by conceptual analysis alone. Likewise, law's nature is not reducible to the ideas that legal actors entertain about law. "The meanings and norms implicit in these practices are not just in the minds of the actors but are out there in the practices themselves, practices which cannot be conceived as a set of individual actions, but are essentially modes of social relation, of mutual action" (Taylor 1971: 27). What we should understand by "law is" may be the result of a dialectic between thick description of actual linguistic practices and a normative social theory. A major philosophical issue will be whether the latter is necessary or helpful for the criticism of actual legal practices, even if only a likely story.

Richard Bernstein (1976: xiv) wrote that any adequate social theory would have to be simultaneously empirical, interpretive, and critical. The same will be true for an adequate philosophy of law, which cannot but be an element in a broader social theory. An adequate philosophy of law will be open to the humanistic or interpretive styles of thought I have been describing. Jurisprudence can never be fully naturalized because the object of its study has the same status as other forms of human spontaneity, to use the Kantian term, and because the most adequate theory for understanding them will have a normative edge. Legal practices are intelligent practices that often serve real human goods. They may be understood in the way a philosophy of science interprets science and literary criticism interprets literary texts or dramatic performances. Humanistic studies of the nature of narrative and of drama will contribute to our understanding of the legal enterprise. Both a philosophy of science and good literary criticism serve to explicate ideals implicit in practices. Neither the philosophy of science nor literary criticism aspires itself to be a science. Nor should jurisprudence.

But an adequate philosophy of law will be open to and interested in the results and methods of the social sciences. Part of what a philosophy of law will do is to develop an adequate philosophy of the social sciences so that the results of those sciences can be integrated into a normative perspective. Those results are quite varied and are dependent for their significance on quite different principles and methods from discipline to discipline. They are not self-interpreting. Sometimes the results of the empirical social sciences may be relevant to traditional normative questions. For example, liberal legal theory generally insists on clear preexistent rules as guarantees of predictability and so of individual autonomy against the intrusion of the state. But whether such rules actually do allow a citizen to predict the likelihood of effective adverse state action is an empirical question to which the methods of several social sciences may be relevant.

Further, an adequate philosophy of law will be dialectical in the manner described previously and will seek to achieve something like reflective equilibrium between our deepest principles and our actual practices. The empirical social sciences can contribute to this effort by offering insight into what our actual practices really are. Part of the efforts of a philosophy of law will be to offer an interpretation of the ways in which the results of the social sciences either conform to or deviate from the internal self-understanding of legal practices to be found in doctrine and theory. There is a place here for both a skeptical hermeneutic of suspicion and a second naïveté. The latter will be open to the ways in which legal practices are necessary to realize human goods and so must be understood not only as so many dependent variables to be explained. Once again, scientific practices may be explained sociologically or economically, but they may also be understood as forms of intelligent and autonomous (to use Kantian language) action. A philosophy of science may provide a rational reconstruction of scientific practices. The same is true for legal practices. They express situated ideals linked to real goods that have a validity to be appreciated and criticized in the process of dialectical reconstruction.

A philosophy of law will not usually be normative in the straightforward way in which classical utilitarianism or even Rawls's early philosophy aspired to be normative. We should not be surprised that we cannot directly derive or deduce results in individual cases. This has implications for what we might call the intellectual style of a good philosopher of law. The apparent ability of a theory to dictate specific results has had too much appeal to legal academics and typically comes at much too high a price. We cannot think of the higher-order principles that have a place in our normative world as objects in the mind of God or in nature from which particular practices are a falling away. This means that the philosopher of law will have to possess intellectual virtues of which political judgment is one. Thus there will be at the theoretical level something like the perception and discrimination that we expected from the judge and the statesman. Sheer intelligence and analytical virtuosity will not identify the most adequate philosophy of law.

One of the most central traditional contributions of philosophy to our understanding of the social world has come in the reformulations of the notion of truth implicit in the actual practices of actors in different social spheres. Thus Kant's critique sought to identify the notion of truth that was implicit in scientific practices, as did John Dewey's philosophy in quite a different way. Implicit in the preceding is the imperative for a philosophy of law to identify forms of truth that are adequate to legal practices. Again, the key task will not be to offer an understanding of doctrine or rules but of valid decisions in particular cases. In resolving particular cases, the decision maker will always be asked to dwell in the logical gaps that always separate circumstantial evidence from fully interpreted narratives (theories of the case) from legal rules from norms embedded in narrative and drama from just outcomes. The law in action is made in those gaps. An important task for an adequate philosophy of law is thus to explain what may and does occur there. The philosophical task is to show how what occurs there can be practically intelligent. The realists made important starts in seeking to understand the event of legal decision as something more than the subsumption of value-free factual narratives under legal rules. The notion of a "situation sense" was an attempt to identify concretely the kind of grasp that a decision maker might have in those grasps. Their notion that cases were decided in the judge's or jury's encounter with meaningful factual patterns was basically correct. At least the sociological wing of realism was thrown off track by the scientism of their age in its pursue of a truly scientific account of judicial decision making.

We now have richer philosophies of practical intelligence than the realists knew. We can illuminate decisions in particular cases by exploring and applying in the legal context what we can learn from a number of different philosophical traditions. An adequate philosophy of law will rely on philosophically sophisticated concepts such as Kantian reflective judgment as explained by Arendt, Aristotelian practical wisdom interpreted by contemporary Aristotelians such as Martha Nussbaum (Nussbaum 1986), and interpretive understanding as interpreted by philosophers in the hermeneutical tradition such as Gadamer and Taylor. Those philosophies allow us to approach the conditions of the possibility of valid results that I mentioned at the beginning as a major task of the philosophy of law at this time. There are five such conditions that can support a concept of legal validity, the elaboration of which in the legal context should be an important task of a philosophy of law. The first condition is that the narratives we employ at the trial and appellate levels really do cut at the joints of the human events they seek to represent. This question has empirical, interpretive, and normative aspects. The second condition is that our practical intelligence, as mediated through our linguistic practices, can converge on the place between the individual features of the particular case and our inevitably overgeneralized public norms where the practical truth of the situation lies. This raises an old question, mentioned by Plato in the *Phaedrus*, where Socrates first asserts, and then retracts, the notion that all we can know about human events are the probabilities that they exhibit, and not the concrete truth of the situation. This is a central issue in the philosophy of legal rhetoric. The third condition that awaits philosophical explication in the context of our adversarial legalism is a notion described by Charles Taylor as a central tenet of modernist thought. This notion is especially important as philosophy shifts its focus from the nature and status of legal rules to the event of judgment in particular cases. The idea is that we can achieve an insight (epiphany or illumination) by dwelling in the tensions that are created "by juxtaposing words." "The epiphany comes from between in the words or images, as it were, from the force field they set up between them, and not through a central reference which they describe" (Taylor 1989: 465–6). The modernist notion is that we can know objective practical truths through subjective resonance. The fourth condition for the validity of legal judgments, which philosophers of law will continue to develop in the context of legal practices, is that fundamentally interpretive methods can converge of the truth of a human situation. This condition is closely related to the second condition. It asserts that we have forms of intelligence that are not instrumental, that reveal rather than control. The final condition is that the forms of legal practice we actually employ can be shown to achieve the human purposes of a legal order. This will require the dialectical tacking described above and will try to establish that the legal order actually does allow us creatively to renew our forms of life by reflecting in our linguistic practices their actual tensions with one another. Because an adequate philosophy of law will be both interpretive and critical, it will not solely seek to reconcile us with our practices. The owl of Minerva need not take flight quite at dusk. But before philosophy offers broad proposals for reform, it should have actually seen and thought what we do with the keenness of vision that an owl is thought to possess.

WORKS CITED

Arendt, Hannah. "Truth and Politics." In *Between Past and Future: Eight Exercises in Political Thought*. New York: Viking Press, 1968: 227–64.

Bernstein, Richard. *The Restructuring of Social and Political Theory*. Philadelphia: Univ. of Pennsylvania Press, 1976.

Burns, Robert P. *A Theory of the Trial*. Princeton, NJ: Princeton Univ. Press, 1999.

Dreyfus, Herbert. "Holism and Hermeneutics." *Review of Metaphysics* 34.1 (1980): 3–23.

Geertz, Clifford. *Available Light: Anthropological Reflections on Philosophical Topics*. Princeton, NJ: Princeton Univ. Press, 2000.

______. "From the Native's Point of View: On the Nature of Anthropological Understanding." In *Interpretive Social Science: A Reader*. Eds. Paul Rabinow and William M. Sullivan. Berkeley: Univ. of California Press, 1979.

Hampshire, Stuart. *Justice Is Conflict*. Princeton, NJ: Princeton Univ. Press, 2000.

Kolb, David. *The Critique of Pure Modernity: Hegel, Heidegger and After.* Chicago: Univ. of Chicago Press, 1986.

Llewellyn, K. N. (Untitled chapter). In *My Philosophy of Law: Credos of Sixteen American Scholars.* Boston: Boston Law Book, 1941, 181–97.

Nussbaum, Martha. *The Fragility of Goodness: Luck and Ethics in Greek Tragedy and Philosophy.* Cambridge: Cambridge Univ. Press, 1986.

Pitkin, Hanna Fenichel. *Wittgenstein and Justice.* Berkeley: Univ. of California Press, 1972.

Rawls, John. *A Theory of Justice.* Cambridge, MA: Harvard Univ. Press, 1971.

Taylor, Charles. *Hegel.* Cambridge: Cambridge Univ. Press, 1975.

———. "Interpretation and the Sciences of Man." *Review of Metaphysics* 25.1 (1971): 3–51.

———. *Sources of the Self: The Making of the Modern Identity.* Cambridge, MA: Harvard Univ. Press, 1989.

PART SIX. QUESTIONING THE RELATIONSHIP BETWEEN PHILOSOPHY AND AMERICAN LAW

28 Law and Philosophy at Odds

LARRY ALEXANDER AND EMILY SHERWIN

In addressing the topic of this symposium – philosophy in American law – we give the term *philosophy* a meaning different from that given by Llewellyn in his article "On Philosophy in American Law." Llewellyn described philosophy as something akin to an ideology or decision-making ethos, which will vary over time according to the interests of decision makers and the needs of society. In contrast, we have in mind a discipline that employs reason to bring clarity, depth, and precision to the process of thinking about a given subject.

Given our understanding of the term *philosophy*, the role of philosophy in law may seem obvious. Legal decision making is supposed to be a reasoned enterprise. Judges, in particular, are supposed to decide cases for reasons and to give reasons for their decisions. Surely philosophical methods, employed by judges and the lawyers who argue before them, will improve the quality of the process.

We shall argue that, in fact, legal decision makers may sometimes do better without the insights of philosophy. Law is a reasoned enterprise, but it is also a rule-governed enterprise. For reasons we shall develop, thorough and meticulous reasoning can undermine the benefits of legal rules. Philosophy is fine for observers of law but not necessarily good for its participants.

In sections that follow, we shall elaborate this point in the context of two practices that are integral to law: general compliance with legal rules and judicial decision making by analogy.

FOLLOWING RULES

Let us assume that the object of a legal system is to settle controversy over the practical meaning of generally accepted values (Alexander and Sherwin 2001: 11–15; Eisenberg 1988: 4–7; Raz 1994: 187–92). The values in question may be moral values or some combination of moral and nonmoral values, as you like. Law settles disagreement and uncertainty about what actions the prevailing values require by translating those values into more determinate rules[1] (Alexander and Sherwin

[1] Members of the society in question may sometimes prefer freedom of action or case-by-case decision making by official adjudicators to settlement by rules. In other contexts, however, they will give first priority to settlement of uncertainty and controversy, and accordingly will authorize officials to make authoritative rules (Hart 1961: 121–3).

2001: 53–95; Raz 1979: 16–19, 22–3, 30–3; 1986: 57–62; Schauer 1991: 42–52, 77–134).

Because legal rules translate indeterminate values into determinate prescriptions for classes of situations, they introduce a certain amount of error to decision making. Most rules will sometimes dictate results that are wrong, judged by the values the rules were designed to implement (Schauer 1991: 31–34, 48–54).[2] Accordingly, if actors follow rules without exception, some of their acts will be wrong, and if judges enforce the rules without exception, some of their decisions will be mistaken.

Yet rules can also prevent error, in several ways. First, rules facilitate coordination. One person's reasons for action often depend on the actions of others. Determinate, generally applicable legal rules make it easier for actors to predict what others will do and so reduce the actor's uncertainty about his or her own reasons for action (Hurd 1999: 214–21; Postema 1982: 172–86; Raz 1986: 49–50; Schauer 1991: 163–6). Second, rules prevent faulty reasoning. Individual reasoners deciding what course of action is best, all things considered, may suffer from bias or lack of information. A well-designed rule dictates outcomes that are correct in most cases (Schauer 1991: 150–2, 158–9). In effect, it eliminates reasoning errors by eliminating reasoning.

Thus, the test of a good legal rule is not whether it always dictates correct results but whether it prevents more decision-making errors than it causes. A sound legal rule is one that, if followed without exception, will result in a lesser sum of errors than will result from unconstrained reasoning by individual decision makers (Alexander and Sherwin 2001: 58–9; Schauer 1991: 149–55; Goldman 2006: 453–56). This is true at the level of private conduct and also at the level of judicial decision making. If judges as a group will make fewer errors overall by enforcing a legal rule than by deciding each case as they believe they should (taking into account the effects of nonenforcement on private conduct), then it is better that all judges follow the rule all the time than that they decide each case by consulting the balance of reasons.

To take an example from property law: suppose that a law-making authority seeks to maximize human welfare, and that welfare maximization is a morally important objective. The authority concludes that under a given set of geological conditions, private property rights in water will advance welfare. Accordingly, the authority enacts a prior appropriation rule for nonnavigable surface water: individuals who divert water for uses of their choosing have priority over subsequent appropriators in a quantity of water measured by the initial diversion.[3]

Assume that overall, the authority's rule is morally sound. Water is scarce and essential to life and commerce. In the absence of well-defined property rights, potential users of water – even those who accept the principle of welfare maximization and do their best to implement it – are likely to err in judging the benefits of different water uses and estimating what other water users are likely

[2] The exception is a pure coordination rule, in which no one has a reason to act one way or the other apart from the coordination benefits of the rule. "Drive on the right" is a possible example (Alexander and Sherwin 2001: 56; Goldman 2006: 453).

[3] *See Coffin v. Left Hand Ditch Co.*, 6 Colo. 443 (1882); Restatement (Second) of Torts, chap. 41, scope note (1979).

to do.[4] At the same time, the prior appropriation rule will cause a loss of welfare in some situations, as when the first appropriator of water uses it less efficiently than subsequent appropriators might have done. The rule is justified if, despite its imperfections, it will produce better results overall than unregulated case-by-case decision making.

The difficulty is that it is not rational for individual decision makers (actors or judges) to follow a rule when they believe the outcome it calls for is wrong (Hurd 1999: 62–94; Kavka 1983). Sensitivity to the potential benefits of rules will not solve this problem, because even a reasoner who understands the reasons for rules may miscalculate the effects of disregarding a rule (Alexander and Sherwin 2001: 61–8; Schauer 1991: 94–100). Sanctions for disobeying rules will not solve the problem because sanctions are imposed by human decision makers, who may (rightly or wrongly) conclude that no sanction is deserved.[5] There is, in other words, a persistent gap between the best course of action for all actors (obey the rule) and the rational course of action for any individual actor (disobey the rule if disobedience appears to the be right thing to do; Alexander 1991; Alexander and Sherwin 2001: 53–95).

Nor can reason itself – philosophy – solve the problem of rule following. Actors may understand that they (and society at large) will fare better if all people, including themselves, follow justified rules in all cases. Understanding this, however, does not make it any more rational to follow a rule in a given instance if the actor believes, all things considered, that the action it requires is wrong. Committing or consenting in advance to follow the rule in all cases does not make such rule following rational because commitment or consent to act against the balance of reasons is not, without more, a reason for so acting (Gauthier 1996; Murphy 1997; Shapiro 1998). Comparing the benefits of universal rule following to the benefits of universal disregard of rules does not make rule following rational because only a single act of disobedience is immediately at stake (McClennen 2004; McClennen 1997; McMahon 2001: 6–30) Nor is the actor rationally obliged to comply in order to fulfill his or her fair share of a collective obligation to realize the benefits of the rule (Goldman 2006: 462–70). As long as the benefits of disregarding the rule appear to outweigh the rule benefits attributable to the actor's contribution to upholding the rule, the rational choice, all things considered, is to disregard the rule. Thus, none of these proposed solutions can overcome the basic difficulty, that a rational actor cannot take a statistical view of his or her own decision making in a particular case.

Experience suggests that, in fact, we do follow rules without reflection. Assuming this is true, we must follow the rules without the assistance of philosophy, which tells us that unreflective rule-following is not rational. If we could clear away

[4] Determinate rules are necessary even when rule subjects endorse the same abstract moral principles and are motivated to act on them. Even under the best conditions of moral harmony, reasoning errors and lack of coordination will lead to morally incorrect actions (Alexander and Sherwin 2001: 232n4; Kavka 1995).

[5] This may be because the actor was right to disobey the rule, or because the actor believed he or she should disobey, and hence was not culpable (Alexander and Sherwin 2001: 77–86; Hurd 1999: 189–225, 297–321).

the effects of habit, training, and convenience, and subject our behavior to the discipline of philosophy, we would no longer be able to treat rules as if they were authoritative in themselves.

REASONING BY ANALOGY

It is widely assumed that common law judges reason by analogy (Brewer 1996; Burton 1995: 25–41; Horty 2004; Lamond 2005; Levi 1948: 1–6; Llewellyn 1960a: 77–87; 1960b: 66–9; Raz 1979: 185–7; Sunstein 1996: 62–100; Weinreb 2005). Faced with a new case that does not fall within the terms of existing legal rules, the judge searches for past cases with similar facts, then reaches a parallel decision in the new case. Faced with a case that appears to be governed by an existing legal rule, but in which the rule produces a questionable result, the judge searches the facts of prior cases that applied the rule. If the facts of those cases are dissimilar to the facts of the new case, the judge may distinguish the rule and reach a contrary result. In both cases, judges' reasoning is thought to be constrained by precedent cases, even when their decisions do not conform to posited precedent rules.

Philosophical analysis suggests that analogical reasoning is a spurious idea (Alexander 1996: 80–6; Alexander and Sherwin 2008: 66–88; Posner 1990: 86–98; Schauer 1991: 183–87). Judges cannot reason directly from one case to another, because particular disputes are like and unlike in innumerable ways. To determine whether a new case is relevantly similar to a prior case, the judge must refer, at least implicitly, to a general proposition that makes certain features of the cases important to their legal outcomes. For example, a nuisance claim against a neighboring property owner who keeps a bear is not simply like a nuisance claim against an owner who keeps a snake. Their likeness, if any, depends on a proposition about the acceptability of placing certain types of risks on other owners in a residential setting. That proposition, rather than the brute facts of the cases, determines whether the two claims should be decided alike.[6]

Intuitive findings of similarity, without the aid of general propositions, may be psychologically possible (Haidt 2001; Sloman 2002: 380–4). They are not, however, a form of legal reasoning in which precedent cases determine the outcome of current cases (Alexander and Sherwin 2008: 72–73; Haidt 2001: 818). An intuitive determination of similarity cannot be explained in terms accessible to others. Moreover, there are no criteria by which it can be judged right or wrong. If one conclusion about similarity is as good as another, past decisions impose no constraint.

A narrower form of analogical decision making might seem more promising as a method of legal reasoning: if the facts of a new case provide at least as much support for the outcome of a precedent case as the facts of the precedent case itself, then, a fortiori, the current judge should reach a parallel outcome in the new case (Horty 2004; Lamond 2005 also defends what appears to be a form of a fortiori decision making). A fortiori analogies occur less frequently than intuitive similarities among cases. Unlike intuitions of similarity, however, they appear to be reasoned, and the outcomes they yield appear to be constrained.

[6] Lloyd Weinreb (2005: 12–13, 44–5, 77–103, 107–16) offers a contrary view.

Yet even this limited form of analogy collapses on close examination. To compare the relative strength of two cases, the judge must determine what weight particular facts bear in favor of an outcome. In doing so, the judge must rely either on a general proposition that assigns both relevance and gravity to the features of each case or on some principle such as utility that provides a metric for numerical comparisons. Once again, the general proposition or the principle of utility, not the facts themselves, determines the likeness of the cases.

Another approach to analogical reasoning is to formulate the best legal principles capable of explaining the bulk of precedents, then to decide new cases according to those principles. This method of decision making is notably defended by Ronald Dworkin (1986: 228–32, 240–50, 254–8; Dworkin 1978: 22–31). Legal principles drawn from precedents become the general propositions that link cases and pick out relevant similarities and differences among their myriad facts. Decision making based on legal principles is a form of reasoning. Moreover, it appears to be a form of reasoning constrained by precedent: because legal principles are shaped by the facts and outcomes of prior cases, the analogy arises from the precedent cases themselves.

The difficulty is that legal principles are too malleable to impose effective constraint, for several reasons. First, the content of legal principles is largely within the control of the current judge. Legal principles are not rules or rationales announced by precedent courts. Instead, the current judge postulates the most morally attractive principle consistent with an unspecified proportion of prior outcomes. Both criteria – moral attractiveness and fit with prior decisions – are matters of individual judgment (Dworkin 1986: 254–8).

Second, legal principles require evaluative judgment at the point of application. Legal principles do not dictate results in the manner of determinate legal rules. Several principles may contend for priority in a given case, in which case the outcome depends on the weight each principle exerts in the context of the case (Dworkin 1978: 26–7). The task of weighing principles, like the task of constructing principles, falls to the current judge. This creates a further opportunity for discretionary decision making.

Third, and perhaps most important, Dworkinian principles are morally unattractive, if not incoherent (Alexander and Sherwin 2008: chap. 4, n53–88). They are not moral principles, the application of which must take into account reliance on past decisions. Rather, they are the most attractive principles available that would account for (some percentage of) past decisions, some of which are sure to have been morally infelicitous. They are the answer to the question, What would be the morally correct principles in a world where certain morally incorrect decisions were actually morally correct? If that question is even coherent, it is nonetheless unclear why anyone should seek guidance from norms that are neither determinate, like rules, nor morally optimal.

If the foregoing analysis is correct, analogical methods impose no meaningful constraint on judicial decision making. Nevertheless, the widespread practice of searching for analogies in past cases as if they were source of law for current judges may have significant indirect benefits for the functioning of the legal system. In particular, a perceived obligation to study the facts and outcomes of prior cases can improve the quality of judicial rule making.

In a legal system that treats rules posited in judicial opinions as binding on later judges, judges perform a dual rule, as rule makers and adjudicators. This is unavoidable, but the vantage point and responsibility that judges assume as adjudicators of particular disputes may impair their judgment as rule makers for future cases (Alexander and Sherwin 2001: 132–3; Alexander and Sherwin 2008: 109–17; Rachlinski 2006; Schauer 2006; Sherwin 1999: 1192; 2000: 315; 2006). When a judge formulates a general rule in the context of a specific dispute, the judge's proximity to the facts of that dispute can obscure the full consequences of the rule. In the terminology of behavioral psychology, the facts of the live dispute the judge must resolve are available – they come more readily to mind than more distant facts or statistical probabilities (Gilovich, Griffin, and Kahneman 1982; Plous 1993: 121–30; Tversky and Kahneman 1982).[7] As a result, the outcome of the rule in the case at hand may appear more representative than it is of the overall operation of the rule.[8] This in turn may lead the judge to adopt a rule that produces a satisfying result but is not justified in the long run or to modify a rule that is justified in the long run but produces an unsatisfying result in the current case (Schauer 2006: 906–11).[9]

Given the circumstances of judicial rule making, a judicial commitment to analogical reasoning has the potential to improve the quality of judicial rules. Close attention to the facts of prior cases will bring to light other applications of a tentative rule, beyond the case at hand. Concrete examples from past cases may expose flaws in a momentarily appealing rule or may show that an established rule that appears to misfire in the present case works well in most of its applications. These positive effects have nothing to do with analogical decision making, but they are likely consequences of the practice of seeking analogies in prior cases (Alexander and Sherwin 2008: 118–20; Sherwin 2006: 927–9).

Analogical reasoning, therefore, presents another instance in which imperfect reasoners – in this case, judges – may do better without the discipline of philosophy. Philosophical rigor calls into question the tradition of analogical reasoning in law; therefore, judges thinking philosophically may no longer feel obliged to consult the facts and outcomes of prior cases. In this way, philosophy may undermine a set of habits that is beneficial to the development of common law, even if analogical reasoning itself is not.

CONCLUSION

We have suggested that philosophical analysis casts doubt on pervasive and possibly salutary features of legal practice. Does this suggestion imply that philosophers

[7] This is also true in the context of legislation (Kuran and Sunstein 1999; Sunstein 2003).

[8] Affect bias can have a similar effect (Rachlinski 2006: 941–2; Slovic et al. 2002). Other heuristics that may affect rule making in the context of adjudication include anchoring, contrast effects, and attribution errors (Plous 1993: 38–41, 180–2; Rachlinski 2006: 938–40; Ross 1977: 174; Schauer 2006: 896–98; Tversky and Kahneman 1974: 1128–30).

[9] We do not mean to suggest that legislative rule making is superior to judicial rule making; legislatures have their problems as well (Rachlinski 2006: 951; Schauer 2006: 912–13). Noncognitive problems also affect legislation (Farber and Frickey 1987; "Symposium" 1988).

should leave the scene and permit the law to continue on its philosophically questionable course? No. Philosophy yields insights that can contribute positively and concretely to the study and practice of law and guide empirical investigation of the legal process. But it may be just as well that few if any philosophers or philosopher-judges are capable of applying the discipline of philosophy to the choices they make in daily life.

WORKS CITED

Alexander, Larry. "Bad Beginnings." *U. Pa. L. Rev.* 145.1 (1996): 57–87.

———. "The Gap." *Harv. J. L. & Pub. Pol.* 14.3 (1991): 695–701.

Alexander, Larry, and Emily Sherwin. *Demystifying Legal Reasoning.* Cambridge: Cambridge Univ. Press, 2008.

———. *The Rule of Rules: Morality, Rules, and the Dilemmas of Law.* Durham, NC: Duke Univ. Press, 2001.

Brewer, Scott. "Exemplary Reasoning: Semantics, Pragmatics, and the Rational Force of Legal Argument by Analogy." *Harv. L. Rev.* 109.5 (1996): 923–1028.

Burton, Steven J. *An Introduction to Law and Legal Reasoning.* Boston: Little, Brown, 1995.

Dworkin, Ronald. *Law's Empire.* Cambridge, MA: Harvard Univ. Press, 1986.

———. *Taking Rights Seriously.* Cambridge, MA: Harvard Univ. Press, 1978.

Eisenberg, Melvin Aron. *The Nature of the Common Law.* Cambridge, MA: Harvard Univ. Press, 1988.

Farber, Daniel A., and Philip P. Frickey. "The Jurisprudence of Public Choice." *Tex. L. Rev.* 65.5 (1987): 873–927.

Gauthier, David. "Commitment and Choice: An Essay on the Rationality of Plans." In *Ethics, Rationality, and Economic Behaviour.* Eds. Francesco Farina, Frank Hahn, and Stefano Vannucci. Oxford: Clarendon Press, 1996, 217–43.

Gilovich, Thomas, Dale Griffin, and Daniel Kahneman, eds. *Heuristics and Biases: The Psychology of Intuitive Judgment.* Cambridge: Cambridge Univ. Press, 2002.

Goldman, Alan H. "The Rationality of Complying with Rules." *Ethics* 116.3 (2006): 453–70.

Haidt, Jonathan. "The Emotional Dog and Its Rational Tail: A Social Intuitionist Approach to Moral Judgment." *Psychological Review* 108.4 (2001) 814–834.

Hart, H. L. A. *The Concept of Law.* London: Oxford University Press, 1961.

Horty, John F. "The Result Model of Precedent." *Legal Theory* 10.1 (2004): 19–31.

Hurd, Heidi M. *Moral Combat.* Cambridge: Cambridge Univ. Press, 1999.

Kavka, Gregory. "The Toxin Puzzle." *Analysis* 43.1 (1983): 33–36.

———. "Why Even Morally Perfect People Would Need Government." *Soc. Phil. & Pol'y* 12.1 (1995): 1–18.

Kuran, Timur, and Sunstein, Cass R. "Availability Cascades and Risk Regulation." *Stan. L. Rev.* 51.4 (1999): 683–768

Lamond, Grant. "Do Precedents Create Rules?" *Legal Theory* 11.1 (2005): 1–26.

Levi, Edward H. *An Introduction to Legal Reasoning.* Chicago: Univ. of Chicago Press, 1948.

Llewellyn, Karl N. *The Bramble Bush.* Dobbs Ferry, NY: Oceana Publishing, 1960a.

———. *The Common Law Tradition: Deciding Appeals.* Boston: Little, Brown, 1960b.

McClennen, Edward F. "The Rationality of Being Guided by Rules." In *The Oxford Handbook of Rationality.* Eds. Alfred R. Mele and Piers Rawling. New York: Oxford Univ. Press, 2004: 222–39.

———. "Pragmatic Rationality and Rules." *Phil. and Pub. Aff.* 26.3 (1997): 210–58.

McMahon, Christopher. *Collective Rationality and Collective Reasoning*. Cambridge: Cambridge Univ. Press, 2001.

Murphy, Marc. C. "Surrender of Judgment and the Consent Theory of Political Authority." *Law & Phil.* 16.2 (1997): 115–43.

Plous, Scott. *The Psychology of Judgment and Decision Making*. Philadelphia: Temple Univ. Press, 1993.

Posner, Richard A. *The Problems of Jurisprudence*. Cambridge, MA: Harvard Univ. Press, 1990

Postema, Gerald J. "Coordination and Convention at the Foundation of Law." *J. Legal Stud.* 11.1 (1982): 165–203.

Rachlinski, Jeffrey J. "Bottom-Up versus Top-Down Lawmaking." *U. Chi. L. Rev.* 73.3 (2006): 933–64.

Raz, Joseph. *The Authority of Law*. Oxford: Clarendon Press, 1979.

———. *Ethics in the Public Domain*. Oxford: Clarendon Press, 1994.

———. *The Morality of Freedom*. Oxford: Clarendon Press, 1986.

Schauer, Frederick. "Do Cases Make Bad Law?" *U. Chi. L. Rev.* 73.3 (2006): 883–918.

———. *Playing By the Rules: A Philosophical Examination of Rule-Based Decision-Making in Life and Law*. Oxford: Clarendon Press, 1991.

Shapiro, Scott J. "The Difference That Rules Make." In *Analyzing Law*. Ed. Brian Bix. Oxford: Clarendon Press, 1998: 33–62.

Sherwin, Emily. "Judges as Rulemakers." *U. Chi. L. Rev.* 73.3 (2006): 919–31.

———. "A Defense of Analogical Reasoning in Law." *U. Chi. L. Rev.* 66.4 (1999): 1179–97.

———. "Rules and Judicial Review." *Legal Theory* 6.3 (2000): 299–321.

Slovic, Paul, et al. "The Affect Heuristic." In *Heuristics and Biases: The Psychology of Intuitive Judgment*. Eds. Thomas Gilovich, Dale Griffin, and Daniel Kahneman. Cambridge: Cambridge Univ. Press, 2002: 397–420

Sloman, Steven A. "Two Systems of Reasoning." In *Heuristics and Biases: The Psychology of Intuitive Judgment*. Eds. Thomas Gilovich, Dale Griffin, and Daniel Kahneman. Cambridge: Cambridge Univ. Press, 2002: 379–96.

Sunstein, Cass R. *Legal Reasoning and Political Conflict*. New York: Oxford Univ. Press, 1996.

"A Symposium on the Theory of Public Choice." *Va. L. Rev.* 74.2 (1988): 167–518.

Tversky, Amos, and Daniel Kahneman. "Availability: A Heuristic for Judging Frequency and Probability." In *Judgment under Uncertainty: Heuristics and Biases*. Eds. Daniel Kahneman, Paul Slovic, and Amos Tversky. Cambridge: Cambridge Univ. Press, 1982: 163–78.

Weinreb, Lloyd L. *Legal Reason: The Use of Analogy in Legal Argument*. New York: Cambridge Univ. Press, 2005.

29 Jurisprudence: Beyond Extinction?

STEVEN D. SMITH

Looking out on the legal world today, we can hardly fail to notice that law – that vast, sprawling enterprise constituted by lawyers, judges, bailiffs, specialized and sometimes arcane procedures, daunting technical jargon, and dusty old books – persists and even flourishes. Meanwhile, jurisprudence in its core or classical sense seems close to moribund. To be sure, the term *jurisprudence* has no set or canonical meaning, so the term can be used to include intellectual inquiries that currently thrive. But in its core sense, *jurisprudence* is understood to name the enterprise of theorizing or philosophizing about the nature of law – about what law is – and that enterprise currently exhibits few signs of life.

Of the various subjects of legal study, jurisprudence is the one in which the most momentous and profound questions about law are presented and in which, as Holmes (1887: 478) put it, we might hope to "connect . . . with the universe and catch an echo of the infinite." Or so we might suppose – but it seems we would be wrong. In recent years, at least, the questions addressed under the headings of "jurisprudence" or "philosophy of law" hold little interest for any but the purest (i.e., the most incorrigibly academic) of theorists. It is hard to resist the impression that the questions are merely semantic, and that some of the most powerful minds in the profession are amusing themselves with word play. In this vein, Dennis Patterson (2006: 258) observes that "[a]nalytic jurisprudence" has been mired in "a long, narrow debate, one that has kept it isolated from virtually all interesting debates in epistemology and metaphysics."

How to account for this peculiar state of affairs? And is there any remedy? Or is jurisprudence a dinosaur that has outlived its time and is being artificially kept alive?

WHAT (AND WHY) IS THE QUESTION?

Jurisprudence, it might seem, is (or should be) to the various subjects of law – contracts, torts, procedure – as metaphysics is to physics and chemistry: just as metaphysics is concerned not with hydrogen and oxygen and carbon but rather with being as such, so jurisprudence is concerned with law in itself. What is law?

Historically, that question has sometimes pushed legal thinkers to sort themselves into two rough camps: proponents of (various versions of) what is often called natural law have contended against partisans of (various versions of) legal positivism. From a contemporary perspective, though, it is not easy to say just what the competing sides are arguing about – or why. A typical contemporary account explains that natural law maintains, while legal positivism denies, that there is a necessary connection between law and morality, or that a moral component is required for something to count as law. "An unjust law is not law": natural lawyers are supposed to affirm and positivists to reject whatever it is that this traditional slogan may be asserting.

But on this account, alas, the classic debate can come to seem quite pointless. After all, we can all agree – can't we? – that governments exist, that they issue directives and enact rules, that there are methods or criteria by which officials determine what the directives and rules are. And we can likewise agree that some of these directives and rules are just and good, while others are inefficient, unfair, or downright oppressive. So, what is the disagreement about? Is it just that some people – the positivists – want to call the wicked rules law (albeit bad law) while the natural lawyers prefer to withhold that honorific designation? Have generations of jurisprudence really been driven by this dispute over labeling?

To be sure, if it were assumed that citizens have a moral obligation to obey anything classified as law, this disagreement might have practical significance. On that assumption, positivists would be saying that we are morally obligated to obey even iniquitous directives coming from government, and natural lawyers would be resisting that distressing dictum. But in fact positivists need not, and typically do not, preach any such duty; indeed, many reject the idea of any general obligation of obedience to law. Thus, in contending that bad or unjust rules are nonetheless law, positivists are not asserting that anyone is morally obligated to obey such rules. And so, once again, we must wonder: what is there in the natural law–legal positivism debate worth arguing about? Why is it not a perfectly adequate response – to both the natural lawyers and the legal positivists – to say, "Well, some people use the word *law* in that way. Other people don't. You're perfectly free to use the word in either sense: just try to be clear about how you're using it."

Given the apparent pointlessness of the classic debate, it is not surprising that people who do jurisprudence sometimes drift off into more intramural disputes. And these disputes may indeed be interesting and meaningful – sometimes, anyway – but unfortunately there is usually nothing particularly jurisprudential in the questions they address. Thus, there are obvious differences of view about morality and justice or about evaluative criteria. How should we determine whether particular laws or legal regimes are good or bad, just or unjust? Is a consequentialist approach the best one? Something more deontological? But there is nothing in this sort of question that is peculiarly within the province of jurisprudence: ethicists, economists, and scholars and citizens generally would seem to have full standing to join in those discussions. And they do: thus, in contract law, tort law, and constitutional law, students, practitioners, scholars, and citizens argue freely and passionately about what is good law and bad law without feeling the least need for certification into the specialized discipline of jurisprudence.

Other potentially meaningful questions have a more positivist aspect. How exactly do officials – how do we ourselves – go about determining what the law is and what it means? Is there in fact some master rule of recognition, as H. L. A. Hart famously contended, and if so what is it, and how does it work? And how is meaning extracted from legal texts? But once again, it is not clear that jurisprudence has any special contribution to make to these debates. On the retail level, lawyers and judges argue about such questions all the time. Is legislative history relevant in determining what a law means? Is the intention of the legislature (or of the framers) determinative? What significance does a prior judicial decision carry in a current case? On the more wholesale level, Hart (1994: vi) famously described his jurisprudence as a kind of "descriptive sociology," and it would seem that social scientists (e.g., sociologists or anthropologists) are better equipped than armchair theorists or philosophers to study how a legal system works in practice – what the operative rules actually are, how officials and subjects determine whether there is a rule, and so forth.

Sensing these limitations, positivist theorists have of late occupied themselves in disputing about exclusive as opposed to inclusive versions of legal positivism. On good grounds (which would be tedious to elaborate here, but see Dworkin 2002), most other lawyers and scholars have regarded these debates as of no conceivable relevance to their own pursuits.

In sum, it seems that the classical natural law–legal positivism debate has a jurisprudential character: but that debate has come to look merely semantic. The term *law* is used in different ways: what more is there to say? By contrast, evaluative questions and, conversely, empirical or sociological questions about law look substantial and potentially interesting, but they do not seem distinctively jurisprudential in character.

So, is there any matter or question of importance for jurisprudence – jurisprudence in the core or classical sense – to address?

THE MODERN DECLENSION

In considering the question, we might begin by noticing that the standard current formulation of the natural law alternative to legal positivism – the formulation that understands natural law to assert some sort of necessary connection between law and morality – is not one that classical legal thinkers from Aquinas to Blackstone employed. What they typically did say, in one way or another, is that nature itself – the cosmos, and particularly human beings – have been created by deity and are subject to some providential scheme or law that transcends us. Remi Brague (2007: vii) explains that in the premodern thought of the West, whether Christian, Jewish, or Islamic, "human action had been conceived of as being in phase with cosmological realities that were presumed to furnish humankind with a model, a metaphor, or at least a guarantee, of right conduct." The classical thinkers added that rules and regulations made by human beings in some sense derive from or are modeled on that more transcendent law, and it is this derivation or modeling that provides the basis for regarding these human enactments as law. We can take Blackstone's (1979: 41) statement as representative: "This law of nature, being coeval with mankind and dictated by God himself, is of course superior in obligation to any other.... [N]o human laws are of any validity, if contrary to this; and such of them as are valid derive all their force, and all their authority, mediately or immediately, from this original."

At the time he made it, Blackstone's statement might have elicited yawns, but someone of Blackstone's stature making a similar claim at an academic jurisprudence conference today would raise eyebrows. The claim would surely generate discussion and strong dissent – at least during the breaks between the formal sessions. (I say that the statement would provoke debate between sessions, and if made by someone of stature, because for reasons to be noted shortly, the claim might not be cognizable at all under current academic conventions, and someone without stature making such a claim would probably be quietly dismissed as some sort of crank.) If we permit ourselves to take it seriously, the claim as Blackstone and other classical thinkers presented it seems somehow meatier, more substantial, more worth arguing about, than the more domesticated contemporary claim asserting a necessary connection between law and morality.

So, how did the classical claim – and hence the classical version of the central question of jurisprudence – come to be reformulated in such soporific terms? We might notice several closely related changes that distinguish our situation from the classical context, and that may help to account for the deflated rerendering of the classical claim.

First, under modern conventions, academic discussion is supposed to be carried on in secular terms – meaning, for the most part, the terms of scientific naturalism and of commonsense everyday experience (Smith 2004: 22–37). In attempting to explain some happening or phenomenon, it is perfectly permissible for modern scholars to refer to religion – or to people's beliefs in God. By contrast, actual appeals to God, or to anything that looks metaphysically suspicious or exotic, are out of bounds. As a result of this drastic narrowing of the range of admissible argument or explanation, claims or positions that would once have been framed forthrightly in theological terms now must be translated into more secular terms – or else abandoned.

Consequently, the assertion made by Blackstone and many others about a law dictated by God himself is cognizable today, if at all, only in secular translation. And the closest available translation, it seems, recasts the divine law as morality – hence the current formulation of natural law as the claim of a necessary connection between law and morality.

But morality itself is a deeply problematic concept – in part because, as Alasdair MacIntyre (1985) has shown, the kind of thinking associated with what we are now pleased to call morality has itself been forced to endure the same sort of denaturing (or at least renaturing) translation process to which appeals to divine law have been subjected. As a consequence, it is by now far from clear what sort of thing or desideratum morality even is. Consequentialists and deontologists, who represent the leading metaethical schools today, seem almost to inhabit different conceptual cosmoses (and the deontological cosmos itself exhibits a decidedly spooky quality within the naturalistic frame of thinking that prevails today). Hence, a leading metaethicist notes that "if one thing becomes clear by reading what philosophers writing in meta-ethics today have to say, if is surely that enormous gulfs exist between them, gulfs so wide that we must wonder whether they are talking about a common subject matter" (Smith 1995: 3).

The result is that outside of metaethics seminars, where the different contemporary answers are directly debated, scholars and thinkers tend to bracket the question, and hence to be latitudinarian in their attitudes. To be sure, legal thinkers, like other people, are likely to have their views about what the best account of morality is. But they are also likely to treat metaethical views and debates as detachable from the jurisprudential debates about whether there is a necessary connection between law and morality. (There are exceptions; see, e.g., Finnis 1980.) Morality in this context thus becomes a sort of placeholder term which, for practical purposes, comes to mean something like "appropriate evaluative criteria, whatever those might be."

And thus the once ambitious and provocative contention that human law is modeled on or derived from a preexisting transcendent or divine law is reduced to the claim that a directive or rule is undeserving of the honorific term *law* unless it satisfies some set of minimal evaluative criteria. As we have noticed, that is a claim more likely to provoke yawns and shrugs – or polite deflections ("well, it all just depends on how you define the terms") – than serious reflection and argument.

THE DIVIDE OF THEORY AND PRACTICE

There is to be sure a seemingly sensible and widely endorsed response to this dispiriting depiction. People once believed, this standard response explains, that human law was somehow derived from some more transcendent law – that law, as Richard Hooker observed, sat "in the bosom of God, her voice the harmony of the world" (Gordon 1997: 1013). "[L]aw was felt as something ordained of god," Karl Llewellyn observed, "or even as something inherently right in the order of nature." Consequently, "the judge was to be regarded as a mouthpiece, not as a creator; and a mouthpiece of the general, who but made clear an application to the particular." But this classical view of law, we now understand, was nothing but "superstition" (Llewellyn 1930: 41–2). Law is not there to be found; it is made – made by human beings for human beings. And the important question – the important normative question, anyway – is how to make law so as best to serve human interests.

Thus, from Holmes on, legal thinkers have overwhelmingly conceived of law in instrumentalist terms (Tamanaha 2006). And on the basis of this understanding, legal thinkers have over and over again predicted and advocated the abandonment of older methods of doing law that were beholden to the classical understanding (Smith 2007).

On this view, jurisprudence in the traditional vein can indeed seem to be a monumental misallocation of intellectual energies. Instead, legal thinkers ought to spend their time and talents pursuing the meaningful instrumentalist questions – doing what is often somewhat grandly thought of as policy science.

But although this diagnosis of our situation is by now close to axiomatic in some quarters, it also encounters a major embarrassment. The embarrassment is this: although for generations lawyers and scholars have disavowed the classical conception of law, when it comes to actually doing law – arguing cases, preparing briefs, writing judicial opinions – it seems that lawyers and judges and indeed even legal scholars continue to talk and act as if the classical conception were still in force. They talk and act, in other words, as if there were in fact a "brooding omnipresence in the sky," as Holmes (1917: 222) famously and mockingly described the notion, and as if the purpose of legal argument were to discover and give effect to the dictates of that brooding omnipresence.

I have argued for this description of our current situation at length elsewhere (Smith 2004, 2006, 2007). For now, it may be enough to quote Lon Fuller's observation about the quintessentially lawyerly practice of invoking, citing, and distinguishing precedents. Consistent with modern conceptions, Fuller accepted that common law judicial decisions are in fact a special kind of judicial legislation. But he acknowledged that judges typically do not talk or think of their decisions in this way: they claim to be "merely applying" a law that in some sense exists before and beyond their decisions (Fuller 1968: 45). And he noted that the way judges actually use precedent seems to reflect this elusive conception:

> [I]t is not too much to say that the judges are always ready to look behind the words of a precedent to what the previous court was trying to say, or to what it would have said if it could have foreseen the nature of the cases that were later to arise, or if its perception of the relevant factors in the case had been more acute. There is, then, a real sense in which the written words of the reported decisions are merely the gateway to *something lying behind them* that may be called, without any excess of poetic license, "unwritten law." (Fuller 1968: 92, emphasis added)

In short, for more than a century now, lawyers and judges and legal scholars have insisted, in their theoretical moments, that contrary to what was once believed, legal arguments and decisions are not attempting to ascertain and give effect to some preexisting hidden or transcendent model. Meanwhile, in their practical activities, lawyers and judges and legal scholars have behaved as if legal arguments and decisions are attempting to do just that.

WHITHER JURISPRUDENCE?

The most significant thing that those engaged in jurisprudence might do at this point, it seems to me, is to think in a sustained way about how to negotiate this embarrassing divergence between theory and practice. In our contemporary situation, in short, the perennial question, What is law? pointedly raises the problem of what to make of a practice that in its theoretical moments persistently insists that it is not the sort of thing that in its practical operations it manifestly appears to be.

Should we understand legal practice as a holdover from an older worldview – one that no longer makes sense on modern assumptions and that we ought, if we could actually raise ourselves to rationality, to phase out in favor of a more straightforwardly instrumentalist approach? And if so, how to account for the durability of the practice based on older, now discarded presuppositions? Perhaps the force of tradition is simply more tenacious than the partisans of Enlightenment have sometimes supposed? Or perhaps, as critics like Duncan Kennedy (1997: 192–209) and Pierre Schlag (1997) have argued, the enterprise of law clings to older forms and methods in bad faith and for self-serving reasons – maybe to enhance its aura of authority and impartiality?

Conversely, it might be that the classical assumptions still reflected in legal practice are not as archaic as they seem. By now it seems widely accepted that the secularization of the world that so many social theorists long regarded as inevitable has not occurred, or at least has not occurred in anything like the way it was supposed to. Widespread belief in more than natural realities now seems destined to persist, even to flourish, into the foreseeable future. So, perhaps it is time to take seriously, or to rehabilitate or revise for modern use, the assumptions that animated and continue to animate the traditional practices of law?

Maybe neither of these assessments is apt. Maybe our current impasse and predicament will generate some new paradigm for understanding law – something that understands law neither as brooding omnipresence (or parasitic thereon) nor as policy science (or the implementation thereof).

In our current unsettled and unstable circumstances, prediction seems hazardous. My modest assertion in this essay is that by contrast to questions about internal and external positivism or some of the other subjects currently discussed in jurisprudence journals, this sort of question is one with the intrinsic interest and potential significance to have a claim on the attention of legal thinkers.

WORKS CITED

Blackstone, William. *Commentaries on the Laws of England*, vol. 1. 1765. Reprint, Chicago: Univ. of Chicago Press, 1979.

Brague, Remi. *The Law of God: The Philosophical History of an Idea*. Trans. Lydia G. Cochrane. Chicago: Univ. of Chicago Press, 2007.

Dworkin, Ronald. "Thirty Years On." *Harv. L. Rev.* 115.6 (2002): 1655–87 (reviewing Jules Coleman, *The Practice of Principle: In Defense of a Pragmatist Approach to Legal Theory* [New York: Oxford Univ. Press, 2001]).

Finnis, John. *Natural Law and Nature Rights*. Oxford: Clarendon Press, 1980.

Fuller, Lon L. *Anatomy of the Law*. New York: F. A. Praeger, 1968.

Gordon, Robert. "The Path of the Lawyer." *Harv. L. Rev.* 110.5 (1997): 1013–18.

Hart, H. L. A. *The Concept of Law*, 2d ed. Oxford: Clarendon Press, 1994.

Holmes, Oliver Wendell. *The Path of the Law. Harv. L. Rev.* 10.8 (1897): 457–78.

———. Dissenting opinion in *Southern Pacific Co. v. Jensen*, 244 U.S. 205 (1917).

Kennedy, Duncan. *A Critique of Adjudication (Fin de Siècle)*. Cambridge, MA: Harvard Univ. Press, 1997.

Llewellyn, Karl. *The Bramble Bush*. Dobbs Ferry, NY: Oceana, 1930.

MacIntyre, Alasdair. *After Virtue*, 2d ed. Notre Dame, IN: Notre Dame Univ. Press, 1985.

Patterson, Dennis. "Notes on the Methodology Debate in Contemporary Jurisprudence: Why Sociologists Might be Interested." In *Law & Sociology*. Ed. Michael Freeman. Oxford: Oxford Univ. Press, 2006, 254–8.

Schlag, Pierre. "Law as the Continuation of God by Other Means." *Cal. L. Rev.* 85.2 (1997): 427–40.

Smith, Michael. *The Moral Problem*. Cambridge, MA: Blackwell, 1995.

Smith, Steven D. "The (Always) Imminent Death of the Law." *U. San Diego L. Rev.* 44.1 (2007): 47–67.

———. *Law's Quandary.* Cambridge, MA: Harvard Univ. Press, 2004.

———. "Metaphysical Perplexity?" *Catholic U. L. Rev.* 55.3 (2006): 639–54.

Tamanaha, Brian Z. *Law as a Means to an End.* New York: Cambridge Univ. Press, 2006.

30 Law and Philosophy in the Hyperreal

PIERRE SCHLAG

Ah the old questions, . . .
Ah, the old answers, . . .
How they love the old answers . . .

– From Samuel Beckett, *Endgame* (*A Play in One Act*), as modified by the author

Neither law nor philosophy are free. Both are beholden to and shaped by cultural and rhetorical logics of which they remain almost entirely unaware. Inasmuch as these logics construct both enterprises rather flatteringly as autonomous and in charge of their own intellectual action, it is doubtful that the resulting comedy of errors will end any time soon. As for legal studies (philosophical or otherwise) its main modus operandi is to misapprehend the character of law in simplistic ways that give rise to a set of pseudo-problems, which in turn enable legal thinkers to go to outrageous lengths in rendering the original misprision complex, intricate, multilayered, and seemingly sophisticated. This too makes it unlikely that the comedy will end any time soon. At this point, one would want to speak to legal philosophers out of both sides of one's mouth. One would want to say: "Look, don't be so philosophical about it all: the law can't take it. It cannot support or sustain such intense philosophical attention. It's just not that sort of thing." At the same time, one would also want to say, "Look, be a bit more thoroughgoing (rigorous?) in your philosophical take: Think harder about whether your philosophical m.o. is saying anything interesting about 'law' or whether instead it is using 'l-a-w' as a site for saying something about itself. Is your philosophy in fact attuned to its ostensible object ('law') or are you merely imposing your own philosophical aesthetics where they do not belong?"

One wants to say these things, but the prospects that the comedy will end anytime soon are not auspicious. The reason is simple: the comedy is itself underwritten by the same cultural and rhetorical logics described above. None of this, of course, means that it is not worth trying to move on. Consider that for some, this comedy might well be rather dark. It might not be comedy at all. Where to start?

Consider that some legal philosophers are profoundly concerned with the social and linguistic contexts within which they frame their inquiries. Such philosophers may be concerned that their thinking is shaped by ideological distortions. Or they may be concerned that the academic frames and protocols within which they operate hinder rather than assist thought. Yet others are concerned that the prison house of language compels them to run the same conceptual mazes over and over again – thinking they are saying something about the world when they are saying something about language. Still others are concerned that language – a particular language or language in general – prevents some ineffable insights from being articulated. Some legal philosophers are concerned with any and all of these things. And some legal philosophers are not.

Who are the latter philosophers? They are not unlike the vast majority of law professors. They are thinkers who understand themselves to be the living end of a great and highly elaborated tradition of established and coherent truths. They understand themselves to be in possession of analytical techniques already vindicated. If one understands one's position in this way, then there really is not much purchase in questioning the social and linguistic contexts within which one frames one's inquiries. The point of legal thought, rather, is to perfect the edifice – to weed out errors, to refine conclusions, to bring ever greater rigor to bear on the reproduction and maintenance of the edifice.

How does one come by such a view of law? A hint may be found by looking at the very beginning of Ronald Dworkin's *Law's Empire*, where Dworkin has just announced that he is going to adopt "the internal perspective." Dworkin then writes: "This book . . . tries to grasp the argumentative character of our legal practice by joining that practice and struggling with the *issues of soundness and truth* participants face. We will study formal legal argument *from the judge's viewpoint . . .* because judicial argument about claims of law is a useful paradigm for exploring the *central, propositional* aspect of legal practice (Dworkin 1986: 13–14).

Now, for most law professors and legal philosophers, this passage is utterly unremarkable: of course, we are going to study law in terms of soundness and truth. Of course, we will be exploring the central propositional aspect of law. Of course, that's what we're going to do. What else would we do?

And yet imagine the perspective of the seasoned transactional lawyer or the young public defender or the serious intellectual: How odd Dworkin's perspective must seem. Indeed, how can a book on law generally – let alone one so grandly entitled *Law's Empire* – presume that "issues of soundness and truth" focused on "formal legal argument" as seen from "the judge's viewpoint" can be a useful, let alone an interesting, paradigm for the study of law? Just what kind of crimped empire is this? Dworkin has an answer to this question and it appears in his next few words: Dworkin, like many other law professors and legal philosophers believes that the propositional aspect of legal practice is *central* to that practice. He takes the implicit view that law's principles, doctrines, holdings, and so forth, viewed as propositions, are central to legal practice and to law itself.

THE CENTRAL PROPOSITIONAL ASPECT OF LAW

This particular move – the subordination of all that might be called law and legal practice to its propositional content – is, for those familiar with legal practice, stunningly reductionist. Reductionism, of course, is not necessarily an objection in itself. More must be said. But, there are plenty of options. Hence, an objection can turn to the importance of what has been left out, ignored, deformed. Or an objection can turn to examine whether the reduction has intensified the right aspect. Or an objection can turn to the question of whether the thing reduced (here, law) is indeed the sort of thing that can be understood or appreciated by reduction. Or an objection can be framed around the question of what the reduction effectively does to the minds of thinkers who will operate within the field. (Often, not surprisingly, it will reduce them.)

Legal thinkers and legal philosophers seldom think about such things. Instead, like Dworkin, they proceed immediately and without argument to an examination of the central propositional aspect of law. They take law's representations of itself – law's idealized self-image as a realm of ordered propositions – as directive of the path of the law itself. Subordinated to this ostensibly rational discourse of propositions are law's other aspects – its stratagems, maneuvers, leveraging, violence, coercion, promises, performances, power, misrepresentations, and so forth. It is somehow assumed that these things will be subject to the disciplining effect of the central propositional aspect of law. But no reason is ever adduced as to why or how this should be so. It is simply taken for granted that the central propositional aspect of law rules.

This is not to say, of course, that there is no slippage. Occasionally, as most legal thinkers will readily acknowledge, the propositional content of law fails at this function. It turns out that in some discrete context, for whatever reason, the central propositional aspect of law fails to govern the way the law is deployed. The stratagems, maneuvers, leveraging, violence, coercion, promises, performances, or power of the law are for some reason left ungoverned or unconstrained. There is a breach between the law in the books and law in action. Or there is breach between the law as it is and law's ideals. There is, to put it in short hand, a gap between the actual and the ideal.

When gaps between the actual and the ideal are detected, law professors and legal philosophers typically step up to craft prescriptions and normative theories that will, if believed, adopted or enacted, bridge the gap. At various points, philosophies or philosophical figures are requisitioned to serve variously as accoutrements, techniques, knowledges, intellectual sledgehammers, diagnostic devices, truth adjudicators, thought-police monitors, barriers to entry, trash-talk talkers, turf protection mercenaries, arms race supplements, and more. Many philosophies cannot survive this sort of juridical conscription: The very attempt deforms them beyond recognition. Other philosophies, by contrast, seem to fit right in. They are the bad ones – the ones that effortlessly join with the ruling jurisprudential conceit that in law, the "central propositional content" is the important thing – the thing that rules.

One could easily think, looking at the vast resulting literature, that American legal scholarship is a vital enterprise highly critical in character – constantly attending to the failures and shortfalls of the law. But such a conclusion would be premature. The reason is simple: At the same time that these discrete failures and shortfalls are recognized, there is a tacit performative reaffirmation that the system of law on the whole "works" pretty well. Indeed, the critical attention and activity is itself organized in terms and in service of law's idealized image of itself. So even in the midst of this ostensibly critical orientation, we have a tacit performative reaffirmation of law's essential integrity.

If one wanted to be intellectually serious about all this, one would have to examine the character of judicial discourse – that is, its propensity and potential for intellectual pursuit and edification or lack thereof. The vast majority of legal thinkers and legal philosophers bypass such an examination and simply join the world of judicial discourse. It's true that many legal theorists have a kind of professional disdain for the verbiage of the courts (Lon Fuller's *tosh*), but on the whole the law professors and legal philosophers do not question the basic conceptual and institutional apparatus – the juridical view of law's role, the high-level distinctions, the advocacy rhetoric of the appellate decision. If one needs evidence here, one need look only to the basic structure of the law review article: it is a dressed up, more sophisticated version of the legal brief, the bench memo, the appellate opinion. Even the conclusion "We should... or the courts should..." becomes an academic mimesis of the court's more imperial "It is so ordered."

When we turn to judicial discourse itself, we find that, on the whole, it is not intellectually edifying. Of course, it is not supposed to be. The primary role of judges is certainly not to be intellectually edifying. Indeed, the converse might be more accurate. Whether as means or ends, their job description is to domesticate the intractable, standardize heterogeneity, and contain deviance. As a job description for judges, this may be serviceable (I take no position here). As a recipe for intellectual pursuit, however, domestication, standardization, and containment seem decidedly less appealing. Nonetheless, by virtue of the legal academy's imitation and adoption of the conceptual apparatus of judicial discourse, this domestication, standardization, and containment are effectively echoed in the discourse of the legal academy (Schlag 2009b).

To dedicate legal studies to the central propositional aspect of law as viewed from the judge's perspective seems, from an intellectual standpoint, a serious category mistake. Rather than a prelude to intellectual rigor (which it is surely not), such a focus is an invitation to intellectual sterility. Nothing of any great value can be created in the first instance (the conceptual apparatus does not allow it). And the paradigm is quickly exhausted (the conceptual apparatus allows only so many interesting moves).

None of this should surprise. The conceptual apparatus of judges is designed and produced not to edify, but to perform the work of the state. When courts are elaborating, reconciling, and rationalizing their doctrines, principles, and policies, they are working on the state (state as organ and state as state of affairs). When legal academics take on this judicial discourse as their own, they too are working on the state – and doing so in accordance with the state's own instructions (e.g., the doctrines, principles, policies). The legal thinkers are elaborating the state's infrastructures and its modes of self-communication. Why or how this should be an enterprise responsive to intellectual imperatives or inclinations is something that legal thinkers and legal philosophers never seem to consider (let alone explain). It does not occur to them. They just take it for granted. They have been trained long and hard to take it for granted.

A few decades ago it was possible to think that the advent of interdisciplinary thought would alter the intellectual situation dramatically. And it does seem, at least, that much recent interdisciplinarity has significantly enriched the discussion. But it also seems that to prove itself in the law school world, interdisciplinary work has (deliberately or not) subordinated itself to the ruling paradigm of judicial discourse. Perhaps it does so at a certain remove – at a more theoretically distanced level. Or perhaps it refrains from being openly normative (while nonetheless operating within an arena charged in conventional normative ways).

One result is that the broad juridical framework remains unchanged: Law and legal theory by and large continue to be seen as regulative; the rule of law is already largely actualized; high-level distinctions such as law and society, public and private, are replicated. All of this is to say that much of this interdisciplinary work has subordinated itself to the propositional content of law – certainly its propositional form – and to dealing with issues of bridging the gap between the ideal and the actual.

Once in a while, of course, legal thinkers are brought back from the heavens of legal propositions to a more terrestrial habitat. They are reminded (and this is a strong refrain in the law schools) that their work needs to be pragmatic, practical, and persuasive. One might think that this would counsel or prompt a turn away from the central propositional aspect of law – toward what it is that lawyers actually do, what clients actually experience, and so on and so forth – all in a vaguely legal realist way. But in point of fact, the most significant effect of this injunction to be pragmatic, practical, and persuasive is – what? It is to produce propositions that are pragmatic, practical, and persuasive. (One never leaves the plane of propositions). This is the Monty Python moment, where the prophet yells out to the assembled multitudes: "You've all got to think for yourselves." And they respond: "We've all got to think for ourselves."

THE MEDIUM IS THE MESSAGE

If one wanted to ascertain to what degree legal thought is intellectually serious, one would have to pay greater attention to the framing of the gap between the actual and the ideal (and the conceptions of both). Here we have a number of critiques worth mentioning. They are old critiques and yet surprisingly still pertinent.

One of them is a specific strain of antiformalism developed in the lineage of Hale, Llewellyn, and Cover. Robert Hale (1923), following hard on the heels of Hohfeld, redescribed law in terms of a distribution of the implements of coercion among all economic and social actors – both public and private. Llewellyn (1935), in his famous article "What Is Wrong with So-Called Legal Education," wrote that law should be considered "a doing." And in a foreshadowing of Robert Cover, Llewellyn (1935) argued that law school should engage in "wolf training." As for Robert Cover (1986) himself, he argued famously that law – its institutional as well as its conceptual apparatus – is shaped and marked by the violence it needs to occasion. Hale, Llewellyn, and Cover – these thinkers understood that one cannot understand the import and character of law by severing, isolating, and interpreting its propositional content. Such a severance and isolation is a misprision. And it is such a fundamental, such a basic misprision, that it is quite simply a waste of time to address works or arguments that depend upon such a misprision.

A second critique, less familiar in the legal academy, issues from Marx, Nietzsche, and Derrida. Each in his own idiom suggests that the ideal (i.e., the ideal of law) never quite escapes the structures of the actual. Instead, the ideal is but an idealized projection of the actual. That is to say, the ideal is not some sort of independently defined normative state of affairs. On the contrary, it bears the limitations, the markings, the birth pangs (social, economic, cultural, and cognitive) of the actual. For normative thinkers who are singularly focused on the discourse of judges, this general point has rather negative implications. The normative ideal is never free: it is always anticipated and limited by the structures and configurations of the actual (Schlag, 1994).

If we put the first critique together with the second, we come to recognize that the actual is already marked by its own idealized self-representations while the ideal is itself already invested with the structures of the actual. That is to say – and this would be the third critique – that the actual already furnishes its own ideal and the ideal already contains its own actual. The distinction is false – and in its falsity, it masks (and Marx at least hinted at this) its own powerlessness, while simultaneously promising transcendence (Schlag 2009a).

So much for the critiques. Put the critical orientation aside for a moment and consider a different question. Could this all be functional in an odd sort of way? What we have here are law professors and legal philosophers trying to repair perceived breaches between the actual and the ideal through the deployment of a discourse modeled on that of judges. Occasionally, the legal academics bring in some extradisciplinary input to aid in the effort. Mostly, of course, this work is subordinated to the imperatives of the judicial discourse, its institutional and conceptual apparatus. To repeat: Can it be that this is all functional in some way?

Of course it can, once one understands that the medium is the message. The argument, the processing, the formal style, the pretense to knowledge, the evaluation of the argument, are all rehearsed and reaffirmed in these scholarly attempts to bridge the actual and the ideal. The identity of the prescriptions offered by legal thinkers falls by the wayside, of course, but those are no longer the point. Rather the point is the rehearsal and maintenance of the discourse. At the institutional level, legal thought is no more about creating or actualizing a normatively appealing prescription than moot court is about deciding which litigant should win.

There is a bit of unwelcome irony here for those legal thinkers who are sincerely committed to the prescriptions they offer. The irony is that, despite their passion and their commitment, the dominant discourse treats their prescriptions merely as an occasion to rehearse the discourse: Is the argument right? Does the argument follow? Is the methodology legitimate? Has all relevant material been considered? Is the presentation rigorous? (And so on.) Ethics has been reduced to technique.

Even the ostensible gap between the actual and the ideal has lost purchase and integrity. In legal thought, the affirmation of a gap between the actual and the ideal has become routinized as a discursive premise, as an opening gambit in highly stylized rightness disputes. It's all a performance where virtually no one thinks the arguments matter to the realization of values or objectives. This is not to say that the arguments do not matter. They do, of course, but what they matter to is the rightness dispute. And what is the point of the rightness dispute, one might ask? To determine whether the arguments are correct, whether they follow (and so on). And what is the point of that? To make rightness determinations, of course. And what is the point of that? To have rightness disputes, of course. Or in short, the point of rightness disputes is rightness disputes.

It is in this way that legal thought folds in on itself. Not so long ago, one might reasonably have believed that rightness disputes were designed and conducted to ascertain the value of the thought or the thinker. Now, however, we seem to be on the other side of an inversion. Now, both the thought and the thinker serve as occasions and vehicles for the prosecution and adjudication of rightness disputes.

Combined with a furious focus on productivity and the ferocious pursuit of self-promotion, the rightness orientation leads legal thought to fold in on itself. This fold is perhaps most easily exemplified in the rankings mania. Once it was thought that the rankings were reflective, or at least supposed to be reflective, of excellence (or the lack thereof). The rankings could be praised or criticized for their success or failure in evaluating excellence. The rankings served as a proxy for excellence. But now rankings mania has folded in on itself. What matters now is not the logic of the proxy, but the logic of self-reference. The whole point of rankings is to rank – just as the whole point of self-promotion is to self-promote and the whole point of publishing is to publish. There is no significant external end. Not long ago, this was the kind of outré claim one might expect of a French philosopher (Baudrillard 1990). Today, it's just a banal observation.

What then can we say of legal thought?

It is what it is. If this seems unduly grim, realize that this ubiquitous phrase, "it is what it is" has a wonderfully ambivalent and ironic cast. On the one hand, it implies resignation, as in "it is what it is and there's not much to be done about it." But the phrase also implies a certain mature reflection as in, "it is what it is and so better to focus your energies elsewhere."

CODA

Be intellectually serious. Drop the received scholarly agendas. Forget reflective equilibrium. Ditch the ideal observer. Throw your copy of "The Concept of Law" into a lake and give "Law's Empire" to a homeless person. Also stop worrying about helping the courts with their various legitimation needs. They don't need you. Really. They'll be just fine.

Instead, try to find the best description you can of whatever might be called the postmodern condition. Maybe Postman or Zengotita or Baudrillard or Lyotard, or whoever. It doesn't really matter. Rather, what matters is that you find some salient description of our contemporary intellectual-cultural condition: A description that seems credible and convincing. Let the condition become your mind and try to think about law *from within* that condition. Think sociologically. Think normatively if you want – but do it *from within* that condition. Try to leave the academic formalizations behind. Avoid rightness disputes. If necessary, leave the room. Abjure and disdain scholasticism in all its forms. Avoid tinkering. If you tinker anyway, don't call it philosophy. If you do call your tinkering philosophy, try not to publish it. Try to think *from within* the as yet undertheorized here and now. Give it a form. Give law a form. Realize that there is no glory, no virtue, and no challenge in theorizing from the exceedingly well-rehearsed formal frames of jurisprudence and legal philosophy. It's been done. And we do not have a lot to show for it. Instead try to rethink law from a position that is at least plausibly our own.

Maybe it'll work for you and maybe it won't. If it does work for you, it's as close as you (and we) are likely to come to doing serious philosophy. Failing that, you can retrieve the soggy book you threw into the lake. But that should be your last, not your first option. Oh hell, it shouldn't be an option at all: Leave the book alone. Just walk away.

WORKS CITED

Baudrillard, Jean. *La transparence du mal: Essai sur les phénomènes extrêmes.* Paris: Galilee, 1990.

Cover, Robert. "Violence and the Word." *Yale L.J.* 95.8 (1986): 1601–29.

Dworkin, Ronald. *Law's Empire.* Cambridge, MA: Harvard Univ. Press, 1986.

Hale, Robert L. "Coercion and Distribution in a Supposedly Noncoercive State." *Pol. Sci. Q.* 38.3 (1923): 470–94.

Llewellyn, Karl N. "On What is Wrong with So-Called Legal Education." *Colum. L. Rev.* 35.5 (1935): 651–78.

Schlag, Pierre. "Values," 6 *Yale J. Law & Hum.* 219 (1994).

———. "The De-Differentiation Problem," *Continental Phil. Rev.* Forthcoming 2009a. Available at http://papers.ssrn.com/sol3/papers.cfm?abstract_id=975810.

———. "Spam Jurisprudence, Air Law and the Rank Anxiety of Nothing Happening (A Report on the State of the Art)." *Georgetown L. J.* Forthcoming 2009b.

31 Philosophy? In American Law?

PHILIPPE NONET

1. Perhaps indeed "philosophy" consists of "theories," the words of which matter less than their "life-in-action," a life they gain insofar as they "serve men's needs." The chief questions regarding "philosophies-in-action" are then: "What needs they serve – and whose."

Talk of such "philosophies" is at bottom nothing but a piece of journalism. Perhaps we should call it gossip. It is now abundant at law, *ad nauseam*, in law practice, where it may well have become indispensable, as well as in legal "education," where it often peddles itself under the nearly transparent disguise of the so-called "sciences of man."

To be more precise, one would have to say, not that this vulgarity has found its place "in law," but rather that law has become immersed in it, having now lost almost all traces of the splendid isolation with which legal institutions were once able to maintain a certain aura of nobility. Vulgarity belongs of necessity to the *vulgum pecus.*

Needless to say, no self-respecting mind will occupy itself with such matters. That is a straightforward and quite easy rule of intellectual hygiene. Let "philosophies-in-action" be the business of newspaper readers and other Llewellyns of this world. We shall find our "philosophy" somewhere else. More questionable than ever is now the question whether any honorable mind can still destine itself to law.

But perhaps we should not let the sense of the phrase "philosophy in American law" be determined by the way Llewellyn used it. What else might it say?

2. Perhaps "philosophy" designates the sort of things that are done and taught in university and college "departments" of the same name. Is there that sort of things "in American law"? What sort of things is that in the first place?

"Philosophy" can concern itself with an extraordinarily wide range of subject matters, but it always, or almost always, distinguishes itself by the peculiar way it approaches whatever it approaches. Its core business is the production and destruction of arguments. It argues and counter-argues, it contends and disputes; it proposes and objects; it analyzes, distinguishes, concedes, evades, uncovers hidden premises and contradictions, and so on. It always has found or will find a ground, i.e., an argument, why some argument fails.

Precisely on account of its argumentative virtuosity, "philosophy" has earned for itself other, and rather less flattering names. "Sophistry" is the most ancient.

Almost as old, but now associated with medieval theology, is "scholasticism." Kant found "dialectics" a threat to the moral law. Somewhere Hegel calls "reasoning" "*die Rabulisterei des Verstandes.*" Heidegger simply says that "philosophizing" endangers thought.

Let us put it our own way: "philosophy" is "lawyering." And with this name, we have also found the answer to our question. Lawyering thrives at law. In that sense, "philosophy" may most properly be said to be "in law," for law is the original ground out of which lawyering grows. Lawyering constitutes a, if not *the*, distinctive disease of law, that is, a disease that law nurtures simply by virtue of being law, and thus posing ever anew the problem of the "application" of rules to singular cases. Casuistry we call it. The lawyer's expertise lies in his readiness to argue for or against anything in any case, unrestrained by considerations of truth, or justice, or any other kind of propriety. Shameless!

In principle, the law should be able to combat its own perversion, but it cannot do so without entering into a virtual war with itself. It used to do so, e.g., by requiring of judges the shortest opinions, straight on point, argumentless; by forbidding lawyers to "spur litigation"; generally by making the service of lawyers inaccessible. American law, and more generally Western European law, now appear to have little or no inclination to do any of that. Can one even dream today of a day when *The Clouds* and *The Provincial Letters* would become texts of the highest legal authority?

Meanwhile, we may have erred in determining "philosophy" on the basis of what is done and taught in academic departments under that name. Perhaps lawyering is a perversion of philosophy proper, which perversion may or may not be native to the latter. Perhaps the "lawyering" in "philosophy" is a corruption that philosophy suffers when it is appropriated by academic industry.

What then is philosophy proper?

3. Philosophy proper is: Metaphysic.

The name is meant here to designate the kind of thinking that has determined the character of Western mankind since Plato and Aristotle. The distinctive trait of Western thought is that it strives to determine the ground of what is, in the sense of *das Seiende* (l'étant, τὸ ὄν), not *das Sein* (l'être, τὸ εἶναι). [Please note in passing that the distinction between *das Seiende* and *das Sein* cannot be said or thought in English, which is grammatically incapable of differentiating the participle from the gerund. We shall shortly have occasion to return to this and other limitations of our language as a possible host of thought.] The ultimate principle of metaphysic is the *principium grande* that was first articulated by Leibniz, and is now widely known as the principle of sufficient reason. It holds, in its abbreviated form, that *nihil est sine ratione*, nothing is without reason, or, to put it positively: All being, in the sense of *das Seiende*, is grounded in reason. Leibniz's is the principle of principles, ground of the nearly irresistible authority with which we ask of all things the question "Why?"

In modern times, namely since the founding of modern natural science in Descartes, metaphysic takes the form of technique, which represents itself as the unconditional will of man to become "lord and possessor of nature." The essence of technique is nothing "technical" (just as the essence of law is nothing "legal," the essence of morality nothing "moral," etc.). Technique asserts a metaphysical stance: it defines the essence of being, in the sense of *das Seiende*; it determines the position of man amidst being, again in the sense of *das Seiende*; it sets the standard of truth by which man's relation to being, in the sense of *das Seiende*, is to be governed. Under the sway of technique, all being, in the sense of *das Seiende*, is reduced in principle to the position of expendable means, available for use at will by man; man himself is turned into an expendable means to uncover and use the expendable means of which being, in the sense of *das Seiende*, consists; the measure of truth becomes the "effectiveness" with which human thinking uncovers "effective" means. It should be apparent that the concept of "means" rests upon the principle of causality, which in turn follows from the Leibnizian principle of sufficient reason. Technique is metaphysic.

If philosophy is metaphysic, and metaphysic today is technique, then we may return to our question and ask: Is there technique in law? Of course there is, although here again, to be more precise, one would have to say not that technique is "in law," but rather that law, like all other domains of modern existence, lies entirely under the sway of technique. In accordance with the technical transformation of all beings into means, law itself is reconstructed as "policy," and legal thinking turns into the calculation of "values." The law as a whole is thus subordinated to a higher "law" – we may call it, as does metaphysic, the *principium rationis* – the being (this time in the sense of *das Sein*) and the imperiousness of which law itself cannot conceive or even name. [Let us note again here how thinking is impaired by the poverty of the English language, which distinguishes itself from other Western languages by having only one word for "law," namely "law." By contrast, German has easily found a fitting word for the "law" of technique; instead of *Gesetz*, it calls it *Gestell*, substituting the root verb *stellen* for the *setzen* of *Gesetz*.]

In consequence of this incapacity, American law fails entirely to see how the sway of technique threatens to bring about a near extinction of freedom on earth. The servitude into which the modern economy drives its "human resources" makes all earlier forms of serfdom – including the "slavery" we purport to have abolished – look benign.

4. One last possibility must still be considered: "Philosophy" might well some day put into question its commitment to metaphysic, and attempt slowly, painfully, laboriously to rethink essential matters free from its inherited apparatus of concepts and modes of "reasoning" (free from "logic" above all, which does the most extreme violence to language). "Philosophy" would then remain the name for a kind of thinking that devotes itself to what is most worthy of thought: What "is" being in the sense of *das Sein*? What "are" time and space? What is language? What is poetry? What is it to think? Who is man? What are art and technique? What is freedom? And so on. We know in advance that all such questions are incapable of ever being "answered." But that is precisely why they are always in need of being thought afresh.

We should not expect such a transformation to happen in anything like present day academic "philosophy," or indeed in any other part of academic institutions, which are all wedded to the pursuit of technique. Of course miracles happen even there: Heidegger did happen in a German university last century.

Might such thinking find a home "in law," if not in a law school, perhaps somewhere else "in" the profession? The answer must be a definite No. Nothing at all in the intellectual make-up of a lawyer prepares him to pose any essential question, not even the question regarding the essence of law. On the contrary, in order to conduct his business, he must at all times assume that he already knows well enough all there is to be known about what is law. Indeed he is a master at "finding the law" in every case that comes on his desk. Were he seriously to question the essence of law, all his practice would *ipso facto* come to a grinding halt. That is presumably why American "jurisprudence" has never added up to anything of substance: Only a few slogans – "the standpoint of the bad man," "realism," "the right answer thesis" – the manifest falseness of which condemns them to oblivion, even if at first they, like scandal, succeed in provoking attention.

The same, *mutatis mutandis*, must be said of every professional or intellectual specialty, "discipline" one hears in certain circles. Every specialty, even the discipline of "philosophy," disables its specialist from asking essential questions. The only qualification that qualifies one for essential thinking is: Being human. Thinking proper is a prerogative of man as man, namely a preeminent way of being human, that is, of enduring the fullness of experience that offers itself to man as his distinctive possibility.

In principle, nothing is to prevent a lawyer, or any other specialist, from letting himself be struck by the necessity of thought, throwing off the mantle and whig, and reassuming the plenitude of his humanity. But in so turning to thought, he will move *out* of law, even if only part of the time and part of the way. The move is in fact nothing easy to accomplish. But no thoughtful man ever lets his profession entirely extinguish his own humanity.

5. That a lawyer can move out of law and turn himself to thought, has been documented in at least two notorious cases: Descartes and Leibniz. But a serious obstacle presents itself in the case of American lawyers. It arises from the fact that American law speaks English, and only English, a language that is, and has so far always been, remarkably unconducive to thought. Not a single great thinker has emerged out of it. In fact only two European languages have ever favored the growth of a tradition of thought: Homer's Greek and Luther's German. How many American lawyers would one find today who can read them both?

Translations have now spread the illusion that Greek and German thought is accessible in English. They are in fact incompetent, all of them, without exception, not so much because of limitations of the translators, as because the poverty of English renders it constitutionally incapable of capturing what the Greek and German texts say.

In two bracketed notes above, I have given examples of the obstacles to thought that one encounters in English: English is incapable of differentiating being in the sense of *das Sein* from being in the sense of *das Seiende*; English is incapable of naming the *Gestell* that sways above all "law" in the age of technique. The two examples are bound together, since *das Gestell* is a name for *das Sein des Seienden* as it manifests itself under the sway of technique, in *die Seinsverlassenheit des Seienden*. Whoever fails to grasp the difference between *das Sein* and *das Seiende*, is incapable of understanding *das Gestell*. He has put virtually all Heidegger out of his reach (not to mention all thought prior to Heidegger), and thereby all the world in which he exists. All attempts by English translations to circumvent these difficulties lead only to misunderstandings, which are not worthy of being reported here. Let them, the translations as well as the misunderstandings, fall into oblivion.

On the same ground, I shall refrain from adding to the examples given above. It would take a couple of volumes for me to collect all those I know. What a waste that would be! Let us instead read a few pages of Kant.

PART SEVEN. COMMENTARIES

32 Optimism and Pessimism in American Legal Philosophy

CARLOS A. BALL

Pity the legal philosopher. Those us of who are academics must to some extent justify our professional existence, insulated as we are from the type of market forces and ongoing performance reviews that most employees are subject to. For academics who help to train professionals – as law professors do – that justification is made somewhat easier by the fact that our students will turn (however indirectly and imperfectly) the doctrinal knowledge that we impart to them in the classroom into doctrinal practices in the outside world. Students of property or of tort law, for example, will to some extent rely on the concepts learned and skills acquired in the classroom in making or interpreting the law as participants in the legal system. Similarly, property or tort scholars can through their writings seek (however indirectly and imperfectly) to influence legal decision makers on the future direction of the law.

But what of jurisprudes? How do they justify their existence? Obviously, there is no practice of jurisprudence as such. There are no causes of action, no claims, no points of legal doctrine that can be passed on from teacher to student. It is possible (at least in theory) that students turned legal actors will bring to bear on their practices concepts related, for example, to pragmatism or natural law or consequentialism that they may have picked up in a jurisprudence class, but the link between knowledge and practice seems considerably more attenuated in jurisprudence than in just about any other course in the law school curriculum.

Jurisprudes, like other legal academics, can always seek to influence legal decision makers on the future direction of the law through their scholarship, but it would seem that neither judges nor legislators bother to grapple directly with issues of theory or philosophy. For instance, even the judges who may come closest to the Dworkinian ideal of the Herculean judge are unlikely to read – or care about – Dworkin's (1986: 239) understanding of what makes a judge Herculean to begin with. Indeed, some judges have complained that much of what is published in law reviews these days is useless to them as legal decision makers, in part because there is too much attention paid to theory. The U.S. Court of Appeals Judge Harry Edwards (2002: 2001), for example, after commenting on how legal scholarship, as of late, has been taken over by theorists, as well as by those interested in interdisciplinary pursuits, puts it simply when he notes that "[t]he most serious concern that I have with legal scholarship is that too much of it is useless." It seems reasonable to assume that the more theoretical or philosophical the scholarly writing, the less likely it is that legal actors will perceive that scholarship to be useful or relevant to their practices.

It appears, then, that legal philosophers are at a considerable disadvantage (at least as compared to other legal academics) in justifying their professional existence. Some may think that this state of affairs might lead jurisprudes to feel hopeless or futile. If this volume is any indication, however, that is by no means the case. Indeed, if we assume that the essays contained in this book represent a fair cross-section of the contemporary state of commentary on the contemporary state of philosophy in American law, jurisprudes (for the most part – there are some exceptions in this collection) are a hopeful bunch.

This optimism is in many ways consistent with the Llewellyn essay whose name provides the title to this book. After skipping and hopping through a century and a half of American jurisprudence in a handful of pages, Llewellyn ended his essay on a rather optimistic note about the state of legal philosophy in the early 1930s. Although he acknowledged that his preferred "sociological jurisprudence" had found "little echo among judges," there was nonetheless reason for hope given what Llewellyn (1934: 212) took to be a correspondence between the ascendant jurisprudence of the realists and "the actual behavior of the better bar." In addition, Llewellyn found much comfort in the fact that the realists, unlike their jurisprudential predecessors, were committed to making judgments about policies in ways that are "backed by facts."

Most of the essays in this book reflect a similar degree of optimism, although the reasons for their sanguinity are quite different from those found in Llewellyn's essay. If indeed, as many have suggested, we are all realists now, then it is difficult to get much frisson from jurisprudential arguments that, in effect, insist on the need to pay attention to conditions on the ground. Jurisprudes in the early twenty-first century, in other words, must get their kicks elsewhere. And many of the contributors to this volume do precisely that, with Backer finding hope in perfectionism, Solum in virtue jurisprudence, Goodrich and Mootz in the discipline of rhetoric, Sarat and Clarke in political philosophy, Thurschwell in continental philosophy, Adler in moral philosophy, Bix in analytical philosophy, Broekman in semiotics, Schroeder and Carlson in psychoanalytical jurisprudence, Pether in theories of discourse and language, West in robust understandings of conceptions of the good, Burns in the multiplicity of philosophical methods and styles, Wright in the ongoing relevance of legal philosophy, Michelman in the correct ordering of law and morality, Patterson in an understanding of law as a shared practice, Garver in the relational justifications for privileging freedom of thought over freedom of action, Hayman and Levit in the power of narrative, Taylor in the power of creativity, Scallen in the importance of contexts and experiences, Balkin in the ability of the law to restrain power, and Fisher in the ability of the law to quell impulses for violence and revenge.

There are, to be sure, common themes that emanate from these essays. For instance, several of the contributions find their hope in the notion of mediation. Backer, for example, contends that the law can play an important and useful role in mediating the tension between faith and reason. For their part, Goodrich and

Mootz (in their respective essays) are sanguine about the ability of the discipline of rhetoric to address (and in many ways overcome) the seemingly inevitable tension between law and philosophy. Solum is confident that a jurisprudence of virtue can help solve the seemingly intrinsic impasse between a jurisprudence of rights and a jurisprudence of consequences. In a similar vein, Sarat and Clarke contend that principles of political philosophy can, if not bridge the gap between law and sovereignty, at least productively illuminate the boundaries between the two.

For the most part, however, the optimistic essays in this volume, which together constitute two-thirds of the book, are a remarkably diverse group of writings that have two main characteristics in common: first, and not surprisingly given the focus of the book as reflected in its title, they all in some way address a topic related to (or arising from) the intersection of law and philosophy; second, they are all (admittedly to different degrees) optimistic about the ability of particular strains of philosophy (or particular theoretical emphases or understandings) to be useful or helpful or relevant to our thinking about the law.

This is not to suggest, of course, that all of these commentators are satisfied with the state of legal philosophy as it currently exists. In fact, many of the essays already noted contend that jurisprudence as an area of academic endeavor should pay more attention to disciplines or fields or theories or ideas that it has (to its peril) so far largely ignored. But these types of arguments are hardly surprising and do not diminish from the sense of hope that emanates from most of the essays in this book. We academics are a notoriously dissatisfied group with the world – including that of ideas – as it is. No scholar has ever built a reputation by exclusively defending the intellectual status quo. There is always room for improvement, and for jurisprudes that often entails paying greater attention to consequential or moral or analytical or deconstructive or naturalist or pragmatist or antifoundational – the list is almost endless – philosophy.

Indeed, several of the essays in this book can be thought of as standing for the straightforward proposition: we need more of *X* in American legal philosophy. I am thinking in particular of the essays by Thurschwell (continental philosophy), Adler (moral philosophy), Bix (analytical philosophy), Broekman (semiotics), Schroeder and Carlson (psychoanalytical jurisprudence), Pether (theories of discourse and language), and West (conceptions of the good). All of these authors express a dissatisfaction with the present state of philosophy in the legal academy because of what it lacks. They also, however, argue (or at least suggest) (1) that the gaps in question can be addressed and (2) that doing so would be beneficial in either providing a better understanding of the types of issues that our society seeks to address through the law or a clearer conception of what the law is (or what it should be). In my estimation, therefore, the "we need more of *X* in American legal philosophy" essays are ultimately jurisprudentially optimistic.

I also do not want to suggest, in noting the hopefulness that emanates from many of the essays contained in this volume, that the optimistic contributions are unbridled in their sanguinity. Several of the essays remind us that there are plenty of reasons to worry, whether they be the (perceived) dangers of foundationalism, or the troublesome legitimizing effects of the law, or even man's inhumanity to man. Nonetheless, it seems to me that in many of the essays that express concerns about the current state of affairs (intellectual or otherwise), a sense of hope ultimately prevails over a sense of doom.

For example, Hayman and Levit, while noting the limits of the move toward empiricism in legal methodology engendered by the realists, are nonetheless hopeful about the role that narrative can play as a tool of persuasion within the law. Hayman's and Levit's faith in the power of narrative is so strong that it leads them to posit that it might even allow (gasp!) the reaching of a form of truth, albeit one that is contingent and culturally bound. In a similar vein, Scallen, while critiquing foundationalism and the search for *the* truth in American legal philosophy, nonetheless urges us to focus on contexts and experiences in order to search for a truth that exists on the ground. For his part, Balkin argues that the law can be used not only problematically to mystify and legitimate unjust exercises of power (as critical legal theorists have argued for a long time), but that it can also be deployed in helpful ways to restrain such power (a point that critical theorists have failed to acknowledge). And Fisher, in elaborating on Paul Ricoeur's understanding of justice, describes a Hobbesian world in which the impulse for violence and revenge is omnipresent but then suggests that law (and morality) represent our only meaningful hope in quelling such destructive impulses.

If jurisprudence were a democracy, then, and the question of whether there is reason to be optimistic about the contemporary state of American legal philosophy – or the potential state of American legal philosophy with some refocusing or tweaking of philosophical priorities – were put to a vote among the contributors to this volume, it would seem that the optimists would win the election by a comfortable margin. There is, however, some dissent; a handful of the essays, it is fair to say, are rather pessimistic about the contemporary state of American legal philosophy. It would seem that Nonet's essay is the least hopeful of the bunch. For Nonet, nothing short of the complete abandonment of both law and philosophy as academic disciplines will help us in thinking productively about the essence of law.

Smith and Schlag do not go as far as Nonet; they do, however, question much of the legal and jurisprudential scholarship that has been written in the past few decades. Smith contends that the issues that legal philosophers have been grappling over for generations (e.g., what is the law and what is the relationship between law and morality) are of little interest to others. For his part, Schlag questions what he takes to be the assumption of most legal scholars that there is a central, propositional aspect of legal practice that can serve as an aspirational benchmark. He also urges academics to cease trying (hopelessly) to make actual law correspond to ideal law.

Clearly, Smith and Schlag are arguing more than simply "we need more of *X* in American legal philosophy." Their essays call less for tweaking and more for paradigm shifting. But it seems to me that there is a silver lining to their otherwise strongly critical assessments of the contemporary state of American legal philosophy in that their essays suggest a way forward: Smith argues that legal philosophers, after they abandon their useless and decades-old debates, grapple with why a traditional conception of the law (which conceives of it as a brooding omnipresence) persists in legal practice even though it has been so thoroughly questioned in legal theory, and Schlag urges us to find peace and comfort, as well as additional time for other intellectual pursuits, in accepting the fact that there is no such thing as imperfections in the law – or, as he puts it, the law is what it is.

There are other pessimistic voices in this collection. Alexander and Sherwin's essay, for example, argues that philosophy is either irrelevant or unhelpful to legal actors. And there are several essays that express dismay over the resilience of powerful and negative ideas or concepts in American legal philosophy. For Allen, the source of the concern is the stubborn pervasiveness of maternalism and paternalism; for Caudill, it is the perseverance of natural law; for Winter, it is the entrenchment of formalism and universalism; and for Tamanaha, it is the universalism of instrumentalism. Although not always explicit on this point, these four essays leave us with the distinct impression that these unfortunate philosophical influences (from the authors' perspective) are unfortunately here to stay.

The pessimistic essays, however, constitute a minority. It seems to me that the philosophical optimism contained in this volume clearly outweighs the jurisprudential despair that can also be found herein.

The question of whether such optimism is justified requires considerable more analysis than I can provide in this short commentary. It is worth noting, however, that, if this collection is any indication, there is a vibrancy and diversity to the contemporary state of commentary on philosophy in American law that was lacking in the historical periods discussed by Llewellyn in his essay. Although Llewellyn's account is clearly simplified, there is some plausibility to the story that he tells of how natural law, the predominant jurisprudential influence in the early days of the republic, was later replaced by positivism, which was, in turn, challenged by realism in Llewellyn's time.

As this book should make clear, the multiplicity of views emanating from American legal philosophy today makes it difficult to divide the field into a handful of self-contained categories as it still seemed possible to do in Llewellyn's day. Indeed, the diversity of contemporary theory-based perspectives in American law becomes even greater once we expand beyond traditional understandings of what constitutes the field of jurisprudence to include ideas and insights from scholars in areas that are largely absent from this book, such as feminist theory, critical race theory, and queer theory. The broad spectrum of perspectives and approaches in American legal philosophy in the early part of the twenty-first century leads to scholarship that is, I believe, considerably more vibrant and rich than (what in hindsight seem to be) the somewhat picayune disagreements, say, between Llewellyn and Pound in the early part of the twentieth century.

To return, then, to the question with which this commentary began, it seems to me that the jury is still out on the question of whether jurisprudes can justify their professional existence through their influence on those who do law. In fact, if Llewellyn were alive today, he would likely be disappointed with the contemporary state of American legal philosophy because, it can be argued, it has little correspondence with the practice (or the making) of law. But if we grant ourselves the right to assess scholarship not through its direct impact on legal actors but through the quality and vibrancy of the ideas and debates expressed therein, it seems to me that this volume of essays should leave us relatively pleased with the contemporary state of American legal philosophy.

WORKS CITED

Dworkin, Ronald, *Law's Empire*. Cambridge, MA: Belknap Press, 1986.

Edwards, Harry T., "Reflections (on Law Review, Legal Education, Law Practice, and My Alma Mater)." *Mich. L. Rev.*, 100.8 (2002): 1999–2007.

Llewellyn, Karl N. "On Philosophy in American Law." *U. Pa. L. Rev.* 82.3 (1934): 205–12.

33 This Jurisprudential Moment

MARIANNE CONSTABLE

> 5. The "true" world – an idea which is no longer good for anything, not even obligating – an idea which has become useless and superfluous – *consequently*, a refuted idea: let us abolish it!
>
> (Bright day; breakfast; return of *bon sens* and cheerfulness; Plato's embarrassed blush; pandemonium of all free spirits.) (Nietzsche 1968: 485–6)

Jay Mootz's aim for this project, according to an early description provided to the contributors, is to "capture the 'moment' in legal philosophy." The thirty-three essays responding to Mootz's call to "a diverse group of people" for papers that "mimic Llewellyn's audacity in describing the relationship between philosophy and law in ten pages in a period of great ferment," present the commentator with a difficult task. Although the actual contributors are on the whole largely affiliated with law schools, their calls on and relations to philosophy run the gamut in terms of tone and involvement. Yet despite their differences and their individual shortcomings, or perhaps because of them, the essays together indeed reveal something of the moment, of its struggles and contradictions. That they show rather than capture this jurisprudential moment says something itself about contemporary philosophy and its possibilities in law.

In keeping with the overall aim of the volume and with Karl Llewellyn's own 1934 commentary "On Philosophy in American Law," the commentary that follows constitutes a provocation. Just as Llewellyn (1934: 206) was interested in implicit philosophy, or with "those premises, albeit inarticulate and in fact unthought, which yet make coherence out of a multiplicity of single ways of doing," so too this commentary finds coherence of sorts in the multiplicity of ways of doing what is done in this collection. It offers apologies to those authors to whom it does not do individual justice.

Llewellyn, himself a U.S. law professor, offered a quite particular understanding of philosophy, as several of the essays point out. Llewellyn is less interested in verbalized philosophy than with what Anita Allen nicely calls the atmospherics of

The author thanks Cheryl Mak, Sarah Misherghi, and Katherine Lemons for excellent comments and research assistance.

law, and what Eileen Scallen identifies with ground truth. Llewellyn is interested in the spirit of the laws, or what Montesquieu might have called the springs that make the nation go. Felt needs rather than reason or Hegelian spirit guide U.S. legal history for Llewellyn through natural law, positivism, and, Llewellyn hopes, a new realism, as Adam Thurschwell shows. The felt needs of Llewellyn's time are social. They are just beginning to articulate themselves, Llewellyn claims in his essay, not so much in the contemporary ways of the law-guild as in the sociological and realist writings that herald the future.

Now, seventy-five years after Llewellyn's essay, this volume shows, Llewellyn's once-implicit philosophy of social needs has become explicit in the law-guild. Contemporary legal theory stands more or less in the space that Llewellyn opened up, as Peter Goodrich points out. We are on the cusp of legal realism, striving – as Llewellyn did at another end of this moment – to move beyond what we are still embroiled in. The essays in this volume recognize the grip that a sociological and realist understanding of law holds over us. Many adopt Llewellyn's realist distinction between theory and practice or philosophy and law. By and large, they then valorize one pole of the distinction, decry the distinction, or seek to overcome it. In so doing, they show how implicated we are in the fifth moment of Friedrich Nietzsche's famous history of the error that is reason.

* * *

I. PHILOSOPHIZING IN RELATION TO LAW-MEN'S DOINGS

In his essay, Llewellyn claimed to have limited use for explicit philosophizing. Not so, many of the contributors to this volume. Identifying philosophy with the writings of philosophers, albeit from different schools of thought, essays in this collection variously take Plato, Aristotle, Kant, Hegel, Ricoeur, Hart, Dworkin, analytical philosophy, moral philosophy, normative theory, Continental philosophy, and critical legal theory to be touchstones for understanding what philosophy in the American legal academy is or should be. The essays suggest that writings of various subfields of academic philosophy may indeed give "fortunate expression to the living currents of their time" (to use Llewellyn's phrase). *Contra* Llewellyn, the essays suggest further that particular philosophical writings can offer guidance to those interested in legal and philosophical issues of our time. Brian Bix, for instance, takes legal scholars to task for their poor reception of analytical legal theorists (he mentions Raz, Coleman, Postema, Schauer, Lyons, Shapiro – none of whom appear in this collection) and for "hiding behind big names in philosophy" (he mentions Wittgenstein, Hegel, Kant, Foucault, Aquinas, Hobbes, Heidegger, Habermas, "and beyond"). Matthew Adler puzzles over the U.S. legal academy's neglect of contemporary moral philosophy (as in Temkin, Hurka, Kamm, Scanlon), in effect confirming Bix's point that academic philosophers address their own ilk. Austin Sarat and Connor Clarke show how the political philosophy of the likes of Carl Schmitt and Giorgio Agamben can help sociolegal scholars understand sovereignty in legal practice. Various essays suggest that virtue

(Solum's aretaic turn), new legal realism (Hayman and Levit), Lacanian psychoanalysis (Schroeder and Carlson), accounts of love and friendship (Garver), and the work of Ricoeur (both Fisher and Taylor) provide insight into or fulfill particular contemporary legal-philosophical needs.

The actual uses to which the essays would put philosophy vary, sometimes surprisingly. Robin West calls for normative jurisprudence to inquire into the legal good, an issue she claims is omitted in contemporary jurisprudence. Brian Bix, by contrast, defends the inability of analytical philosophy to be practical. Jeanne Schroeder and David Gray Carlson agree that philosophy ultimately cannot tell us what to do but find what they call "cash value" in psychoanalytic approaches to law that enable freedom. George Taylor's reflections on creativity lead him to call for greater inculcation of imagination in legal education.

Most of the essays do share Llewellyn's (1934: 205n*) belief that "philosophers' writings and law-men's doings meet rarely on the same level of discourse." Mootz himself begins (in his essay) with the irrelevance of contemporary academic philosophy for law and the need to bridge the theory-practice divide. By contrast, Larry Alexander and Emily Sherwin argue that judges and legal decision makers would do better to stay away from philosophy, which discipline they identify with reason. Philosophical reasoning, they argue, undermines the unity and consistency of obedient rule-following and of common-law precedent.

Few essays, other than those of Larry Catá Backer and Steven Winter, however, explore "the *why* of either [the philosophers' writings and law-men's doings]" that Llewellyn thought important. Llewellyn in his appeal to legal realism yet to come had, as mentioned, offered the functionalism of felt needs as the ostensibly philosophical spirit that made law what it is in U.S. history. Backer explains U.S. legal history, by contrast, as a function of American aspirations to perfection, a "religion without religion." Winter explains the "strange recrudescence of formalist [as opposed to realist] understandings of law" in the legal academy during the past two decades in terms of world events and an unconscious yet "deeply held cognitive model of law." He addresses in functionalist terms what Steven Smith, like Mootz, identifies in a different register as a significant problem for legal thinkers: "what to make of a practice that in its theoretical moments persistently insists that it is not the sort of thing that in its practical operations it manifestly appears to be."

For many of the essays, then, their point of contact with Llewellyn lies less in concern for the spirit of legal doings or with explanations of legal history than with social reality and the ability of philosophical knowledges of society to ground law or modern policy. When Frank Michelman inverts Llewellyn's use of unarticulated premises that make sense of law, by offering a philosophical argument for the use of law as a premise on which certain ostensibly moral demands can rest, he nevertheless does so in the service of substantively Llewellyan socioeconomic rights. Most essays raise a more troubling sense of legal realism than does Michelman, though. They appear uncomfortable with the legacy of legal realism, invoking it as a specter that haunts contemporary U.S. law. Fully six of the essays quote or play with the old "chestnut" (according to Thurschwell), "we are all legal realists now" (Caudill, Goodrich, Pether, Solum, Tamanaha, Thurschwell). Citing the phrase in all seriousness, Brian Tamanaha deplores the emptiness of a law mired in the instrumental mind-set of a legal realism that offers means but no ends.

* * *

II. THE USE OF LEGAL REALISM

What is the use of legal realism, ask Tamanaha and, more subtly, West, when one does not know what to use law for? Their plaints echo those foretold by Nietzsche as belonging to the fifth moment of his pithy six-moment history of philosophy in *Twilight of the Idols.* In less than 250 words, Nietzsche traces transformations in truth since the Greeks. The "true world" of the empiricists is no longer the "true world" of the Platonic idea nor the "true world" of the Christian heaven nor the "true world" of Kantian things-in-themselves. Reason posited the truth of these worlds, which worlds were used as ideals or standards with which to judge *this* world – the actual, ephemeral, temporal, apparent world – as lacking. With the empiricism of Nietzsche's fourth moment, as with Llewellyan legal realism, truth or knowledge comes down to earth; formal doctrine, like now-former ideals – of the polis, of natural law, of moral law – cannot be empirically known. It follows for legal realists of today, as for those of Nietzsche's fifth moment (quoted in the epigraph), that the "'true' world" (in quotation marks for the first time) is simply "an idea." In the empirical world that rejects the "truth" of worlds that lie beyond this empirical one, law that relies on the old truths or ideals of natural or moral law is no longer any use. Law is not good *for* anything. It does not constitute obligations or duty.

Furthermore, insofar as law, as means to empirically or sociologically knowable ends, grounds itself in empirical knowledge of the social reality that it governs, it lacks ends beyond itself. For some, such as Tamanaha, this produces an impasse. Others, such as Jack Balkin and Pierre Schlag, revel in the ways in which they are no longer bound to particular concepts of law and morality. In the brightness and daylight of this paradoxically rational moment in which reason encounters its limitations, Nietzsche's "free spirits" run wild. Balkin declares himself all in favor of critical legal studies' ambivalence about relations between law and justice. Schlag wittily celebrates the absence of ends external to law.

Others experience the moment less riotously, if still dynamically. If the social policy or modern law of legal realism is without purpose other than itself, if it has become "useless and superfluous," as Nietzsche writes, then it is "*consequently*, a refuted idea: let us abolish it!" Lawrence Solum, David Caudill, Penelope Pether, and others indeed respond to claims as to the inability of sociological knowledge to provide external ends for law with calls for jurisprudence to move on from the limitations of that reality. They disagree among themselves though about the direction in which to go. Standing in for today's Kantians and Greeks, Solum proposes a return to virtue as a way to break out of antinomies that include the realism-formalism divide. Caudill shows that Llewellyn's legal realism already contains a "hangover" of natural law from back in jurisprudential history. Smith agrees. So does Jan Broekman, who in his important essay on Llewellyn and life, argues also that Llewellyn was unaware of the metaphysics of representation. Llewellyn did not realize, Broekman argues, that reason could turn not only against the foundations of law, but also against the transparency of language and its correspondence to reality. Thurschwell, however, like Mootz and Goodrich and *contra* Broekman's analysis of Llewellyn's own views, tries to recuperate a foreshadowing of a challenge to language from Llewellyn's text. And finally, in a postrealist passion that Llewellyn might appreciate, Pether turns to the insights of the humanities into what language does, to generate ways of seeing what ostensibly real, sociologically-knowable law cannot see about itself.

Understanding law as linguistic or rhetorical practice rather than as (legal realist) instrument or as moral end as such, opens one to the "return of *bon sens*" ("good sense") and "cheerfulness" in such relatively grounded and optimistic accounts of law as those of Dennis Patterson and Robert Burns. Patterson and Burns – to some degree like Goodrich and Pether – turn to locally situated rhetorical practice to understand law. Rhetoric, Mootz argues, exceeds or escapes the constraints of ostensibly universal reason and logic and hence avoids the "practice-theory quandary" that frames so many of the essays (including Llewellyn's). Patterson discards concepts and definitions concerned with rules and structures of law in favor of a future practice-theory of law as dynamic doing. Burns offers the possibility of an even more sense-oriented (rather than reason-oriented) phenomenological account of legal practice and its aspirations.

* * *

III. THE END OF AN ERROR?

Can rhetoric and the turn to language "capture the 'moment' in legal philosophy"? The essays in this volume recognize and respond, in manners variously helpless and hopeful, flippant and serious, irrelevant and engaged, to the limitations of the contemporary legal realism of a law-guild that posits its findings as *the* truth of and about law. From within a space of legal realism that acknowledges some of its own limitations, this volume asks what one is to make of contemporary law and jurisprudence. Several essays refuse to guide or to predict. Only one, that of Philippe Nonet, says directly that making something – or anything worth thinking – of our law and jurisprudence may not be within our reach rhetorically or otherwise. For not only has law become pure instrument, Nonet writes, but the English language too has become technique, a strategy in the service of ends and an obstacle to thinking – not only about law but also about thought.

What, then, does this volume show? As legal realism extends its grasp, the essays show how we seek to extend our grasp over law: to master it as practitioners and to capture it as scholars. The impossibility of these tasks brings some to strive at them ever more desperately. Some come to believe that we may succeed; others, that we are doomed. To a few, the impossibility of the task so conceived brings revelations into the ways of language or speech. In law no less than in philosophy and in other domains, speech shows – thankfully without capturing – moments that are not completely of our making nor within the control of legal realism and our law.

WORKS CITED

Llewellyn, Karl N. "On Philosophy in American Law." *U. Pa. L. Rev.* 82.3 (1934): 205–12.
Nietzsche, Friedrich Wilhelm. "Twilight of the Idols." In *The Portable Nietzsche.* Trans. and Ed. Walter Kaufman. New York: Viking Press, 1968, 463–563. [Nietzsche, Friedrich. "Gotzendämmerung." *WERKE.* Fünfter Band. Leipzig: Alfred Fröner Verlag, 1930.]

34 Fresh Looks, Philosophy-in-Action, and American Law

MICHAEL SULLIVAN

Mootz's premise: ask a large number of talented and wide-ranging legal thinkers to share their thoughts about the ongoing development of American law, and more specifically about the intersection of philosophy and law in America at this moment in time. Don't give them much space. Discourage footnotes. As a shared point of provocation, refer them to a short piece of critical reflection, speculation, and exhortation by a man who seventy-five years ago asked himself a similar question. Could today's academics, legal and otherwise, play along? Would they embrace Mootz's license to think out loud? If they did, what would happen?

In what follows, I offer my view on some of these matters. The essays in this volume are impressive on several fronts. Many would be, even if published in isolation, superb pieces of work. For example, Balkin's penetrating account of critical legal theory suggests new roles and critical possibilities in the present for a movement that is seldom mentioned outside of obituaries these days. But the volume does something more than provide space for tantalizing hypotheses, though it certainly does this. It draws attention to philosophy and American law in a way which exemplifies the key moments of Llewellyn's short essay.

Llewellyn encouraged us to take a fresh look at matters of theoretical and practical concern. He drew our attention not to dusty tombs of arid and abstract philosophical speculation, but to what he called philosophy-in-action. He wanted to investigate not what was said about legal philosophy but what was done by the philosophical commitments embodied in law. How does American law live its philosophy? What American social experience has produced such philosophy? How and why has it changed over time, and how might we expect it to change or encourage it to change in the future?

A FRESH LOOK

As Broekman points out in his essay, Llewellyn wants to take "a fresh look," and his "desire for lawyers to see legal facts 'fresh,' without philosophical ideological connotations, was captured by his effort to define the 'grand style,' which he opposed to the 'formal style'." Although it is clear that the great majority of contributors to this volume do not hold out much hope for accessing legal facts unencumbered by ideological presuppositions (e.g. Balkin, Hayman and Levit), there is nonetheless a sense of the fresh look that permeates the volume and manifests itself in a variety of different ways.

I will detail some specific impressions along these lines below, but perhaps more important is a general impression that, for the reader, the juxtaposition of views on philosophy and American law embodied in the volume enables a fresh look. What we see is a collection of thoughts on philosophy and American law by highly intelligent individuals with advanced training in multiple disciplines who are highly invested in the questions under discussion that embody very different assumptions about the meaning of the topics under discussion. For some, philosophy is a highly technical discipline committed to conceptual analysis. Among thinkers with this view, some view such analysis as underappreciated while others see it as overrated. Others view philosophy more loosely as the name of a collection of practices which includes cultural studies, rhetoric, and a variety of other disciplines that, for contingent reasons, have developed tools to facilitate cultural self-understanding and critique. Impressions of American law are equally varied among the contributors.

The authors have been given only a short space for their observations. They have not been asked to defend their views against critique, but rather to take this occasion to reflect on the present situation of philosophy and American law. And that's one of the things that makes reading the essays together so interesting. It's not a matter of sorting through a variety of complex arguments to see who does the best job of demonstrating the plausibility of their view, but rather of simply taking a look at what people think. What are the salient features of philosophy and American law that have grabbed their attention? What do they think needs to be done in response to the present situation? And, when read together, what to make out of the wide range of different assumptions and proposed remedies? What strikes me, as a reader, is how the collection itself facilitates a fresh look at philosophy and American law by presenting so many interesting, but competing, ways of looking at the key terms under discussion.

For example, many in the volume take the opportunity offered by Mootz to revisit Llewellyn's 1934 essay "On Philosophy in American Law" and discover a departure point for rumination on the trajectory of how philosophy of law has developed in the United States. It's probably not too surprising to discover a number of participants in an academic volume calling, at least in some sense, for more philosophical sophistication. It's interesting that a number of participants observe that greater philosophical sophistication has been attained since Llewellyn's day, but note that American law, by and large, pays little attention to philosophy (here understood as an academic discipline) generally.

Brian Bix, for example, charts a history of the development of legal philosophy, in particular analytical legal philosophy, that has become increasingly sophisticated since Llewellyn's time. One mark of this sophistication is that nowadays analytical legal philosophy is written primarily by academics who have advanced philosophical training. However, Bix worries that the achievement of this very sophistication may marginalize the discourse because so few have the necessary training to fully participate. The implication, as I read it, is that although legal philosophy has come of age since Llewellyn, much needs to be done to facilitate its appreciation. Matthew Adler raises a similar concern. He wonders why, despite the vast growth in interdisciplinary legal studies, there has not been greater attention to the potential contributions of academic moral philosophy to law. Perhaps, he suggests, this is tied to the fact that much of the most interesting recent work in moral philosophy is not nonconsequentialist in character. What's interesting is that in the fresh look taken by both Bix and Adler, we see increasingly sophisticated philosophy available to a culture of American law that, by and large, ignores it – a fact that they both lament. The implicit call is not so much for better philosophy but for a legal culture that takes philosophy seriously. One sees optimism about the potential for philosophical contributions to law but pessimism about the likelihood that this potential will be widely appreciated.

Adam Thurschwell reaches a similar conclusion, but from a very different vantage point. Llewellyn, on Thurschwell's view, is looking to explicate the philosophy "concretely embodied in the history of American law as it has been practiced, done, and lived, and not as it has been written about or theorized by legal philosophers." One might expect, from this description, that no philosophers per se would have the right orientation given the typical preference for theory over practice. If one did find such a philosopher, one would expect that she would be steeped in American culture in the manner of some American pragmatists. In both cases, one would be surprised. It turns out, on Thurschwell's analysis, that a post-Hegelian orientation is in order. Llewellyn's call to explicate the implicit philosophy of American law can be seen as a piece of Hegel's philosophy of history, which recognizes in history a "sequence of embodied forms of consciousness captured in the habits and attitudes of the community." Thurschwell argues that Llewellyn would be not content to stop with a Hegelian project, however, precisely because he, unlike Hegel, holds out hope that such philosophers might not only explicate the philosophy embodied in our legal and social practices but also contribute to shaping those practices. Hence, the philosophy appropriate to American law is group of post-Hegelian thinkers who, perhaps ironically, are currently identified primarily with the tradition of Continental philosophy. If it is a shock that Thurschwell would have us turn to Continental philosophy to help us articulate the felt needs of American legal culture, he reminds us that the thinkers to which Llewellyn turned for inspiration in his own day, including Holmes and Pound, appeared, as Llewellyn himself remarks, "hopelessly unorthodox" at the time. Continental philosophy, like Llewellyn, understands that philosophy is implicit in our social practices but that this realization need not commit us to some form of historical positivism wherein the values thus embodied are immune from critique. The crucial task is to find resources for such criticism without seeking to transcend history, and Thurschwell offers us such luminaries as Hans-Georg Gadamer, Giorgio Agamben, and Jacques Derrida as models. So, like Bix and Adler, there is an effort to draw attention to the potential for increasingly sophisticated philosophy to contribute to American law, though in this case the philosophical contributions with the most to offer come from the Continental rather than the analytic tradition.

In contrast, Larry Alexander and Emily Sherwin suggest that American law might be better served by avoiding philosophy. Indeed, philosophy might interfere with the ability of legal decision makers to do their job. They take pains, however, to distinguish their account of philosophy from Llewellyn's: "Llewellyn described philosophy as something akin to an ideology or decision making ethos, which will vary over time according to the interest of decision makers and the needs of society. In contrast, we have in mind a discipline that employs reason to bring clarity, depth and precision to the process of thinking about a given subject." More interesting still, however, is the distinction they make between participants in legal decision making (which includes judges and lawyers) and observers (which presumably include academics). "Philosophy is fine for observers of law but not necessarily good for its participants." They develop a number of reasons for this conclusion. Central among them is their contention that the practice of law is built around following rules, which often proves valuable even if done unreflectively, whereas philosophy demands that we should not follow rules unreflectively.

So, we have promising philosophy of analytic and continental stripes that might contribute if the practices of American law would consider them. We have a view of philosophy as committed to conceptual clarity and reason-giving that suggests such philosophy might interfere with and undermine central goals of American law. What if we take an even broader view on the meaning of philosophy?

Robert Burns, Penelope Pether, and Anita Allen take a fresh look that sends them in a different direction, looking for something more than philosophies which focus on questions of epistemology, method, and even hermeneutics. Like Bix and Thurschwell, Burns believes we have richer philosophies today, but he believes that an adequate philosophy of law must not merely explain and justify legal doctrine, but also "provide a constructive account of legal practices that reveals how and when they achieve valid results." To do this involves moments of both interpretation and justification and thus deploys resources from philosophy, anthropology, and rhetorical studies. He suggests that we can "illuminate decisions in particular cases by exploring and applying in the legal context what we can learn from a number of different philosophical traditions."

Pether wants to take up Llewellyn's effort to take a fresh look while eschewing what she sees as his ambitions for a totalizing philosophy anchored in the advance of social science. The crucial effort, on her view, concerns "restoring the subject of American law to the possibility of justice." In this way she shares Thurschwell's concern with issues of justice but relies on rhetoric, cultural studies, critical linguistics, and the privileging of nontotalizing theory, which, following Norris, "enables the familiar to be seen with estranged eyes." She recommends comparative and critical legal studies to help theorists undertake an ontology of legal subjects which is "as much as if not more than a coherent and principled account of legal epistemology and hermeneutics . . . the most critical project for those of us who profess the philosophy of American law." The introduction of the self-reflective question here is of particular note. What is it that we who profess the philosophy of American law are committed to? Pether's fresh look is a startling interruption of sorts, not just a call for more philosophy, even a radical philosophy understood as an ontology of the subject, but a reminder of the responsibility of the inquirer whose inquiry shapes the object and the subject, too.

Perhaps it is not so surprising to discover that many who revisit Llewellyn's essay discover within it an earnest, if misguided in some respects, effort to discover a substantial philosophical basis in American law. But when Anita Allen takes a fresh look at Llewellyn's essay, she is struck primarily by Llewellyn's inattention to philosophy in a strict sense, inasmuch as we understand philosophy in a contemporary vein to focus primarily on conceptual issues. Rather, she argues that "by 'philosophy' Llewellyn only meant atmosphere." And for him, the atmosphere within which law operated included legal philosophy like natural law, positivism, and realism, but also, as she reminds us, racism, maternalism, and paternalism. Her fresh look leaves her questioning not so much why American law hasn't taken interest in the availability of increasingly sophisticated philosophical discourses, but why American law has failed to critically assess the philosophy or atmosphere to which Llewellyn's essay draws our attention. When Llewellyn talks about philosophy in American law, according to Allen, he means the atmosphere that surrounds and shapes it but too often is taken simply as given and remains critically unquestioned. She demonstrates the persistence and effects of such unacknowledged philosophical orientations by uncovering how maternalism and paternalism are guiding forces in recent Supreme Court cases concerning partial-birth abortion. Subsequently, she raises critical questions about the conditions of the atmosphere that facilitate this persistence.

Many of the other authors in the volume also have interesting perspectives on what philosophy consists in, how best to characterize American law, and whether one can advance or improve the other. There are a wide range of views here. Philosophy can help us attain a clearer view of our fundamental legal commitments, or alternatively, it distracts us into conceptual puzzles. Some say it confronts us with the unavoidable existential challenge of how to live our lives; others suggest it all too often leads to detachment, which obfuscates our implication in the functioning of the system. American law is primarily about the decisions of judges and development of doctrine. No, it's about lawyerly practices of litigation and advocacy. Perhaps it encompasses our entire social structure. Ordinarily, in an academic context, one would immediately subject the expression of such differences to a unifying question – who is right? But here, inasmuch as the authors weren't asked to defend their views, the more interesting observation is simply the fact of this wide range of descriptions and the sense of central problems in the present that are tied up with these descriptions. Contra some recent obituaries for legal theory which suggest that there is little of interest to be done, one sees whole sets of problems appear and disappear depending upon the underlying assumptions of what it means to engage American law philosophically.

PHILOSOPHY-IN-ACTION: THEORIZING PRACTICE AND PRACTICING THEORY

A second moment in Llewellyn's article that is highlighted in this collection is his insistence that we study not philosophy in the abstract, but philosophy-in-action. Llewellyn was not interested in philosophy as a set of propositions about the nature of truth, justice, beauty, or the good to be understood theoretically and subsequently applied to practice. Theory and practice are not two separate realms that must somehow be reunited. Rather, Llewellyn's philosophy-in-action suggests, in a manner consistent with the pragmatism of Peirce, James, and Dewey, that we discover our philosophical commitments by investigating our practices. On what assumptions and beliefs are they based? What are their consequences? What do they produce? There is something akin to a use theory of meaning at work here – our practices mean what they do. If you want to know our philosophy of law, don't ask us what it is; look! Our actions and practices, critically understood, belie our philosophy. "Thus what is here before the telescope is the changing array not of verbalized philosophies, but of philosophies-in-action as the history of law in these United States has gone its way. . . . I am concerned with philosophy-in-action, with implicit philosophy, with those premises, albeit inarticulate and in fact unthought, which yet make coherence out of a multiplicity of single ways of doing" (Llewellyn 1934, 206).

Several of the essays collected here do just this – they look at our practices and ask what assumptions underlie them. Steven Smith points to what he sees as a huge chasm between theory and practice. Theoretically, legal scholars insist that "legal arguments and decisions are not attempting to ascertain and give effect to some preexisting hidden or transcendental model." Practically, judges, scholars, and lawyers "have behaved as if legal arguments and decisions are attempting to do just that." How do we square this circle? One might think that the theorists could easily be dismissed on Llewellyn's philosophy-in-action model simply by insisting that what we are after is the philosophy implicated in the practice, but of course the theorists take themselves to be offering a critical view of the practice that better describes the practice despite how things may appear on the surface.

Smith's analysis suggests that when we undertake to spell out the implications in American law what we find is incoherence similar to the kind of incoherence Alasdair MacIntyre has famously charted in our contemporary moral discourse. Having stripped our theory of theological resources we find "a drastic narrowing of the range of admissible argument or explanation, claims or positions, that would have been framed forthrightly in theological terms, now must be translated into more secular terms – or else abandoned." Under these conditions, "jurisprudence – the activity of theorizing or philosophizing about law, about the nature of law – seems close to moribund." There's just not much to do, on Smith's view, if you are uncompelled by the rehashing positivist/natural law disputes about whether bad law is really law. Moreover, because the only resources admissible in contemporary discussions for making sense of our present practices are instrumentalist in character, legal theory naturally turns away from questions about the nature of law to a variety of evaluative, sociological, and normative questions that "do not seem in any way distinctively jurisprudential in character." Perhaps we might recover jurisprudence if we allow ourselves to "take seriously, or to rehabilitate or revise for modern use, the assumptions that animated and continue to animate the traditional practices of law." Said otherwise, there is a philosophy implicit in our practice that our theory now ignores. Perhaps we should make it explicit and see what that makes possible?

Robin West, like Smith, sees that something significant has changed with the secularization of law. We have lost our focus on the concept of the human good and the study of human nature that would help us understand that good. Jurisprudence has suffered because attention to the question, What is law? has excluded attention to the legal good. Contemporary theorists have "conflate[d] the legal is and moral good." "This has the effect, desired by Dworkin and Fuller both, of morally enriching the legal craft, but it also had the effect of subjecting the law only to internal legal – albeit higher or constitutional critique but legal all the same, thus muting the purely moral criticism of law, or jurisprudential inquiry into law's potential goodness." West wants to encourage sustained inquiry into the concept of the human good. Unlike Smith, she does not suggest this is impracticable given secularization, but she does think that contemporary theory has, to the detriment of jurisprudence generally, ignored this central task. West is less interested in asking what theory of the good is implied by our present legal practices than in asking how it is that we understand our legal practices to contribute to the human good. Of course, to do this, we must inquire after the human good in the first place and we must not ignore these questions, as she thinks we do, in our jurisprudence.

For both Smith and West, our present legal practices depend on theological or philosophical commitments that remain obscure and are insufficiently investigated. American law can't make sense of itself let alone reveal a philosophy-in-action that is substantially well formed. In part, American law either doesn't ask the relevant questions, namely, what good law can do, or it doesn't allow itself the tools necessary to investigate these. One might think in light of these critiques that, in some sense, legal practice is parasitic upon larger moral, religious, or ethical questions. While not denying that there are other needs that condition the development of law, Michelman sees something different about the philosophy-in-action in American law. He sees an American law that doesn't simply respond to the demands of an external morality, but rather an American law that creates its own moral demands. So, we have an amazing range of understandings and interrelations at work wherein law responds or fails to respond appropriately to moral demands, wherein law needs or doesn't need religious language to explain itself, and wherein law may generate its own moral terrain independent of general moral concerns.

WHAT DOES AMERICAN LAW PRODUCE? WHAT DOES IT DO?

Political theory that focuses on the legitimacy of social and legal institutions and arrangements tends to give pride of place to legitimacy concerns. How do we know that a particular set of legal rules is just? Perhaps one can provide an argument for a substantive theory of justice that shows which rules must be chosen. Some versions of natural law proceed in this manner, but it has proved impossible to secure anything close to universal agreement on which theory is better or more correct than the others. Another alternative has been a procedural or social contract approach that secures agreement on a set of ground rules, which when enforced are justified by the prior agreement of the parties. There is still no shortage of thorny problems, but the theoretical demands become a bit easier to meet since, absent knowing one's interest in a particular concrete controversy, it's easier to come to agreement about our abstract commitments to justice, fairness, and the like. And yet, as a theoretical matter, it's not enough to know that individuals agreed to a set of rules, because we must also ask about the background morality that made that very agreement possible. It would seem that there must be a background morality in place that would make promising possible. You couldn't begin by signing on to an agreement to respect agreements because there would be nothing prior to warrant respecting that agreement; there must be some sort of background morality in place that enables the ball to begin rolling. What else, aside from promise keeping, does such background morality enable or constrain?

Llewellyn's famous insistence that to understand the development of law one must understand the development of the society in which it operates changes matters. He insists that to understand law one must understand how social pressures have influenced the development of law. This insight changes how we look at the law, even philosophically. Instead of asking solely about the legitimacy conditions necessary for law to grow – that is, instead of merely focusing on the abstract theoretical story about how we can derive a legitimate social order from a state of nature, we instead ask how law responds to social needs. More than this, insofar as law changes the social terrain within which needs are expressed, satisfied, and frustrated, law itself influences the development of future needs such that it both responds to and shapes social needs. It is this last point that Michelman takes and runs with.

Whether a particular set of legal rules is required given our understanding of the moral background conditions, Michelman argues that certain obligations may follow from implementing a legal system, even if there is no obligation to implement a legal system in the first place. His fresh look turns matters upside down and has us asking not the usual question of how morality fits in with law, but the more provocative question of how morality might flow from law. What if we started with a system of law as premise and derived our moral obligations accordingly? As Nietzsche famously asked in the preface to *Beyond Good and Evil*: "Supposing truth is a woman – what then? Are there not grounds for the suspicion that all philosophers, insofar as they were dogmatists, have been very inexpert about women?" (Nietzsche 1966, 1). What if we start with law as premise? Here we don't simply ask whether our law embodies a coherent philosophy but consider what the law itself gives rise to.

CONCLUSION

Judging from the essays collected in this volume there is no shortage of philosophy in, around, alongside, in support of, outside of, and at odds with American law. We're not all realists now – if we ever were. Not so much because we are against finding ways to use the law to serve our ends, but because we have a pluralism of ends that is large and extends to competing descriptions of our practices (including legal practice). American law harbors instrumental and deontological moments, secular proclamations, and persistent theological overtones. We celebrate descriptive conceptual analysis even as many call for making explicit our normative commitments. In short, taken as a whole as part of an effort to take a fresh look and reveal the implicit working philosophy in American law, the volume reveals a range of legal values, methods, strategies, procedures, and commitments that are both mutually supportive and antagonistic in turn.

The many calls to action contained herein persuasively, if depressingly, diagnose a range of problems that American law faces in trying to respond to our ever-changing community. In these calls one hears not just philosophy-in-action, but theorists in action. For the most part, the efforts comment not only on what American law has become but what it should become, how it should move forward. The authors have noted both potential theoretical resources and the absence of such resources for addressing the problems at hand. The invitation implicit in the theoretical conversation about American law calls one not merely to join in predicting the future development of the discourse, but to an engagement that will help direct that development. Whether one finds American law sufficiently philosophical, the impressions shared here suggest that ideas have mattered and will continue to matter in the development of American law. Moreover, as troubling as many of the observations presented about American legal culture are, the wide-ranging, nuanced criticism, cautious idealism, and the repeated demonstrations of creative theoretical engagement show that American law in general, and Llewellyn's essay in particular, are good for philosophy.

WORKS CITED

Llewellyn, K. N. "On Philosophy in American Law." 82.3 U. Pa. L. Rev. (1934): 205–12.
Nietzsche, Friedrich. *Beyond Good and Evil: Prelude to a Philosophy of the Future.* Walter Kaufmann trans. (New York: Vintage Books ed., 1989) (1886).

Contributors and Selected Bibliography

Matthew D. Adler
Leon Meltzer Professor of Law
University of Pennsylvania Law School
madler@law.upenn.edu

Well-Being and Equity: Framework for Policy Analysis. Oxford: Oxford University Press (forthcoming 2010).
With Eric Posner. *New Foundations of Cost-Benefit Analysis.* Cambridge, MA: Harvard Univ. Press, 2007.
"Popular Constitutionalism and the Rule of Recognition: Whose Practices Ground U.S. Law?," *Nw. U.L. Rev.* 100.2 (2006): 719–805.
With Chris Sanchirico. "Inequality and Uncertainty: Theory and Legal Applications," *Univ. Pa. L. Rev.* 55.2 (2006): 279–377.

Larry Alexander
Warren Distinguished Professor of Law
University of San Diego School of Law
larrya@sandiego.edu

With Emily Sherwin. *Demystifying Legal Reasoning.* Cambridge: Cambridge Univ. Press, 2008.
With Emily Sherwin. *The Rule of Rules: Morality, Rules, and the Dilemmas of Law.* Durham, NC: Duke Univ. Press, 2001.
"Bad Beginnings." *U. Pa. L. Rev.* 145.1 (1996): 57–87.
"The Gap." *Harv. J.L. & Pub. Pol.* 14.3 (1991): 695–701.

Anita L. Allen
Henry R. Silverman Professor of Law and Professor of Philosophy
University of Pennsylvania Law School
aallen@law.upenn.edu

Privacy Law and Society. St. Paul, MN: Thomson West, 2007.
The New Ethics: A Guided Tour of the Twenty-First Century Moral Landscape. New York: Mirimax, 2004.
Why Privacy Isn't Everything: Feminist Reflections on Accountability. Lanham, MD: Rowman and Littlefield, 2003.
Ed. with Milton C. Reagen. *Debating Democracy's Discontent: Essays on American Politics, Law and Public Philosophy.* Oxford: Oxford Univ. Press, 1998.

Larry Catá Backer
Professor of Law
The Pennsylvania State University Dickinson School of Law
Director, Coalition for Peace and Ethics
lcb911@mac.com

"Fides et Ratio: Religion and Law in Legal Orders Suffused by Faith." *Law at the End of the Day*. July 30, 2007 (available at http://lcbackerblog.blogspot.com/2007/07/fides-et-ratio-religion-and-law-in.html).
"Reifying Law – Government, Law and the Rule of Law in Government Systems *Penn State Int'l. L. Rev.* 26.3 (2007): 521–63, and *Law at the End of the Day*, Oct. 22, 2006 (available at http://lcbackerblog.blogspot.com/2006/10/reifying-law.html).
"Retaining Judicial Authority: A Preliminary Inquiry on the Dominion of Judges." *Wm. & Mary Bill of Rights J.* 12.1 (2003): 117–78.
"Chroniclers in the Field of Cultural Production: Interpretive Conversations Between Courts and Culture." *B. C. Third World L.J.* 20.2 (2000): 291–343.

Jack M. Balkin
Knight Professor of Constitutional Law and the First Amendment
Director, The Information Society Project
Yale Law School
jack.balkin@yale.edu

With Martin Lederman et al. "The Anti-Torture Memos." *Balkinization*, 2001–2007 (available at http://balkin.blogspot.com/2005/09/anti-torture-memos-balkinization-posts.html).
"The Proliferation of Legal Truth." *Harv. J. Law & Pub. Pol'y.* 26.1 (2003): 5–16.
Cultural Software: A Theory of Ideology. New Haven, CT: Yale Univ. Press, 1998.

Carlos A. Ball
Professor of Law
Rutgers University School of Law (Newark)
cball@kinoy.rutgers.edu

"Against Neutrality in the Legal Recognition of Intimate Relationships." *Geo. J. of Gender & L.* 9.2 (2008): 321–36.
"This Is Not Your Father's Autonomy: Lesbian and Gay Rights from a Feminist and Relational Perspective." *Harv. J. of Gender & L.* 28.2 (2005): 345–79.
"Looking for Theory in all the Right Places: Feminist and Communitarian Elements of Disability Discrimination Law." *Ohio State L.J.* 66.1 (2005): 105–75.
The Morality of Gay Rights: An Exploration in Political Philosophy. New York: Routledge, 2003.

Brian H. Bix
Frederick W. Thomas Professor of Law and Philosophy
University of Minnesota
bix@umn.edu

"Legal Philosophy in America." In *The Oxford Handbook of American Philosophy*. 551–77. Ed. Cheryl Misak. Oxford: Oxford Univ. Press, 2008.
Jurisprudence: Theory and Context, 4th ed. London: Sweet and Maxwell; Durham, NC: Carolina Academic Press, 2006.

A Dictionary of Legal Theory. Oxford: Oxford Univ. Press, 2004.
Law, Language, and Legal Determinacy. Oxford: Oxford Univ. Press, 1993.

Jan M. Broekman
Distinguished Visiting Professor of Law
The Pennsylvania State University Dickinson School of Law
Dean Emeritus, Catholic University of Leuven, Belgium
jmb56@psu.edu

"Trading Signs: Semiotic Practices in Law and Medicine." *Int'l. J. for the Semiotics of Law* 20.3 (2007): 223–36.
The Virtual in E-education. New York: IIS, 2004.
"Legal Education, Institutional Skills and European Opinions." *Int'l. J. for the Semiotics of Law* 14.3 (2001): 249–61.
A Philosophy of European Union Law. Leuven: Peeters, 1999.

Robert P. Burns
Professor of Law
Northwestern University School of Law
r-burns@law.northwestern.edu

"How Law Knows in the American Trial Court." In *How Law Knows*. 126–55. Eds. Austin Sarat et al. Stanford, CA: Stanford Univ. Press, 2007.
"The Distinctiveness of Trial Narrative." In *The Trial on Trial: Truth and Due Process*, Eds. Antony Duff et al. Oxford, UK: Hart Publishing, 2004: 157–77.
"Some Philosophical Resources for An Account of Truth Practices in the American Trial." *Pol. & Legal Anthropology Rev.* 26.2 (2003): 109–35.
A Theory of the Trial. Princeton, NJ: Princeton Univ. Press, 1999.

David Gray Carlson
Professor of Law
Benjamin N. Cardozo School of Law
dcarlson@yu.edu

A Commentary to Hegel's Science of Logic. London: Palgrave MacMillan, 2007.
"Hegel and the Becoming of Essence." *Cosmos & History: J. Nat. & Soc. Phil.* 3 (2007): 276–390. Reprinted in *Rethinking the Place of Philosophy With Hegel*. 118–35. Eds. Paul Ashton, Toula Nicolacopoulos, and George Vassilacopoulos. Melbourne: Melbourne Univ. Press, 2007.
Hegel's Theory of the Subject. London: Palgrave MacMillan, 2006.
Ed. with Peter Goodrich. *Law and the Postmodern Mind*. Ann Arbor: Univ. of Michigan Press, 1998.

David S. Caudill
Professor and Arthur M. Goldberg Family Chair in Law
Villanova University School of Law
caudill@law.villanova.edu

With L. H. LaRue. *No Magic Wand: The Idealization of Science in Law*. Lanham, MD: Rowman and Littlefield, 2006.

"A Calvinist Perspective on the Place of Faith in Legal Scholarship." In *Christian Perspectives on Legal Thought.* Eds. M. McConnell, R. Cochran, and A. Carmella. New Haven, CT: Yale Univ. Press, 2001, 307–20.

Lacan and the Subject of Law. Atlantic Highlands, NJ: Humanities Press, 1997.

Connor Clarke
Amherst College Class of 2008

Mr. Clarke writes for *Slate* and the *New Republic.*

Marianne Constable
Professor, Department of Rhetoric
University of California, Berkeley
constable@berkeley.edu

Just Silences: The Limits and Possibilities of Modern Law. Princeton, NJ: Princeton Univ. Press, 2005.

Ed. with Austin Sarat, David Engel, Valerie Hans, and Susan Lawrence. *Everyday Practices and Trouble Cases in Law and Society Research.* Evanston, IL: Northwestern Univ. Press, 1998.

Ed. with Austin Sarat, David Engel, Valerie Hans, and Susan Lawrence. *Crossing Boundaries: Traditions and Transformations in Law and Society Research.* Evanston, IL: Northwestern Univ. Press, 1998.

The Law of the Other: The Mixed Jury and Changing Conceptions of Citizenship, Law and Knowledge. Chicago: Univ. of Chicago Press, 1994.

David H. Fisher
Professor of Philosophy and 2007–11 Ruge Fellow
North Central College
dhfisher@noctrl.edu

"Or Image of That Horror? Imagining Radical Evil?" In *This Thing of Darkness: Perspectives on Evil and Human Wickedness.* Eds. Richard Paul Hamilton and Margaret Sonser Breen. Amsterdam and New York: Rodopi, 2004: 51–68.

"Loyalty, Tolerance, and Recognition: Aspects of Morality in a Multicultural Society." *J. of Value Inquiry* 31.3 (1997): 339–51.

"The Function of Images and the Imagination in Moral and Ethical Reflection." In *Picturing Cultural Values in Postmodern America.* Ed. William Doty. Tuscaloosa: Univ. of Alabama Press, 1995: 173–86.

Eugene Garver
Regents Professor of Philosophy
Saint John's University (Minnesota)
egarver@csbsju.edu

Confronting Aristotle's Ethics: Ancient and Modern Morality. Chicago: Univ. of Chicago Press, 2006.

For the Sake of Argument: Practical Reasoning, Character and the Ethics of Belief. Chicago: Univ. of Chicago Press, 2004.

Aristotle's Rhetoric: An Art of Character. Chicago: Univ. of Chicago Press, 1994.

Machiavelli and the History of Prudence. Madison: Univ. of Wisconsin Press, 1987.

Peter Goodrich
Professor of Law
Director, Program in Law and Humanities
Benjamin N. Cardozo School of Law
goodrich@yu.edu

Ed. with Francis J. Mootz III. *Nietzsche and Law*. Aldershot, UK: Ashgate, 2008.
Laws of Love: A Brief Historical and Practical Manual. New York: Palgrave Macmillan, 2006.
Oedipus Lex: History, Psychoanalysis, Law. Berkeley: Univ. of California Press, 1995.
Legal Discourse: Linguistics, Rhetoric and Legal Analysis. New York: St. Martin's Press, 1987.

Robert L. Hayman Jr.
Professor of Law
Widener University School of Law
rlhayman@widener.edu

With Leland Ware, *Choosing Equality: Essays and Narratives on the Desegregation Experience*. Harrisburg: Penn State Univ. Press, 2008.
With Michael J. Cozzillio, *Sports and Inequality*. Durham, NC: Carolina Academic Press, 2005.
With Nancy Levit, Richard Delgado, and Jean Stefancic, *Jurisprudence: Classical and Contemporary – From Natural Law to Postmodernism*. St. Paul, MN: West Group American Casebook Series, 2002.
The Smart Culture: Society, Intelligence, and Law. New York: New York Univ. Press, 1998.

Nancy Levit
Curators' and Edward D. Ellison Professor of Law
University of Missouri-Kansas City School of Law
levitn@umkc.edu

"Confronting Conventional Thinking: The Problems Heuristics Pose for Feminist Legal Theory." *Cardozo L. Rev.* 28.1 (2006): 391–440.
With Robert R. M. Verchick, *Feminist Legal Theory: A Primer*. New York: New York Univ. Press, 2006.
With Robert L. Hayman Jr., Richard Delgado, and Jean Stefancic, *Jurisprudence: Classical to Contemporary – From Natural Law to Postmodernism*. St. Paul, MN: West Group American Casebook Series, 2002.
The Gender Line: Men, Women, and the Law. New York: New York Univ. Press, 1998; 2000.

Frank I. Michelman
Robert Walmsley University Professor
Harvard University
fmichel@law.harvard.edu

"The Constitution and Social Rights." *I. Con* 1.1 (2003): 13–34.
"Morality, Identity, and Constitutional Patriotism." *Ratio Juris* 14.3 (2001): 253–71.

Brennan and Democracy. Princeton, NJ: Princeton Univ. Press, 1999.
"Law's Republic." *Yale L.J.* 97.8 (1988): 1493–1537.

Francis J. Mootz III
William S. Boyd Professor of Law
William S. Boyd School of Law
University of Nevada, Las Vegas
Jay.Mootz@unlv.edu

Gadamer and Law. Ed. Francis J. Mootz III. Aldershot, UK: Ashgate, 2007.
Rhetorical Knowledge in Legal Practice and Critical Legal Theory. Tuscaloosa: Univ. of Alabama Press, 2006.
"Psychotherapeutic Practice as a Model for Postmodern Legal Theory." *Yale J. Law & Human.* 12.2 (2000): 299–395.
"Law in Flux: Philosophical Hermeneutics, Legal Argumentation and the Natural Law Tradition." *Yale J. Law & Human.* 11.2 (1999): 311–82.

Philippe Nonet
Emeritus Professor of Law
University of California – Berkeley
pnonet@law.berkeley.edu

"Time and Law." *Theoretical Inquiries in Law*. 8.1 (2007): 311–32.
"Antigone's Law." *Law, Culture, & the Human.* 2.2 (2006): 314–35.
"Sanction." *Cumberland L. Rev.* 25.3 (1995): 489–532.

Dennis Patterson
Board of Governors Professor of Law and Philosophy
Co-director, Institute for Law and Philosophy
Rutgers University, School of Law (Camden)
Professor of Jurisprudence and International Trade
Swansea University, School of Law, Wales, UK
dpatters@camden.rutgers.edu

The New Global Trading Order. Cambridge: Cambridge Univ. Press, 2008.
Mind, Meaning and Law. Aldershot, UK: Ashgate, 2007.
Law and Truth. Oxford: Oxford Univ. Press, 1996.

Penelope Pether
Professor of Law
Villanova University School of Law
pether@law.villanova.edu

"Sorcerers, Not Apprentices: How Judicial Clerks and Staff Attorneys Impoverish U.S. Law." *Ariz. St. L.J.* 39.1 (2007): 1–67.
"Praxis; or the Benefits of Shedding Hostility to Theory." *Law, Culture and the Human.* 2.1 (2006): 51–66.
"Take a Letter Your Honor: Outing the Judicial Epistemology of *Hart v. Massanari*." *Wash. and Lee L. Rev.* 62.4 (2005): 1553–95.
"Inequitable Injunctions: The Scandal of Private Judging in the U.S. Courts." *Stan. L. Rev.* 56.6 (2004): 1435–1579.

Austin Sarat
William Nelson Cromwell Professor of Jurisprudence and Political Science and Five College Fortieth Anniversary Professor
Amherst College
adsarat@amherst.edu

Ed. with Lawrence Douglas and Martha Umphrey. *The Limits of Law*. Stanford, CA: Stanford Univ. Press, 2005.
Mercy on Trial: What It Means to Stop an Execution. Princeton, NJ: Princeton Univ. Press, 2005.

Eileen A. Scallen
Professor of Law
William Mitchell College of Law
eileen.scallen@wmitchell.edu

"Evidence Law as Pragmatic Legal Rhetoric: Reconnecting Legal Scholarship, Teaching and Ethics." *Quinnipiac L. Rev.* 21.4 (2003): 813–91.
" 'Mere' Rhetoric about Common Ground and Different Perspectives: A Comment on Twining's 'Evidence as a Multi-disciplinary Subject'." *Law, Probability & Risk* 2.1 (2003): 109–16.
"Classical Rhetoric, Practical Reasoning, and the Law of Evidence." *American U. L. Rev.* 44.5 (1995): 1717–1816.

Pierre Schlag
Byron R. White Professor of Law
University of Colorado School of Law
schlag@colorado.edu

The Enchantment of Reason. Durham, NC: Duke Univ. Press, 1998.
Laying Down the Law: Mysticism, Fetishism and the American Legal Mind. New York: New York Univ. Press, 1996.
Tactics of Legal Reasoning. Durham, NC: Carolina Academic Press, 1986.

Jeanne L. Schroeder
Professor of Law
Benjamin N. Cardozo School of Law
schroedr@yu.edu

The Four Lacanian Discourses or Turning Law Inside-Out. London: Birkbeck Press, 2008.
"His Master's Voice: H. L. A. Hart's Positivism and Lacanian Discourse Theory." *Law & Crit.* 18.1 (2007): 117–42.
The Triumph of Venus: The Erotics of The Market. Berkeley: Univ. of California Press, 2004.
The Vestal and the Fasces: Hegel, Lacan, Property, and the Feminine. Berkeley: Univ. of California Press, 1998.

Emily Sherwin
Professor of Law
Cornell University Law School
els36@cornell.edu

With Larry Alexander. *Demystifying Legal Reasoning.* Cambridge: Cambridge Univ. Press, 2008.
"Judges as Rulemakers." *U. Chi. L. Rev.* 73.3 (2006): 919–31.
With Larry Alexander. *The Rule of Rules: Morality, Rules, and the Dilemmas of Law.* Durham, NC: Duke Univ. Press, 2001.
"A Defense of Analogical Reasoning in Law." *U. Chi. L. Rev.* 66.4 (1999): 1179–97.

Steven D. Smith
Warren Distinguished Professor of Law
University of San Diego School of Law
smiths@sandiego.edu

"The (Always) Imminent Death of the Law." *U. San Diego L. Rev.* 44.1 (2007): 47–67.
Law's Quandary. Cambridge, MA: Harvard Univ. Press, 2004.
With Paul Campos and Pierre Schlag. *Against the Law.* Durham, NC: Duke Univ. Press, 1996.

Lawrence B. Solum
John E. Cribbet Professor of Law and Professor of Philosophy
University of Illinois College of Law
lsolum@gmail.com

"Natural Justice." *American J. Juris.* 51.1 (2006): 65–105.
"Public Legal Reason." *Va. L. Rev.* 92.7 (2006): 1449–1501.
"Procedural Justice." *S. Cal. L. Rev.* 48.1 (2004): 181–321.
"Virtue Jurisprudence: A Virtue-Centered Theory of Judging." *Metaphilosophy* 34.1–2 (2003): 178–213. Reprinted in *Moral and Epistemic Virtues.* Eds. Michael Brady and Duncan Prichard. Oxford: Blackwell Publishing, 2003, 163–98.

Michael Sullivan
Associate Professor of Philosophy
Emory University
michael.sullivan@emory.edu

Legal Pragmatism: Community, Rights, Democracy. Bloomington: Indiana Univ. Press, 2007.
With Daniel Solove. "Can Pragmatism Be Radical? Richard Posner and Legal Pragmatism." *Yale L.J.* 113.3 (2004): 687–741.

Brian Z. Tamanaha
Benjamin N. Cardozo Professor of Law
St. John's University School of Law
tamanahb@stjohns.edu

Law as a Means to an End: Threat to the Rule of Law. New York: Cambridge Univ. Press, 2006.
On the Rule of Law: History, Politics, Theory. New York: Cambridge Univ. Press, 2004.
A General Jurisprudence of Law and Society. New York: Oxford Univ. Press, 2001.
Realistic Socio-Legal Theory: Pragmatism and a Social Theory of Law. Oxford: Clarendon Press, 1997.

George H. Taylor
Professor of Law
University of Pittsburgh School of Law
gtaylor@pitt.edu

"Ricoeur's Philosophy of Imagination," *J. French Phil.* 16.1–2 (2007): 93–104.
"Derrick Bell's Narratives as Parables," *N.Y.U. Rev. Law & Soc. Change* 31.2 (2007): 225–71.
Editor of Paul Ricoeur, *Lectures on Ideology and Utopia.* New York: Columbia Univ. Press, 1986.

Adam Thurschwell
Civilian Defense Counsel
Office of the Chief Defense Counsel
Office of Military Commissions
United States Department of Defense
(Affiliation provided for identification purposes only. The views expressed are the author's alone and are not those of the Office of Military Commissions – Defense or the United States Department of Defense.)
athurschwell@gmail.com

"Specters of Nietzsche: Potential Futures for the Concept of the Political in Agamben and Derrida." In *Nietzsche and Law.* Eds. Francis J. Mootz III and Peter Goodrich. London: Ashgate Publishing, 2008: 357–426.
"Specters and Scholars: Derrida and the Tragedy of Political Thought." In *Derrida and Legal Philosophy.* Eds. Peter Goodrich, Florian Hoffman, Michel Rosenfeld, and Cornelia Vismann. New York: Macmillan Palgrave, 2008: 152–64.
"Cutting the Branches for Akiba: Agamben's Critique of Derrida." In *Politics, Metaphysics, and Death: Essays on Giorgio Agamben's* Homo Sacer. Ed. Andrew Norris. Durham, NC: Duke Univ. Press, 2005: 173–97.
"On the Threshold of Ethics." *Cardozo L. Rev.* 15. (1994): 1607–55.

Robin West
Professor of Law
Georgetown University Law Center
west@law.georgetown.edu

Marriage, Sexuality and Gender. Boulder: Paradigm Press, 2007.
Re-imagining Justice: Progressive Interpretations of Formal Equality, Rights and the Rule of Law. Aldershot, UK: Ashgate, 2003.
Caring for Justice. New York: New York Univ. Press, 1997.

Steven L. Winter
Walter S. Gibbs Professor of Constitutional Law
Wayne State University Law School
swinter@wayne.edu

"What Is the 'Color' of Law?" In *Cambridge Handbook of Metaphor and Thought.* Ed. Ray Gibbs. Cambridge: Cambridge Univ. Press, 2008. 363–79.
"What Makes Modernity Late?" *Int'l. J. Law in Context* 1.1 (2005): 61–80.
A Clearing in the Forest: Law, Life, and Mind. Chicago: Univ. of Chicago Press, 2001.
"The Next Century of Legal Thought?" *Cardozo L. Rev.* 22.3–4 (2001): 747–72.

R. George Wright
Lawrence A. Jegen Professor of Law
Indiana University School of Law – Indianapolis
gwright@iupui.edu

"Personhood 2.0: Enhanced and Unenhanced Persons and the Equal Protection of the Laws." *Quinnipiac L. Rev.* 23.4 (2005): 1047–95.
Selling Words. New York: New York Univ. Press, 1997.
Does the Law Morally Bind the Poor? New York: New York Univ. Press, 1996.

Name Index

CPSIA information can be obtained at www.ICGtesting.com
Printed in the USA
LVOW071050101011

249833LV00002B/4/P

9 781107 661240